T0284808

Advance Praise for
Defenders of the West

"*Defenders of the West* is engaging storytelling of fascinating people and forgotten events at its best. Although anchored in arcane or archaic texts, it reads and flows like an adroitly crafted novel, buttressed by a scholarship that allows those of the past to speak for the past."

—**Victor Davis Hanson**, Martin and Illie Anderson Senior Fellow,
Hoover Institution

"Relying primarily on contemporary sources, Raymond Ibrahim vividly tells the story of 'eight eminently violent men' who played leading roles fighting Muslims back in the era 1100–1500, when Christianity was a 'muscular religion.' By recalling those exploits, the author hopes not just to pay tribute to distant accomplishments but to inspire today's Christians again to 'stand against Islam.'"

—**Daniel Pipes**, president, Middle East Forum

"For two decades, Raymond Ibrahim has been one of the few historians telling us the truth about Islam and its thousand-year assault on the West. With narrative force, clarity, and a command of primary sources, his new book *Defenders of the West* tells the story of that millennium of aggression and the heroic resistance that saved the West from its oldest enemy."

—**Bruce S. Thornton**, Research Fellow at Stanford's Hoover Institution, and
Executive Member of the Working Group on the
Role of Military History in Contemporary Conflict

"Military historian Raymond Ibrahim is of Egyptian origin, fluent in Arabic, and an expert on the centuries-long armed conflicts between the West and Islam."

—**National Association of Scholars**

"In a brilliantly written and highly dramatic book, Raymond Ibrahim brings to life eight Christian heroes who stood up against evil and injustice to fight for human dignity and the Christian faith in various theatres of war. Remarkable tales from a time of massive upheaval—not unlike our own age. While the book outwardly documents a history of fierce warfare, it also manages to invoke matters of the heart that are relatable to the average reader."

—**Hanne Nabintu Herland**, African-born historian of religions
and bestselling author in Norway

"Raymond Ibrahim is a highly intelligent student of history and the civilizational warfare of Islamic jihadism."

—**Allen West**, retired U.S. Army lieutenant colonel
and former Member of the U.S. House of Representatives

"With his trademark erudition and intellectual courage, Raymond Ibrahim chronicles the exploits of eight Western Christian Defenders against Islamic imperialism, including four—Ferdinand, Hunyadi, Skanderbeg, and Vlad Țepeș—who defended or liberated their home territories from Islam. An unapologetic, pellucid reminder for our era about the necessity of standing resolute against the unprovoked aggression of Islam's timeless institution, jihad."

—**Andrew Bostom**, MD, MS, author of *The Legacy of Jihad*, *The Legacy of Islamic Antisemitism*, and *Sharia Versus Freedom*

"This exciting and very well-researched book introduces us to the lives and heroic deeds of courageous men who, against great odds, defended their people and their culture from an implacable enemy."

—**Darío Fernández-Morera**, Associate Professor Emeritus of Northwestern University, author of *The Myth of the Andalusian Paradise: Muslims, Christians, and Jews Under Islamic Rule in Medieval Spain*

DEFENDERS OF THE WEST

The Christian Heroes Who Stood Against Islam

RAYMOND IBRAHIM

BOMBARDIER
BOOKS

Published by BOMBARDIER BOOKS
An Imprint of Post Hill Press

Defenders of the West:
The Christian Heroes Who Stood Against Islam
© 2022 by Raymond Ibrahim
All Rights Reserved

ISBN: 978-1-64293-820-3
ISBN (eBook): 978-1-64293-821-0

Cover Design by Tiffani Shea

No part of this book may be reproduced, stored in a retrieval system, or transmitted by any means without the written permission of the author and publisher.

Post Hill Press
New York • Nashville
posthillpress.com

Published in the United States of America
2 3 4 5 6 7 8 9 10

Contents

To all the Past, Present, and Future Defenders
of that which is Good, Right, and True.

Foreword

by Victor Davis Hanson

Raymond Ibrahim is well known for translating and editing the mostly unknown writings and communiques of Osama bin Laden and Dr. Ayman al-Zawahiri in *The Al Qaeda Reader* (2007). In the post-9/11 climate, Ibrahim revealed to Western readers the sharp dichotomy between the terrorists' filtered Islamism that appeared in English, and the fiery jihadism they spoke and composed in Arabic to inflame their own constituencies.

In the following years Ibrahim focused on yet another little known but increasingly worsening tragedy—the systematic oppression of Christian minorities throughout the Islamic world, culminating with his book, *Crucified Again: Exposing Islam's New War on Christians* (2013).

With *Sword and Scimitar: Fourteen Centuries of War between Islam and the West* (2018), Ibrahim offered an analysis on how and why for nearly a millennium-and-a-half, the Islamic world and the West fought so violently and seemingly endlessly—and why outmanned Western militaries in often far-off, hostile theaters were able to persevere due to superior technology, logistics, and organization. In so doing, Ibrahim was returning to the same academic focus he had over a quarter of a century earlier as a university student, when he and I first met in the mid-1990s and I eventually became his MA thesis advisor on the first major military encounter between the Christian West and Islamic East, the Battle of Yarmuk.

Now in *Defenders of the West*, Ibrahim revisits these historical themes of West-East adversity. But he focuses on individuals—specifically eight important Christian warriors who fought Islamic armies in various iterations of nearly endless conflict.

Some are familiar names, known from Hollywood epics (El Cid and Richard the Lionheart). A few survive in sensationalized form in popular culture (Vlad the Impaler, now more popularly "Dracula"). Others may be vaguely recognized by eponymous place names in America and Europe (St. Louis and San Fernando). And yet the most impressive are now mostly unknown to contemporary readers (Godfrey of Bouillon, John Hunyadi, and Skanderbeg).

Even so, for centuries, all were canonized in the West for their largely successful roles in beating back Islamic invasions of Europe or reversing Islamic occupations of lands of the former Roman Empire, in the Iberian Peninsula, the Balkans, and the Holy Land. Such Western-centric characterizations may seem controversial today, given both the postmodern mood of Western society, the later nineteenth/twentieth century European colonial and imperial occupational presence in the Mideast and North Africa, and, more recently, the successful propaganda of radical Islamists, ranging from Osama bin Laden to Recep Tayyip Erdoğan, concerning how the West today illegitimately occupies or controls land still belonging to various caliphates and sultanates of the past.

Ibrahim's biographical theme is that all these quite diverse European leaders saw themselves as defenders not just of religion alone, but of a civilization antithetical to those of their enemies. In what now may seem an archaic sensibility, they were fighting for a unique way of life—or often a restoration of it—against a rising challenge completely foreign to everything in their experience, from the aspirations voiced on the Sermon of the Mount to Classical traditions of individual liberty.

In this and past books, Ibrahim sees the strife between the West—formerly though now anachronistically called Christendom, given its widespread agnosticism and atheism—and Islam as unending. The tenets of these two religions, he posits, have for centuries been seen as incompatible, given that Western pacifism has no counterpart in the Koran and the Hadith. Yet the postmodern attractions of globalism and materialism, combined with Western-style consensual government and free-market capitalism, make it ever more difficult to convince affluent and leisured Western publics that many leaders in the Islamic world have never dropped its ancient ideas of jihad. Few now comprehend that many in the Muslim world want no part of a Westernized "end-of-history" or ecumenical vision of global harmonization. And those that do partake in Western consumer capitalism often blame the purveyors, not the consumers, of such addictive materialism.

So, there is a political as well as historical message in these military biographies of the wartime careers of Christian resistance leaders to Islam. They were realists who saw defeat as a guarantee of extinction—and even victory as a brief reprieve against a dynamic Eastern ideology that demanded either their conversion, submission, or annihilation.

Mutatis mutandis, Ibrahim argues that these men's careers can still offer some guidance in a far more dangerous modern world of nuclear, biological, and economic warfare—in which the Khomeinist regime of Iran boasts of an impending nuclear destruction of democratic Israel; the moribund Islamic State and its sub-Saharan offshoots institutionalize beheadings and promise a new caliphate to launch attacks against Westerners; imams brag of demography as destiny as the European population shrinks and the Muslim immigrant community grows; and a loosely organized group of post-al-Qaeda terrorists still intimidates Western writers, film directors, journalists, and political officials to censor themselves—and others—even within their own supposedly free Western societies.

Post-9/11 long lines at airport security checkpoints, the endemic Western fear of referring to Mohammed in the deprecatory fashion habitually accorded to Christ, and the one-way immigrations to Western nations from Muslim countries, for Ibrahim, all follow historical and predictably asymmetrical patterns. It is within this larger landscape that Ibrahim expresses sympathy for the eight defenders, whose own fierceness would today be written off by most of their Western descendants as abject fanaticism and cruelty.

Ibrahim's eight heroes fought in three great iterations of this perennial rivalry—the Crusades, the Reconquista, and the battles in Eastern Europe to deflect Ottoman advances—with mixed successes, given their smaller numbers, internal religious schisms, and political differences. We sometimes forget that at the high tide of the Ottoman Caliphate, Islam was imperial and for centuries mostly united. In contrast, late fifteenth- and sixteenth-century Europe was splintered into Catholicism, Orthodoxy, and Protestantism, and relied on new transatlantic exploration routes as a way of bypassing or altogether escaping rather than confronting the Ottoman threat in the east.

The Iberian Peninsula, along with most of Eastern Europe and the Balkans, eventually reclaimed their earlier Western and Christian pedigrees, while the Middle East, after the nihilist Fourth Crusade, gradually reverted to pre-Crusader Islamism and later Ottomanization. Yet another subtext of Ibrahim's biographies are the contributions of these little remembered leaders in leaving lasting legacies. After all, without some of them, there was no inherent reason why Muslim Albania should not have become the current model for all Eastern Europe. Why is the contemporary southern Iberian Peninsula a part of Europe rather than of Morocco? And why are there still slivers of Westernism in Lebanon and the state of Israel?

It would be easy to caricature Ibrahim as an ideologue offering up "propaganda" to a diminishing number of Christian readers—except that he is not and for several reasons. One, he is an accomplished historian; two, he is a Coptic-Egyptian-American with long familial roots and experience in the Middle East; and, most importantly, he is a linguist. His academic training in classical and Byzantine Greek, his fluency in Arabic and deep knowledge of classical Arabic texts, and his familiarity with canonical medieval Latin chronicles have resulted in a book that cites and quotes hundreds of contemporary sources, some little known, thus allowing Ibrahim to assess secondary scholarship by firsthand knowledge of primary texts.

Although he quotes warnings about Islamic agendas from several Western luminaries—Hilaire Belloc, Teddy Roosevelt, Winston Churchill—Ibrahim's use of contemporary Muslim sources best characterizes the asymmetry, not just between the divergent mores of Islam and Christianity, but also in the vast differences between the freedom to criticize and the fear to dissent. If Western leaders are now embarrassed by five-hundred-year-old fiery and fierce expressions of their ancestors' resistance to Islam, many influential Muslims still take pride in reading about the roots of their own ongoing jihad. So, from Ibrahim's careful documentation of both primary and secondary sources, there emerges a candor about Islamic violent chauvinism. If contemporary Westerners are today ashamed of their past militarists who saw themselves as saviors of Christendom, most Muslims share no such self-doubt. Islam worries not so much over the methods of those who fought the West but far more whether the ends that justified them were achieved.

In his concluding chapter, Ibrahim sees Western self-inquiry as a positive, but he notes that it often can devolve into license and nihilism. And in the current mood, whether in academic circles or popular culture, Western browbeating manifests itself in virtue-signaling damnation of Western civilization—while quite timidly practicing self-censorship, or keeping silent, about Islamic pathologies, including those, ironically, most illiberal to race and gender, diversity, equity, and inclusion.

Again, Ibrahim is not really a polemicist; he is a historian who wishes to retell the often-forgotten military careers of an extraordinary group of great captains. He reflects many themes from his past work, including by emphasizing the dependence of Western troops on shock, technology, and the Classical military tradition, pitted against the Islamic reliance on missiles, and indirect and more mobile warfare. In his chapters on the Cid and Skanderbeg, modern readers may find incomprehensible the physical suffering, courage, and ordeal that both endured from near constant warring.

After the failures of the Crusades to recapture Jerusalem, and the success of the Reconquista, it soon became ever more difficult to enlist papal and Western European kingdoms in the defense of Christendom. Their factionalism, their distance from Istanbul, and their growing interest in the New World diluted their attentions to the dangers threatening Eastern Europe. I once asked a middle-aged Greek friend why he harbored such hostility to Roman Catholicism and Western Europe; without hesitation he answered, "We paid the price for keeping the Turks out of Western Europe." By "we" he meant that fellow Greeks of five hundred years past were near living entities. By "price" he inferred the now less dynamic economies of the frontline nations of Eastern Europe.

Similarly, Ibrahim notes that many of these Christian generals are still revered in Eastern Europe, precisely because these countries have for centuries been "garrison" states, whether facing Ottoman invasions or more modern threats from imperial, communist, and now Putin's Russia, or their sense of ingratitude or even betrayal from their Western kin. They have no margin of error in their defense calculations, given that they have always lived on the proverbial edge of Europe without a vast ocean of protection, far distant from the Americas, and more proximate to the centers of Islam. If Hungarians, Poles, Romanians, and Serbs continue to see eternal threats to their precariousness, whereas Western Europeans envision the advantages of open-borders immigration and a more diverse society, it may well be because their respective histories—and current geographies—are so different.

In the end, *Defenders of the West* is engaging storytelling of fascinating people and forgotten events at its best. Although anchored in arcane or archaic texts, it reads and flows like an adroitly crafted novel, buttressed by a scholarship that allows those of the past to speak for the past. And it recaptures a mentality now long buried in the West—that its defenders never demanded perfection to justify their sacrifices, but simply trusted that their cause was far preferrable to an unendurable alternative.

Victor Davis Hanson
The Hoover Institution, Stanford University
December 29, 2021

"He that hath no sword, let him sell his garment, and buy one."

—JESUS CHRIST (LUKE 22:36)

"Like a trampled spring and a polluted well is a righteous man who gives way before the wicked."

—PROVERB 25:26

"Praise be the Lord my Rock. He trains my hands for war, my fingers for battle."

—PSALM 144:1

Introduction

> "It is especially pleasing to the living…when the deeds of brave men (particularly of those serving as soldiers of God) are either read from writings or soberly recounted from memory.…"
>
> —FULCHER OF CHARTRES (c. 1100)[1]

To understand the nature and purpose of this book, a brief recap of its 2018 predecessor is required, for the two books very much complement one another. In keeping with its subtitle, *Sword and Scimitar: Fourteen Centuries of War between Islam and the West* documented the perennial conflict between the two civilizations; it showed how from its inception in the seventh century, Islam identified itself in contradistinction to Christianity—"God does not beget nor is he begotten!" the Koran thunders (112:3)*—and became the chief adversary of the West, then known as Christendom.

Between especially the seventh and seventeenth centuries, an array of Muslim peoples (beginning with Arabs and Berbers, ending with Turks and Tatars), waged one devastating jihad after another on Christians. As a result, three-quarters of the original Christian world, including the older, richer, and more developed regions—namely, the Middle East, North Africa, and Asia Minor (now "Turkey")—were permanently

---

* Many other Koran verses make this point explicitly. For example, "Infidels are they who say Allah is one of three," a reference to the Christian Trinity (5:73); also, "Infidels are they who say Allah is the Christ, son of Mary" (5:17; cf., 4:171). To be referred to as an infidel (كافر in Arabic, *kafir*) is to be categorized as an existential enemy of Islam that must be either eliminated or subjugated, in keeping with Koran 9:5 and especially 9:29, which contains Islam's final word on Christians (and Jews): "Fight those among the People of the Book who do not believe in Allah nor the Last Day, nor forbid what Allah and His Messenger have forbidden, nor embrace the religion of truth, until they pay the *jizya* with willing submission and feel themselves subdued."

conquered and Islamized.[2] Seen as the final bastion of Christianity—the final "infidel" holdout—Muslims continuously bombarded Europe, or "the West" (so named for literally being the *westernmost* appendage of what was once a much larger civilizational block that Islam permanently severed). In the words of Bernard Lewis,

> For almost a thousand years, from the first Moorish landing in Spain to the second Turkish siege of Vienna, Europe was under constant threat from Islam. In the early centuries it was a double threat—not only of invasion and conquest, but also of conversion.... All but the easternmost provinces of the Islamic realm had been taken from Christians.... North Africa, Egypt, Syria, even Persian-ruled Iraq, had been Christian countries, in which Christianity was older and more deeply rooted than in most of Europe. Their loss was sorely felt and heightened the fear that a similar fate was in store for Europe.... It was this fear, more than any other single factor, which led to the beginning of Arabic scholarship in Europe [in keeping with the dictum, "know your enemy"].[3]

In between the millennium separating Islam's invasions of Spain and Vienna, from 711 to 1683, virtually every corner of Europe—as far as distant Iceland—was pummeled and savaged in the name of jihad with untold millions of Europeans slaughtered or, often worse, enslaved.[4] Few now can comprehend the traumatic impact this had on Europe's development. As historian Franco Cardini puts it, "If we...ask ourselves how and when the modern notion of Europe and the European identity was born, we realize the extent to which Islam was a factor (albeit a negative one) in its creation. Repeated Muslim aggression against Europe [over the centuries]...was a 'violent midwife' to Europe."[5]

Nor was the United States of America spared; its very first wars as a nation—the Barbary Wars (1801–1805; 1815)—were against Muslim slavers. Years earlier, when Thomas Jefferson and John Adams met with and asked one of Barbary's ambassadors why his coreligionists were raiding U.S. vessels and enslaving American sailors, the Muslim relied on the same exact logic that the Muslims who had savaged Europe for over a millennium had always relied on: "The ambassador answered us," the Framers of the Constitution wrote to Congress in a letter dated March 28, 1786, "that it was founded on the laws of their Prophet, that it was written in their Koran, that…it was their right and duty to make war upon them [all non-Muslims] wherever they could be found, and to make slaves of all they could take as prisoners…."[6]

This, of course, is a near perfect paraphrase of that one Koran verse most associated with jihad, 9:5: "Kill the idolaters [non-Muslims] wherever you find them—capture them, besiege them, and sit in wait for them at every place of ambush."

The same nineteenth century that witnessed the Barbary Wars also witnessed the meteoric rise of Western power and concomitant nose-dive of Muslim power, so that by the early twentieth century, what was once a constant threat became a forgotten nightmare. By 1922, the last standing and long moribund Islamic power—the Ottoman Empire, for centuries, the scourge of Europe—died, and Turkey became a secular republic.

Even so, those few Europeans able to rise above the myopic triumphalism surrounding them continued to appreciate, not only the historic life and death struggle the West had experienced with Islam, but its existential and permanent nature. Writing around 1938—at the absolute peak of European power and nadir of Islamic power—European historian Hilaire Belloc (1870–1953) made the following prescient observation:

> Millions of modern people of the white civilization—that is, the civilization of Europe and America—have forgotten all about Islam. They have never come in contact with it. They take for granted that it is decaying, and that, anyway, it is just a foreign religion which will not concern them. It is, as a fact, the most formidable and persistent enemy which our civilization has had, and may at any moment become as large a menace in the future as it has been in the past…. In Islam there has been no dissolution of ancestral doctrine—or, at any rate, nothing corresponding to the universal break-up of religion in Europe. The whole spiritual strength of Islam is still present in the masses of Syria and Anatolia, of the East Asian mountains, of Arabia, Egypt and North Africa. The final fruit of this tenacity, the second period of Islamic power, may be delayed—but I doubt whether it can be permanently postponed.[7]

While Belloc's warnings were widely dismissed as hyperbolic—well into the 1970s, ivy league scholars were still convinced that Islam, like Western Christianity, had become obsolete, a mere outer trapping—today his words seem prophetic. After all, since Belloc penned them nearly a century ago, not only has the West "forgotten about Islam"; it has become sympathetic to this creed that for over a millennium terrorized and negatively impacted the West's development.

Conversely, not only does Islam continue to exhibit its historic hostility; it continues reasserting itself all around the world—including if not especially against the West: the Taliban, an Islamic extremist group, which the U.S. spent much by way of blood and treasure to declare victory against twenty years ago, is back in power in Afghanistan (with billions of dollars' worth of U.S. weapons to boot); Iran, which is driven by apocalyptic visions and eschatological dreams of the jihadist kind, is close to becoming a nuclear power; millions of Muslim "refugees" are flooding the West, especially Europe, where they overtly and especially covertly continue the work of their jihadist ancestors, either by engaging in bouts of thuggery, violence, and outright terrorism or, more commonly, by subverting the continent's identity; and Christian minorities throughout the Islamic world are being oppressed and killed in ways reminiscent of the great era of Christian persecution under Rome—though the legacy media keeps all of these inconvenient facts suppressed. Everywhere the threat is real and palpable, even as a somnolent if not comatose West slumbers on.

The words of British statesman, Winston Churchill (1874–1965)— who once likened religiosity in Muslims to rabies in dogs*—seem pertinent here:

---

* The full, notorious quote, as excerpted from Churchill's 1899 book, *River War: An Historical Account of the Reconquest of the Soudan* (vol.1), follows: "How dreadful are the curses which Mohammedanism lays on its votaries! Besides the fanatical frenzy, which is as dangerous in a man as hydrophobia in a dog, there is this fearful fatalistic apathy. The effects are apparent in many countries, improvident habits, slovenly systems of agriculture, sluggish methods of commerce, and insecurity of property exist wherever the followers of the Prophet rule or live. A degraded sensualism deprives this life of its grace and refinement, the next of its dignity and sanctity. The fact that in Mohammedan law every woman must belong to some man as his absolute property, either as a child, a wife, or a concubine, must delay the final extinction of slavery until the faith of Islam has ceased to be a great power among men. Individual Muslims may show splendid qualities, but the influence of the religion paralyses the social development of those who follow it. No stronger retrograde force exists in the world. Far from being moribund, Mohammedanism is a militant and proselytizing faith. It has already spread throughout Central Africa, raising fearless warriors at every step; and were it not that Christianity is sheltered in the strong arms of science, the science against which it had vainly struggled, the civilization of modern Europe might fall, as fell the civilization of ancient Rome" (Churchill 1899, 249).

Introduction

[I]f you will not fight for the right when you can easily win without bloodshed; if you will not fight when your victory will be sure and not too costly; you may come to the moment when you will have to fight with all the odds against you and only a precarious chance of survival. There may even be a worse case. You may have to fight when there is no hope of victory, because it is better to perish than to live as slaves.[8]

Such words underscore the grand irony: Islamic advances and Western retreats are currently happening when the West's might vis-à-vis Islam is at an all-time high. As one historian put it back in 2006, "At a time when the military superiority of the West—meaning chiefly the USA—over the Muslim world has never been greater, Western countries feel insecure in the face of the activities of Islamic terrorists.... In all the long centuries of Christian-Muslim conflict, never has the military imbalance between the two sides been greater, yet the dominant West can apparently derive no comfort from that fact."[9]

What explains this strange and ironic dichotomy? What did the West's past possess that its present—which seems to be far superior in every conceivable way, including militarily—does not? The answer is *men who had something worth fighting for*—from their faith and family, to their countries and cultures.

And that is what this book is about: eight men who, driven by something greater than themselves, devoted much of their lives and went to great lengths—most of them died in their forties or fifties—to make a militant if not desperate stand against Islamic aggression.[*] (The epic natures of their conflicts are such that, by the close of this book, the reader may well wonder why—though the Conclusion will explain precisely why—the lives of these men have not been turned into blockbuster movies.[†])

---

[*] The eight chapters contained herein do not purport to be *complete* biographies—much more can be and has been said about the totality of these men's lives—but rather highly detailed and panoramic views of their conflicts with Islam.

[†] With the possible exception of *El Cid* (1961) starring Charlton Heston. Yet even this sixty-year-old film—which predates full-blown "wokeism" by several decades—artificially and anachronistically tried to juxtapose supposedly "good and tolerant" Christians and Muslims (the Cid and the Moors of Zaragosa) with "bad and intolerant" Christians and Muslims (King Alfonso and the Almoravids), a rather exaggerated dichotomy, as Chapter 2 shows. Nor are the countless "Dracula" movies worth mentioning as they have virtually nothing to do with the real Vlad III Dracula of history, as more fully expounded in Chapter 8.

As intrinsically rewarding as it may be to read heroic biographies, focusing on and drawing lessons from heroes was, in fact, once a serious and well regarded historical endeavor. One modern school of thought maintains that "The history of the world is but the biography of great men," to quote British philosopher of history, Thomas Carlyle (1795–1881). Much—not least much-needed inspiration—could be gained by studying these shakers and movers, argued Carlyle: "Great men, taken up in any way, are profitable company," he wrote. "We cannot look, however imperfectly, upon a great man, without gaining something by him."[10]

This view came at a time when its antithesis—that material and economic factors were the *only* molders of history—was making deep inroads in the historical method. Of its practitioners—especially its chief advocate, whose name would become conflated with it, Karl Marx (1818–1883)—Carlyle was unsympathetic: "Such small critics [of great men] do what they can to promote unbelief and universal spiritual paralysis," he charged.[11] Projection explained the rejection: "No sadder proof can be given by a man of his own littleness than disbelief in great men."

To be sure, Carlyle and his allies did not reject the importance of material and mundane factors; rather, they likened them to "dry dead sticks," always present, idly littering the floor until that rare man of genius or courage ignites them into an epoch-making conflagration. The British thinker wrote as much in the context of lamenting the creeping dominance of the materialist worldview of history: "I am well aware…[that] this is an age that denies great men—denies the desirableness of great men…. There is no sadder symptom of a generation than such general blindness to the spiritual lightning [individual actors], with faith only in the heap of barren dead fuel [material factors]. It is the last consummation of unbelief."[12]

Be that as it may; above and beyond the fact that this book approaches "history as biography"—the value of which is ultimately for the reader to decide—the non-biographical lessons it offers are significant.

First, the history contained herein has been intentionally ignored or suppressed because it directly gives the lie to the popular, mainstream mantra that Islam is a perpetually "misunderstood"—including by its own practitioners—"religion of peace." As mentioned, and as the coming pages will further demonstrate, right from Islam's birth, Muslims and Christians became entangled in a perennial, nonstop war—punctuated only by the exigencies of realpolitik and other practical considerations that modern day academics inordinately emphasize and exploit to substantiate their pro-Islamic theses.

The following history further demonstrates that premodern Christians understood—the educated classes explicitly, the masses implicitly or just instinctively—that, whatever their label, national designation, or temporal iteration, Islamic polities were inherently hostile. Consider how Konstantin Mihailović—a fifteenth century Serb who was forced to convert to Islam and made to fight as a slave-soldier for the Turks until he escaped—conflated the main enemies of Christendom: "the Persians, the Turks, the Tatars, the Berbers, and the Arabs; and the diverse Moors...[all] conduct themselves according to the accursed Koran, that is, the scripture of Mohammed."[13]

Another useful aspect of this book is that it offers a close and colorful look at the important differences between the Western and Islamic ways of war—elements of which are still evident today.

Before proceeding, yet another irony concerning the West's past and present needs accounting for: irrespective of what any professional historian thought, the eight men profiled in this book were for centuries held by their respective posterities as iconic exemplars of heroism and self-sacrifice; today, however, they are largely seen by their Western descendants as embarrassments—exemplars *only* of the patriarchy, "toxic masculinity," xenophobia, and, of course, "racism." How and why such a change came about is more fully explored in this book's conclusion.

For now, addressing the greatest factor behind this dramatic turn in opinion should suffice: although the Christian faith of this book's Defenders was, as will become very clear early on, central to their desperate and defiant stance against Islam, it is precisely their descendants and coreligionists—namely, contemporary Western Christians—who are most prone to denouncing these men who fought and died for their faith as unworthy of the name "Christian." Rather ironically, such modern day Christians fail to realize that without their ancestors' sacrifices, they themselves would very likely be Muslims today (as most of the descendants of the once fiercely Christian Middle East, North Africa, and Turkey are today).

One reason for this conundrum should be obvious enough: because the overwhelming majority of warfare between Islam and Western

Europe occurred in the thousand years before the sixteenth-century Protestant Reformation, almost all* of this book's Defenders were adherents of the only form of Christianity then recognizable: what is today called Catholicism—that is, what is today looked upon with deep suspicion, and worse, by most Western Christians.

Put differently, whatever improvements the Reformation may have led to, it also created a discontinuity in and—perhaps more importantly—*how* Christian history is understood (including against its "most formidable and persistent enemy"). Everything preceding the Reformation—meaning the first fifteen centuries of Christian history—was and often continues to be seen through a jaundiced lens, especially the notion of violence, or "holy war," on behalf of Christendom, and those who advocated it—which naturally includes this book's eight men.

Worse, the evolution of Christianity from its premodern to modern to now *postmodern* forms has created insurmountable ruptures between the past and present that now transcend and have little to do with the traditional Catholic/Protestant divide. In other words, a great many Catholics—indeed, mainstream Catholicism itself, particularly as defined under the current pope and in keeping with the predominant "spirit of the age," or *geist*—disavow their heritage and its heroes as much as if not more so than their Protestant counterparts.

None of this, of course, tells us if these eight eminently violent men were—as some inquisitive readers may be wondering—"true" Christians. Nor, happily, is it for me to say who was or wasn't a Christian—or "saved," or "born again," or had a "personal relationship with Jesus," to use Evangelical terms the contemporary significance of which would have been unintelligible and therefore anachronistic to at least the first 1.5 millennia of Christian history. Instead, I hereby focus on those aspects of Christianity that are both answerable and germane to this book. (Incidentally and for full disclosure: I'm not now, nor have I ever been, a Catholic or a Protestant, and am merely endeavoring to call it as I see it).

For starters, it must be understood that premodern Christianity was for at least the first three-quarters of its existence a *muscular* religion: not only does recorded history, including the forthcoming one, make

---

* Only one of the eight, Vlad III Dracula, was an adherent of the only form of Christianity recognizable in Eastern Europe: Orthodoxy.

this abundantly clear; vestiges of the "glories of Christendom" still surround us. Consider the impulse of faith that erected so many massive if not imposing cathedrals and churches all throughout Europe. Once thundering with the booming, masculine voices of confident worshippers, they are today the haunt of little old ladies lighting candles for their departed loved ones—that is, when such buildings are not actively being pawned off or donated (in the name of "Christian charity") to Muslims who transform them into mosques.

Much of this evolution revolves around the modern Christian penchant to "internalize" the faith and express it only in passive, never active, terms. From here, one begins to understand the modern Christian aversion to the seemingly oxymoronic notion of "Christian warriors"—an aversion that cries, "But Christians must always turn the other cheek!"

In reality, many centuries before Islam burst onto the scene, Christian theologians had concluded that "the so called charity texts of the New Testament that preached passivism and forgiveness, not retaliation, were firmly defined as applying to the beliefs and behavior of the private person [and not the state]," to quote Crusades historian Christopher Tyerman.[14]

Christ himself—who called on his followers to render unto Caesar what is Caesar's and unto God what is God's (Matt. 22:21)—differentiated between the social and spiritual realms. In the only recorded instance of Jesus being slapped, he did not offer his other cheek but rather challenged his slapper to explain himself (John 18:22–23). The Nazarene further praised a Roman centurion without calling on him to "repent" by resigning from one of the most brutal militaries in world history (Matt. 8: 5–13). Similarly, when a group of soldiers asked John the Baptist how they should repent, he advised them always to be content with their army wages (Luke 3:14)—and said nothing about their quitting the Roman army.

This is because "there was no intrinsic contradiction in a doctrine of personal, individual forgiveness condoning certain forms of necessary public violence to ensure the security in which, in St. Paul's phrase, Christians 'may lead a quiet and peaceable life in all godliness and honesty' (1 Tim. 2:2)."[15] Or in the words of that chief articulator of "Just War" theory, Saint Augustine (354–430), "It is the injustice of the opposing side that lays on the wise man the duty to wage war."[16] Crusades historian Jonathan Riley-Smith elaborates:

> What was evil in war itself? Augustine had asked. The real evils were not the deaths of those who would have died anyway, but the love of violence, cruelty, and enmity; it was generally to punish such that good men undertook wars in obedience to God or some lawful authority.... Expeditions to the Levant, North Africa, or the Iberian Peninsula could be justified as responses to present Muslim aggression or as rightful attempts to recover Christian territory which had been injuriously seized in the past.[17]

Perhaps a more difficult idea to fathom—yet one pivotal to understanding nearly half of this book—is that premodern Christian notions of "self-defense" transcended today's boundaries: not only were conquered territories and peoples to be liberated; so too were sacred sites. From here, one begins to appreciate why "Jerusalem and the Holy Land had a primacy of importance in medieval minds that is scarcely conceivable to moderns"—and hence why the Crusades were every bit as defensive as the wars of liberation in Spain and the Balkans were.[18]

Premodern Christians were also much more familiar with and moved by the logic of righteous warfare contained in the Jewish scriptures (the Christian "Old Testament") than their modern counterparts. In 1217, for example, a Crusades preacher paraphrased Lamentations 5:2—"Our inheritance has been turned over to strangers, our homes to foreigners"—to express Christian outrage that the Holy Land and its many sacred sites were in Muslim hands: "the Land of Promise is our inheritance and the place where Christ was buried and suffered is our home. And this inheritance is given into the hands of [Muslim] gentiles.... Now our holy inheritance is seized; the holy places are profaned; the holy cross is made a captive."[19]

In short and from the start, mainstream Christian teaching has always supported violence and war for *just* causes—repulsing an enemy or reclaiming conquered territory or sacred spots from him. Violence itself was always seen as a neutral means to a desired—meaning, just—end. In this light, none of this book's eight Defenders can be accused of being "un-Christian" for their wars against Muslims, though that is, of course, the chief reason that they are. As the popular pseudo-historian

Karen Armstrong once chided, "During the 12th Century, Christians were fighting brutal holy wars against Muslims, even though Jesus had told his followers to love their enemies, not to exterminate them."[20] No word, of course, that it was Muslims who had initiated these "brutal holy wars" and first began to "exterminate" Christians or that the Crusaders were trying to protect their coreligionists.

At any rate, the point here is less about correct Christian *doctrine*— which one may argue has also been "reformed" in recent centuries—and more about correct Christian *history*. As Riley-Smith observes,

> The issue I have with these leading representatives of the consensus [that Christian "holy wars" were a betrayal of Christian teaching] relates not to their theology but to their knowledge of history, because underlying their opinions is the belief that the crusading movement was an aberration, a departure from the norm in Christian history. This is wish-fulfillment, stemming from a desire to reshape the past of one's religion into a more acceptable form. As recently as the seventeenth century, and perhaps more recently still, most Christians—Catholic, Orthodox, Protestant—had in general no problem with the idea of holy war.[21]

Indeed, virtually no major religion—apparently not even Buddhism*—has a "problem with the idea of holy war." (Any premodern religion that might have is now naturally extinct.) As such, although the Defenders of this book fought for the historic faith of their European homeland—Christianity—people of all religions can now respect, if not draw inspiration from, the firm conviction and implacable determination that drove them to fight tooth and nail against Islamic aggression, which other non-Christian civilizations have done and continue to do.

In short and for our purposes, any Defender who identified himself as Christian and defined his conflict with Islam as on behalf of

---

* Those—especially dilettante Western converts or admirers—who would argue that Buddhism is certainly and most inherently peaceful need to take it up with Ashin Wirathu (b.1968), an immensely popular Buddhist monk, whom the *New York Times* refers to as "the Burmese bin Laden." With a "rock star following" in Burma, he leads a "new generation of militant anti-Muslim Buddhist organisations." Their vociferous vehemence against Islam rivals, if not exceeds, the premodern Europeans profiled in this book. "You can be full of kindness and love, but you cannot sleep next to a mad dog," the Buddhist leader is on record saying: "I call them [Muslims] troublemakers, because they are troublemakers." For more, see https://www.raymondibrahim.com/2015/03/02/west-misses-point-and-lesson-of-buddhist-anti-muslim-sentiment/.

Christianity—as did all eight men profiled in the coming pages—was, by my standards, deemed eligible for inclusion in this book on "Christian heroes." Readers unsatisfied with such simple but ascertainable criteria are welcome to take it upon themselves to determine whether these men were "true" Christians above and beyond the facts of recorded history.

A word on the selection process—deciding which Defenders to profile. The ultimate consideration was "innate." I have long thought that these eight men and their wars with Islam deserve sufficient presentation. Proof of this is evident in the fact that, although it would have been more ideal to include men of widely different backgrounds, times, and places—there are, after all, nearly fourteen centuries to cull from—two of my eight selections were first cousins and another three were acquainted contemporaries.

Despite such seeming parochialism, the general story of the eleventh to fifteenth centuries, the high age of Christian resistance, is amply told in the following pages, as all eight chapters focus on the three main theaters of war: the Holy Land (three chapters), Spain (two chapters), and the Balkans (three chapters).

That only eight men made it through the selection process does not reflect a dearth of heroes but rather practical considerations. First, figures from before the eleventh century are generally so underrepresented in the historical record that they were disqualified from consideration. This is not to say that men such as Charles Martel, Leo III the Isaurian, and Charlemagne do not warrant inclusion, but that there is simply not enough primary source information to do them justice in a full chapter. For these and other heroes of early Christendom, readers are directed to Chapters 1–3 of *Sword and Scimitar*.

Relatedly, because this book and its predecessor have such a strong synergy and affinity to one another—they are in fact best seen as companion books—those many Defenders who received adequate coverage in *Sword and Scimitar* were excluded from consideration: faced with a fresh blank page, I much preferred to write and offer something new rather than rehash and paraphrase something old. As such, men that might have warranted inclusion in this book but already received a fair bit of mention in *Sword and Scimitar*—I especially have in mind Nikephoros II Phocas, Don Juan of Austria, and Jan Sobieski—were also passed over to make room for the others.

This leads to perhaps the primary difference between this and that book: the men who appeared in *Sword and Scimitar* were connected to its main theme—decisive battles. In reality, however, great heroes are defined by their courage, commitment, and self-sacrifice irrespective of actual victory on the battlefield, which, as even Carlyle acknowledged, was often a byproduct of several other factors beyond their control. As such, there is, happily, little overlap in the histories contained in these two books. For whereas *Sword and Scimitar* is about decisive *battles*, this book is about decisive *men*, meaning it has less to do with historical outcome and more to do with the human heart—something the West is sorely lacking these days.

A final word on sources: The reader will quickly note that I quote liberally if not voluminously from the primary sources of history, the earliest and most original accounts written by both Christians and Muslims, most of them contemporaneous with their subjects. (Of this book's more than twelve hundred endnote citations, the majority are primary sources.) I chose this approach for two main reasons.

First, primary sources contain information that is, as they say, "from the horse's mouth." While it is true that they should not be accepted uncritically, all subsequent ("secondary") histories must, if they wish to be taken seriously, trace back to and at least grapple with the original writings on their subjects, for that is where it all begins.

Instead, many popular histories, documentaries, and movies, especially in the last few decades, have ignored if not downright contradicted much of what these primary sources relay. As for scholarly secondary histories, and as I for one have learned over the decades, no matter how well credentialed or esteemed a modern academic may be, their histories—and even translations and direct quotes therein—sometimes do not agree, even if in subtle but important ways, with the primary sources they purport to trace back to.* Still more vexing is when such writers,

---

* To be clear, I am not suggesting that there are *no* serious or objective modern historians who base their academic work—their secondary histories—on a close and careful reading of the primary sources. On the contrary and for example, several professional Crusades historians have long been frustrated that what they have been writing for many decades continues to be ignored by popularizers, film makers, journalists, and, above all, many of their colleagues, in favor of a whole spectrum of fanciful interpretations and myths that comport only with the current spirit of the age. As an example of those academics that not only ignore, but willfully distort the primary sources of history, see https://www.meforum.org/middle-east-quarterly/pdfs/58687.pdf.

behaving as if they are not to be questioned over trifles, do not even bother to cite their sources—the reader is to accept everything at face value, on the fallacy of authority.

Unsuspecting readers may well assume that whatever these new histories dismiss deserves to be dismissed—being, say, an obvious byproduct of medieval superstition or propaganda unworthy of mention. All too often, however, the creators of such histories ignore or gloss over precisely those things they simply *do not like*, not least because they contradict the theses—that "Islam is a religion of peace" or that "the Crusades were unjust wars of European colonialism"—they may be trying to peddle.

Moreover, because primary sources often do indeed contain information that invariably strikes the modern reader as unintelligible (and therefore better ignored without any further ado), readers have naturally become that much more receptive or susceptible to such ideologically-charged histories. After all, unlike the original sources, these revisionist histories readily comport with our preconceived paradigms; they confirm what one already "knows"—or was systematically indoctrinated into believing—and therefore require little thinking outside the box. In reality, many of the "oddities" contained in premodern histories are less indicative of untrustworthy sources and more indicative of our own idiosyncratic worldviews—epistemologies we should transcend rather than project onto or seek to understand the past through.

One pertinent example: it has been rather difficult for some modern historians and their readers to accept what the primary sources insist on—that, over the centuries, millions of Europeans, including kings, sacrificed everything they had, including their lives, in an effort to "liberate" the tomb of their otherwise risen Lord.

In place of this well attested motive of the Crusades, more cynical and material reasons—because they are more palatable to our cynical and material worldview—have been posited and accepted without any primary source documentation: that, for example, such Christians were *really* motivated by greed, xenophobia, racism, colonialism, a penchant for violence and conquest, and so on and so forth. But as Crusades historian Thomas Madden writes,

> It is easy enough for modern people to dismiss the Crusades as morally repugnant or cynically evil. Such judgments, however, tell

us more about the observer than the observed. They are based on uniquely modern (and, therefore, Western) values. If, from the safety of our modern world, we are quick to condemn the medieval Crusader, we should be mindful that he would be just as quick to condemn us. Our infinitely more destructive wars waged for the sake of political and social ideologies would, in his opinion, be lamentable wastes of human life. In both societies, the medieval and the modern, people fight for what is most dear to them. That is a fact of human nature that is not so changeable.[22]

It is for all these reasons and more that I have opted to rely on a (possibly inordinate) amount of both Christian and Muslim primary sources and quotes*—to capture the original context as much as possible. This decision was not taken lightly. It is, after all, much easier for an author to put things in—not to mention make them more engaging by using—his own words. Even so, I expect that my primary-source heavy approach is in the best interest of the reader (whom I for one do not expect to "take my word" on anything).

---

* Here it seems appropriate to share some of the historiographical perspectives of this book's earliest chroniclers, if only to show how they approached their subjects. According to William of Tyre (b.1130), "[T]he writer of history usually meets with a…formidable difficulty, which he should endeavor to avoid in so far as in him lies. It is, namely, that the lofty dignity of historical events may suffer loss through feeble presentation and lack of eloquence. For the style of his discourse ought to be on the same high plane as are the deeds which he is relating. Nor should the language and spirit of the writer fall below the nobility of his subject. It is greatly to be feared, therefore, that the grandeur of the theme may be impaired by faulty handling and that deeds which are of intrinsic value and importance in themselves may appear insignificant and trivial through fault in the narration" (1943, 54). Spanish chronicler Juan Mariana's (b.1536) humble consideration for his predecessors' otherwise curious claims are also interesting: "I write more than I believe, because I would not wholly omit what others affirm" (157).

CHAPTER 1

Duke Godfrey:
Defender of Christ's Sepulchre

"Allah Akbar…was no longer heard in the city. It was replaced by the returning sounds of 'Christ conquers, rules, and commands.'"
—URSINUS, A FIRST CRUSADER[1]

"The Lord bestowed on you, Duke Godfrey, the highest reward, the rule of the city. But not for long did you discharge this function, for by nature's command you passed away. With the sun arising under Leo's sign, you, happy, arose to Heaven with Michael [the Archangel] coming to meet you."
—FULCHER OF CHARTRES[2]

Beginning in the fourth century, when the Roman Empire started to Christianize, Jerusalem—where Christ was crucified, buried, and resurrected—took on great importance and became *the* center of pilgrimage. In the 330s, Constantine the Great ordered the construction of the Holy Sepulchre, a massive temple complex over the site of Christ's burial; and the True Cross, believed to consist of fragments of the instrument of execution, was unearthed. Both would take on great importance for Christendom and shape the course of this book.

Precisely three hundred years after Constantine's death in 337, the Arabs, who had recently unified under the banner of Islam, conquered Jerusalem from the Eastern Roman Empire in 637. Thereafter, the

Christians of the Holy Land were, "generation after generation,"* persecuted, "to the point of slaughter and destruction, suffered at the hands of Muslim rulers."[3]

Not every Muslim leader was committed to the destruction of churches and persecution of Christians; some were more pragmatic, leaving *dhimmis* alone on payment of *jizya* and acceptance of social inferiority.[†] That said, and as in other Muslim-occupied territories, whether the next ruler would be "radical" or "moderate"—to use an anachronistic but familiar dichotomy—was always a coin flip away. As for the Muslim populace, then as now, mobs were always ready to rise against and plunder Christians under any pretext.

Even the Holy Sepulchre, Christendom's most sacred church, was not spared. In 936, "the Muslims in Jerusalem made a rising and burnt down the Church...which they plundered, and destroyed all they could of it," records one Muslim chronicler. Similarly, in 1009, Fatimid Caliph Hakim bi-Amr Allah (r. 996–1021) ordered one of his officials "to destroy the [Sepulchre] church and have the people plunder it so thoroughly all traces of it were obliterated. He did exactly that."[4] Such wanton vandalism "plunged the entire church and the city of Rome into deep grief and distress," to quote the pope of the time, Sergius IV (d. 1012). Not content, Hakim further ordered the destruction of, according to Muslim accounts, some thirty thousand churches throughout Egypt and Greater Syria.[5]

---

* For example, in the early eighth century, seventy Christian pilgrims in Jerusalem were tortured and executed for refusing to convert to Islam (seven who converted were spared). Some years after that, another sixty pilgrims were crucified in Jerusalem. In the late eighth century, Muslims destroyed two churches and a monastery near Bethlehem and slaughtered its monks. In 796, Muslims burned another twenty monks to death. In 809, and again in 813, multiple monasteries, convents, and churches were attacked in and around Jerusalem; Christians—of both sexes—were gang raped and massacred. On Palm Sunday of 929, another wave of atrocities broke out; churches were destroyed and Christians slaughtered.

† *Dhimmis* are conquered non-Muslims who, on submitting to Islam and accepting their inferior position in the Islamic order of things, are allowed to keep their religion, subject to several stipulations, including payment of *jizya*. Although that Arabic word is often translated as "tribute," its root meaning is to "repay," "recompense," or "compensate" for something. In other words, conquered non-Muslims were to purchase their lives, which were otherwise forfeit, with money. Some jurists spell this out, writing that "their [infidels'] lives and their possessions are only protected by reason of payment of jizya" (Ibrahim 2013, 22–24). For a comprehensive overview of the discriminatory and humiliating rules dhimmis were expected to adhere to, see "The Conditions of Omar" in *Crucified Again* (Ibrahim 2013, 24–30).

Although a much smaller church was rebuilt over the Sepulchre of Christ in 1048—subsequent Muslim rulers preferred the vast revenues raised by Christian pilgrimages to the destruction of yet another "infidel" church—it too remained under threat. As William of Tyre (1130–1186), an important Crusades chronicler born and raised in the Holy Land, writes, when the Muslims "desired to exact anything by force from either the patriarch or the people, any delay in rendering obedience was immediately followed by the threat that the church would be pulled down."[6]

Around the same time the Sepulchre was being rebuilt, the Seljuk Turks rose to power in Afghanistan and eastern Iran in the 1040s, occupied Baghdad in 1055—keeping the Abbasid caliphs as figureheads—and continued marching westward into Syria. No other Muslim peoples would come to spearhead the jihad as the Turks had; both friend and foe attest to their martial prowess and religious zeal. As Bernard Lewis writes, "the converted Turks sank their national identity in Islam as the Arabs and Persians had never done." Accordingly, "under Turkish influence, Islam regained the zeal of the early Arab conquests and reopened holy war against its Christian foes on a significant scale."[7]

Matters went from bad to worse for the people of the ancient Christian region of Asia Minor—the future "Turkey"—particularly those on its easternmost edge, where the Turks first began to invade, namely, the Armenians. Hundreds of thousands of these Christians were either massacred or enslaved; and thousands of churches were torched or transformed into mosques. The pivotal moment came in 1071, after the decisive Turkish victory over the Eastern Roman Empire at Manzikert, which opened the rest of the Anatolian plain to Turkic Islam. Then, the Seljuk sultan, Muhammad bin Dawud Chaghri ("Alp Arslan") called on his followers to run "through the countryside day and night, slaying the Christians and not sparing any mercy on the Roman nation." Eagerly they obliged and penetrated westward; as a result, "cities were obliterated, lands were plundered, and the whole of Rhomaioi [Anatolia] was stained with Christian blood," writes the Eastern Roman princess, Anna Komnene.[8] "All that was left were devastated fields, trees cut down, mutilated corpses and towns driven mad by fear or in flames."[9] Like the Armenians before them, hundreds of thousands of Anatolian, Greek-speaking Christians were massacred, enslaved, or compelled to convert to Islam (this latter point was recently confirmed by DNA studies[10]).

Anna's father, Emperor Alexios I Komnenos (r.1081–1118) recounted his people's travails in a letter addressed to his friend, "Count [Robert] of Flanders and to all the princes of the whole kingdom, lovers of the Christian faith." In it, he lamented "how hard the most holy Roman Christian Empire is being pressed" by the Turks, "pillaged daily and constantly raided, with Christians being murdered and mocked in various indescribable ways."

Not only did the Muslim invaders "defile the holy places in innumerable ways, and destroy them," continued the emperor, but they would "circumcise Christian boys and youths above Christian baptismal fonts, pour the blood from the circumcision into the fonts in mockery of Christ, force them to urinate on it, and then drag them round the church and force them to blaspheme the name and faith of the Holy Trinity. Those who refuse are subjected to various punishments and eventually killed."[11] As for Christian women,

> [The Muslim invaders] took virgins and made them public prostitutes…. Mothers were violated in the presence of their daughters, raped over and over again by different men, while their daughters were compelled, not only to watch, but to sing obscene songs and to dance. Then they changed places, and the suffering, which is painful and shameful to speak of, was inflicted upon the daughters, while the filthy activity was adorned by the obscene songs of the unfortunate mothers…. When the female sex was not spared (an action which might be excused since it is at least in accord with nature), they became worse than animals, breaking all human laws by turning on men. Their lust overflowed to the point that the execrable and profoundly intolerable crime of sodomy, which they committed against men of middle or low station, they also committed against a certain bishop, killing him.[12]

Things fared little better in the Holy Land. Jerusalem's Christians "endured far greater troubles [under the Turks]," writes William of Tyre, "so that they came to look back upon as light the woes which they had suffered under the yoke of the Egyptians [Fatimids] and Persians [Abbasids]…. Death threatened them every day and, what was worse than death, the fear of servitude, harsh and intolerable, ever lowered before them."[13] William proceeds to offer a typical example:

Even while they were in the very act of celebrating the holy rites, the [Turkish] enemy would violently force an entrance into the churches which had been restored and preserved with such infinite difficulty [since being destroyed earlier under the Egyptians and Persians]. Utterly without reverence for the consecrated places, they sat upon the very altars and struck terror to the heart of the worshipers with their mad cries and whistlings. They overturned the chalices, trod underfoot the utensils devoted to the divine offices, broke the marble statues and showered blows and insults upon the clergy. The Lord Patriarch then in office was dragged from his seat by hair and beard and thrown to the ground…. Again and again he was seized and thrust into prison without cause. Treatment fit only for the lowest slave was inflicted upon him in order to torture his people, who suffered with him as with a father.[14]

Nor were European pilgrims to Jerusalem spared: "As the Turks were ruling the lands of Syria and Palestine, they inflicted injuries on Christians who went to pray in Jerusalem, beat them, pillaged them, [and] levied the poll tax [jizya]," writes Michael the Syrian (b.1126). Moreover, "every time they saw a caravan of Christians, particularly of those from Rome and the lands of Italy, they made every effort to cause their death in diverse ways."[15]

It was in this abysmal context that, at the Council of Clermont on November 27, 1095, Pope Urban II called for what came to be known as the First Crusade. After describing to the assembled lords and nobles the plight of Eastern Christendom under Islam, he cried, "who is to repair this damage, if you do not do it?…. Rise up and remember the manly deeds of your ancestors, [including] the prowess and greatness of Charlemagne…."[16]

For the martial knights of the West, hearing of the aforementioned Muslim atrocities against Christendom was intolerable. Thus, when Urban concluded by calling on them to undertake an armed pilgrimage to Jerusalem—with the twin goals of defending fellow Christians and liberating the Sepulchre of Christ—with one voice, all in assembly cried out, "God wills it!" Thereafter, and in the words of the contemporary Armenian chronicler, Matthew of Edessa (c.1075–1144):

[A]ll the peoples of Italy and Spain, right up to the confines of Africa, and even the distant Frankish nation, began to move and surged forth in a formidable and immense throng; they were very much like…the sands of the seas which are beyond the mind's calculation…. [T]he noblemen of the Frankish nation rose up and came forth. Each of them came with his troops to aid the Christians, to deliver the holy city of Jerusalem from the infidels, and to free the holy sepulcher… from the hands of the Muslims; they were illustrious men of royal blood, endowed with piety and faith, and brought up in the practice of good works. Here are the names of these Franks.[17]

First to be named in Matthew's list is "Godfrey, a mighty man from the lineage of the Roman emperors."[18]

Godfrey of Bouillon

Godfrey of Bouillon—widely known in the sources simply as "the Duke"—was born around 1060 in territory that is now part of northeast France or Belgium. Of Germanic stock and maternally descended from Charlemagne and Charles "the Hammer" Martel—both scourges of Islam—he was fluent in eleventh century German and French. The second of three sons (Eustace the eldest, Baldwin the youngest) he was born to Eustace II of Bouillon, one of the most important vassals of the king of France, and Ida, daughter of Godfrey III, the duke of lower Lorraine, whom Godfrey was named after. When he was about six, his father fought alongside William the Conqueror at the battle of Hastings. His mother, who was known for her piety and funding monasteries, "took the best care of her children, nursing them herself lest they be contaminated by evil influences."[19]

Like all future knights, Godfrey began military training before the age of ten. His days were spent learning how to fight, including on horseback.[20] When he was sixteen, German chronicler Lambert of Hersfeld, then aged forty-eight, described Godfrey as "an energetic young man, very eager for military action."[21]

Of his appearance on reaching manhood, William of Tyre gives the following description: "He was tall of stature, not extremely so, but still taller than the average man. He was strong beyond compare, with solidly built limbs and stalwart chest. His features were pleasing, his beard and hair of a medium blond."[22] Robert the Monk (1055–1122), a contemporary, adds that "Godfrey was handsome, of lordly bearing, eloquent, [and] of distinguished character."[23] William of Tyre continues:

He was a man of deep religious character, devout and God-fearing, merciful and just.... He scorned the vanity of the world, a trait rare at his time of life, and especially in one belonging to the military profession. He was constant in prayer, assiduous in good works, and noted for his liberality.... In the use of arms and in the practice of military tactics he was, in the judgment of all, without a peer.[24]

Even those biographers who may have had reason to downplay Godfrey in favor of their own subjects—such as Ralph of Caen (1080–1120), a Norman friend and biographer of another First Crusader, Tancred—confirm that Godfrey was known for "many virtues," including "charity to the poor, mercy to wrongdoers, humility, clemency, sobriety, justice and chastity. In fact, the Duke demonstrated more of the qualities of a monk than he did of a soldier. However, he was not less experienced in secular virtues. He knew how to wage war.... As a youth, he was first or among the first in learning to kill the enemy." Godfrey was, in short, "a man totally devoted to war and God."[25]

Although he possessed all the qualities of a natural born leader, in this era of primogeniture, his elder brother, Eustace, inherited all of their father's holdings. However, their maternal uncle, Godfrey IV, duke of the Lower Lorraine, who had no children, took a liking to his young namesake and designated him his heir. In 1089, when Godfrey was about twenty-nine, he became the Duke of the Lower Lorraine, an especially important duchy that buffered between Germany and France.

The Duke's renown spread well before the First Crusade. Once, for example, another noble voiced a territorial grievance against him before Holy Roman Emperor, Henry IV, and demanded single combat to resolve the matter. Godfrey preferred a more amicable resolution, but the other insisted and the emperor decreed it. During their battle, Godfrey broke his sword at the hilt from an especially powerful blow to his opponent's shield, so that "barely half a foot beyond the hilt remained in his hand." Seeing this disadvantage, the nobles called for a truce and pled with the emperor to stop the duel and settle on a compromise, at which point "the duke declared positively that he declined to take advantage of the efforts of the would-be peacemakers, and with determined obstinacy returned to the field to renew the combat" with naught but a broken blade. His properly armed opponent renewed the duel with increased ferocity. "Urged on by anger" at the other's lack of honor, Godfrey "rushed forward with the hilt of his broken sword in his hand and dealt his adversary such a mighty blow on the left temple that he was thrown half dead to the ground." The duke cast aside his broken sword, picked up his vanquished enemy's weapon, and stood over him. Instead of exacting vengeance, however, he again suggested that a peaceful compromise be reached so that his opponent might be spared an "ignominious death," and it was so granted.[26]

Despite his own chivalrous nature in times of peace, once all-out war was declared, Godfrey was brutally fierce. After writing that the Duke gave "the impression of being a monk rather than a soldier," Robert the Monk adds, "However, when he realized that the enemy was at hand and battle imminent...he feared the attack of no man. What breastplate or shield could withstand the thrust of his sword?"[27] (As shall be seen, this last assertion manifested itself in an especially dramatic anecdote before the walls of Antioch.)

One anecdote preceding the First Crusade is especially telling: when the emperor chose Godfrey as leader of an expedition against Rudolph, the so-called "pseudo king" of the Great Saxon Revolt (1077–1088), Godfrey "very reluctantly and unwillingly accepted" the eagle from the hands of Henry IV and did as he was bid. During battle, Godfrey forcefully broke through the lines of the enemy and "before the very eyes of the emperor and some of his nobles, the duke plunged the standard which he was bearing into the heart of the king [Rudolph]. Then throwing the lifeless body on the ground, Godfrey again raised aloft the imperial standard, all stained with the blood of the king."[28]

Six years after this fierce display, in 1095, came Urban's call from Clermont. Earlier, Godfrey had once declared, "What assistance, fellow warriors, can we hope for from God, we who, while His churches are perishing, not only do not come to their defense, but do not even put forward any word of objection?"[29] Considering this sentiment, the thirty-five-year-old duke was among the first nobles to take the cross; his brothers, Eustace and Baldwin, joined him. The religious fervor of their mother, whose "teachings seem to have had a lifelong influence" on the brothers, was especially instrumental in their joining the First Crusade.[30]

Before setting out, the brothers "made a series of unusually rich donations to different churches and religious houses between 1090 and

1096."[31] To help fund their Crusade, they sold or mortgaged much of their lands and properties, often cheaply; this included Godfrey's castle of Boullion, founded by Charles Martel. According to a charter from 1096 recording Godfrey's and Baldwin's land donations to the abbey of Nivelles, the brothers did all this, "moved by the hope of an eternal inheritance and by love, [and] are preparing to fight for God in Jerusalem [after having] sold and relinquished all their things."[32]

Finally, on August 15, 1096, Godfrey, at the head of eighty thousand Crusaders—ten thousand knights and seventy thousand infantry, most of whom were Germanic and drawn from the regions of Belgium, Luxemburg, northern France, and the Lower Rhine—set off for Constantinople, the gateway to Muslim-held Asia Minor and thence to Jerusalem. He also "led with him in his train monks from well-regulated cloisters, religious men notable for their holy lives. During the entire pilgrimage, at the regular hours, night and day, these monks celebrated the divine offices for him after the custom of the church."[33]

There were, of course, other "great and distinguished men," who, "voluntarily embracing poverty, left fatherland, relations, friends, and extensive ancestral estates to follow Christ," writes William of Tyre.[34] These included the other well-known leaders of the First Crusade: Hugh the Great, younger brother of Philip I, king of the Franks; Robert, Duke of Normandy and eldest son of William the Conqueror; Robert II, Count of Flanders, recipient of the aforementioned letter from Emperor Alexius; Bohemond, a giant Norman imbued "with every warlike attribute"; and Raymond IV, Count of Toulouse, leader of the Provençal contingent, a wealthy magnate experienced in war against the Muslims of Spain.[35]

Godfrey was among the first lords to arrive with his army at Constantinople in late 1096 (not counting the rag tag participants of the "People's Crusade," who had arrived a few months earlier). Alexius would not open the way to Godfrey or any other leader until they took an oath to return to him any formerly Eastern Roman cities they might reconquer from the Turks. In exchange, the emperor would offer his support, provide them with food and supplies, and ferry them into Anatolia.

When that old Norman enemy of Alexius, Bohemond I—who was still smarting from his loss against the emperor's forces at Larissa in the region of Thessaly thirteen years earlier—sent a message to dissuade Godfrey from cooperating with the emperor until he arrived so they could both wage war on him, the Duke, according to the oldest account of the First Crusade, the *Gesta Francorum* (c. 1100), written by someone attached to Bohemond's army, "replied that neither for gain nor for the destruction of Christians had he left his country and kindred, but, rather, in the name of Christ to pursue the way to Jerusalem."[36] Or, in Godfrey's own words in another version: "I shrink from turning against a Christian people the arms which are pledged to combat the infidel."[37]

After the emperor and Crusaders came to terms, Godfrey was the first to leave Constantinople and enter into the lion's den—Asia Minor, which for decades had been ravaged and conquered by the Turks. On landing in Nicomedia in early May 1097 and realizing that there were no routes sufficient to support the massive army following him, he "sent ahead three thousand men with axes and swords to cut and clear" a road to Nicaea. Though they "sweated blood" in the effort, they succeeded and "cut a road through a very narrow and very great mountain," says the *Gesta Francorum*. Then they fixed "iron and wooden crosses on posts, so that the pilgrims would know the way."[38]

The Siege of Nicaea

By May of 1097, the entire Crusader army—or rather armed pilgrimage, which by now consisted of some six hundred thousand people, women and children included—reached and surrounded Nicaea, site of Christendom's first ecumenical council (325 AD), where the Nicean Creed, still professed by all major Christian denominations, was articulated. Now capital of the Seljuk sultanate and occupied by the enemies of the cross, the Crusaders put it to siege on May 14.

Although the besiegement was brutal, the Turks held their own; from their high walls, the Muslims "shouted their war-like battle-cry in the horrible tones of their language"—shrill, jihadist cries such as "Allahu Akbar!" were still indecipherable for early chroniclers—and "fired poisoned arrows so that even those lightly wounded met a horrible death," writes Guibert of Nogent (b.1055).[39] Moreover, in order to defend their walls from being "struck and shaken repeatedly by the battering ram, the Turks created a combustible mixture and poured it over the walls, which torched the battering ram."[40] Smoke and fire rose as the siege went on for weeks.

During this time, a certain Turk, described as a ferocious giant of "most warlike spirit,"[41] wreaked havoc among the Christians with his bow—all while hurling taunts and blasphemies. "In this impudent manner, he was raging along that section of the wall which the duke and his cohorts were attacking" and "Godfrey could not endure this ignominy. He took a heavy bow, sought a suitable position, and directed his aim so accurately that the weapon pierced the vitals of that miscreant and he fell lifeless to the ground."[42]

On May 20, the Seljuk sultan, Kilij Arslan, appeared with a massive Muslim army to deliver Nicaea, his capital. A wild battle ensued. "Duke Godfrey and Bohemond," writes the chief biographer and near contemporary of the duke, Albert of Aachen (1060–1120),* "did not curb their horses but...flew in the midst of the enemy, piercing some with lances, unsaddling others, and all the while urging on their allies, encouraging them with manly exhortations to slaughter the enemy. There was no small clash of spears there, no small rings of swords and helmets heard in this conflict of the war, no small destruction of Turks...."[43]

But it was the greater force of the Crusader army under the command of Raymond of Toulouse with aid from Robert of Flanders that gave the Muslim army its death stroke.[44] "The Arabs, Persians, and ferocious Turks soon fled," concludes Guibert of Nogent: "It was a rout.... Prodigious was the slaughter of the fleeing army.... From the third until the ninth hour the destruction, or rather Arabian slaughter, of this battle raged."[45]

Having butchered countless Muslims, the bloodstained knights resumed the siege of Nicaea. As a material reminder for its inhabitants not to hope for deliverance from their coreligionists, the Crusaders "lobbed the severed heads of the slaughtered Turks from their throwing-machines and catapults into the city."[46]

Another reason fueled this tactic. Earlier, on first landing in Nicomedia, the Crusaders had encountered a horrific sight: "a mountain of considerable height and depth and width," to quote Anna Komnene,

---

* Because it greatly praises Godfrey and his exploits during the First Crusade, it has become fashionable to sideline or present Albert of Aachen's account as exaggerated or unreliable. But as Godfrey-scholar Susan Edgington replies, "The simplified view that [Albert's] *Historia* is a deliberately slanted account of Godfrey and the house of Bouillon is not borne out by an objective reading. Similarly, we should reject the opinion...that Albert was not only writing a 'hagiography' of Godfrey, but was deliberately overstating the part played by the Germans in the First Crusade. Albert's close interest in Godfrey and his family and followers is only to be expected since he lived in Godfrey's home territory and seems to have gained his information from Godfrey's followers" (from Edgington's introduction, Albert of Aachen, 6).

made up entirely of the bones and decapitated heads of the participants of the People's Crusade—peasant men, women, and children who had impatiently crossed into Anatolia without waiting for the professional Crusaders. Kilij Arslan's forces had ruthlessly fallen upon and slaughtered them.[47]

Others, the Crusaders learned, were ritually tortured and decapitated for refusing to renounce Christ and embrace Muhammad. The fate of those kept alive—as usual, the young and comely—was even worse: "[They] were given away as gifts, while others were sold outright," writes Guibert. "[T]hey would endure wretched slavery under the worst masters imaginable. They underwent a torture much longer than that endured by those whose heads were severed swiftly by the sword."[48]

If the same Turks now holed up in Nicaea had laughed then—having annihilated the indigenous Christian population of Anatolia, European peasants had willingly marched into their hands for the same treatment—they were certainly not laughing now, as the heads of their coreligionists rained down on them from the hands of Europe's warrior aristocracy.

Some weeks later, on June 19, 1097, the Turks—these longtime scourges of Eastern Christendom—surrendered Nicaea, on condition that they capitulate, not to the heavily armored newcomers from the West who had so terrorized them, but to Emperor Alexios, who had followed the Crusaders with his own army.

The Battle of Dorylaeum

The Crusaders resumed their march southward through Anatolia, even as Sultan Kilij Arslan, "mindful of the injury done him, constantly brooded…. With all his heart he yearned to retaliate" and "lay an ambush for his foe."[49] He got his chance at Dorylaeum, where the Crusader army divided its forces to better forage during their march.

On July 1, 1097, Bohemond's small force beheld some thirty thousand mounted Muslims flying towards them while "shrieking heaven knows what barbarisms in loud voices."[50] Along with these hysterical cries of "Allahu Akbar," which "seemed to rise to the skies," was the "clang of armor, the neighing of horses, the trumpet's blast," and "the awe-inspiring roll of the drum"—all of which "struck terror to the hearts of the [Christian] legions, unaccustomed as they were to such a scene."[51] Intent on annihilating the insolent infidels, the Turks let loose a torrent of arrows, killing hundreds. On getting closer, they targeted the weak and even "slaughtered mothers with their children."[52]

Bohemond instantly dispatched a quick rider to inform the other leaders that "what they want is now here: come quickly." Godfrey and his men were first to the rescue and "wondered where in the world such an infinite number of people had come from. Turks, Arabs, and Saracens stood out among the others." The Duke and other leaders exhorted their men to fear only God, not "this pile of husks,"[53] whereupon "the Christians with unwonted energy made a furious attack upon the foe with swords."[54] Even as "the Duke pressed and pursued the Turkish battle line"—and despite the "carnage" created among the Muslims—"like the regenerating heads of the Hydra, where a few fell, countless others took their place."[55]

After much bloodshed on both sides, Christian heavy cavalry charges eventually "broke up the battle lines of the infidels and put them to flight with dreadful slaughter."[56] All the chroniclers indicate that Godfrey fought with distinction; the *Gesta Francorum* simply says he was "reckless"—a word with no pejorative connotation then—"and brave."[57]

In the gory aftermath, four thousand Christians were massacred, including nobles, such as Tancred's brother, William, a "youth of more than usual promise." Tancred himself—who was seen in the thick of battle "hurling destruction upon the enemy"—nearly died, "when he was forcibly rescued in spite of himself by the efforts of [his uncle] Bohemond." As for the Muslims, about three thousand were killed, "including Arabs, Turks, [and] Persians."[58]

Not only was Dorylaeum the first pitched battle between the Crusaders and Turks, it was also where the Europeans first truly experienced the Turkic way of war. Unlike their heavily armored Christian counterparts, the Turkish army consisted primarily of light cavalry. It would gallop around, always avoiding what the Crusaders sought and excelled at— cavalry charges and close combat—and let fly volley after volley of arrows (regularly described in both Muslim and Christian sources as blotting out the sun) that would kill or incapacitate their enemy (sources tell of Crusaders looking like "hedgehogs" or found dead with forty arrows protruding).[59] Finally, when the time was right, the Turkish horsemen would go for the kill, that is, when their enemy's army was disunited.*

---

* William of Tyre offers a succinct summary of the Turkish way of war which dominated most encounters between Turks and Christians, including before and after the First Crusade (e.g.,

After Dorylaeum, the Crusaders marched largely unopposed for three months. Rather than confront them again, the Turks turned to more ignoble tactics. "We have defeated the Christian armies and deprived them of all desire for combat," they told other Muslim-controlled fortresses on the Crusaders' route: "Therefore let us into your cities, and welcome gratefully those who go to such lengths to protect you." Once inside, they "stripped the churches," plundered whatever was valuable, and "abducted the sons of Christians as slaves, and consigned to the flames other things that were less useful, constantly in fear of our [men] coming up behind them," writes Guibert.

"Afterward, in searching for the infidels through pathless solitudes," the chronicler continues, "our men entered a deserted, pathless, waterless land, from which the pitiful men emerged scarcely alive. They suffered from hunger and thirst; nothing edible could be found.... [M]any noble knights died there."[60]

Thus where the Turks failed, mortality triumphed. Once proud knights were seen "smashing their fists, tearing their hair, begging for the relief of death" as a result of thirst, starvation, disease, exhaustion, and delirium.[61] Many died; some deserted; others persisted to the bitter end. Fulcher of Chartres (1059–1127), an important chronicler and participant of the First Crusade, summarizes how this once massive army of six hundred thousand was decimated: "[S]ome, refusing hardships, had returned to their homes.... Others, going on with us, though weak, died.... You could see the many cemeteries where our pilgrims were buried along the footpaths, on the plains, and in the woods."[62]

On Bears and Forbearance

During this trying time, the Crusaders passed through the wild and mountainous region of Pisidia. In an effort to help alleviate the people's suffering, a number of knights put aside their armor, took up bow and arrow, and entered the dense woods in search of game. During this

---

Manzikert, 1071; Hattin, 1187): The Turks, he writes, would "let fly a shower of arrows which filled the air like hail.... The first shower had barely ceased when another no less dense followed. From this no one who had haply escaped from the former attack emerged unscathed." Then, whenever the Crusaders charged, the Turks "purposely opened their ranks to avoid the clash, and the Christians, finding no one to oppose them, had to fall back deceived. Then...the Turks again closed their lines and again sent forth showers of arrows like rain" (1943, 170–171).

hunt, Godfrey heard a roar that "roused all the forest and mountains… so that all who were able to hear it wondered."[63] Quickly galloping to it, the Duke saw an "enormous" bear—a man-eater, as later confirmed by locals—chasing a bloodied pilgrim:

> Ever full of sympathy for his brethren, he quickly rushed to the assistance of the sufferer. As soon as the beast caught sight of the duke, who was in the act of raising his sword to strike, it at once spurned its former victim and hurled itself with teeth and claws upon the braver foe. His horse was seriously wounded; nevertheless, the duke, now necessarily on foot, attacked the bear with his sword. The beast, roaring horribly, met him with open jaws.[64]

As the animal charged, "the duke drove it back with his sword" and, as he was known for powerful strokes, "endeavored with all his might to give it a deadly thrust." The bear avoided the swing, knocked Godfrey down, threw its mammoth weight on and pinned him under it and "wasted no time before tearing his throat with its teeth." During this life-and-death struggle, the Duke, "lamenting that he who had up to now escaped splendidly from all danger was about to be choked by this blood-thirsty beast in an ignoble death, recovered his strength" and tried to deal another desperate sword swing; but, being smothered by the overbearing bear and with no room to maneuver, he instead "mutilated the calf and sinews of his own leg with a serious cut."[65]

Despite the excruciating pain, Godfrey "clung to his sword, and, as he was a man of great strength, he seized the monster with his left hand and with the right plunged the sword up to the hilt in the side of the struggling beast." Simultaneously, a knight who had heard the commotion rode to and also smote the bear, which finally expired.

The Duke fared little better and "lay on the ground, so weakened by loss of blood that he could not rise," including from a ruptured artery.[66] His near-lifeless and mutilated body was carried back to camp, whence loud wails erupted. At least the emaciated pilgrims had the bear's carcass to feast on, "saying that they had never seen anything like it in size."[67]

The Crusaders eventually began to receive succor from an unexpected source: the indigenous Christians, primarily Syrians and Armenians, who marveled at the sight of their armor-clad coreligionists. "When we passed by the villages of the Armenians," wrote Fulcher of Chartres, "it was astonishing to see them advancing towards us with crosses and standards, kissing our feet and our garments most humbly for love of God, because they had heard that we would defend them from the Turks under whose yoke they had been oppressed for a long time."[68]

Similarly, when Godfrey's younger brother set off for Edessa, and because the "Christian cultivators of the land abhorred the overlordship of the [Muslim] infidels, as soon as Baldwin entered the region they turned over the fortified places to him."[69] Some indigenous Christians even rose up against their Muslim masters, as when the Crusaders arrived before the city of Artah:

> The Armenian citizens, whom those same Turks had long oppressed with slavery and who were with them within those same defenses, called to mind the injustices which they had borne from those same Turks for a long time—the rape of their wives and daughters; the other crimes they committed; the levying of unjust tributes [jizya]—and now, relying on the arrival and support of the [Western] Christians, they attacked the Turks and killed them with the sword's edge, they cut off their heads and threw them from the windows and the walls, and, opening the city gates to their Christian brothers, they delivered it up safe by the massacre of the gentiles.[70]

The Siege of Antioch

By October 1097, the Crusaders were at and besieging the walls of Antioch, one of ancient Christendom's greatest cities—where the word "Christian" itself was coined (Acts 11:26). Even when "all the East was shaken and the successors of Muhammad were subjugating by force entire provinces to their impious superstition and perverse dogma," William of Tyre explains, Antioch had "as long as possible refused to bear the domination of an infidel nation," that is, until its capture by the Turks in 1084.[71]

Now, more than a decade later, its indigenous Christians were much oppressed by their Turkish master, Yaghi-Siyan, who had demanded more jizya payments, launched sporadic persecutions, forced Christians to convert to Islam, and converted Antioch's main cathedral into a horse stable.[72]

Moreover and "Alas!"—to quote Fulcher of Chartres—"How many Christians, Greeks, Syrians, and Armenians, who lived in the city, were killed by the maddened Turks," once the Crusaders arrived. "With the

Franks looking on, they threw outside the walls the heads of those killed, with their catapults and slings. This especially grieved our people."[73]

But the Crusaders were a different breed of Christian than the Muslims were accustomed to. Far from being cowed by these macabre missiles, they responded in like manner by catapulting into the city the decapitated heads of several Turks they had fought and killed before its walls; other Muslims were "impaled upon stakes and set up before the city."[74]

But Antioch was not Nicaea; founded on the mountainous slopes of the Orontes Valley and surrounded by walls with four hundred towers, it would not fall so easily, and the siege dragged on for months. At one point, Count Raymond and Bohemond led their men to the port of Saint Simeon to bring hired workers to help build a tower near and thus blockade the Bridge Gate, the only exit from Antioch to the Orontes River. While returning around March 7, a Turkish ambush routed and massacred a thousand of these Crusaders.[75] The news reached and stunned Godfrey—who finally reappears in the sources having "recover[ed] fully from the serious illness which had long troubled him, the result of the wound which he had suffered from a bear."[76]

As they hurried back to Antioch, Bohemond and Raymond sent another swift messenger ahead of them to advise Godfrey, who was stationed by the Bridge Gate, to withdraw and so avoid the enemy's onslaught. The hitherto convalescent Duke ignored the advice, for he was "unafraid and thirsting for revenge for the destroyed Christians, and he refused absolutely to move from there or to desert this place out of any fear, but he declared with an oath that either he would today ascend the mountain [near the Bridge Gate] on which the fortress had been built, or he would lose his life with his men on that same mountain."[77]

Godfrey arrayed his forces in battle line formations, even as hordes of Turks arrived and poured out of Antioch, with the other Crusaders coming behind them. Before engaging the enemy, he likely harangued his men with words similar to those he had used earlier against the Turks:

> We are followers of the living God and Lord Jesus Christ, for whose name we serve as soldiers. [The Muslim] men are gathered in their own strength; we are gathered in the name of God. Let us trust in his favour and not hesitate to attack the wicked and unbelieving foe, because whether we live or die we are the Lord's.[78]

A great battle of wrath ensued, replete with "such clashing of arms and ringing of gleaming swords, such neighing of horses and tumult of shouting men…."[79] Godfrey managed to "cut off many heads there, even though they were helmeted," writes Albert of Aachen, adding for the incredulous that "this is said by those who were present and saw it with their own eyes."[80]

The duke further "performed there a famous deed worthy of remembrance forever," adds Robert the Monk—"a feat which rendered him illustrious in the eyes of the entire army." During the carnage, a Turkish chieftain, "bolder than the rest, unusually heavily built and of greater strength…saw the Duke savaging his men mercilessly."

> [So the Muslim] urged his horse towards him with bloodstained spurs, and lifting his sword high, he sliced through the whole shield of the Duke, which he held above his head. If the Duke had not parried the blow with the boss of the shield and twisted over to the other side, he would have paid the debt of death…. The Duke, ablaze with furious anger, prepared to return the blow and thus aimed for his neck. He raised his sword and plunged it into the left side of his shoulder blades with such force that it split the chest down the middle, slashed through the spine and vital organs and, slippery with blood, came out unbroken above the right leg. As a result, the whole of the head and the right side slipped down into the water, whilst the part remaining on the horse was carried back into the city. All those inside rushed together to see this horrible sight, and were struck with amazement, panic and fear, overcome with terror; here there were screams like those of a woman in labor, their voices raised in misery, because he had been one of their emirs.[81]

The terrified Muslims retreated back to Antioch and unleashed a "hailstorm of missiles and arrows" directly onto Godfrey, but he successfully absconded.[82] It was a great victory and allowed the Christians to tighten the noose around the city, which, nonetheless, continued to hold out.

During this time, and although the Fatimids of Egypt and the Turks of Asia had been warring enemies when the Crusaders arrived, the Fatimids sent a delegation to chide the Europeans before the walls of Antioch. Their Egyptian masters, the emissaries said, were "amazed that you should seek the Sepulchre of your lord as armed men, exterminating their people [Muslims] from long-held lands—indeed, butchering them at sword point, something pilgrims should not do."

Of course, these diplomats said nothing about what "their people"—Muslims—had been doing to Christian pilgrims, that is, extorting, torturing, raping, and massacring them which is what occasioned the First Crusade in the first place. Even the Crusaders, responding with "one accord," replied that "No one with any sense should be surprised at us coming to the Sepulchre of Our Lord as armed men and removing your people from these territories. Any of our people who came here with staff and scrip [i.e., as unarmed pilgrims] were insulted with abominable behavior, suffered the ignominy of poor treatment and in extreme cases were killed."[83]

This was an understatement. As just another of countless examples, a pilgrim wrote the following of a "noble abbess of graceful body and of a religious outlook," who had joined a German pilgrimage to Jerusalem in 1064: "The pagans captured her, and in the sight of all, these shameless men raped her until she breathed her last…. Christ's enemies performed such abuses and others like them on the Christians."[84]

Before the walls of Antioch, Godfrey and the other leaders continued their response by noting that the land "belonged to our people [Christians] originally and your people [Muslims] attacked and maliciously took it away from them, which means it cannot be yours no matter how long you have had it." Accordingly, "payback will be exercised by Frankish swords on your necks!"[85] Speechless, the emissaries returned to Egypt.

Seven months had passed since the siege began and by now starving Crusaders were reduced to eating dogs, rats, and thistles. Once again, many died of thirst and pestilence. Even the leaders were going hungry and suffering greatly, especially Godfrey, "in part because of his generous alms to the poor and to hard-pressed knights."[86]

Eventually, "Bohemond, who had a gift for fluent and winning speeches," secretly won over a Muslim captain in charge of a section of the wall—an Armenian Christian converted to Islam during Yaghi-Siyan's persecutions.[87] They made a deal and, on June 3, 1098, under the cover of night, the emaciated Europeans, having clandestinely been brought up over the walls into the city, were running wildly and slaughtering anyone in the streets.

"Those who were Christians chanted Kyrie Eleison"—the Christian mantra, "Lord have mercy," in Greek—"to make it clear to our men that they were not Turks but Christians."[88] Once their startle was over, however, these same Christians, "Syrians, Armenians, and the true believers of other nations, rejoiced exceedingly over what had happened. They at once took arms and joined forces with the army."[89]

The result was a bloodbath not unlike those Muslims had visited upon Christian cities all throughout Anatolia in the preceding decades. Yaghi-Siyan managed to escape the carnage, but local Christians tracked, killed, beheaded and hurled their former tormentor's head "into the view of all the Christian princes. The head was of enormous size, the ears very wide and hairy, his hair was white and he had a beard which flowed...."[90]

Just War Theory in Action

Before they could celebrate, or even recuperate, Kerbogha, the Turkish lord (or *atabeg*) of Mosul, arrived with a "countless and innumerable throng" of forty thousand fighters, consisting of Turks, Arabs, Egyptians, Africans, and Persians.[91] "It is quite obvious that these people are completely mad," the atabeg observed of the hopelessly outnumbered Crusaders: "They are a presumptuous race.... Doubtless they have every confidence in their courage. But by Muhammad, it was a bad day for them when they entered Syrian territory...."[92]

He quickly blockaded Antioch; and they who only yesterday were the besiegers became the besieged. Worse, by the time the Crusaders took Antioch, most of its stores had been depleted by the Turks during their lengthy besiegement, forcing the feral Franks to eat leather shoes and drink horse blood. At one point, Godfrey led a small sortie of knights in a desperate effort to break the siege. The fighting was fierce—nearly two hundred Crusaders were killed—but so outnumbered were the Christians that they retreated to Antioch.[93]

Now desperate, Godfrey and the other leaders "met for deliberation, and it was decided by common consent to send a deputation" to Kerbogha, "proposing that he agree to do one of two things: either let him depart and leave the city to the Christians as a possession forever—the city which had been theirs in the first place and which now by the will of God had been restored to them—or let him prepare for battle and submit to the decision of the sword."[94]

This—Just War logic*—was at the heart of the message delivered to the Turkish leader by the Christian delegation:

Kerbogha, the Frankish lords send the following message to you. What staggering audacity has possessed you that you should have marched against them with armed forces when in their view you and your king and your people [in a word, Muslims] are guilty of invading Christian lands with unbridled covetousness and insulting and killing them all…. If you had any kind of rule of law and wanted to act fairly towards us, we would negotiate, reserving the rights of honor, and demonstrate to you with incontrovertible arguments what ought to belong to the Christians.[95]

Further underscoring the religious nature of the quarrel, the delegation continued by telling Kerbogha that if he were to embrace Christianity, they would surrender Antioch to him and take him for their lord.[96] But if he still refused, then "fly immediately or prepare your necks for our swords…."[97]

As might be expected, Kerbogha, who "was so transported with anger that he could barely speak"—to say nothing of "the arrogant Turks who accompanied him [and] raged when they heard these things"—responded by saying that "we took" Christian lands "by means of our remarkable strength, from a nation [Byzantines] scarcely better than women."[98]

Moreover, we think that you are mad to come from the ends of the earth, threatening with all your might to drive us from our homes, when you have insufficient supplies, too few arms, and too few men. Not only do we refuse to accept the name of Christians, but we spit upon it in disgust. To respond briefly to the message you have brought: return, you who form this delegation, to your leaders swiftly and tell them that if they are willing to become [Muslims] like us and renounce the Christ upon whom you seem to rely, we shall give them not only this land, but land of greater wealth and size.[99]

Should the Crusaders refuse this offer, "they will undoubtedly die horribly," continued the *atabeg*, "or endure the exile of eternal imprisonment, as slaves to us and our descendants…[and] I shall save all

---

* For a discussion on Just War theory, see the Introduction, pp. 9–12.

those who are in the flower of youth of either sex, for the service of my master."[100]

The Christian delegation returned to Antioch. As its head relayed Kerbogha's response, Godfrey interrupted and took him aside; he asked him to be discrete and refrain from describing the mammoth Muslim camp lest whatever little morale remained among the Christians dissipate.[101] After hearing Kerbogha's retort, the famished, exhausted, and vastly outnumbered men concluded that there was nothing left but to sally forth and meet the hordes besieging them head on.

A three day fast was ordered; the little food available was given to the horses. Then everyone in Antioch, lord and commoner, "marched through the city squares, stopping at churches and calling on God's aid, barefoot and crying, beating their breasts, so grief stricken that father would not greet son, brother would not look at brother," to quote Raymond of Aguilers, who was present.

On the morning of June 28, 1098, "everyone received the Eucharist and offered themselves to die for…God, if he should wish."[102] Then some twenty thousand Crusaders—the entire army minus two hundred left to defend the city—issued out of the Gates of Antioch to the sound of blaring horns.

Commanding one of four contingents, the once wealthy Duke had been reduced to borrowing a horse from Count Raymond, for "Godfrey and the other chiefs also had already expended all the money they had brought with them in generous almsgiving and in works of piety, especially those which concerned the common welfare."[103]

Never expecting the outnumbered and weakened Franks to sally forth and meet their much larger and well rested army, the Muslims were shocked—doubly so, as the desperate Christians fought with a feral fury. Contemporary accounts speak of "knights bristling like porcupines with arrows, darts, and javelins, but still moving forward and fighting ferociously."[104] Although a "company of mujahidin [Muslim jihadists] stood firm and fought zealously, seeking martyrdom," writes chronicler Ali ibn al-Athir (b.1160), "the Franks slew thousands of them."[105]

The Crusaders' tight formations eventually caused the Muslim horsemen—used as they were to overwhelming their enemies with darts—to panic and retreat. "To pursue them more effectively," the relentless Crusaders "mounted the horses of those [Muslims] who were dying and left their horses—gaunt and suffering from hunger—on the battlefield."[106] Although their berserker-like determination won the day, "most of the Franks perished" at Antioch, continues Ibn al-Athir, retrospectively if not relievedly adding, "Had they remained in the numbers they set out with, they would have overwhelmed the lands of Islam."[107]

The Holy Land

In early 1099, while other Crusading lords were bickering over Antioch— which ended up going to Bohemond—and/or trying to carve out their own kingdoms, Godfrey, "who was greatly anxious for the journey [to Jerusalem], and incited people to it," became the first of the major leaders to resume the Crusade.[108] In the end, he and the others led a tiny fraction of the original number of First Crusaders—twelve hundred knights and twelve thousand infantry—to their final destination: Jerusalem.

As usual, their journey was fraught with dangers; near Sidon in modern Lebanon their camp was harried by highly venomous snakes called "tarenta"; more Crusaders died.[109]

Indigenous Christians continued to hail them as liberators, especially near and in Bethlehem, which the Muslims had "turned into a stable for pack animals, and all the churches around it had for many years been subject to the ridicule of the pagans," to quote Ekkehard of Aura (1080–1126).[110] According to Fulcher of Chartres,

> When the Christians, evidently Greeks and Syrians...found that the Franks had come, they were especially filled with joy.... Immediately, when they had taken up their crosses and [Christian] banners, they proceeded to meet the Franks with weeping and pious singing: with weeping, because they feared lest such a small number of people at one time or other would be very easily slain by such a great multitude of heathen, whom they knew to be in their own land; with singing, because they wished joy to those whom they had desired to come for a long time, those who they knew would raise Christianity again to its proper and former honor, after it had been ruined by the wicked for such a long time.[111]

Because his reputation preceded him, many of these Christians specifically sought out Godfrey.[112] Even from the high mountain tops of Lebanon, the Maronites descended "to offer their congratulations to the pilgrims and to pay them their tribute of brotherly affection," writes William of Tyre. They too "in all good faith," offered advice on the best routes to take.[113]

Raymond of Aguilers heard and recorded the travails of these indigenous Christian minorities who "possessed that land and mountains for a long time":

> But when the Saracens and Turks arose…[these Christians] were in such great oppression for four hundred and more years that many of them were forced to abandon their fatherland and the Christian law. If, however, any of them through the grace of God refused, they were compelled to give up their beautiful children to be circumcised, or converted to Mohammedanism; or they were snatched from the lap of their mothers, after the father had been killed and the mother mocked. Forsooth, that race of [Muslim] men were inflamed to such malice that they overturned the churches of God and His saints, or destroyed the images; and they tore out the eyes of those images which, for lack of time, they could not destroy, and shot them with arrows; all the altars, too, they undermined. Moreover, they made mosques of the great churches.… In addition, too harsh to relate, they placed [male] youths in brothels, and, to do yet more vilely, exchanged their sisters for wine. And their mothers dared not weep openly at these or other sorrows.[114]

After leaving the local Christians, and during the final stages of their march, Godfrey and the Crusaders ascended a hill whence they received their first glimpse of Jerusalem—a sight that so transported them that the hill was later named Montjoie ("Mount of Joy").[115]

Meanwhile, the Muslims of Jerusalem, currently under Fatimid rule, were long aware of the Crusaders' arrival; and they knew why they had come—to take Jerusalem. Outraged and operating on the logic of collective punishment, which, past and present, always figured prominently in Muslim thinking, they "decided to slay all the Christian inhabitants and then to overthrow from its very foundations" and "utterly destroy" the rebuilt Sepulchre of Christ. "On further consideration, however," continues William, "they feared that such a course would intensify the hatred of the Christians. It might still goad them to more furious efforts." So instead they "extorted all the money and goods in possession of the

Christian inhabitants" living in Jerusalem, before ejecting all males outside the city walls.[116]

The War for Jerusalem

At long last, on June 7, 1099, the Crusaders finally reached their destination. They had suffered much over the last two years—three for Godfrey, who was one of the very first leaders to set out, in the summer of 1096. Historian Mary Noyes Colvin summarizes the Duke's and other pilgrims' reaction on reaching the Holy City:

> Never before or since, in the history of the world, probably, has a scene of such intense emotion, on so large a scale, been seen, or have such transports of joy and reverence been witnessed. Strong, stalwart men, who had endured untold suffering and privations to behold this sight, sobbed aloud; some cast themselves upon their knees in prayer; others kissed the earth on which they stood, in an ecstasy of rejoicing.[117]

It was short-lived; on seeing the Muslims' "military strength, the defense of the city, and the[ir] resistance," the Christians immediately set to work. According to Albert of Aachen, they "blockaded and surrounded the walls. They stationed Duke Godfrey, because he was powerful in counsels and forces, with the Germans, who were very fierce in battle, on the side of the Tower of David." Tancred and Robert of Flanders went with him.[118] The rest of the forces were arrayed along the northern and southern walls.

Considering that the Crusaders consisted of a skeleton crew (compared to their original numbers) and did not have enough or suitable siege equipment, their initial assaults on the highly fortified city bore little fruit. Many fell by arrows from sneering Muslims safe behind their high walls.

At the same time, their water supply was quickly dwindling, for there were no natural springs near Jerusalem, and the Muslims had plugged all the nearby wells with refuse and filth, while lying "in ambush for the Christians and dealing death to those who came looking for water."[119] Before long, "their thirst was so great" that "they dug in the earth and put damp clods on their mouth, and licked damp marble."[120]

As time was not on their side, the Crusaders decided on an all-out effort set for June 13. But without the necessary siege equipment, their otherwise valiant assault remained impotent, and many more lay dead or dying around the city's walls.

Wild desperation set in; they had suffered and sacrificed much to get here and would now rather die for the mere chance to touch the outer walls of their Lord, than hold back and perish from sunstroke, thirst, or Muslim projectiles. Thus, as Ralph of Caen explains, maddened Christians "hurried headlong in a joint rush toward the walls as if to the embrace of their wives."

> It was as if there were one thought for each of them: "I shall kiss my desired Jerusalem before I die." The kisses of these poor men were met by a storm of swords, stones, and sometimes burning stakes that brought sudden death to those who tried to embrace the wall. But this devotion, once taken up, could not be frightened away. Often, yes very often, the death of some led others to this same embrace.[121]

Once again, a dark time set in for the Crusaders. The extreme July heat and lack of water killed many; the futility of their predicament set more to despair. "You might see the plague," wrote Gilo of Paris (d.1142), "which had lain dormant deep in a man's bones, suddenly bring on its own madness, his walk become unsteady, as his strength was impaired, and his ability to speak was suppressed."[122] Many horses and beasts of burden died; their blood was instantly drunk by the parched people. The camp became pestilent. "Each day our ranks grew less than on the previous day. Almost daily many perished.... Nor did fresh recruits come from elsewhere to take the places and assume the duties of those who had succumbed."[123]

Their immediate problem—lack of water—was eventually ameliorated, though at no small price. Indigenous Christians familiar with the region came and directed the Crusaders to unknown water reserves some five miles away. Even then, many continued to be "killed by the Saracens lying in ambush around the narrow passages, or were abducted by them."[124]

On June 17, refreshing news arrived: six Italian ships containing material to construct the much-needed siege equipment they lacked—wooden towers, catapults, and ladders—had arrived in Jaffa. As the port was some forty miles away, transporting this material in the Crusaders' bedraggled condition—to say nothing of assembling it—was itself something of a crusade. As Raymond of Aguilers observes, "for the construction of machines at Jerusalem fifty or sixty men carried on their shoulders a great beam that could not have been dragged by four pair of oxen. What more shall I say?"[125]

Three weeks were feverishly spent building the necessary siege equipment, which included two movable war towers and a battering ram with an ironclad head. Once everything was ready, these engines of war were transported to and established in each leader's respective camp: "You who read this must not think this was a light undertaking," continues Raymond of Aguilers, "for the machines were carried in parts almost a mile to the place where they were to be set up. When morning came and the Saracens saw that all the machinery and tents had been moved during the night, they were amazed."[126]

But they had not been idle. As soon as the Muslims learned that the Christians were constructing siege equipment, they too got busy adding fortifications and constructing catapults. Gilo of Paris summarizes these developments:

> [A] siege-engine was built, at the earnest prompting of Godfrey; it resembled a castle in shape, and took a great deal of effort to construct. Its timbers gave raw material to the carpenters, and fear to the city. With equally careful provision, Raymond [of Toulouse] also raised up an equal siege-castle, and its towers were built up to face the turrets of the city. The wretched heathen were astonished to see these massive structures suddenly rise up, and they themselves toiled by night to raise their own towers higher.... [127]

Once all was ready, the Christians agreed to launch another all-out assault on July 14. Before that day came, they again "embrace[d] a painful regime of fasting and of continual prayers of devotion."[128] On July 8, the Muslim defenders atop the walls watched in astonishment as the Crusaders became a large, barefoot, and unarmed procession. With crosses held high, the pilgrims marched around the walls of Jerusalem—in conscious emulation of the ancient Hebrews' procession around Jericho—before congregating at the Mount of Olives, where they heard impassioned sermons.

Safe behind their walls, the Muslims jeered; they shot arrows and catapulted projectiles at the crowded procession killing a few and injuring many. Moreover, and "to show their scorn and contempt for the

Christians," the Muslims "set up crosses on the walls, and on these they vented all kinds of shameful insults."[129] They broke and smashed the crucifixes against walls, spat on them and "did not shrink from urinating on them in full view of everyone"[130]—all while "pouring forth blasphemous words and taunts against our Lord Jesus Christ and His doctrine of salvation."[131]

As Near Eastern Christians had more than four centuries earlier called the invading Arabs "friends of demons" for desecrating Christian symbols and sacraments, so now the "enemies mocking us in the city," the Crusaders were told in sermons, were "limbs of those other enemies [demons], lesser and weaker versions of their masters." The Crusaders were exhorted to ignore the sacrilege and "think on Christ, who until today has been outlawed and crucified in this city!"[132]

By the evening of July 13, preparations were complete, the city surrounded. One of the wooden castles, set against the northwestern wall, was under Godfrey's command. Fighters filled the various levels of the tower, with Godfrey and his brother Eustace on the highest platform; at the base of the tower, which had wheels, were those who, as the Crusaders made progress, would push the tower closer and closer to the wall.[133] To the south, Raymond commanded the other tower. William of Tyre captures the pre-battle zeal of the Western warriors on the morning of July 14:

> At daybreak, according to arrangement, the entire Christian army stood before the city, fully armed and ready for the attack. One single purpose fired the hearts of all—either to restore Jerusalem to the enjoyment of Christian liberty or to give up their lives for Christ's sake. There was not one person in that great throng, whether aged or sick or even very young, who did not fervently and zealously long for battle. Even women, regardless of sex and natural weakness, dared to assume arms and fought manfully far beyond their strength. Thus the Christians advanced with one accord to battle. All tried to push the newly constructed engines closer to the wall so that they might more easily attack those who were putting up a strenuous resistance on the ramparts and the towers.[134]

The initial phase of the assault saw Muslims rain down "showers of arrows and missiles" on the Crusaders; moreover, "stones, hurled both by hand and from machine, fell with fearful force" and wreaked havoc among the Christians, "as the infidels tried by every device to keep our people from approaching the wall." Even so, "the pilgrims, undismayed, strove to approach closer to the fortifications…. Thus, as both sides were exerting themselves to the utmost and fighting with bitter hatred, the conflict continued from morning to night. It was persistent and terrible beyond belief."[135]

For those who participated in this siege, such as Raymond of Aguilers, the conflict could only be understood on theological grounds: "We gladly labored to capture the city for the glory of God," he wrote, "they less willingly strove to resist our efforts for the sake of the laws of Mohammed. It is hard to believe how great were the efforts made on both sides during the night."[136]

By nightfall, Christian progress had been made. The forces of Godfrey and Raymond, the former especially, had managed to penetrate the exterior walls and fill in parts of the moat. Now exhausted, both besiegers and besieged disengaged and retired.

Godfrey's Tower

On awakening to the sound of battle in the early hours of July 15, the Muslims were shocked to find Godfrey's camp completely gone; looking again they saw it was right up against another section of their wall—tower and all. While the weary Muslims had slept, the equally exhausted but indefatigable Christians had, under Godfrey's leadership and the cover of night, continued to pursue the war. The siege recommenced with implacable determination. William offers a snapshot of the Muslims' desperate response:

> [I]n the hope of putting an end to our efforts once for all, they hurled down fire upon the machines in fragile jars and in every other possible way. They also threw down sulfur and pitch, grease and fat, wax, dry wood and stubble—anything, in fact, that might help to feed the flame by acting as fuel. As a result, in both armies frightful havoc was wrought, and many, both knights and foot soldiers, perished by various mishaps and unforeseen accidents. Some were crushed to atoms by missiles hurled from the engines; others collapsed suddenly, pierced through both breast plate and shield by the showers of arrows and spears. Some died immediately, struck by sharp rocks hurled either by hand or from the machines. Others lived on with shattered

44

limbs disabled for many days or, perchance, forever. Nevertheless, these many perils could not deter the contestants from their undertaking nor lessen their fervent determination to fight. Nor was it easy to judge which people contended with the greater enthusiasm.[137]

All this time, "Duke Godfrey was up high in his tower, not as a soldier but as an archer," writes Robert the Monk. "[T]he arrows he fired pierced right through the chest of the enemies, in at one side out at the other." He and his brother Eustace "withstood the hard blows of darts and stones and paid them back with fourfold interest…. They rained blows on each other the whole day."[138]

Amazingly to modern sensibilities, even as "this battle was taking place on top of the walls, there was a procession around them in which the crosses and relics and holy altars were carried."[139] Especially adding Christian insult to Muslim injury was a large "cross shining brightly with gold" fixed atop Godfrey's tower. "The Saracens were striving keenly to destroy this by the bombardment of mangonels," to no avail. One massive stone did, however, strike a knight stationed alongside Godfrey, crushing his skull and killing him. "The duke, who missed so narrowly a blow, fought back fiercely with his crossbow," even as he held up collapsing sections of his tower "by bracing his massive strength against them until repairs could be made."[140]

Meanwhile, "Godfrey's men, with unrelenting exertion and zeal, sent arrows and boulders against the Saracens, and…wrought considerable havoc by hurling firebrands wrapped in cotton into the city"[141]—even as the Duke's wooden tower continued to edge closer and closer to the wall. In desperation, the Muslims reportedly had two female "sorceresses" who "tried to bewitch one of the hurling machines, but a stone struck and crushed them…."[142]

The Muslims' only hope was to torch Godfrey's tower. Twice did they attach massive tree trunks together and, setting them aflame, drop them between Jerusalem's wall and his tower; and twice did Godfrey and his men, who were prepared for such a maneuver, extinguish the blaze, including with vinegar. Thus "Mohamet was defeated twice and Christ was twice the victor," observed Ralph of Caen.[143]

The Duke fought fire with fire by ordering sacks of straw set aflame so "that those who were trying to defend that wall could not open their mouths or eyes." In this smoky inferno, Godfrey, with his renowned strength, single-handedly heaved a platform from his tower to the city's wall. It was quickly bridged by two of his men, German brothers, Ludolph and Engelbert, followed by Godfrey and his brother, Eustace.

The walls of Jerusalem had finally been breached; scores of enflamed Crusaders followed the Germans.[144] Having descended or jumped into the city, Muslims were dismayed to see the "duke and those who were with him"; the Christians "united their forces and, protected by their shields and helmets, swept hither and thither through the streets and squares of the city with drawn swords. Regardless of age and condition, they laid low, without distinction, every enemy encountered. Everywhere was frightful carnage...."[145]

Following close on his heels were Tancred, the counts of Flanders and Normandy, and Count Raymond. The gates were flung open from the inside and "the entire army rushed in pell-mell without order and discipline."[146] Indeed, "the pressure and anxiety of those entering this gate was so great that even the horses themselves, vexed by the excessive pressure, attacked very many with their teeth" and "were sweating incredibly."[147] Holed up in the citadel, Jerusalem's Muslim governor eventually surrendered to Raymond on assurance that he and his would be granted mercy.

"Meanwhile," writes Albert of Aachen, "Duke Godfrey had no desire for the citadel, the palace, gold, or silver or any kind of spoils."[148] He was instead "desperate to make the enemy pay for the blood of the servants of God which had been spilt around Jerusalem, and wanted revenge for the insults they had heaped on the pilgrims. In no battle had he ever found so many opportunities to kill, not even on the bridge at Antioch where he had cut in half the Turkish giant."[149] The legend of Godfrey's wrath grew over the years, so that, writing some two decades later, Matthew of Edessa asserted that, once inside Jerusalem, "Godfrey fell upon the infidels with all his might and slaughtered sixty-five thousand men."[150]

All Christian sources indicate that the carnage was so horrific that, once the battle frenzy had subsided, "even the victors experienced sensations of horror and loathing," writes William, adding, "It was impossible to look upon the vast numbers of the slain without horror.... Still more dreadful was it to gaze upon the victors themselves, dripping with blood from head to toe, an ominous sight which brought terror to all that met them."[151] (One historical point of view holds that the chroniclers exaggerated the slaughter in apocalyptic terms as a way of underscoring "God's righteous judgment against the heathen.")

In the end, and as picturesquely described by Edward Gibbon, "Godfrey of Bouillon stood victorious on the walls of Jerusalem. His example was followed on every side by the emulation of valour; and about four hundred and sixty years after the conquest of Omar, the holy city was rescued from the Mohammedan yoke."[152]

First to enter Jerusalem and exercise his vengeance, Godfrey was also first to decide that "prayer rather than bloodshed befitted their first hours in Jerusalem, and set the example to the others by withdrawing from the carnage, and going barefooted, clad simply in a clean linen garment, to the sepulchre of our Lord, to return thanks that He had thus allowed them to accomplish their pilgrimage and fulfil their vows. Godfrey was followed by all."[153]

Jubilant that their impossible mission had been accomplished, and eager to do what they had come all this way to do, "all approached it [the Sepulchre] not on foot but on their elbows and knees and flooded the floors with tears running down."[154]

There they "were met by the [indigenous] clergy of the faithful citizens of Jerusalem. These Christians who for many years had borne the heavy yoke of undeserved bondage were eager to show their gratitude to the Redeemer for their restoration to liberty. Bearing in their hands crosses and relics of saints, they led the way into the church to the accompaniment of hymns and sacred songs."[155]

Henceforward, "Allah Akbar...was no longer heard in the city. It was replaced by the returning sounds of 'Christ conquers, rules, and commands.'"[156]

Defender of Christ's Sepulchre

Once order was restored, it "became necessary to debate the question of who should be King; one individual needed to be chosen from amongst them all to rule such a great city and population."[157] An election was agreed to and candidates, which included Godfrey, set forward. However, and to quote William of Tyre,

[I]n order that the...merits of the candidates might receive due consideration, individuals from the households of those proposed for the honor were secretly interviewed. Each man was forced to take an oath that, when questioned concerning the life and character of his lord, he would speak the truth without deviating from the facts. This course was adopted so that the electors might obtain full and accurate information as to the worth of the several candidates.[158]

Many of the questions sought to ascertain the worst or most immoral aspects of the nominees. When it came to Godfrey, his men, on oath, said that the most vexing thing they recalled him doing was spending an inordinate amount of time in church after mass had concluded and questioning the clergy on theological issues, so that they, his companions, became "excessively bored." Worse, the meal prepared for them after mass had grown cold and tasteless.[159]

Although the followers of other leaders made strong cases, in the end, "Duke Godfrey was chosen by unanimous agreement of all in a clear vote and with general agreement, on the eighth day after the taking of the city [July 23]," writes Robert the Monk.[160] The fact is, following the capture of Antioch, Godfrey had become the "dominant figure" of the First Crusade, especially popular with the rank and file—a fact which was sealed by his prominent role in capturing Jerusalem.[161]

Even so, the Duke appears to have been reluctant to take on the honor. He had only vowed to go on pilgrimage in an effort to liberate Jerusalem and had "no intention of expatriating himself forever."[162] Besides, he had the important duchy of Lorraine in his charge, where—no doubt, and due to his heroic exploits—he would be more honored than the emperor upon his return. On the other hand, remaining in Jerusalem—in this small Christian island surrounded by a tumultuous Muslim sea—meant nonstop threats, privations, and warfare.

In the end he accepted, though under one condition: that he not be called King of Jerusalem, but rather Defender of the Holy Sepulchre—for, "God forbid," said he, "that I should be crowned with a crown of gold, where my Saviour bore a crown of thorns."[163]

Such was Godfrey: "his piety, though blind, was sincere," writes the normally cynical Edward Gibbon, a paragon of the Enlightenment, before elaborating: "he reserved his enmity for the enemies of Christ... and his pure and disinterested zeal was acknowledged by his rivals.... In the mind of Godfrey of Bouillon every human consideration was subordinate to the glory of God and the success of the crusade."[164]

The Battle of Ascalon

Days after his coronation, in early August, Jerusalem's new Defender received his first challenge: a massive Muslim army, consisting of Egyptians, North Africans, Arabs, sub-Saharan Africans, and Turks, led by al-Afdal Shahanshah (1066–1122), the vizier and effective ruler of Fatimid Egypt, was making its way to besiege Jerusalem and annihilate the insolent Christians once and for all. Although the Sunni Turks and Shia Fatimids had been at each other's throats for decades, "fear of the Christians…drew them together."[165] For Robert the Monk, who tended to see temporal conflicts as reflective of eternal ones, that "writhing serpent" Satan had "in his venom" stirred up the "whole of the Orient."[166]

Rather than taking a defensive posture and barricading Jerusalem, Godfrey, as usual, decided to go out and give battle with his entire army on August 10, leaving only a small contingent to guard his new kingdom. Knowing that everything was on the line—and that they were outnumbered by and far from refreshed as the Fatimid army—the knights marched barefoot in the desert heat, carrying a fragment of the True Cross, which had been recovered on May 5 in Jerusalem, while loudly imploring God for aid.

They met and were augmented by the forces of Count Raymond and the two Roberts, the counts of Normandy and Flanders. Altogether the Crusader army consisted of about one thousand knights and ten thousand infantrymen; the Muslim army was as much as five times larger (though some sources say it consisted of as many as three hundred thousand).[167]

On August 11, the Franks, having neared the coastal city of Ascalon, where al-Afdal's forces were encamped, captured Muslim spies and ascertained the opposing army's status and layout. With such information, Godfrey decided that a surprise attack was in order. Thus, at the crack of dawn on August 12, the tired Christian fighters attended mass, partook of communion, and then, once again, rode out to victory or death.[168]

And again, as at Antioch, the much larger and overconfident Muslim army was taken unawares; the vizier was shocked to learn that, instead of abandoning or at least barricading themselves inside Jerusalem, the

Christian infidels had actually dared to rush out and intercept him. "Either they have lost their senses," he exclaimed before his chiefs, "or they love death as much as life." Either way, "exterminate them from the earth!"[169]

A wild battle ensued and continued for the greater part of the day, though the Christians had the upper-hand. "[W]ith drawn swords in the hands of his followers," Albert writes, "Godfrey visited severe destruction on the enemy...."[170] Robert of Normandy also distinguished himself in battle, slaughtering the vizier's own standard bearer; and Raymond "killed innumerable enemies and forced many more to plunge in the sea." By late afternoon, thousands of Muslims lay dead or dying on the sands outside the walls of Ascalon. The rest fled back to Egypt—even as the Crusaders "pursued the enemies of the Cross of Christ."[171]

According to Robert the Monk's account, which was informed by a Muslim deserter, right before the Fatimids were routed, Vizier al-Afdal was heard lamenting to Allah and his prophet:

O Mahommed, our master and protector, where is your strength?.... Why have you abandoned your people like this to be mercilessly destroyed and dispersed and killed by a wretchedly poor and ragged people, a people who are the scrapings of other races, the lees, rust and slag of the whole human race.... Are those who have such power really men or are they in fact gods from Hell? Maybe Hell split asunder and let these men spew forth.... If they were really men they would fear death; but as it is they have no fear of returning to the Hell from which they emerged.... O Mahommed, Mahommed.... This is what the Christians say to insult us: that the power of the Crucified One is greater than yours because he is powerful on earth and in heaven. And it certainly seems to be the case now that those who place their trust in him win, whilst those who revere you are defeated.... So whose fault is it that we are reduced to this state? Why should we give you every honor and receive nothing in return? O Jerusalem...if you ever fall into our hands I shall raze you to the ground and completely destroy the Sepulchre of the One buried in you.[172]

By now, Godfrey's renown had reached even distant Muslims. One notable story concerns an Arab sheikh who traveled to and met with the Defender of Christ's Sepulchre under a flag of truce, simply to test "the amazing strength of Godfrey, whose drawn sword turned one Turk into two [at Antioch]," writes Ralph of Caen.[173] William recounts the story:

> When he stood in the presence of the duke and had greeted him with all due reverence, the Arab chief earnestly begged Godfrey that he would deign to smite with his own sword an immense camel which he had brought for this purpose. He wished to be able to testify to others of the duke's strength as seen with his own eyes. Since the chief had come from a long distance to see him, Godfrey consented. Unsheathing his sword, he cut off the animal's head as easily as if it had been some fragile object. The Arab was amazed at the evidence of such great strength, but, in his own heart, he attributed the feat largely to the sharpness of the sword. Accordingly, begging leave to speak freely, he asked Godfrey whether he could accomplish a similar feat with the sword of another. The duke, smiling a little, requested that the Arab's own sword be brought to him. Taking it, he commanded another animal of the same kind be brought before him.* This done, he raised the sword and without difficulty struck off its head also at one blow.[174]

Finale

Soon after the battle of Ascalon, most of the great lords of the First Crusade—including Raymond, Robert of Normandy, and Robert of Flanders—having fulfilled their vows and accomplished their pilgrimage, "revealed to the duke their intention of returning home," that is, their intention of leaving him to his fate. Perhaps to their surprise, "they found him agreeable to all things which they had in mind." Albert continues:

> The duke, fulfilling in all things the will of his brothers, decided to remain in Jerusalem, because the power of the city was granted to his protection and defense, and, embracing his comrades' necks for a long time and graciously kissing them, he beseeched them tearfully with all his strength, while wishing them well, that they should be mindful, and should impress on their Christian brothers [in the West], that they should not hesitate to come to the Lord's Sepulchre,

---

* Although this anecdote might be suggestive of animal cruelty, it should be borne in mind that in the late eleventh century every ounce of both camels—skin, meat, and bone—would have been put to good use.

but should flock daily to assist him and the other comrades who were staying in exile to oppose so many barbarous peoples.[175]

If fact, the threats were constant and from every direction. As William writes, "The entire country surrounding their possessions was inhabited by infidel Saracens, who were most cruel enemies of our people. These were all the more dangerous because they were close at hand.... Any Christian who walked along the highway without taking due precaution was liable to be killed by the Saracens, or seized and handed over as a slave to the enemy."[176]

However, rather than shrink into a defensive posture, which always contradicted his nature, Godfrey again took to the offensive and carved out a secure perimeter around Jerusalem, reducing various Muslim cities—Acre, Tyre, Sidon, Tripoli, and Beirut—to tributaries, for "fear of the most Christian duke was instilled in all the lands and regions of the gentiles."[177] He even, it is said, vowed to travel to Mecca to overthrow "Mahon"—that is, Muhammad—from his seat of power.[178]

Perhaps it was precisely because of his relentless drive that the Duke's reign was destined to be a short one. On July 18, 1100, slightly less than one year after his coronation, the Defender of the Holy Sepulchre died, aged forty.

What exactly happened is unclear, as the chroniclers, both Christian and Muslim, give different accounts. Some say he died after contracting and suffering from a prolonged illness brought on by his indefatigable activity; others say he was struck by and eventually died from a Muslim arrow during his siege of Acre. Perhaps the most plausible explanation, because it bridges the two others—personal illness and Muslim animosity—is that he was poisoned.

On marching to and reaching Caesarea, the "Muslim chiefs came to him on the pretext of making peace and brought food and set it before him," writes Matthew of Edessa. At first, Godfrey politely declined, but on being pressured and not wishing to be rude, he "ate the food, not knowing that it was poisoned."[179] He quickly fell ill and, barely able to sit upright atop his horse, returned to Jerusalem.

As he lay in his deathbed, he called for his leading men and said, "Behold, I am about to enter the path of the universal world. While I am still alive, I would have your counsel about who should be appointed to rule in my place in Jerusalem." The warrior-monk had never married and had no heir. "We place our trust in your providence," they responded with some emotion. "Whomever you choose for us, we will obey him without any doubt."[180] He named his younger brother, Baldwin, the conqueror and count of Edessa, a proven and popular leader; and then Godfrey died on July 18, 1100.

According to Albert of Aachen, after the "noble champion of Christ" died, there followed five days of "very great lamentation and bitter weeping by all the Christians there—Gauls, Italians, Syrians, Armenians, [and] Greeks."[181] The Defender of the Sepulchre was honored by being buried in Golgotha, near the entrance of his Lord's tomb. On Christmas Day of that same year, Baldwin was crowned king of Jerusalem; his blood would flow in generations of kings in the Holy Land.

Due to his exemplary life (by at least Medieval Christian standards), Godfrey became the quintessential model of Christian virtue for the descendants of the First Crusaders. "To us he seems not merely a king, but the best of kings, a light and mirror to others," wrote William of Tyre, who was born in Jerusalem thirty years after Godfrey's death and interviewed those who knew the duke: "he scorned the pomp and vanity of the world to which every creature is prone. It was in the spirit of humility that he declined the crown which would perish, in the hope of attaining hereafter one that would never fade."[182]

Almost immediately after his death, Godfrey's fame spread far and wide; he was seen as *the* chivalrous hero par excellence of the First Crusade—his very name eventually becoming "shorthand for the entire crusading movement."[183] Before long, fabulous accretions and supernatural exploits were also heaped upon his name, particularly in those French *chansons de geste*, poetic epics concerning knightly deeds, that centered around him.

Memory of him lived on for long, including in Jerusalem. Although his tomb was destroyed in 1808, one thing of his remained, as described by Mark Twain, who, in 1867 explored the Holy Land with a group of other Americans. While visiting the Holy Sepulchre, "the relic that touched us most," Twain wrote, "was the plain old sword of that stout Crusader, Godfrey of Bulloigne—King Godfrey of Jerusalem":

No blade in Christendom wields such enchantment as this—no blade of all that rust in the ancestral halls of Europe is able to invoke such visions of romance in the brain of him who looks upon it— none that can prate of such chivalric deeds or tell such brave tales of the warrior days of old.... This very sword has cloven hundreds of Saracen Knights from crown to chin in those old times when Godfrey wielded it.[184]

"I can never forget old Godfrey's sword, now," the American continued, adding, apparently satirically, that he would like to use it to kill "all the [Muslim] infidels in Jerusalem," in revenge for the massacres they were still visiting upon the Christians of the Holy Land. As Twain explained, a few years before his visit, in 1861,

> [Five thousand] men, women and children were butchered indiscriminately and left to rot by the hundreds all through the Christian quarter [of Damascus] ....[T]he stench was dreadful. All the Christians who could get away fled from the city, and the Mohammedans would not defile their hands by burying the "infidel dogs." The thirst for blood extended to the high lands of Hermon and Anti-Lebanon, and in a short time twenty-five thousand more Christians were massacred and their possessions laid waste. How they hate a Christian in Damascus!—and pretty much all over Turkeydom as well. And how they will pay for it when Russia turns her guns upon them again![185]

In the end, and without taking anything away from Godfrey's well-earned reputation, it must be acknowledged that without the other Crusade leaders—not to mention the nameless foot soldiers who bled and died on the road to Jerusalem—there would be no Duke to speak of. The success of the First Crusade was above all a collective effort: his brothers, Eustace and Baldwin; the Normans, Bohemond and his nephew Tancred; Count Raymond of Toulouse; Count Robert of Flanders; Count Robert of Normandy—and so many more named and unnamed—each played important roles in the recovery of Jerusalem from Islam; and there are not a few historians who might argue for one of these in the place of Godfrey.

Still, in electing him as effective king of the Holy Land—a land so important to them that they were willing to sacrifice everything, including their lives and possessions—it was these other lords who decided who was greatest among them (a choice that I for one shall not gainsay).

As William of Tyre writes, "For no one can doubt that one who was unanimously singled out as the best by famous princes who are said to be unequalled in the world was a very great man indeed."[186]

CHAPTER 2

The Cid:
Lord and Master of War

"The Moors called on Muhammad and the Christians on St. James. In a short time one thousand three hundred Moors fell dead upon the field. How well the Cid…fought…. [H]e approached a Moorish leader mounted on a fine horse and dealt him such a blow with his sword that he cut him through the waist and hurled the rest of his body to the ground…. What a great day it was for Christendom when the Moors fled from the place!"
—*POEM OF THE CID*[1]

"Do you see my bloodstained sword and my horse dripping sweat? That is how Moors are vanquished in battle."
—THE CID[2]

After the Arabs had conquered Christian North Africa in the seventh century—from Egypt in the east to Mauretania (Morocco) in the west—the only way to continue the jihad was by crossing the Pillars of Hercules (now Straits of Gibraltar) into Europe. Thus in 711, fleets of Arabs and African Berbers—collectively known as "Moors" in Western sources—"godlessly invaded Spain to destroy it," says the Latin *Chronicle of 754*.[3]

After meeting and defeating Visigothic king Roderick at Guadalete in 711—"never was there in the West a more bloody battle than this," writes the Muslim chronicler Ibn 'Abd al-Hakam (b.803), "for the Muslims did not withdraw their scimitars from them for three days"—the invaders continued to penetrate northward into Spain, "not passing a place without reducing it, and getting possession of its wealth, for Allah Almighty had struck with terror the hearts of the infidels."[4]

Such terrorism was intentionally cultivated in keeping with the Koran (e.g., 3:151, 8:12). In one instance, the invaders slaughtered, boiled, and ate—or rather pretended to eat—their captives, prompting hysteria among the Christians of Spain that "the Muslims feed on human flesh," and thereby "contributing in no small degree to increase the panic of the infidels," writes another Arab chronicler.[5]

Emboldened by the Muslims' initial victories, swarms of North Africans "crossed the sea on every vessel or bark they could lay hold of," and so overwhelmed the peninsula that before long "the Christians were obliged to shut themselves up in their castles and fortresses, and, quitting the flat country, betake themselves to their mountains."[6] This is not to say that the Spaniards did not fight back; even Muslim chroniclers note how "the Christians defended themselves with the utmost vigor and resolution, and great was the havoc that they made in the ranks of the faithful." In Córdoba, for example, a number of Spaniards holed themselves up in a church; although "the besieged had no hopes of deliverance, they were so obstinate that when safety was offered to them on condition either of embracing Islam, or paying jizya, they refused to surrender, and the church being set on fire, they all perished in the flames."[7]

One year after the Islamic invasion, in 712, the Muslims had, in the words of the *Chronicle of 754*, "ruined beautiful cities, burning them with fire; condemned lords and powerful men to the cross; and butchered youths and infants with the sword." As for their leader, Musa bin Nusayr—the Yemenite governor of Africa who followed his jihadists— "He terrorized everyone."[8]

Other early sources corroborate the devastation. The oldest account, the *Tempore belli*, a Latin church hymn written soon after the fall of the Visigoths, "describes an 'implacable enemy,' 'full of enthusiasm in the exercise of war,' 'forcing Christian troops to turn around and flee in panic,' sacking Christian temples and homes, burning the cities of those who resisted, and taking their young women as sexual slaves, all creating an 'indescribable terror.'"[9]

There is, in fact, no dearth of chronicles documenting how "the Muslim conquerors killed the men, burned cities, wasted the land, took young women as sexual slaves"; "cut down fruit trees, destroyed churches, regarded sacred music as blasphemy, and profaned chalices"; "changed the towers of ancient cities [to mosques]; destroyed castles… [and] monasteries; burned the books of the sacred [Christian] law, and committed many bad deeds."[10]

Native Spaniards had two choices: submit to Muslim rule—which often meant be exposed to exploitation and humiliation if not outright treachery—or "flee to the mountains," continues the *Chronicle of 754*, "where they risked hunger and various forms of death." This is a reference to the inhospitable regions of Asturias and Galicia in the northwest quadrant of Spain; due to its rough terrain and remoteness, it remained largely free of Muslim control, and—despite the severe difficulties of eking out a living off it—was the destination of every Visigothic fugitive who wished to live free of Islam.[11]

Pelagius (Pelayo in Spanish, 685–737), a relative of and "sword-bearer" to King Roderick, and a survivor of the battle of Guadalete, eventually consented to become a vassal of Munuza, a local Muslim chief. When the Moor seized upon Pelagius's sister, the sword-bearer rebelled, and, like other Christians before him, fled to a nearby mountain, where he "joined himself to as many people as he found hastening to assemble."[12] There, in the deepest recesses of the Asturian mountains the assembled Christian fugitives declared Pelagius their new king; and the Kingdom of Asturias, the first Christian kingdom after the Muslims overthrew the Visigoths, was born.

Before long, a large Muslim army was sent to bring these infidel rebels to heal. Oppa, a Visigothic bishop of noble descent, now serving the Muslims, was sent to parley with Pelagius at the mouth of a deep cavern: "If when the entire army of the Goths was assembled [at Guadalete], it was unable to sustain the attack of the Ishmaelites [meaning Arabs], how much better will you be able to defend yourself on this mountaintop?" he rhetorically asked. "To me it seems difficult. Rather, heed my warning and recall your soul from this decision, so that you may take advantage of many good things and enjoy the partnership [of the Arabs]."[13]

"I will not associate with the Arabs in friendship nor will I submit to their authority," Pelagius angrily retorted, adding, "Christ is our hope that through this little mountain"—which he likened to the "mustard seed" of the famous parable that eventually grows into something great (Mark 4:30–32)—the "well-being of Spain and the army of the Gothic people will be restored."[14] Battle commenced there at Covadonga—meaning "Cavern of the Lady"—sometime around 720, and, due to the terrain which was conducive to their guerilla tactics, the vastly outnumbered Christians prevailed, thereby permanently establishing their presence in the northwestern most tip of Spain.

Ahmad bin Muhammad al-Maqqari (1578–1632), a chief historical source on Islamic Spain, or al-Andalus as it was known in Arabic, had access to many now lost accounts and offers the Muslim perspective on this pivotal development:

> [A] despicable barbarian, whose name was Belay [Pelagius], rose in the land of Galicia [later part of Asturias], and, having reproached his countrymen for their ignominious dependence and their cowardly flight, began to stir them up to revenge the past injuries, and to expel the Moslems from the land of their ancestors. From that moment the Christians of Andalus began to resist the attacks of the Moslems on such districts as had remained in their possession, and to defend their wives and daughters.... The commencement of the rebellion happened thus: there remained no city, town, or village in Galicia but what was in the hands of the Moslems, with the exception of a steep mountain.... [There, Belay/Pelagius] took refuge with three hundred followers, whom the Moslems ceased not to pursue and to attack, until the greater part of them died of hunger, and Belay remained with only thirty men and ten women, whose sole food consisted of honey which they gathered in the crevices of the rock.... However, Belay and his men fortified themselves by degrees in the passes of the mountain until the Moslems were made acquainted with their preparations; but, perceiving how few they were, they heeded not the advice conveyed to them, and allowed them to gather strength, saying, "What are thirty barbarians, perched upon a rock?—they must inevitably die."[15]

Several jihads were subsequently launched to conquer the tiny Asturian kingdom, and the "Christians of the North scarcely knew the meaning of repose, security, or any of the amenities of life."[16] Even so, the resilient mustard seed continued to grow—not least because "all who were dissatisfied with Moorish dominion, all who clung to the hope of a Christian revival, all who detested Mahomet," fled to and augmented its ranks.[17]

In an effort to snuff them out once and for all, in 793, Córdoban Emir Hisham I (757–796) declared a jihad to end all jihads against the Christian rebels of the north. One hundred thousand Muslims, coming from as far as Arabia, answered his call. For months, they "traversed this land in every direction, raping women, killing warriors, destroying fortresses, burning and pillaging everything, driving back the enemy who fled in disorder," writes Ibn al-Athir. The Muslim general "returned safe and sound, dragging behind him Allah alone knows how much booty."[18]

As other sources make clear, much of this "booty" consisted of Christian women and children; for Muslims "particularly valued blond or red-haired Franc or Galician women as sexual slaves"—so much so that Muslim Spain "became a center for the trade and distribution of slaves" to the rest of the Islamic world.[19] Christian subjects were sometimes even required to make an annual tribute "not of money, or horses, or arms, but of a hundred damsels (all to be distinguished for beauty) to ornament the harems."[20]

Even so, the Christians of the north persevered and, in 844, scored another significant—miraculous, even—victory over the Muslims at Clavijo. During that battle, the Apostle James the Greater (son of Zebedee)—whose relics had long rested at his shrine of Santiago de Compostela in Galicia—is said to have appeared on a snow-white charger, slaughtering thousands of Muslims. (The apostle—now better known as Santiago Matamoros, that is, "Saint James the Moor-Slayer"—would go on to play an inspirational and symbolic role in Spain's wars against Islam and remains its patron saint.)

By the eleventh century, the Asturian "mustard seed" had morphed into or alongside several Christian kingdoms, including León, Castile, Navarre, Aragon, and Catalonia. Eventually a scorched no-man's-land, roughly along the Duero River, separated Muslim-ruled Spain (al-Andalus) from the northern Christian states. Because "service in the holy war, according to [the prophet] Muhammad, was the most meritorious of all works," the "opportunity to participate in the holy war in Spain and to obtain religious merit and even entrance into paradise drew many volunteers to the peninsula."[21] The Christian-Muslim frontier was utterly devastated.

Then came Muhammad bin Abi Amir (938–1002)—a highly pious ruler of Córdoba who always meditated over the Koran before battle. His overriding goal was to annihilate the Christian north. Once he proclaimed jihad—and because "every young Moor of ambition, every aspirant for a paradise, either in this world or the next…sought his career and his field in Christian Spain"—they flocked to his banner in droves.[22] With these hordes, Muhammad "made war, summer and winter, against the Christians," boasts a Muslim chronicler.[23] He personally participated in fifty-seven jihads—all successful—earning him the appellation of Almanzor (from Arabic *al-munsoor*), "the Victorious One."

During these campaigns, the Muslims massacred, raped, and enslaved tens of thousands of Christians, and plundered, desecrated, and torched hundreds if not thousands of churches and shrines—including Spain's most sacred, Santiago Compostela, the shrine of Saint James the Moor-Slayer. Almanzor sent its church-bells on the backs of Christian slaves as trophies of war to adorn the Great Mosque of Córdoba. Indeed, with each of Almanzor's jihads, "hosts of captives and long trains of carts, laden with the heads of the vanquished or with crosses, censers, holy vessels, and other rich spoil, kept pouring into Cordova." Hoping to placate the jihadist warlord, terrified Spanish nobles even "surrendered their daughters to be his [sex] slaves."[24]

But even the Victorious One could not live forever; worse for Islam, twenty-nine years after Almanzor's death, the Córdoban caliphate collapsed in 1031, and al-Andalus splintered into over thirty infighting Muslim kingdoms (or *taifas*). Before long, some of their petty kings, certainly not all, ignored the duty of jihad—it had become overly onerous against the Christians who, having withstood centuries of jihad, had become as hard as adamantine—and turned to the pleasures of life.

Seeing their opportunity, the long harried Christians of the north, who by now shared in the same chivalric and knightly culture of Medieval Europe, moved fast, particularly under Ferdinand I of León-Castile (c.1015–1065), better known as "Ferdinand the Great." His "ambition was to subjugate the whole of Moslem Spain"; he is sometimes credited with formally setting the Reconquista, or the recovery of Spain, in motion.[25] This "God-fearing man," says the *Chronicle of the Kings of León*, began to make "a great slaughter of the Saracens and each and every year he received from their kings the appointed tribute."[26] The tables were slowly but surely turning.

Roderick Díaz of Vivar

In this backdrop, Roderick (Rodrigo in Spanish) Díaz was born in Vivar, a village near Burgos, the capital of León-Castile, around 1043. Raised in the arts of war by his father, a minor noble, Roderick was knighted during his late teens and entered into Ferdinand's service by joining the entourage of Sancho, the king's eldest son and heir apparent. By the age of twenty-three, and as a testimony to his prowess, Roderick had risen to become the prince's second and standard bearer. It was during these early years that he became known among his compatriots as "the Campeador"—"the master of the battle field" in Old Spanish (from the Latin, *campi doctor*).

As for the Arabic epithet that posterity would come to know him by—El Cid and Mío Cid, "the lord" and "my lord," respectively—chronicler Juan de Mariana (b.1536) offers the following account:

> [Roderick] adventured with his own forces, to make excursions into the territories of the Infidels, and in battle overthrew five Moorish kings...but released them upon condition that they should pay him a yearly tribute. At this time King Ferdinand was busy, in rebuilding the City Zamora, which had not been repaired since the Moors destroyed it.... It happened whilst the King was there, the Moors came to pay the tribute they had agreed upon to Roderick Díaz, and called him Cid, which in Arabic signifies Lord. All this was done in the presence of the King and his Courtiers, whence many took an occasion to envy and hate him.[27]

Alas for Roderick, such "envy and hate" would hound him for the rest of his life.

The one aspect of his personality that has most been lost to modernity is his severity and extreme ferocity in war: "Solidity, seriousness—these were his most obvious characteristics," writes historian Louis Bertrand:

> He was also a strong willed and obstinate man who followed his path without deviating from it. Fundamentally tempestuous and violent by nature, he learnt how to hold himself in check. He got the better of his enemies by a perfect mastery over himself, even though he was

sometimes subject to terrible gusts of passion. He restrained them almost immediately. This violent man was able to pass himself off as a man temperamentally moderate.[28]

In other words, he was able to pass himself off in "polite society," among which he received the typical, noble education—in grammar, rhetoric, logic, and law; he was certainly literate (Latin inscriptions from him exist). Due to the many years he spent among the Moors, he was at least acquainted with and possibly fluent in Arabic. As Ibn Bassam relays, "Books were studied in his presence. The doings and the deeds of the paladins of Arabia of old were read to him, and, when one came to the story of Mohallab [a legendary Arab warrior of great renown*], he was enchanted to the point of ecstasy."[29]

Such "ecstasy" for all things dealing with battle and bloodshed further underscores his fundamentally warlike demeanor. Indeed, Roderick's prowess often manifested itself in ways reminiscent of the berserker's fury in the Viking sagas; during "emergencies such as a surprise attack by night he would tremble with excitement and grind his teeth; whenever there was the prospect of a battle his heart would leap with joy."[30]

Of his physical appearance, the best that can be surmised is that he was a "sturdy man, very tall and very hairy, a rough warrior in a leather jerkin."[31] His most distinctive feature in later years was, in the words of the *Poem of the Cid* that would later immortalize him, "his long, flowing beard [which] was a wonderful sight!" He strokes it when pondering weighty matters, and ties it around his waist during battle. Those who see it cannot keep their eyes off it. When his court adversary, García Ordóñez, accuses Roderick of "allow[ing] his beard to grow long to strike terror in the hearts of all," the Cid responds: "Thanks be to almighty God, it is long because it has much loving care lavished on it. What reproach can you cast on my beard? All my life it has been my chief delight. No woman's son has ever plucked it out and no one, Moor or Christian, ever tore it—as happened to yours."[32]

---

* Considering that the Cid would have been much better acquainted with and seeking to emulate the heroes of his own heritage—of which there was no shortage from the ancient Greco-Roman epics to the exploits of Charlemagne and Roland—more than one historian have suggested that Ibn Bassam is here trying to credit his own Islamic heritage with inspiring the Christian Cid to great feats of arms.

First Exile

In 1065, King Ferdinand died. Roderick continued serving as general commander under now King Sancho II, until the latter was assassinated in 1072, at which point he served his younger brother and new king, Alfonso VI. This would make for an awkward relationship; for when he was Sancho's captain, Roderick had fought and defeated Alfonso's forces during the brothers' civil war.

Far from doing what most other nobles would have done—ingratiate himself with his new lord—during Alfonso's crowning ceremony in the Church of Santa Gadea in Burgos, Roderick managed only to further scandalize the soon-to-be-king by compelling him to swear publicly—thrice no less—that he had nothing to do with his brother's assassination. It was only after Alfonso complied that the Cid—this man whose audacious sense of honor and loyalty would continue to work against him more than once—finally knelt and swore fealty to his new lord.[33]

If the new king was vexed with his popular vassal, he did not show it, and their relationship soon stabilized. In 1075, Alfonso even had his own third cousin, Jimena, married to Roderick. She would give the Campeador a son and two daughters—as well as a large crucifix that he would always carry into battle (and which was only recently rediscovered in a Spanish cathedral in 2020).[34]

Suddenly, in 1081, Alfonso banished the Cid. The official story is that Roderick had conducted an unauthorized raid on Moors paying tribute to and thus under the protection of the king—and this at a time when a number of court nobles envious of the growing fame of Roderick were regularly defaming him before the king. (Although these reasons appear legitimate, one historical view suggests that they were ultimately pretexts for Alfonso who was still smarting from the Cid's cheek during his coronation.)

On pain of death, Alfonso's subjects throughout León-Castile were forbidden from offering the Cid any aid—no food, water, or shelter. Roderick left his wife and young children in the care of a religious order in Burgos. As he set off, the locals, huddled by and watching from their windows, remarked, "What a good vassal was here had he but a good lord!"[35]

Homeless and destitute, this once great captain of men set out to the northeast, the only region of Christian Spain not under Alfonso's rule.

To his surprise and comfort, some three hundred men chose to go into voluntarily exile with him. Roderick first went to and offered his services to Ramon Berenguer II, the count of Barcelona, to fight the surrounding Muslims. The latter ignored and, aware and possibly envious of his renown, spurned him as a lowly exile. So Roderick went to Berenguer's sometime enemy, Yusuf al-Mu'taman ibn Hud, the petty king of Zaragoza, the northern most Moorish kingdom of al-Andalus, who was only too happy to take this renowned warrior into his services.

Several factors unique to eleventh century Spain made this possible. Along with the aforementioned fracturing of the Córdoban caliphate and essential "secularization" of several though not all petty kings—some were still very much committed jihadists who persecuted Christians under their authority—most of the northern Muslim kingdoms had become vassals, and therefore allies, of the Christian kingdoms they bordered, especially León and Castile.[36]

Moreover, unlike the southernmost Moors, those of the north were racially intermingled with the Spaniards—particularly their rulers, who were often born to European slave girls and had fair hair and eyes* and "could thus understand their Northern brothers who had remained true to Christianity."[37] In short, for a destitute knight, exiled by his king and spurned by other Christian rulers to offer his services to the Moorish ruler of Zaragoza was far from surprising and arguably reflective of loyalty to his native Castile (as Zaragoza was a sometime vassal of it).

Al-Maqqari offers a valuable snapshot of the realpolitik behind such "*convivencia*":

> [N]ot only were the different independent [Muslim] chieftains at that time waging unrelenting war against each other, but they would not unfrequently avail themselves of the arms of the Christians to attack and destroy their own countrymen and brothers in religion.... The Christians, perceiving the state of corruption into which the Moslems had fallen, rejoiced extremely; for, at that time, very few men of virtue and principle were to be found amongst the Moslems, the generality of whom began to drink wine and commit all manner

---

* According to the calculations of Spanish Arabist Julian Ribera, due to the constant sexual intercourse with white slave women, the genetic Arab component of each generation of Umayyad rulers was reduced by half, so that the last Umayyad, Hisham II (976–1013), was approximately only 0.09 percent Arab (Fernandez-Morera, 162–163).

of excesses. The rulers of Andalusia thought of nothing else than purchasing singing-women and slaves, listening to their music, and passing their time in revelry and mirth, spending in dissipation and frivolous pastimes the treasures of the state, and oppressing their subjects with all manner of taxes and exactions, that they might send costly presents to Alfonso [VI], and induce him to serve their ambitious projects…. [In short,] the entire society was corrupted, and the body of Islam, deprived alike of life and soul, became a mere corpse.[38]

Roderick's reputation among the Moors as a formidable warrior was sealed over the next few years of service at Zaragoza—so much so that its ruler, Yusuf al-Mu'taman, confided to fellow Muslims that "Roderick is a hard man, a very brave and invincible fighter, such that I do not care to engage him in battle."[39] That he, the king of Zaragoza, and every other Muslim in that kingdom, referred to the infidel Roderick as *al-sayyad*—"the lord"—further underscores his steely reputation among them.

The Almoravids

Some years before exiling the Cid, in 1074, Alfonso VI, "being a man of great resolution," writes al-Maqqari, "and well acquainted with the pitiful state of Mohammedan affairs," sought to "subject the whole country to his detestable rule," and, like his father, Ferdinand, "began to attack all those among the rulers [of al-Andalus] who refused to pay him tribute."[40] He "traversed all the towns and castles of the Saracens," adds the *Chronicle of the Kings of León*, "and whilst he lived he received from them the appointed tribute every year."[41] Indeed, by 1077, he was confident enough to proclaim himself "Emperor of All Spain."

Alfonso's greatest triumph came in 1085 (often considered the official start date of the Reconquista): the great Moorish kingdom of Toledo capitulated to him after being financially bled dry and then besieged. Alfonso explained his actions in terms intelligible to Medieval Christians:

The city, by the hidden judgment of God, for three hundred and seventy-six years had been held by the Moors who commonly blasphemed the name of Christ…. [So] I directed my army against this city…thinking that it would be pleasing in the sight of the Lord, if I, Alfonso, the emperor, under the leadership of Christ, were able to restore to the devotees of his faith, the city which wicked people under the evil guidance of their leader Muhammad had taken from the Christians.[42]

The re-conquest of Toledo was a watershed moment and caused a great noise far and wide. Not only was this kingdom in the very center of Spain, making it strategically important; it was the ancient capital of the Visigoths, the forbears of Spain's Christians, such as Pelagius. The symbolism was not missed on either Christian or Muslim.

And it was just the start: "When the tyrant Alfonso saw himself master of Toledo, his nostrils dilated with pride," continues al-Maqqari; "his ambition was kindled, and he imagined that he could easily conquer the rest of Andalus." Nor was he alone, for "the arrogance of the Christian dogs waxed so great."[43] According to the contemporary Moor, Ibn Bassam (1058–1147), "Alfonso began to govern the people with justice and moderation, hoping to gain them over to polytheism [*shirk*, Trinitarian Christianity], and make them embrace his abominable religion; but, seeing that he could not accomplish this, he set about polluting the principal mosque and turning it into a church for the celebration of his detestable rites."[44]

The result was jihad—of a ferocity not seen since the days of Almanzor. Knowing that they could no longer withstand the Christian advance, the petty kings of al-Andalus called on the aid of their coreligionists across the Straights of Gibraltar in North Africa; there, the Almoravids, a brutal Islamic sect, had recently forged an empire across modern day Morocco and the Western Sahara.

Austere and pious—today, "radical"—the Almoravids were Muslim zealots who, as their name denotes,* devoted their lives to waging jihad along the frontiers of the Niger and Senegal rivers. They enforced the draconian dictates of sharia on their subjects and warred on infidels. They were, in short, what groups such as the Islamic State ("ISIS") aspire

---

* "Almoravid" comes from the Arabic word *al-murabit* (المرابط), a generic term for those Muslim fighters who man the *ribat* (الرباط) or frontier zone with infidels. Considered Islamic history's jihadists par excellence, all *al-murabitun* were dedicated to expanding or defending the domains of Islam. Along with the *ribat* that developed along the Duero River separating the Christian kingdoms of northern Spain from Islamic al-Andalus, other famous *ribats* include the Anatolian no-man zone that developed between the Umayyads and Eastern Romans beginning in the seventh century, and the ever westward expanding *ribat* of the Ottomans between the fourteenth and seventeenth centuries. In jihadist lore, Muslims who fought along these *ribats* are considered great heroes.

to be—including in appearance: their traditional attire consisted of black tunics, black turbans, and black veils covering all but their eyes.

The Almoravid leader, known as *amir al-mu'minin*, the emir or commander of the "believers" (Muslims)—an honorific attributed to leaders of the jihad—was Yusuf ibn Tashfin (b.1009). Described as being of average build, a dark complexion, having curly hair, a sparse beard, a hooked nose and a unibrow, this Berber sheikh was renowned for being "a wise and shrewd man," who "passed the greater part of his life in his native deserts, exposed to hunger and privation, [and] he had no taste for the life of pleasure."[45] Most strangers, certainly most infidels, only saw a wizened man in black—black tunic, turban, and veil covering all but the fanaticism in his eyes. For, despite his age—seventy-six at the time he was summoned—Yusuf possessed all the zeal of a neophyte (even though his Berber ancestors had been ruthlessly and forcibly Islamized in the eighth century) and eagerly accepted the invitation to aid his coreligionists against the uppity infidels.

Fearing that they risked falling out of the frying pan and into the fire, the eldest son of al-Mu'tamid ibn Abbad, the king of Seville, warned his father that, once invited, these fanatics might prove more onerous than the northern infidels. "I would prefer anything rather than be accused of surrendering al-Andalus to the Christians," al-Mu'tamid retorted. "I do not want to be cursed from the pulpit of every mosque of Islam; and, since I am bound to choose, I would sooner be a cameleer with the Almoravids than a swineherd among the Christians."[46]

He was not alone. After noting the "abject condition to which the Moslems have been reduced, paying tribute [to Christians], after being so long in the habit of receiving it [from them]," a number of leading *qadis*, or sharia judges, in Córdoba concluded that "If the present state of things continue for any length of time, we may be sure that the Christians will soon regain in this country the position they held [before the Muslim conquest of 711]." So they, too, resolved "to write to the Arabs of Africa [to come to us], and to lavish upon them on their arrival half of our riches. We will then go out with them to fight for the cause of Allah."[47]

And so the Commander of the Believers agreed to come and "prop up the tottering edifice of Islam, and to humble the pride of the insolent Christians."[48] The Muslim petty kings of al-Andalus, al-Maqqari continues, quickly "acknowledged his sway, hoping that he would stop the victorious course of the infidel, and thus open, for the prosecution of jihad, those gates which they had hitherto kept criminally locked."[49]

Just months after the fall of Toledo, Yusuf and his hardened jihadists set off for Spain. "If this crossing, O Allah, be of service to Islam," the emir implored his deity while preparing to cross the strait, "let good fortune attend it; but if not, then let some mishap on the voyage compel me to turn back."[50] The Almoravid fleets landed safe and sound in southern al-Andalus.

Now thousands of "the wearers of the veil, and the Sheikhs"—as well as their horses, camels, and engines of war—emerged from barges and marched onto Seville. Of the camels, Ibn Khallikan (b.1211) writes that they were transported "in such numbers that the country was actually filled with them, and their cries reached the sky. The people of Andalus had never seen camels, and their horses were greatly frightened at them. The sight of one of those animals, or his cry, was enough to make a horse rear and throw his rider."[51]

Yusuf and al-Mu'tamid of Seville met and "congratulated each other upon their determination to wage war against the infidel." The latter was impressed to see that, among the many fighters the emir brought from Africa were "great numbers of virtuous Moslems, who privately flocked under his banners for the purpose of taking part in the jihad."[52]

Such an Islamic force was of a quality and quantity that could easily reverse Alfonso's gains. Unlike many of the effete and libertine petty kings of al-Andalus, the North Africans were jihadists of the old variety: ruthless and uncompromising. Accordingly, not only did Alfonso hurry to intercept them, but "he summoned to arms all the men of his own and the neighboring kingdom, as well as those of the countries beyond them; his priests, bishops and monks raising everywhere their crosses and displaying their gospels. By these means he collected round him an innumerable host of Franks and Galicians."

The Christian knights certainly seem to have made an impression on the Muslims: "His warriors," continues al-Maqqari, "clad in bright mail, and armed with sharp-edged swords, with steel caps on their heads, marched, animated with desperate courage, under broad pennons and fluttering banners, looking like the black gathering clouds on a spotless sky."[53]

But there was one notable absence. There was no Cid.

DEFENDERS OF THE WEST

The Battle of Sagrajas

By mid-October 1086, the Christian and Muslim forces were camped at Sagrajas, near Badajoz. Although exact numbers are unclear, the Muslims outnumbered the Christians by at least three to one. According to al-Maqqari, prior to battle,

> As the two armies were in the presence of each other, Yusuf wrote to Alfonso offering him one of the three [conditions] prescribed by the [sharia] law; namely, Islam, tribute, or death.... At the receipt of this letter, the infidel was highly indignant; he flew into a most violent passion, and returned an answer indicative of the miserable state [of his mind].[54]

Certainly, for the proud liberator of Toledo and Emperor of All Spain who had laid al-Andalus to tribute, the idea of embracing Islam—or even paying tribute to Muslims—was anathema.

On October 23, 1086, the Christians charged the front lines of the Muslim army, where Yusuf had placed the petty kings, while he and his Berber warriors held the rear. The battle quickly "became fiercer than ever, and the furnaces of war burned with additional violence," writes the Muslim historian; "death exercised its fury." As expected, it was not long before the Moorish front line began to crumble and retreat before the Christians who "repeated their attacks with increasing fury."[55]

Yusuf's unperturbed reaction belies the contempt he held for his "moderate" Muslim allies: "Let the slaughter continue a little while longer," he told a concerned general; "they no less than the Christians are our enemies."[56] Moreover, the Christians would tire themselves out, added the shrewd sheikh, and then "we shall vanquish them without great difficulty."[57]

Before long, Alfonso and his knights had penetrated to the Muslim rear camp. Yet Yusuf was nowhere to be found. He had divided his forces into three: one (finally) to aid the nearly routed petty kings and another to directly engage Alfonso; the last, led personally by the aged emir, had circumvented the field of battle. "Advancing with drums rolling and banners flying," they went straight to and put the Christian rear camp to fire and sword.[58]

Realizing he had been outflanked, Alfonso ordered an about-face back to his own camp. It was a mistake; the Christian knights crashed into their own men, and in the chaos "the Moslems began to thrust their swords into their backs and their spears into their flanks."[59] The camels, which Yusuf had "trained...to war and surrounded his camp with," further offered "great assistance to him by throwing into disorder the Christian cavalry."[60]

All this time in the background was "this weird drum beating, which so dumbfounded the Christians." It was, in fact, part of the new tactics brought into play by the Almoravids, whereby military units rhythmically advanced to the beat of drums.[61] As one Spanish authority explains:

> The thundering roll of the Almoravide drums, now heard for the first time on Spanish soil, shook the earth and resounded the mountains. And Yusuf, galloping along the serried ranks of the Moors, nerved them to bear the fearful sufferings inseparable from holy war, promising Paradise to the dying and the richest booty to those who survived the day.[62]

Soon even the effete petty kings that had been driven off returned to the fray, which Muslim and Christian sources now describe in epic terms; al-Maqqari's rendering follows:

> [T]he earth quaked under the hoofs of their horses; the sun was obscured by the clouds of dust rising under the feet of the warriors; the steeds swam through torrents of blood.... [T]he stormy din of drums, the clash of clarion and trumpet, filled the air; the earth quaked [under the weight of the warriors], and the neighboring mountains echoed the thousand discordant sounds.... Both parties, in short, fought with equal animosity and courage.[63]

At just the right moment, Yusuf unleashed his elite African guard— four thousand naked black slaves, armed with light blades, spears, and hippo-hide covered shields—towards where Alfonso and the bulk of his knights were fighting. According to Yusuf's biographer, Ibn Khallikan, he ordered them "to dismount and join the fight, which they did with awful execution, cutting the horses' houghs, spearing their riders when on the ground, and throwing confusion into the enemy's ranks":

> In the middle of the conflict Alfonso attacked, sword in hand, a black slave who had spent all his javelins, and aimed at his head; but the black avoided the blow, and, creeping under Alfonso's horse, seized

the animal by the bridle; then, taking out a *khanjar* [J-shaped dagger] which he wore at his girdle, he wounded the Christian king in the thigh, the instrument piercing both armour and flesh, and pinning Alfonso to his horse's saddle. The rout then became general, the gales of victory blew, and Allah sent down his spirit to the Moslems, rendering the true religion triumphant.[64]

Exhausted, bloodied, and now partially impaled, Alfonso and his few remaining men—just five hundred, almost all of whom were seriously wounded—retreated, even as the relentless Muslims gave chase deep into the night and slaughtered some more. Thus Alfonso "fled from the field of battle like the timid hare before chasing dogs," concludes al-Maqqari, "and reached Toledo, beaten, dejected in spirits, and wounded."[65]

Meanwhile, a grisly scene was unfolding on the field of battle. In keeping with the modus operandi of four centuries of jihad, stretching back to the prophet Muhammad's treatment of the Jewish tribe of Banu Qurayza, "Yusuf caused the heads of all the Christian slain [to the number of two thousand-four hundred] to be cut off and gathered together in massive piles. And from the tops of those gruesome minarets the muezzins called to morning prayers the victorious soldiers, now worked into a frenzy by the sight of this bestial treading under-foot of human remains: 'In the name of Allah, the Compassionate, the Merciful.'"[66]

The emir later had the now rotten heads hauled off in carts to all the kingdoms of al-Andalus as material proof of victory—and a reminder of the fate of *all* who dared resist Allah's advance.

Yusuf bin Tashfin is still revered among Muslims, particularly those of a jihadist bent, for his pious exploits during this battle. Indeed, with the exception of the battle of Yarmuk, few if any other jihads of Islamic history are as extolled in Muslim historiography as Sagrajas, known in Arabic as the battle of *al-Zallaqa*, meaning "slimy"—a reference to the slippery conditions caused by the copious amounts of blood spilt on the battlefield, as echoed by another early Arabic source quoted in al-Maqqari: "For many years after the field of battle was so covered with carcasses of the slain, that it was impossible to walk through it without treading on the withering bones of some infidel."[67]

Strategically speaking, "this memorable battle and defeat of the Christian forces," concludes al-Maqqari, "inspired new life into the body of [Andalusian Islam]."[68] Now fear beset the Christian kingdoms of the north; the jihadist nightmare that was Almanzor had returned to terrorize them—not least as the Almoravids excelled at desecrating and destroying or turning churches under their sway into mosques. Pope Urban II, who appreciated the significance of this turn in events, beckoned the whole of Christendom to Spain's aid—a decade *before* he called for the First Crusade to the East. After all, "whereas the Turks were causing concern in the East alone, the Almoravides were reckoned a powerful danger to Europe."[69]

Although offered the lion's share of the plunder (in keeping with Koran 8:41), Yusuf declined: "I came not to this country for the sake of plunder; I came for no other purpose than that of waging war against the infidel, and thereby deserving the rewards promised to those who fight for the cause of Allah."[70]

Unfortunately for Yusuf, he was unable to capitalize on his victory. Many of his own warriors were killed at Sagrajas; worse, his own son and heir had died unexpectedly in Marrakesh, the Almoravid capital in Morocco, and his African subjects were rebelling. All this prompted the emir to rush back home, though he left three thousand fighters under al-Mu'tamid of Seville—who of all the petty kings had actually proved his mettle at Sagrajas—to help dislodge the Christians from their recent advances. Emboldened by this turn of events, all of al-Andalus's Muslim kingdoms stopped paying tribute to Alfonso.

The Cid and the Jihad Meet

Soon after the Sagrajas disaster of 1086, and rather unsurprisingly, Alfonso recalled and pardoned Roderick—this warrior who, if present at Sagrajas, would have, as the whisperers had it, led to a different outcome. Alfonso further offered his reconciled vassal much autonomy, granting him complete control of any Moorish territory he could conquer.

Given the green light, the hitherto idle Cid now ruthlessly "fell upon the Moors that dwelt upon the Borders of Aragon and Castile."[71] So sudden and violent was his onslaught that "not one stone was left upon another, nor was there any sign of life," to quote Ibn al-Qama (1036–1116), a contemporary native of Moorish Valencia.[72] Several of the Muslim kingdoms that had declared themselves free after Sagrajas were again reduced to paying tribute.

Indeed, during this time, "Alphonso was completely overshadowed by the Cid." Although the "Almoravide armies, with their religious zeal, their strong, cohesive, warlike spirit, and the new tactics of mass formations maneuvered by the beat of the drum, had paralyzed all Christian action in the south [where King Alfonso held sway]," they could do little along the eastern seaboard, where the Cid dominated.[73]

Perhaps unsurprisingly, and once again, Alfonso exiled Roderick one year after pardoning him—this time with extreme severity: not only did he strip the Campeador of all lands and titles; he even temporarily threw his wife and children (Alfonso's own relatives) in a dungeon.[74] Whether it was intentional or not, the Cid's crime was that he had failed to rendezvous with the emperor at the Christian fortress of Aledo, which was under siege by the Almoravids in 1088. The earliest chroniclers assert that Alfonso's extreme response was exacerbated by envy—which itself was wildly exacerbated by the jealousy and thus slander of his own nobles and entourage, many of whom by now vehemently disliked Roderick.

Wherever the truth may lie, it seems that, while loyal to Castile, the Cid also possessed a sort of unshakable headstrongness that—as seen at Alfonso's coronation—inevitably caused him to fall into disfavor among his "betters." It may even have been him that the twelfth century *Chronicle of Alfonso the Emperor* had in mind when it said, "The men of Castile were rebellious down the ages. Noble Castile, eager for terrible wars, could scarcely bring herself to bow her neck to any king."[75]

Yusuf returned to Spain in June of 1089. Not only was he set on finishing what he had started—"to rid the peninsula of the Christians is our sole purpose" he regularly declared—but word had reached him of an especially impudent infidel that was not only subjugating Muslims, but being honored by the Arabic honorific *al-sayyad*—"lord."[76]

Before long, however, and as had happened between Alfonso and Roderick, dissensions arose between the petty kings and their Berber guest. With each passing day and gruff remark from the curmudgeon sheikh, the kings of al-Andalus began to weary of Yusuf. Thus when the emir besieged Toledo—and although he "made havoc of its walls, cut down the trees, and laid waste the country for miles around"[77]—none of the petty kings joined him, and he ultimately failed to take it. Matters were not helped when he learned that "whilst his own troops were performing a service of danger on the frontier, waging incessant war against the Christians, and leading at the same time a life of hardship and privation, the kings of Andalus were plunged in pleasure and sloth, and their subjects were enjoying a happy and easy life."[78]

Realizing that he could never conquer the Christian infidels until he had first conquered the quasi-apostates—that is, by reuniting all of al-Andalus under strict Islamic rule—he abandoned Toledo and turned his displeasure on his unreliable allies. "I well know your conniving ways and mendacious utterances," Yusuf casually told Abdullah, the king of Granada, who had made a secret pact with Alfonso; "do not pin your hopes on the long term. The near future is what matters to you."[79] Abdullah and his family were fettered and shipped to North Africa.

The other Moorish kings suffered a similar fate as Yusuf moved against them one by one. "Did I not tell you," al-Mu'tamid's son reminded him, "that this man from the Sahara would be our ruin if we brought him over?"[80] Then, the king of Seville had said that he preferred to be a cameleer for the Almoravids than a swineherd for the Christians—but now he would not even be that: he was exiled to Morocco in 1090, where he was later assassinated.

The fact is the petty kings' time was up. Through *fatwas*, their own *ulema*, experts in Islamic law, had long ago thrown their weight behind the Commander of the Believers: "Far from keeping their promises, [the kings] have allied themselves with Alphonso against you that you might fall into his hands," they inveighed before Yusuf. "Depose them! We will answer for you to Allah, and if we sin, eternal punishment shall be ours; but, if you leave them in peace, they shall surely surrender the lands of Islam unto the Christians, and yours will be the blame." Even in distant Baghdad, the Abbasid ulema "endorsed the opinions of their western brethren and authorized Yusuf to carry out the sentence of Allah on the Andalusian emirs."

As a result, al-Andalus's radical clerics "installed themselves in the important posts and through their fatwas, so respected by Yusuf, conducted the highest affairs of State, dethroned kings at will, and instigated the persecution of the Mozarabs," that is, Christians living as dhimmis under Muslim rule.[81]

In 1090, the Almoravids finally took the strong fortress of Aledo, just south of the Cid's sphere of activity. Now more than before, "the steady approach of Yusuf's soldiers encouraged Moslems everywhere to rebel against Christian domination, and soon there was not a city or castle where the Almoravide party, swollen with political malcontents and religious fanatics, might not suddenly rear its head."[82]

By 1093—after virtually all of the kings of al-Andalus had been overthrown, their Moorish kingdoms swallowed up by Yusuf's Almoravid Empire—only two Muslim kingdoms remained outside the fold: Valencia and Zaragoza in northeast al-Andalus—and the Cid was overlord of both.

Mío Cid

Now began the final and most dramatic stage of the Cid's career, as evidenced by his own words overheard by a Moor: "A Roderick lost this peninsula"—he said of his namesake, the Visigothic king who lost Spain to the Muslims following his defeat at Guadalete in 711—"but another Roderick shall save it."[83] The Cid's premiere modern biographer, Professor Ramón Menéndez Pidal (d.1968), summarizes the mood and stakes:

> With the Almoravide invasion, the struggle between the two civilizations had reached its height. Before, as we have already seen, the slight racial differences between the Caliphate and the northern kingdoms had been more or less satisfactorily settled.... But now, with the invasion of the desert races and the recrudescence of Islamic fanaticism, a new chasm opened out between the two. And, on the Christian side, it was the Cid who, as the leader of the resistance against the victorious invaders, showed himself the most determined to carry on the war without giving or seeking quarter.... [I]t was upon the Cid that the task devolved of resisting, unaided, the whole might of Islam....[84]

He began by expending all his energies to the defense of Spain's eastern seaboard, which was dominated by Moorish Valencia, then his tributary. In 1092, while fighting elsewhere he learned "that the barbarian Saracen peoples," to quote from the *Historia Roderici* ("History of Roderick") an important and contemporary biography, "had penetrated the eastern region and laid them to waste most savagely; that they had even got as far as Valencia, and had already obtained control of it," where they "were carrying on with their evil deeds."[85]

A secret plot between the Almoravids and the Moors of Valencia, led by its *qadi* (sharia judge) Ibn Jehhaf, resulted in the overthrow of its king,

Yahya (John) al-Qadir, who had "increased their [Valencians] hatred by being a friend to the Christians"—that is, by being a vassal to the Cid.[86] During the uprising, fanatical Muslims discovered al-Qadir trying to abscond out of Valencia dressed in and concealed by a woman's burqa. To cries of "Allahu Akbar," the mob slaughtered him as an apostate and hurled his body in a camel dung pit.

On learning of the Valencians' treachery and murder of his vassal, the Cid's "anger was kindled, and his soul was inflamed," writes al-Maqqari.[87] Like a fierce storm he came and with extreme violence thrashed the Valencian countryside, taking all the castles and suburbs up to the city's very walls. He "fought so fiercely," writes Ibn al-Qama, "that the Moors were terrified at the havoc he played among them."[88]

From the wreckage of the lands he stormed through, and as an indication of Roderick's iron determination, he had a small town built in a few weeks—complete with granaries, ramparts, and even churches—near and to launch operations against the walls of Valencia. In short, "with growing harshness," he "gave the Spanish Moslems to understand that no mercy would be shown to any who sought an alliance with the Africans."[89]

Several months into the siege, the terrified Valencians "sent envoys to him, asking and indeed beseeching him to be peaceable towards them and to allow the Moabites [Almoravids*] to live with them. But he would in no wise allow himself to live at peace with them unless they cut all connections with the Moabites and expelled them from the city altogether. But they were not willing to do this and shut themselves up together in the city." During this time, the *Historia* continues, Yusuf, who was in Africa, "sent letters to him strictly forbidding him to dare to enter the land of Valencia."

When he heard this Roderick was mightily angered. Warmed by the flame of his rage he spoke of Yusuf in terms of the strongest contempt and mocked him with daring words. He sent letters to all the princes and leaders of the Spains, telling them that for fear of him Yusuf did

---

* Medieval chroniclers typically employed biblical terminology and imagery: Moabites here (and throughout) signifies the Almoravids, that is, strange and savage Muslims from distant Africa; Ishmaelites, on the other hand, tends to signify the Muslims of al-Andalus proper, the so-called Moors who had long been in and were familiar to Spain.

not dare to cross the sea and come to Valencia. When Yusuf heard this he ordered that an immense, innumerable army be gathered and prepare to cross the Strait without delay.[90]

By July, 1094, Valencia's besieged Muslims had become desperate; but still there was no sign of this "immense, innumerable army" to relieve them. So they opened talks with Roderick and indicated a willingness to surrender. Knowing that they much preferred Muslim over Christian rule, and hoping to once and for all win their sincere submission, the Cid made the Valencians a magnanimous offer: "Men of Valencia," declared he, "I freely offer you a period of truce until the month of August. If Yusuf should come in the meantime to your assistance, and should defeat and expel me from these lands and liberate you from my dominion, serve him and remain beneath his rule. But if he should not do this, serve me and be mine."

The Moors of Valencia enthusiastically agreed and wrote letters to Yusuf, urging him "to come to Valencia with a huge army" to overthrow "the hand and authority of Roderick," the *Historia* continues: "If this were not done before the month of August, they emphasized, they would undoubtedly have to bow to Roderick's power."[91]

When August came and went without the Almoravids appearing, the Valencians "dishonored the agreement which they had made with him." Their logic was that, sooner or later, their African coreligionists would arrive; and, so long as the Cid and his much smaller force could be kept outside of the walls of Valencia, the Almoravids would eventually overwhelm and crush the Christians. In reneging, however, "they made themselves in every way rebels against Roderick and [became] his enemies," asserts the *Historia*: "and he well understood this. So he again laid siege to Valencia with intense hostility, and pressed the city from every side with the most aggressive tactics possible."[92] Mass starvation soon plagued the Moorish kingdom.

At long last, an immensely large host of Almoravids was espied marching to Valencia's relief. Acting fast, the Cid destroyed all of the bridges leading to the city and flooded the countryside with water from the canals, so that only one strip of land, which he now controlled, was dry. Done none too soon, a massive dust storm heralded the arrival of the Islamic hordes of North Africa.

[Now] when the news came that the Africans had arrived at Alcira, the Valencians, frantic with joy, rushed to the walls to scan the horizon for signs of their saviors and watch by night the twinkle of the numberless fires of the Almoravide bivouacs…. And all the time the citizens prayed unceasingly for Allah's aid against the Cid and agreed in council to plunder the Christian camp and the stores and hostels of the suburb when the battle reached the wall.[93]

When morning came, the Cid and the Valencians awoke to a strange sight: empty fields. The jihadist saviors of Valencia had retreated in the dark over the flooded plains, abandoning the city to its fate. Roderick's chronicler allots two sentences to this ignominious event: a large "army of Moabites, swiftly on its way to relieve the siege, approached Valencia. But they did not dare to commit themselves to battle with Roderick. Greatly fearful of him they dispersed by night and retired to their bases in confusion."[94]

Black despair now fell on the Moors of Valencia: "they were like drunkards who understand not one another," wrote Ibn al-Qama, who was present; "their faces grew as black as pitch, their memories deserted them; and they became as one that falls into the sea."[95] Their mood was not helped by the Cid's army. Completely unopposed, it now surrounded the city's walls and loudly reviled the oath-breaking Moors with vows of unrestrained vengeance. Topping it all off, the famine had reached the point that "the poor were driven to eating the flesh of human corpses."[96]

With no hope, Valencia finally surrendered to "the *kanbittur* [Campeador]—may the curse of Allah fall on his head!" to quote al-Maqqari—on June 15, 1094, after a nearly nineteen-month-long besiegement; and Roderick Díaz of Vivar became its undisputed lord—literally, its *sayyad*, Cid.[97]

Although it did not ostensibly concern them, even Europeans outside of Spain rejoiced at this outstanding feat; for "the conquests by the Cid" were seen as "a barrier protecting, not only Spain, but the whole of Western Europe from the Moslem peril."[98] Henceforward, and as lord of Valencia, he formally adopted the title, "Prince Roderick Campeador," as seen in one of his extant signatures affixed to the dedication of the Virgin Mary Cathedral at Valencia, "in the year of the Incarnation of Our Lord in 1098."[99]

The Battle of Cuarte

With the loss of the great Moorish city, the pride and prestige of the glorious jihadist victor of Sagrajas, who had subsequently unified virtually all of Muslim Spain under his authority, was shaken to its core: "He has forcibly invaded my territory and he attributes all his success to Jesus Christ!" blurted Yusuf, who, on hearing of the fall of Valencia, "was powerfully moved to anger and bitterness," and, according to Ibn Bassam, "determined to recover the city at all costs."[100]

The contemporary Muslim adds that "the news of the fall of Valencia filled every Moor in Spain with grief and humiliation."[101] Nor did this disaster affect the western world of Islam alone. Having acknowledged the supremacy of the Abbasid caliph in Baghdad, Yusuf had only recently "been proclaimed in every mosque of Islam as ruler of Spain, the Maghreb, and the other territories under his dominion."

The humiliation was too much; a showdown was inevitable: "Islam and the Occident were now each represented by an outstanding personality," writes Pidal: "Yusuf the Saharan and the Castilian Cid stood face-to-face in the struggle between the two civilizations."[102]

The elderly sheikh responded by sending the supreme Almoravid general of Spain, his nephew, one Muhammad, "with an infinite number of barbarians and Moabites [Almoravids] and Ishmaelites [Moors] drawn from all over Hispania to besiege Valencia and to bring Roderick to him captive and in chains."[103] Reportedly consisting of some fifty thousand fighters, the Almoravids dwarfed the Cid's Valencian garrison of four thousand men. By late 1094, "the infidel hordes" had arrived and "pitched their tents and encamped" at Cuarte, three miles from Valencia.[104]

Now, "all the Moors in the vicinity"—the same who had only recently pledged their loyalty to the Cid—"came forward with barley and food supplies, which they either sold or gave away" to their invading coreligionists. "As a matter of fact," asserts Pidal, "the Cid never could count on the loyalty of the Valencian Moors, who, far from being resigned to their subjection, supported every attempt of the Africans to extend their dominions."[105] On learning of their treacherous designs, and to safeguard against having to fight on two fronts, Roderick ordered the Valencians to surrender all their weapons—including all iron tools—on pain of death and ejected the most able-bodied male Muslims outside the city.[106]

The final showdown between the Cid and his African adversaries—both contenders being then undefeated—had come and is recorded in both song and chronicle. According to the *Historia Roderici*,

> This Moabite army lay about Valencia for 10 days and as many nights, and remained inactive. Every day indeed they used to go around the city, shrieking and shouting with a motley clamor of voices and filling the air with their bellowing [references to the *takbir*, i.e., spasmodic cries of "Allahu Akbar," and other jihadist battle-cries]. They often used to fire arrows…. But Roderick…comforted and strengthened his men in a manly fashion, and constantly prayed devoutly to the Lord Jesus Christ that he would send divine aid to his people.[107]

The sources emphasize the ominous beat of the African drums, the thundering roll of which seemed to rend the earth asunder. It filled the hearts of all—especially those unacquainted with its booming sounds, including Roderick's wife and daughters, who were then holed up with him in Valencia—with dread and consternation.

With every day that the Cid remained on the defensive, the Muslims became more emboldened and encroached closer to his city's walls. Before long they had surrounded Valencia's gates in very tight formations—precisely what the Cid was waiting for. On October 21, 1094, when "the enemy were as usual going around outside the city yelling and shouting and scrimmaging, confident in the belief that they would capture it," Roderick Díaz, "trusting with his whole mind in God and his mercy, courageously made a sortie from the city," whereupon "a major encounter ensued."[108]

Thus, at the height of Muslim confidence, heavily armored knights astride even heavier steeds of war burst out of one of the gates, taking the jihadists by complete surprise. Before they could effectively retaliate, another Christian sortie burst out from another gate. Though unclear which, the Campeador led one of these two forces which now crisscrossed each other in a medieval style blitzkrieg, causing mass confusion and carnage among the densely packed Muslims. After a "multitude" of the enemy "fell to the sword," the panicked Africans and Andalusians "turned their backs in flight," the *Historia* concludes, many of them falling and drowning in the river Jucar.[109]

Not unlike Yusuf's strategy at Sagrajas, the Cid's "was the classic tactic of feint followed by attack from a different quarter, carefully planned and boldly executed."[110] A modern biographer of the Cid summarizes its effectiveness:

The maneuver Rodrigo used that day has come to be known as "la tornada," or, the tornado. Once the Christian knights had charged through the enemy lines in one direction, they turned and passed through again in a different direction. Whole units were disrupted, broken apart and irreversibly separated. The Africans were packed so tightly together, and their shouts and screams and the clash of steel so loud, that few commands could be heard over the din of battle. Besides, the attack was so swift that there was no tactic that could be successfully employed to neutralize it.[111]

A document drawn up by Valencian clerics three years later confirms that the Cid won "in a moment with incredible speed and very few casualties on the part of the Christians."[112]

After the battle, and now "sated with slaughter," the twelfth century *Poem of the Cid* resumes the narrative: "the Cid returned to his wife and daughters, his helmet gone, the hood of his coat of mail thrown back and the linen under-cap pushed over his brow. His sword was dripping with blood, which had run up the blade to the hilt and along his arm up to the elbow." With the other arm he hurled a mutilated drum at their feet, crying "Thus are Moors vanquished!" In terror and awe, they fell to the ground before him—"We are thy servants!"[113]

The battle of Cuarte was a shattering blow to the hitherto undefeated Almoravids: four thousand knights had defeated and driven off fifty thousand jihadists. Christians everywhere wildly celebrated. Even one modern historian, who specializes in Cid "reductionism," concedes that the battle of Cuarte's "fame spread far and wide. It was *the* event of the year."[114]

Having reestablished his authority over Valencia, Roderick again treated its traitorous Moorish inhabitants leniently. In a post battle speech meant to create reconciliation between Christian and Muslim in Valencia, the Cid said:

Now that he [king Yahya al-Qadir, whom the Valencians assassinated] is dead and God has willed that I be Lord of Valencia, I want her for myself and for those who helped me win her, subject to the overlordship of Alfonso of Castile, my liege Lord, whom God preserve for many years. Now are you all in my power to do with as I will. Easily could I take your all, your persons, your women, and your children; but it is not my wish to do so. I desire rather and command of those among you who have always been loyal, remain with your folks in Valencia, and in your own homes. ...I desire you to have your mosques in Valencia and Alcudia, your fakirs, your laws, your qadi, and you're vizier, whom I have appointed. You shall retain all your lands, paying me the tithe of the fruits thereof, and I will administer justice and mint such coin as I please. Those who wish to remain under my rule, let them remain! Those who do not let them go whither they will, though taking naught with them, and I will grant them safe conduct.[115]

For those who remained, there was another word of advice: "[Y]ou must bow to my ruling in all such things as I shall tell you. Fail not to do so, nor disobey my commands! Keep strictly whatever pact you make with me and abide by whatsoever I ordain, for I love you and desire your weal."[116]

These were no idle threats. Ibn Jehhaf, the Islamic jurist who led the pro-Almoravid rebellion that led to the butchering of the Cid's vassal, al-Qadir, was arrested and, as a lesson to all, burned alive. "Rodrigo de Vivar was certainly a hard man," observes Bertrand while discussing this incident, but "in the environment in which he lived, it was essential that he should be."[117] Only extreme punishments could be hoped to keep such a recalcitrant people at bay.

Given the two choices, most Moors profusely thanked him and kissed his hands, swearing fealty; a few purists, not deigning to be ruled by an infidel, left, as required by sharia, unmolested. For those who remained, and based on the admission of an Almoravid, "He dispensed justice so fairly that none had any grievance against him or his officials, for he strictly observed the Moslem Law [meaning he allowed Muslims to govern themselves according to sharia] and exacted only the legal tithes."[118]

The Battle of Bairén

Despite their losses to Roderick, the Almoravids continued to terrorize the Christians elsewhere. Even on the same year of their humiliating defeat at Cuarte, in 1094, distant Lisbon fell to the jihadists and "vast numbers of Christians were slaughtered or taken captive."[119] Yet, for every Almoravid victory, one insolent infidel continued to counter. After a brief respite, the now fifty-two-year-old Roderick resumed the offensive and expanded his territories in the eastern seaboard of al-Andalus, taking Olocau and the castle of Serra in 1095.

Rage turned to fury in the lands of Islam. "Valencia was a mote in Yusuf's eye that robbed him of all ease," writes Ibn Bassam; "it was constantly in his thoughts and on his tongue; his one aim was to recover it, and he sent troops and money for that to be done; but the results he achieved were negligible."[120] Sometime in 1097, he dispatched Muhammad—the same disgraced nephew who fled the carnage at Cuarte—with another massive host of Almoravids and Andalusians. On learning that they were headed to besiege his fortress in Benicadell, Roderick, with the aid of Peter I, the young king of Aragon (1068–1104)—who, although formerly an opponent of Castile and the Cid, had entered into an alliance with him "against our common foes"—rushed to fortify Benicadell.[121]

On their way, "they encountered Muhammad," continues the *Historia*. "He had a huge army of 30,000 well-armed soldiers and was intent on battle. However, that day the Ishmaelites and Moabites did not offer battle with them but throughout the day remained in the mountains thereabouts howling and shouting," evidently in an effort to lure and finish off the Christians in the high places.[122] The Cid ignored them and continued to fortify Benicadell.

On its way back to Valencia, the Cid's army camped at Bairén, a narrow strip of land between the coast and mountains. There, on an unknown date in 1097, the Muslims sprung their trap: the Christians found themselves pinned between rising ground on one side, and water on another—and both were packed with enemy forces. The *Historia* explains:

> Here, on the hill, was the Saracen camp. Opposite it was the sea, and on it, a great number of Ishmaelite and Moabite ships, from which they harassed the Christians with bow and arrow. And from the mountain quarter they attacked them with other weapons. When the Christians realized what was happening, they were not a little afraid.[123]

Vastly outnumbered and surrounded by the Muslims—who held both the high ground and sea—this is certainly an understatement. Yet the Cid maintained his reserve; he instantly armed himself and sprang atop his war horse: "Hearken, my followers and allied knights!" he cried as he galloped around his disheartened men. "Let each of you bear himself in the field like a man. Fear not their numbers. Smite them!... For, of a surety, Christ has delivered them into our hands this day."[124] With that, "he embraced his shield, lowered his lance, put spurs to Babieca, his fiery white stallion, and dashed into the fray, laying about him with heart and soul. The Campeador, bursting through the first ranks, overthrew seven and killed four."[125]

Once again, "the Cid's presence had its magical effect: confidence in their leader took the place of fear and all plunged into the fray."[126] As they charged,

[T]he Christian knights reached the enemy's front line and smote them with a terrific, irresistible blast.... The Moors reeled at the shock of the thunderous Christian onslaught, but the sheer press of thousands of Muslim horsemen eventually slowed the dramatic, uphill charge [of the Christians]. Now, sword bent against scimitar, and the Cid fought with such vehemence that he became a relentless, unstoppable force. He knew that the battle must be won quickly, or else the superior numbers of the Moors would decide the outcome.[127]

In the end, and because the Christians "attacked with such impetuosity...the Moslems gave ground, broke and fled in all directions."[128] "Some were killed by the sword," concludes the *Historia*; "some fell in the river, and enormous numbers fled into the sea where they were drowned."[129] The aftermath is vividly described by the *Poem of the Cid*:

When they had driven them out they fell to the pursuit. You might have seen many a mailed arm hacked off, many a head with its helmet fall to the ground, while riderless horses ran hither and thither.... [The Cid] killed King Bucar [Abu Bakr, an Almoravid general and another relative of Yusuf]...and won his sword, Tizon, which was worth a thousand golden marks.... The far-famed Campeador, carrying two swords* which he valued highly, rode swiftly over the

---

* The swords mentioned here, known in the sources as Tizona and Colada, were forged of Damascene steel—meaning sharpened to a razor's edge and lethal in capable hands such as Roderick's. In 2008, Tizona sold for €1.7 million and is reportedly on display in a Burgos museum. https://english.elpais.com/elpais/2011/03/11/inenglish/1299824444_850210.html

scene of slaughter with his mail thrown back, showing his creased face and his coif somewhat rumpled on his hair.[130]

As he celebrated this great victory with his men, the "Cid raised his hand and grasped his beard," saying "Thanks be to Christ, Lord of this world, I have seen my desire fulfilled!"[131] Months later he would celebrate the marriage of his daughter Maria to his young ally, King Peter I of Aragon, a union that would ensure that the Cid's blood would course in the veins of future kings (including one featured in this book).

Loyalty and Enmity

Not one to be granted a break, the crowned champion returned to his Valencian kingdom only to find another Muslim rebellion brewing. Although his Moorish subjects were free to worship and enforce sharia on themselves, and although they paid fewer taxes to the Cid than to their former Muslim overlords, they always rebelled whenever the opportunity—in this case, his absence—presented itself.[132]

In fact, the Valencians could never be loyal to both infidels and Islam. The tribalistic doctrine of al-wala' wa'l bara' ("loyalty and enmity") places an existential wedge between Muslims and non-Muslims.[133] It requires Muslims always to side with their coreligionists, while feeling only "enmity and hatred" for non-Muslims—"even if they be their fathers, their sons, their brothers, or their nearest kindred"—until they "believe in Allah alone," to quote the Koran (60:4; 58:22).

Relatedly, Muslims are banned from pledging allegiance to infidels. "Oh you who have believed!" declares Allah: "Do not take the Jews and Christians as friends and allies" (Koran 5:51). There is, of course, one caveat: Muslims may perform taqiyya*—that is, feign loyalty to infidel

---

* Koran 3:28 is one of the primary verses that sanction taqiyya: "Let believers [Muslims] not take infidels [non-Muslims] for friends and allies instead of believers. Whoever does this shall have no relationship left with Allah—unless you are but guarding yourselves against them, taking precautions." Al-Tabari (d. 923), author of a mainstream Koran commentary, offers the following exegesis of 3:28: "If you [Muslims] are under their [non-Muslims'] authority, fearing for yourselves, behave loyally to them with your tongue while harboring inner animosity for them…[Know that] Allah has forbidden believers from being friendly or on intimate terms with the infidels rather than other believers—except when infidels are above them [in authority]. Should that be the case, let them act friendly towards them while preserving their religion." Taqiyya was especially on display towards the close of the Reconquista, when the Muslim populations of Spain were significantly weaker than and under the rule of Christians (see Sword and Scimitar, pp.199–203). As one frustrated Spaniard remarked, "With the permission and license that their accursed sect accorded them, they could

authority while biding their time for the opportune moment to subvert or revolt—as the Valencians did time and time again. Ibn Taymiyya (b.1263), arguably the most influential Muslim cleric of Medieval Islam, summarized the matter by writing that every Muslim "is obligated to befriend a believer—even if he is oppressive and violent toward you, while he must be hostile to the infidel—even if he is liberal and kind to you."[134]

Thus, no matter how fairly the Cid ruled, or allowed the Muslims of Valencia freedom of worship, they could never sincerely accept his authority; and the more he indulged them, the more they projected their own divisive doctrines onto him. Because Christians "are the natural enemies of Islam," they argued, the Cid's "lenience" must be "prompted by falseness and cunning, which in the end must strengthen the inveterate antipathy of all true Moslems to the Christians."[135]

Not, of course, that the Cid was naïve; for "he begins by treating the Valencians with benevolence; but, when he finds that they continue to intrigue with the Africans, he ceases to respect Moslem law and resorts to the mailed fist of the conqueror"—as he did with this latest revolt.[136]

Finale

In the end, Roderick became undisputed master of Valencia—which for nearly four centuries had been an integral part of al-Andalus, Muslim Spain—and the votaries of Allah, both domestic and foreign, could do nothing about it. Now aged eighty-eight, Yusuf gave up on Valencia and turned his attention to reconquering Toledo from Alfonso. Apparently finding the "Emperor of All Spain" a more manageable foe than his lowly vassal from Vivar, the Almoravids again met, and again crushed, Alfonso in battle on August 15, 1097—for "the Almighty [Allah] threw the Christian vanguard into confusion," asserts Ibn al-Kardabus, a twelfth century chronicler from Tunisia.[137]

Tragically for Roderick, his only son and heir, Diego, aged twenty-two, had fought and died in Alfonso's army. "The Cid's grief when he learned the news nearly proved fatal.... [T]he loss of his son, weighed on his soul as if he were paying in sorrow for a lifetime of prodigious

feign any religion outwardly and without sinning, as long as they kept their hearts nevertheless devoted to their false impostor of a prophet. We saw so many of them who died while worshipping the Cross and speaking well of our Catholic Religion yet who were inwardly excellent Muslims [waiting for a chance to revolt; Ibrahim, 2018, p.201–202]."

victories. His son's death not only meant the failure of his line through future generations, but was an irreparable social loss that deepened his despair."[138] So he abandoned himself to vengeance and heaped victory atop victory over the Almoravids. He furiously put their fortress at Almenara to siege; three months after his son's death it capitulated; and he conquered Murviedro, west of Valencia, in 1098, thereby further consolidating his hold over the eastern seaboard.

By now, the undefeated Castilian was fifty-five-years-old; and although his spirit remained indefatigable and his will indomitable, the scars of a lifetime of war riddled his body and mind and boded ill—so much so that a "short life had been prophesied for the hero five years before by his tax-gatherer, Ibn Abdus.... [T]he sagacious Moor had already perceived the wastage brought about by ceaseless action, the loss of vital power being consumed by his enthusiasm and everlasting struggle against enmity and hatred."[139]

And so, on Sunday, July 10, 1099, Roderick Díaz of Vivar—the master of war, the lord—died in his bed in his Valencian kingdom, aged fifty-six. News of it cast a shadow of gloom over Christendom in the midst of the triumph of the First Crusade, which had culminated in the liberation of Jerusalem from Islam on the same week of Roderick's death. The Cid's subjects "gave vent to bitter and unrestrained grief.... [T]he expression of grief assumed proportions that to us are inconceivable. The men beat their breasts, rent their garments, and tore out their hair; the women scratched their faces until the blood flowed, and covered their foreheads with ashes; and the weeping and wailing went on for many days." In short, and in the words of a contemporary chronicle written in Poitou, Roderick's death caused "great lamentation among the Christians and exceeding joy among the Paynim [pagans, i.e., Muslims]."[140]

Indeed, "when the news of his death spread," the *Historia* says, "all the Saracens who lived across the seas mustered a considerable army and marched against Valencia. The Almoravids laid siege to it on all sides and attacked the city for seven months."[141] Under the Cid's grieving widow, Jimena, his men managed to hold the Muslims off for a while; when matters became desperate, Alfonso himself came to his kinswoman's aid. Before long he concluded that Valencia—the only Christian kingdom inside and surrounded by Muslim al-Andalus—could never be held. He torched and evacuated it. Jimena brought her husband's mortal remains with her; they were eventually buried at the center of the Burgos Cathedral.

Although the Almoravids conquered Valencia on May 5, 1102, the victory was soured for Yusuf by his nemesis's death; for "the last thing the Emir wanted to do was meet Roderick, on whom he devoutly called down the curse of Allah."[142]

After a forty-five year reign as the great Commander of the Believers, Yusuf died in 1106, aged ninety-seven. Three years later, Alfonso VI followed him to the grave, aged seventy-nine. "Despite his personal faults, his arrogance, and his unhappy relations with the Cid," writes one authority on Spanish history, "he was indeed a great king," not least for inaugurating the Reconquista with the liberation of Toledo in 1085.[143]

Legacy

As for Alfonso's indomitable vassal, due to the Cid's deeds of renown—never once was he defeated, no matter the odds or situation—he went on to become Spain's national hero. Of his many exploits—including beating (or simply scaring off) the hitherto undefeated Almoravids in every encounter—it is perhaps the Campeador's conquest of Valencia that, when closely examined, truly underscores his iron will and implacable determination. Pidal elaborates:

> It savors of madness that a single man, unsupported by any national organization and lacking resources even for a single day, should appear before [the walls of] Valencia determined upon restoring a rule that had been overthrown this second time by an enemy [the Almoravids] who had proved irresistible to the strongest power in Spain [Alfonso VI]: that he should dream of doing what the Christian Emperor had failed to do, and in the teeth of the Moslem Emir's opposition [and succeed is]...the most extraordinary achievement ever performed in Spain by anyone but a king.... [E]ven had the king of Castile, the most powerful monarch of Spain, engaged his whole forces in the effort, he would have found it extremely difficult to conquer so populous a city in the very heart of the Moorish country. Alfonso did, in fact, throw his whole strength in the attempt, and failed.[144]

Equally significant is that the Cid showed to his countrymen that Africa's most fanatical Muslim hordes were not invincible and could be beat; this was an important and inspiring lesson for every Spaniard—not least as worse was about to come (Chapter 4).

For all these reasons, Roderick became a legend in his own lifetime. The *Carmen Campidoctoris*, a poem, was composed and sung during his final years; and the *Historia Roderici*—Spain's very first chronicle devoted to, not a king, but rather a "warlike man" who forged his own destiny— was written by a cleric who followed the Cid in his wanderings and appeared a few years after his death (much of the aforementioned narrative is based on it).[145] Other "Castilian chronicles," moreover, "devoted more pages to him than to the most famous kings."[146]

Roderick is best known as the subject of one of Medieval Europe's greatest epic poems, *El Cantar de Mío Cid* ("The Song of My Lord," commonly known as "The Poem of the Cid"), which appeared a few decades after his death. Unlike the Greek and Roman epics, which cast their heroes in a superhuman light, it presents the Cid as a man devoted to the well-being of his family. Further ironic, and "although poetic exaggeration clothes all heroes in the mantle of invincibility, it is surprising to find that, so far as the Cid is concerned, fact agrees with fiction."[147]

As another sampling, here is how the Poem describes the situation when Roderick and his womenfolk were holed up in Valencia, besieged by Almoravid hordes, days before the battle of Cuarte, when "the Cid of the flowing beard routed them":[148]

> Day dawned over the Moorish camp, and soon the Moors began to beat their drums. This made the Cid happy, and he cried out, "What a good day this is going to be!" His wife was terrified, and so were his daughters and their ladies; they had never been so frightened in their lives. The Campeador stroked his beard and said: "Do not be afraid, for it will all turn to your advantage. Before a fortnight is up [we shall capture] those war drums, please God, and I shall set them before you for you to see what they are like." [And so he did.][149]

During combat, the Cid is vividly—though accurately—described as "wielding his sword" and "killing countless Moors while the blood dripped down to his elbow." After the slaughter is done, he says, "Do you see my bloodstained sword and my horse dripping sweat? That is how Moors are vanquished in battle."[150]

Till this day, nearly a millennium after the Cid walked the earth, he remains a popular folk hero and national icon in Spain; countless movies, plays, novels, songs, and even video games feature him.

Even so, and as might be expected, the naysayers and scoffers—that is, not a few modern academics, the same who vehemently deny Carlyle's "great man" thesis—have marred the Cid's reputation, specifically by portraying him as something of a charlatan, a mercenary who cared little about religion or defending Christian Spain against Islam. The basis for this charge is that during his first exile he fought for and defended Moorish kingdoms such as Zaragoza against the Christians of Aragon.

This argument is misleading. For starters, and as seen, the Islam of the racially watered down petty kings of northern al-Andalus was itself watered down, allowing them to fit into a realpolitik paradigm. Moreover, offering them protection in exchange for tribute was, under Ferdinand I and Alfonso VI—that is, during the entirety of the Cid's lifetime—the primary strategy of the Reconquista: fiscally weakening Moorish kingdoms until they were ripe for conquest or capitulated peacefully. Alfonso VI's own ambassador, Count Sisnando, once casually explained the logic to Abdullah, king of Granada:

> Al-Andalus originally belonged to the Christians. Then they were defeated by the Arabs.... Now that they are strong and capable, the Christians desire to recover what they have lost by force. This can only be achieved by weakness and encroachment. In the long run, when it [al-Andalus] has neither men nor money, we'll be able to recover it without any difficulty.[151]

Roderick's actions at Zaragoza—offering it protection in exchange for tribute—perfectly conformed to this strategy. But when this status quo changed—when the Almoravids, a truly fanatical regime and existential threat, came onto the scene—all deals were off, and the Cid essentially became a Crusader for Spain.

In many respects, it is perhaps the words of his most inveterate enemies—the many contemporary Arabic writers who describe him as the "accursed of Allah," the "Galician dog, Allah's curse on him"—that inadvertently most vindicate the Cid's reputation. For example, written ten years after Roderick's death, the account of Ibn Bassam, a Muslim contemporary who suffered much from the Castilians, is, as might be expected, redolent with resentment and accusations against the Cid. "The power of this tyrant became ever more intolerable," he complains, "it weighed like a heavy load upon the people of the coast and inland regions, filling all men, both near and far, with fear. His intense ambition, his lust for power…caused all to tremble."

All the same, Ibn Bassam could not but confess what all of Christian and Muslim Spain knew: "Yet this man, who was the scourge of his age, was, by his clear-sighted energy, his virile character, and his heroism, a miracle among the great miracles of the Almighty."[152]

CHAPTER 3

King Richard:
The Lion that Roared at Islam

"[T]here is something especially amazing about one of them. He threw our people into disorder and destroyed them. We have never seen his like nor known anyone similar.... It is he who mutilates our people. No one can stand against him, and when he seizes anyone, no one can rescue them from his hands. They call him in their language *Melech* [King] Richard."

—A MUSLIM EMIR[1]

"King Richard always aspired to stamp out the Turks, to crush their shameless arrogance, and to confound the law of Muhammad, so as to vindicate Christianity."

—A CONTEMPORARY CHRISTIAN CHRONICLE[2]

The moment the Crusader states and the Kingdom of Jerusalem were founded by Godfrey of Bouillon and the other First Crusaders between 1097 and 1099, surrounding Muslims gave them no peace. Although they made inroads—the brutal jihadist sack of the County of Edessa in 1144 prompted the Second Crusade—most Crusader kingdoms, including Jerusalem, remained secure, until the rise of Salah al-Din, Saladin, founder of the Ayyubid dynasty (1171–1260). A master propagandist of jihadist rhetoric, after uniting Egypt and Syria under his rule, he riled the lands of Islam against the tiny Crusader states.

After various engagements, on July 4, 1187, the combined forces of Saladin and the Crusaders fought at Hattin. It was a resounding Muslim victory, replete with symbolism of Islam's triumph over Christianity. Saladin had the True Cross, Christendom's most precious relic, seized and paraded upside down in dirt and dung to Muslim jeers and spits;* and, rather than ransom or merely enslave them, he had the most committed of all fighters for Christ, the warrior-monks of the military orders of the Temple and Hospital, butchered before him in a scene that has long informed ISIS's propagandistic execution videos.†

Because most professional fighting men had been annihilated, the Crusader kingdoms were left vulnerable. Accordingly, by July 10, just six days after Hattin, Saladin had speared through and captured several Christian strongholds, including Acre, Jaffa, and Sidon. Next, the indefatigable sultan sped to and besieged Jerusalem; after being in Christian hands for some eighty-eight years, it capitulated on October 2, 1187. Now "a great cry went up from the city and from outside the walls, the Muslims crying the Allahu Akbar in their joy, the Franks groaning in consternation and grief," wrote Ibn al-Athir. "So loud and piercing was the cry that the earth shook."[3]

Saladin reestablished sharia. Churches were pillaged and vandalized; their bells were silenced, their crosses broken off. Although such anti-Christian animus is nowadays portrayed as a bit of triumphalism against those who had long humiliated Islam—namely, the Crusaders—Saladin's intrinsic hate for Christians far transcended his wars with the Franks. He

---

* This, of course, was the usual treatment for the sacred things of Christendom. Here, as another example, is what the Muslims did to the "cross fixed on top of the spire of the Hospitallers' church [in Jerusalem]. They tied ropes around it and threw it down, spat contemptuously on it, hacked it into pieces, then dragged it through the city dung-pits" (Nicholson, 39).

† After boasting "I shall purify the land of these two impure races [Templars and Hospitallers]," Saladin "ordered that they should be beheaded, choosing to have them dead rather than in prison," writes eyewitness Baha' al-Din: "With him was a whole band of scholars and Sufis and a certain number of devout men and ascetics; each begged to be allowed to kill one of them, and drew his scimitar and rolled back his sleeve. Saladin, his face joyful, was sitting on his dais; the infidels showed black despair, the troops were drawn up in their ranks, the amirs stood in double file. There were some who slashed and cut cleanly, and were thanked for it." After saying that some of these would-be executioners did not have the stomach to continue in the grisly ritual, Baha' al-Din focused on one who "killed unbelief to give life to Islam": "I saw there the man who laughed scornfully and slaughtered, who spoke and acted; how many promises he fulfilled, how much praise he won, the eternal rewards he secured with the blood he shed, the pious works added to his account with a neck severed by him" (Gabrieli, 138–139; cf. Mourad & Lindsay, 95–96).

severely persecuted Egypt's indigenous Christians, the Copts—including by crucifying or hanging many thousands of them and routinely breaking the crosses off and tarring their churches—even though the Copts, who knew Saladin as "the Oppressor of the Cross Worshippers," had nothing to do with the Franks or the Crusades.[4]

As for Jerusalem, now that "the Koran was raised to the throne and the [Old and New] Testaments cast down," Saladin ordered some fifteen thousand Christians sold into slavery.[5] "Women and children together came to eight thousand and were quickly divided up among us, bringing a smile to Muslim faces at their lamentation," wrote Muhammad al-Isfahani, one of Saladin's secretaries who was present at Jerusalem's capitulation, before launching into a sadomasochistic tirade extolling the sexual debasement of European women at the hands of Muslim men:

> How many well-guarded women were profaned...and miserly women forced to yield themselves, and women who had been kept hidden [nuns] stripped of their modesty...and free women occupied [meaning "penetrated"], and precious ones used for hard work, and pretty things put to the test, and virgins dishonoured and proud women deflowered...and happy ones made to weep! How many [Muslim] noblemen took them as concubines, how many ardent men blazed for one of them, and celibates were satisfied by them, and thirsty men sated by them, and turbulent men able to give vent to their passion.[6]

News of Jerusalem's fall rocked Europe, "stirring some to tears and inflaming others to revenge."[7] From a combination of shock and grief, Pope Urban III died the day word reached him, on October 20, 1187, aged sixty-seven. His successor, Gregory VIII, immediately issued the *Audita Tremendi*, calling "for the recovery of that land [Jerusalem] in which for our salvation Truth has arisen." Men from everywhere—primarily England, France, Germany, and Italy, but also Denmark, the Netherlands, and East Europe—responded and took the cross. According to a contemporary, even a "great number" of monks "threw off their cowls, donned mailshirts, and became knights of Christ in a new sense, replacing alms with arms."[8]

Such were the origins of the Third Crusade—or the "Kings' Crusade," for several monarchs pledged themselves to it—Medieval Europe's grandest enterprise, one that fused chivalry with faith. "Distinguished warriors had come to avenge the injuries inflicted on the Cross," wrote one chronicler. "Summoned by their devoted fervor, from everywhere famous champions had come for your consolation, O Jerusalem!"[9]

Richard I of England

Among Christendom's great lords, Richard, the thirty-year-old count of Poitou, a descendant of the Norman conqueror of England, "was the first to receive the sign of the cross.... He preceded everyone in this action, inviting them to follow his example."[10] This was unsurprising: from his youth, Richard was given to war—particularly when its cause was righteous; and, in late twelfth century Europe, nothing was more righteous than fighting for the faith. As he himself later explained, "To serve the living God we too have accepted the sign of the cross to defend the places of His death that have been consecrated by His precious blood and which the enemies of the cross of Christ have hitherto shamefully profaned, and we have taken upon us the burden of so great and so holy a work."[11]

Born on September 8, 1157—the third son of King Henry II of England and Queen Eleanor of Aquitaine—few men conformed to the chivalric ideal of knightly courage, honor, and magnanimous self-sacrifice as Richard. "For so great were the man's strength of body, mental courage, and entire trust in God," writes Richard of Devizes (b.1150), a contemporary English chronicler.[12] While such praise may appear exaggerated and biased, even Muslims would later confirm that "He, the accursed one...was brave, valiant, and expert in battle."[13]

At six foot five inches tall, and of an athletic build, Richard was an imposing figure of a man.[14] "The sight of him," wrote another contemporary, "was a pleasure to the eyes."[15] His "hair was between red and gold," and his arms were powerfully made "for drawing a sword and wielding it most effectively." In short, and "with the not insignificant addition of his suitable character and habits"—Richard was well educated, articulate, and even a sometime poet—"his was a figure worthy to govern," concludes the anonymous author of the *Itinerarium Peregrinorum et Gesta Regis Ricardi* ("The Journey of the Pilgrims and the Deeds of King Richard"), the most comprehensive and contemporaneous account of the Third Crusade (henceforth referred to as "the chronicle").[16]

On July 6, 1189, his father, Henry II, who had also taken the cross, died, and Richard was elevated to the throne of England. Though this development delayed his setting out for the Holy Land, he used it to his advantage by raising money, including through the "Saladin Tithe"—a tax on those not taking the cross—and selling much of his own properties and privileges to increase his war chest, whence he spent liberally.

Barbarossa's Crusade

Meanwhile, the nearly seventy-years-old Holy Roman Emperor himself, Frederick "Barbarossa" (so-called for his long flowing red beard)—a consummate Crusader in his youth—had already set out from Regensburg on May 11, 1189, at the head of a gargantuan German army, to recover Jerusalem from Saladin, whom the emperor first berated in a scalding letter. Despite his great age, "Frederick remained vigorous and eager to use, in the service of Christ, the considerable power he had built up in Germany."[17]

His, however, would be one of the most disastrous episodes in the entirety of Crusading history. On June 10, 1190, Frederick died—either from stroke, the extreme heat, or because his horse lost its footing—while crossing a river on horseback in Asia Minor.

Without his charismatic person at its center, the vast Crusader army the Holy Roman Emperor had assembled dissolved. His son, Frederick, the duke of Swabia, persisted to the Holy Land with a much smaller force, and buried his father with honors in Antioch. He then went to join the rest of the indigenous Crusaders, who were then desperately besieging Muslim-held Acre. There, famine and pestilence were ravaging the Christians' ranks, as many thousands died "from the foul air, polluted with the stink of corpses, worn out by anxious nights spent on guard, and shattered by other hardships and needs. There was no rest, not even time to breathe."[18] The recently arrived young duke of Swabia himself died there, in 1191, aged twenty-three.

With Barbarossa's much anticipated Crusade at a premature end, King Richard's only counterpart and close ally was Philip I Augustus, king of France, who had also taken the cross. In early summer of 1190, they met in Vezelay, Burgundy. "There was great love between the king of England and the king of France," writes the continuer of William of

Tyre's chronicle, "as they had sworn together to be loyal companions and keep good faith with one another."[19]

This would not last. Although Richard was technically Philip's "vassal" for his lands in France, the English king's lordly bearing and charisma, compared to the king of France's diminutive stature and closed persona, did not lend much credence to this bit of feudalism, and everyone sensed it—especially Philip. The chronicle well summarizes why they found it difficult to cooperate: "Both of them refused to give way to the other: the king of France felt he would demean himself if he committed himself to the judgment of an inferior, while Richard thought he would be dishonored if he submitted to a man whose feats were less impressive than his own."[20]

On July 4, 1190, three years to the day since the disaster at Hattin, they sailed off separately from Vezelay. As he had managed to raise more money than Philip, Richard's fleets were impressive—as many as two hundred fully manned vessels—and one more reason to antagonize his nominal superior.

Adventures to the Holy Land

Richard first stopped at Sicily to collect his sister, Joan. Her husband, William II, had recently died and his throne was usurped by Tancred of Lecce. Now Richard wanted his sister—and her dowry—back. Tancred stalled, weeks passed, tempers flared, and Richard laid siege to and captured Messina on October 4. Tancred finally capitulated, and Richard withdrew. Before leaving Sicily, he awaited his mother, Eleanor, who was bringing her preferred future daughter-in-law with her, Berengaria, daughter of King Sancho VI of Navarre (yet another slight against Philip, for Richard was expected to marry his sister, Alice).

On April 10, 1191, Richard set sail from Sicily. Due to a terrible storm, some of his ships, including one holding the treasury coffers, were shipwrecked off the coast of Cyprus. Its ruler, Isaac Comnenus, a Byzantine rebel and self-styled "emperor," imprisoned the survivors and plundered their ships. On arriving, Richard furiously demanded the instant release of all his men and gold. Isaac scoffed and incited his men to war.

Frightened at the nighttime approach of Isaac and his vast army, a clerk ran to and presumed to advise Richard, who then only had about fifty knights with him: "My lord king," implored the man, "it would seem well-advised to avoid engaging such a great and powerful crowd of opponents at this moment." "Lord clerk," coolly responded the king as he continued strapping on his gauntlets and greaves, "it is best for your profession to stick to your scriptures, leaving the fighting to us, and concentrate on keeping yourself out of the thick of it." Others offered the same advice: "Yet their trepidation only made him more courageous," continues the chronicle. "Putting spur to horse, he charged into the enemy, broke through and scattered their battle line, destroying them on this side and that. In a moment he routed the lot of them."[21]

Days later Isaac surrendered himself on condition that he not be put in iron fetters; Richard agreed and had him put in silver shackles. Before long, Cyprus had capitulated and "was subjected to him in everything, just like England."[22] In their earlier parleys, Richard had berated Isaac:

> I am most amazed that you, who are a Christian and have seen the loss of the Holy Land in which God died and rose and the destruction of Christendom, have never sent counsel or aid there. In particular, while the siege of Acre has been in progress, the Christians have endured great hardships and have been short of both food and men, but you have done nothing to suggest that it means anything to you. Instead, you have shown them enmity, for you have harmed or oppressed many of those who have gone to their aid.[23]

Now that Richard had taken Cyprus, all this was about to change: being so near to the Holy Land, the east Mediterranean island would become a major bastion of the Crusades, and for nearly four centuries, until 1571, a chief thorn in Islam's side.

Richard left Cyprus in early June, 1191, at the head of a massive armada. "Impatient of delay as was his wont," the chronicler says "he always advanced first in the front line."[24] Around June 8, the desperate besiegers of Acre finally espied what they had long hoped for—the banners of the Lionheart fluttering atop the mast of the first vessel to appear over the horizon. Immediately, "the land shook with the Christians' rejoicing," while the "besieged Turks...were terrified and devastated by his arrival."[25] Muslim sources confirm that the appearance of "the accursed king of England"—who came with "twenty-five galleys, full of men, weapons, and stores" thereby "greatly strengthening the Frankish threat"—had "a dread and frightening effect on the hearts of the Muslims."[26]

Before Richard's fleets could harbor, on June 11, a friendly "merchant ship of immensely large dimensions" was seen approaching Acre. Richard, "astonished at its enormous size," sent envoys and received vacillating replies (first that the ship was owned by the French, then by the Genoese, etc.).[27]

It was in fact a Muslim ship come from Beirut or Egypt. Islamic relief forces had been sneaking into Acre by pretending to be Christian vessels (including by dressing as Franks, shaving their beards, and displaying pigs on deck). The ship was "loaded with heaps of stuff" to reinforce the Muslim besieged, including:

> 100 camel loads of every sort of weapon: great piles of crossbows, bows, bolts and arrows. There were seven Saracen emirs and 800 elite Turks on board, and overwhelming quantities of every kind of food, beyond calculation. They also had plenty of Greek fire in phials, and 200 very deadly snakes to destroy the Christians.[28]

Concerning that last creepy commodity, "the Muslims," writes one historian, "with characteristically evil cunning, had planned to release" these "venomous snakes" into "the camp of the Christian army."[29]

Fearful of the English king's encroachments and inquiries, the large Muslim vessel, which "was fortified with towers and bulwarks," eventually took the initiative and opened fire on his fleets. Because "our people were unable to stand up under the shots fired from the great height of the ship," they panicked. So the Lion flew into action—roaring, "you all ought to be hanged on the cross or suffer the ultimate penalty, if you let these people get away."[30] Being thus upbraided, "our sailors made a virtue of necessity, eagerly threw themselves into the sea, dived under the [enemy] ship and tied up the rudder with ropes to turn the ship and impede its progress.

> Others crept up with great care and perseverance, grabbed hold of cables and jumped into the ship. The Turks met them with determination and cut them to pieces as they boarded, cutting off here an arm, there a hand, or heads, and hurling the bodies into the sea. When the rest saw this they seethed with anger and thirst for revenge. Gaining courage, they made a more bitter assault, climbed over the ship's bulwarks and fell on the Turks, slaughtering them as they bravely resisted. The Turks gained boldness from despair and

tried with all their strength to resist the attacking sailors, cutting off...a great many heads.... [And so] they fought for a long time, and many fell on both sides.[31]

The Christians eventually returned to their ships, at which point Richard "ordered each galley to ram the ship with its spur, i.e., the iron-covered beak on the prow."

> The galleys drew back; then with many strokes of the oars they slammed forward to hole the sides of the ship. The ship was stove in...and began to sink.... To escape death in the ship the Turks leapt out into the sea. They died there nonetheless because our people met them with weapons, killed some and drowned the rest. The king, however, kept thirty-five alive, i.e., emirs and those who were skilled at constructing siege engines. All the others perished, and their weapons were lost; the snakes were drowned and scattered by the waves of the sea.[32]

Muslim sources claim the ship was ultimately sunk by the self-sacrifice of its captain, Yaqoub of Aleppo. On seeing that death was inevitable, he reportedly capsized the ship to prevent its rich stores from being appropriated by the "accursed" infidels.[33] (In fact, modern day jihadist groups regularly cite this anecdote to justify "martyrdom operations."*)

It was a major and demoralizing defeat: "Seeing what had happened from far off in the mountains," where Saladin was stationed, "the Saracens were devastated" and "carried on a terrible lamentation over this misfortune.... For in that ship all their outstanding young warriors had perished, in whom all their confidence had been placed." As for the sultan, "on hearing the news," he reportedly "pulled out his hair and tore his beard in his furious rage. Afterwards he sighed, and burst into these words: 'O Alla kibir ychalla!' [O Allah, all-powerful]."[34] On recomposing himself, Saladin more characteristically added, "Allah will not neglect the reward of those who do right."[35]

---

* "Look you to these valorous heroes," writes al-Qaeda leader Ayman al-Zawahiri to would-be jihadists, "how they punched a hole in their ship, thereby killing themselves, in order to gain two legitimate and great advantages: (1) preventing their deaths at the hands of their enemies, or falling hostage to them; (2) preventing booty from falling to their enemies. Men such as these are truly the horsemen of *tawhid*, who defend the *sunna* of the Prophet, the enemies of America and Israel" (Ibrahim 2007, 151).

In such a manner—or with such a "big splash"—did the thirty-three-year-old English king announce his entry into the Third Crusade. It instantly revitalized the siege: "the man whose arrival we sought, the king more skilled in warfare than any Christian, is come," the exhausted besiegers cried.[36]

Considering that Richard was Philip's vassal, this, too, did not sit well with the French king. Even Baha' al-Din, Saladin's confidant and court historian, sensed the incongruity: "This king of England was a mighty warrior of great courage and strong purpose," he writes. "He had much experience of fighting and was intrepid in battle, and yet he was in their eyes below the king of France in royal status, although being richer and more renowned for martial skill and courage."[37]

The Siege of Acre

Richard immediately ordered the construction of more siege engines, including a moveable tower, which housed archers and crossbowmen on each floor; the top floor, taller than Acre's walls, had a drawbridge to drop onto and storm over the walls—the same set up that Godfrey and the First Crusaders employed at Jerusalem. More ditches around Acre were filled, thereby allowing these new engines of war to encroach upon and bombard the city; and defensive trenches were dug around the Crusaders' camp, to prevent sorties from Saladin's marauding troops.

Soon all the engines of war rained down death dealing destruction. Massive boulders—some aflame and setting anything inside Acre not built of stone ablaze—rocked the city. The brothers-in-arms of those ritually massacred by Saladin at Hattin also made their presence felt: "the Templars' stonethrower wreaked impressive devastation, while the Hospitallers' also never ceased hurling, to the terror of the Turks."[38] As Muslim chronicler Ibn al-Athir observes, after Richard's arrival, "The damage they did to the Muslims increased greatly. The king was the outstanding man of his time for bravery, cunning, steadfastness and endurance. In him the Muslims were tried by an unparalleled disaster."[39]

Before long, however, Muslim spies "reported the great fatigue they [the Crusaders] endured on account of all the various tasks they had constantly to put up with since the arrival of the accursed king of England. Then the latter fell seriously ill and was on the verge of death."[40] More robust than most men, even Richard had succumbed to the pestilent

Crusader camp and contracted a form of scurvy which caused hair and fingernails to fall out, and in extreme cases, blindness.[41] Even so, he continued inciting his men to war from the sickbed. The chronicle offers a snapshot of these times:

> King Richard's stonethrowers hurled constantly by day and night.... [O]ne of them killed twelve men with a single stone. That stone was sent for Saladin to see, with messengers who said that the diabolical king of England had...[come] to punish the Saracens. Nothing could withstand their blows; everything was crushed or reduced to dust. Yet the king was confined to bed suffering from a severe fever, completely wretched because he saw the Turks insolently challenging and attacking our people with increasing frequency but he could not engage them in battle because he was ill.[42]

This, the chronicler adds, is what truly "burned" him up—for Richard "suffered more torture from the insolent Turkish raids than from the burning fever."[43]

The long awaited Lion from England had come; his men had fiercely contributed to the siege; dead men and animals littered the inside and outside of Acre, which was plagued by disease and starvation; even the Accursed Tower, the main citadel of Acre, had been demolished—and yet still no surrender from the Turks came, a testimony to their resilience.

"Disgusted at the great delay" and hoping to end matters—and thus upstart his upstart—on July 1, Philip "launched a very fierce assault on it, with crossbows and siege machines shooting bolts and stones without a pause." The besieged Muslims, driven to despair, "raised to heaven such an uproar and bellowing of war trumpets" while "beating drums and making a racket in various other ways as well as raising smoke from a fire," so that "the air seemed to resound with thunder and flashing lightning." It was, in fact, "a prearranged signal to Saladin and the outer army to come to their assistance."[44]

Soon the Crusaders were fighting on two fronts: Acre to their front, where they had managed to place and climb scaling ladders, even as fire rained down atop and smoldered them; and Saladin's horsemen to their rear. The Franks managed to beat them back, but also made little headway in capturing the city. When, after yet another promising assault, the Muslims torched Philip's wooden siege engines with Greek fire, "the king of France was thrown into a violent rage. He began to curse all those under his command, using terrible language....["45]

On July 3, Phillip ordered another full-scale assault. This time, "picked warriors of exceptional valour" were stationed in the ditches to protect the besiegers' rear from Saladin's advances. A wall was partially undermined and the horsemen came: "It was a bitter battle: they fought hand-to-hand with drawn swords, and daggers and two-headed axes, and clubs bristling with sharp teeth.... A great many perished *en masse.*"[46]

All this time Saladin had also been resorting to terror tactics, for he "enrolled 300 robbers from amongst the thieving Bedouin to infiltrate the enemy." Baha' al-Din explains how, after a day of exhaustive fighting, these cutthroats would slip into the Crusader camp during the thick of night. The common soldier would be rudely awoken "by a dagger which was held at his throat." He and his belongings would then be spirited away or, if he resisted, slaughtered on the spot.[47]

By now, Richard, though still sick, had become even more sick of his impotence. He ordered his moveable tower hauled into "the ditch outside the city wall"; he then "had himself carried out" on his sick bed and placed near his "most skilled crossbowmen" under the tower. The wounded warrior-king did this "to discourage the Saracens with his presence and encourage his own people to fight. There he used his crossbow, with which he was skilled, and killed many."[48]

Meanwhile, "the Christians' stonethrowers kept up a constant battering of the walls, day and night."[49] Acre was holding on by a thread. Although the Christian chronicler praised the martial spirit of its Turkish garrison—they were "fit and ready for anything" and "certainly not inferior to our people"[50]—by now many desperate Muslims "hurled themselves from the walls at night in a desperate attempt to escape." On being captured, a "great many of them begged to be given the sacrament of the Christian baptism," though, as the chronicle observes, "they asked for this more as a means of escape."[51]

Finally, on July 12, 1191, the day after another extremely savage attack spearheaded by the English and Italians, and considering that large sections of Acre's walls had by now collapsed into and filled the moat, "the Franks—Allah curse them!—conquered the city of Acre," writes Ibn al-Athir.[52] The Muslims offered terms of surrender: in exchange for the garrison's lives, Saladin would return the True Cross, release all his Christian hostages, and pay two hundred thousand dinars in indemnities.

The gates were opened and the Crusaders reclaimed the city. "With Acre once again a Christian city, the first task of the crusaders was to reconsecrate the churches," and thank God in them.[53] Many of the Muslim garrison converted to Christianity and were, on good faith, set free—only to cross over to Saladin's camp.

Two weeks later, Philip announced his imminent return to France, despite tearful pleading by even his own men. He had had quite enough of Crusading, and was tired of being overshadowed by Richard—even when he was sick. Before leaving, he reconfirmed his oath that he would not attack the English king's holdings in France and, to his credit, left ten thousand of his men under the command of Hugh of Burgundy. Then, on July 31, "Philip, king of the French, having left his companion Richard, king of the English, in the territory of Jerusalem amongst the enemies of the Cross of Christ—neither the liberation of the Holy Cross nor of the Sepulchre being obtained—returned to France," to quote Richard of Devizes.[54]

Apparently King Richard himself felt betrayed; in a letter to home, he lamented how, "to the eternal dishonor of his kingdom, [Philip] so shamelessly failed in his vow."[55] It was, however, a sort of good riddance as well; for so long as Philip was present, Richard was destined to be "like a cat with a hammer tied to its tail."[56]

As for the Muslims' terms of surrender, when the first payment was due, Saladin asked for more time, and was given an additional three weeks, until August 20. It was widely believed, and certainly consistent with the wily sultan's modus operandi, that he was intentionally delaying for strategic purposes. In the meantime, "Saladin sent the king frequent gifts and messengers, gaining time with deceitful and crafty words; but he never carried out any of his promises. He aimed at keeping the king hanging on for a long time through his myriad subtleties and ambiguities."[57] Worse, on the day before payment was due a rumor spread among the Crusaders that instead of freeing them, Saladin had slaughtered all his Christian captives.

When, therefore, August 20 came and the first payment remained undelivered—no envoys even appeared to ask for more time—an already disgruntled Richard flew into a rage, marched some twenty-six hundred

Muslim captives outside in full view of Saladin and ordered their execution. The Crusaders eagerly complied in order to "take revenge for the deaths of the Christians whom the Turks had killed."[58] Saladin instantly replied in kind, beheading all his Christian captives, over a thousand, and many more later.

Although some in modern academia have obsessed over this incident—a few to the point of arguing that contemporary Muslim terrorism is partially motivated by grievances concerning this massacre—contemporaries were not overly shocked. After all, in the end, it was Saladin's fault: he had not stuck to the terms of surrender—and this in an era when such terms were taken deadly seriously. As he had reneged, so did Richard—even if in a decisively ruthless manner. At least he had offered to ransom the Muslims' lives at a time when not a few Crusaders were clamoring for their blood. As the chronicler observed after explaining all of the Christians' sufferings and "countless" deaths—reportedly "300,000 pilgrims and more died from infection and hunger"[59]—before the walls of Acre: "In the eyes of God and humanity the Turks certainly deserved their fate because of their destruction of churches and slaying of people."[60] Richard himself explained his rationale in a letter sent home:

> On Saladin's behalf it had been agreed that the Holy Cross and 1,500 living prisoners would be handed over to us, and he fixed a day for us when all this was to be done. But the time-limit expired, and, as the pact which he had agreed was entirely made void, we quite properly had the Saracens that we had in custody—about 2,600 of them—put to death. A few of the more noble were spared, and we hope to recover the Holy Cross and certain Christian captives in exchange for them.[61]

Many Muslim leaders throughout history had treated their hostages similarly or worse*—including Saladin himself, who ordered the ritual massacre of his Templar and Hospitaller captives at Hattin in keeping with sharia, which says that Muslim leaders can do one of three things with their captives: release them, ransom them, or simply kill

---

* As one example, consider the unprovoked Muslim sack of Amorium, an ancient Christian city in Anatolia, in 838. Half of the city's population of seventy thousand was massacred or burned alive, while the other half was enslaved. Because there was such a surplus of human booty, when Caliph Mu'tasim came across four thousand male prisoners, he ordered them executed on the spot.

them in cold blood. Even Baha' al-Din offers two prosaic reasons for this mass execution: in "revenge for their men who had been killed" or else because Richard had to move on with his Crusade and naturally did not want to leave behind and spend resources on the upkeep of such a large, hostile force.[62]

The Battle of Arsuf

With Acre secure and the Crusaders unified under the sole command of Richard, talk of marching onto and liberating Jerusalem began. The problem, however, was that Jerusalem was inland, whereas all Crusader holdings were coastal. Any march into the hilly and desolate interior from Acre would require a line of supplies too vast to secure. So Richard decided to head for and take Jaffa; while coastal and directly south of Acre, it was the closest port to and directly west of Jerusalem. At the head of some ten thousand Crusaders, he marched out of Acre on August 22 and, "directing his arms to the storming of castles along the sea-shore, he took every fortress that came in his way," writes Richard of Devizes, "though after hard fighting and deep wounds."[63]

During their seventy-five mile march from Acre to Jaffa, Saladin sought every opportunity to annihilate the infidels; his horsemen repeatedly "harassed the Franks on their march and loosed arrows at them which well nigh veiled the sun," writes Ibn al-Athir. The Muslims also "fell on the Frankish rearguard, killed several and captured several others."[64]

Richard tried to safeguard against this by keeping the army in remarkably tight formation. The van and rear were entrusted to the most veteran Christian warriors, the Templars and Hospitallers, respectively. It was a long, arduous, and miserable trek. Marching in the Syrian sun during summer was exhausting—particularly for the heavily armored knights. Richard kept the march short by day, even as "swarms" of the same venomous snakes that had harried the First Crusaders a century earlier stung and caused "terrible agony" for the wearied men by night.[65]

All the while, "the Turks raged in their stubborn wickedness," writes the chronicler, "keeping alongside our army as it advanced, struggling to inflict what injury they could on us, firing darts and arrows which flew very densely, like rain." It got so bad that wherever "the army passed through you could not have found a space of four feet of ground free of darts." During these arrow-deluges, even Richard, while "driving away the Turks with slaughter," was wounded. He pulled the arrow out—the pain of which only "incited him to attack the enemy" more fiercely, until the Muslims withdrew. Many horses were also "transfixed" and died from these downpours; they were put to good use. Because Saladin was always ahead of the marching Crusaders, his men had destroyed all of the land's crops and resources. Thus the starving Crusaders "ate horse-meat as if it was game. Flavoured with hunger rather than sauce, they thought it was delicious."[66]

After writing of another raid to occur during this march—when Muslim arrows again "blotted out the sky"—Baha' al-Din writes: "The battle raged furiously. His [Saladin's] aim was to provoke them into a charge, so that, when they did charge, he would hurl his troops against them and Allah would give the victory to whomsoever he willed." In other words, the sultan was counting on the same tactic that had won him the day at Hattin—and Richard knew this. "They did not charge, however," continues the Muslim historian, "but controlled themselves and marched on in their battle lines according to their custom."[67]

Indeed, despite it all—despite the casualties from arrows, sunstroke, starvation and disease, despite the wounds, snake bites, and overall misery—the Christian warriors remained undaunted. Saladin's own biographer expressed his dismay: "I saw various individuals amongst the Franks with ten arrows fixed in their backs, pressing on in this fashion quite unconcerned.... Consider the endurance of these people, bearing exhausting tasks without any pay or material gain."[68] (Baha' al-Din's shock is ultimately reflective of the major differences between Crusading and Jihading—differences that are today often glossed over and conflated.*)

The Christians were nearing Jaffa and Saladin was running out of time. So he decided to ambush them in a full-scale attack. For the field of battle, he chose the vast plain between Arsuf and the dense woods just north of it, which the Crusaders were passing through on September 6.

---

* For example, because Just War demanded the restoration of a particularly important piece of Christian territory—Jerusalem—the Crusaders marched for years over thousands of miles deep into hostile territory, suffering hunger, thirst, disease, and a host of other plagues to reach their goal—and they usually had nothing, no plunder or slaves, to show for it. Conversely, the jihad took place wherever Muslim territories conveniently abutted against infidel territory (the *ribats*). Thus jihadists rarely suffered hardships or deprivations and were always a short march away from Muslim territories, whence supplies, recruits, and refreshments of all sorts were easily attainable. Hence Baha' al-Din's admiration for the Crusaders, who embodied self-sacrifice in ways the jihadists did not.

They were on high alert, lest Saladin set the wood ablaze as they passed through. Relieved to emerge unscathed, they soon saw why. A huge army, consisting of at least some twenty-five thousand horsemen—more than double the Christians—was awaiting them in battle formation under Saladin's command. "All the forces" of Islam had merged together, "from Damascus and Persia, from the Mediterranean Sea to the East," writes the chronicler. There was not a single warlike Muslim peoples "whom Saladin had not summoned to aid him in crushing the Christian people," for he "hoped to wipe the Christians completely off the face of the earth."[69]

Battle commenced on the morning of September 7, 1191. A wild din erupted from the Muslim camp; drums, horns, and cymbals banged and brayed to reverberant cries of "Allahu Akbar" and other "horrible yells." As the Crusaders knelt in prayer and went into battle formation, the "land all around resounded with the echo of their [Muslims'] harsh cries and roaring noise." Suddenly, in the midst of this "terrifying racket," some ten thousand Turks "rushed down on our people" on horses "driven like lightning." The dust storm caused by this stampede "filled the sky like a dark cloud."[70] Behind the galloping Turks "ran a devilish race, very black in colour," and "Bedouins, savage and darker than soot, the most redoubtable infantrymen, carrying bows and quivers and round shields."[71]

In this manner, the Muslims "fell on our army from all sides…. There was not a space for two miles around, not even a fistful, which was not covered with the hostile Turkish race…. As they kept up their persistent assaults they inflicted very grave losses on our people."[72] Unlike the better rested and provisioned Muslims, the already exhausted Crusaders fought back as best they could: unhorsed knights were seen "walking on foot" and "returning blow for blow as far as means and strength allowed," even as the Turks galloped about and continued to rain down darts on them.

Before long, a "very fierce race of people," one "proud and insolent, rendered unyielding by demonic instigation," pummeled the Christian rearguard, led by the Hospitallers. The latter bravely held their ground, prompting the frustrated Muslims to "rage with even worse barbarity," for they lamented "that our people were made of iron and could not be harmed." Even so—and although they were burning to do so—the Crusaders were forbidden to charge the enemy, in keeping with Richard's orders not to break ranks until he gave the word, prompting one frustrated Hospitaller to cry, "Christianity is perishing because she is not fighting back against this unspeakable race!" The Master of the Hospital repeatedly implored Richard but he refused. The king's plan was sound: only when the entire Muslim army had gotten close enough, and their horses had tired, would he give the signal for a counteroffensive.

Inevitably, "two knights who could not bear to wait" any longer "burst out of the line," whereupon "everything was thrown into confusion." They charged at and began slaughtering their enemies. "The rest of the Christians heard these two calling with loud voices for Saint George's aid as they charged boldly on the Turks," and so immediately followed suit—"charging as one into the relentlessly attacking enemy."[73]

On seeing this, Richard signaled for the general assault, and sped to where the fighting was thickest. He broke through the Hospitallers and crashed with thunderous violence into the enemy. "Stunned by the strength of the blows he and his force inflicted on them," the Muslims "fell back to the right and the left." Many were butchered on the spot, while a "great number were but headless corpses trodden underfoot by friend and foe regardless." Driven into a battle frenzy, and in the words of the chronicler:

> King Richard pursued the Turks with singular ferocity, fell upon them and scattered them across the ground. No one escaped when his sword made contact with them; wherever he went his brandished sword cleared a wide path on all sides. Continuing his advance with untiring sword strokes, he cut down that unspeakable race as if he was reaping the harvest with a sickle, so that the corpses of Turks he had killed covered the ground everywhere for the space of half a mile. The rest panicked at the sight of the dying and gave him a wider berth.... Constantly slaying and hammering away with their swords, the Christians wore down the terrified Turks, but for a long time the battle was in the balance. Each struck each other, each struggled to overcome; one drew back stained with blood, the other fell slain. How many banners and multiform flags, pennons and innumerable standards you would have seen fall to the ground![74]

In the end, the Christians prevailed, and the "rout of the enemy was so complete that for two miles there was nothing to see except for people running away, although they had previously been so persistent, swollen with pride and very fierce."

Arabic sources confirm the magnitude of this defeat: "The Muslims were routed, a great number of them were killed," writes Ibn al-Athir, before indicating how terror-stricken his coreligionists had become: "When the Franks made camp, the Muslims did so too—though keeping their horses' reins in their hands."[75]

It was a Christian victory of the first order. "So great was the slaughter among Saladin's more noble Saracens," Richard wrote a few weeks later, "that he lost more that day near Arsuf…than on any day in the previous 40 years."[76] The sultan's lofty and invincible stature as Defender of Islam collapsed overnight. He had lost Acre and Arsuf; as for Jaffa—the ultimate destination of the Crusaders—after seventy-five miles of warfare and travails, they now marched onto it without impediment, for Saladin had quickly ordered its fortifications destroyed before fleeing.

Henceforth Saladin would never again risk a pitched battle with Richard. As the latter later wrote, "Since his defeat that day, Saladin has not dared do battle with the Christians. Instead he lies in wait at a distance out of sight like a lion in his den, and he is intent on killing the friends of the cross like sheep led to the slaughter."[77]

Meanwhile, sultan and servant lost respect for one another. Before the battle, Saladin's emirs had, with "boastful tongues and pompous words," revived his hope, saying that "without doubt and with Muhammad's help the Christians would be wiped off the face of the earth on the day of that battle"—only to end up fleeing before the Crusaders' wrath.[78] "Now look!" the sultan berated his leading men as they stood crestfallen in his tent: "The Christians travel through the land of Syria just as they like without meeting any opposition or resistance."

> Where are my soldiers' great boasts and brilliant exploits now? … [W]here is the victory they boasted of? How the people of today have degenerated from our noble ancestors who gained so many brilliant and justly memorable victories against the Christians, victories which are retold to us daily and whose memory will endure forever![79]

One of Saladin's emirs dared offer reply: "Most sacred sultan, saving your majesty's grace, you have blamed us unjustly, for we attacked the Franks with all our effort [to no avail]." He continued by lamenting Christian armor, which "is not like ours" but rather "incalculable, impenetrable." But that was not all:

[T]here is something especially amazing about one of them. He threw our people into disorder and destroyed them. We have never seen his like nor known anyone similar. He was always at the head of the others; in every engagement he was first and foremost.... It is he who mutilates our people. No one can stand against him, and when he seizes anyone, no one can rescue them from his hands. They call him in their language *Melech* [King] Richard.[80]

If Acre had not done it, Arsuf did: from now on, Saladin's jihadists were in mortal dread of this man-mountain and his men from the West. Thus, when the sultan ordered a Muslim contingent to hold Ascalon, another strategically important coastal fortress for whoever would be master of Jerusalem, and which was next on the Crusaders' route, according to Ibn al-Athir, they told him "If you wish to hold the place, then come in with us yourself and one of your older sons. Otherwise none of us will enter lest we suffer what the men at Acre suffered."[81] As with Jaffa, Saladin destroyed Ascalon and withdrew to and holed himself up in Jerusalem.

Twice to Jerusalem

While stationed in and rebuilding Jaffa, the Crusaders took council on what to do next. Despite their victories, their strength, numbers, and morale had diminished: "[W]e consistently endure the heat of day and have already exhausted all our money—and not only our money but both our strength and our body also," Richard wrote in a letter addressed to his "most dear friend in Christ, the abbot of Clairvaux," dated October 1, 1191.[82] Talks resumed; the English king, relying on reason, sent the following message to the sultan:

> The Muslims and the Franks are done for. The land is ruined, ruined utterly at the hands of both sides. Property and lives on both sides are destroyed. This matter has received its due. All we have to talk about is Jerusalem, the Holy Cross and these lands. Now Jerusalem is the centre of our worship which we shall never renounce, even if there were only one of us left. As for these lands, let there be restored to us what is this side of the Jordan [those Crusader holdings captured by Saladin after and because of Hattin]. The Holy Cross, that is a piece of wood that has no value for you, but is important for us: Let the sultan

bestow it upon us. Then we can make peace and have rest from this constant hardship.[83]

Saladin sent the following reply to Richard:

> Jerusalem is ours just as much as it is yours. Indeed, for us it is greater than it is for you, for it is where our Prophet came on his Night Journey and the gathering place of the angels.[*] Let not the king imagine that we shall give it up, for we are unable to breathe a word of that amongst the Muslims. As for the land, it is also ours originally. Your conquest of it [during the First Crusade] was an unexpected accident due to the weakness of the Muslims there at the time.[84]

Saladin continued by saying that "The destruction of the Holy Cross would in our eyes be a great offering to Allah, but the only reason we are not permitted to go that far is that some more useful benefit might accrue to Islam."[85] The sultan knew the importance of the True Cross—he rejected a two hundred thousand dinar ransom for its return from the king of Georgia—and would never give it up. Since then, its status and/or whereabouts remain unknown.

Saladin did, however, try to flatter Richard with gifts, including "seven valuable camels and a tent."[86] He also sent his brother, Safadin, who—and despite the meaning of his name, "Sword of Islam"—was a consummate diplomat, to Richard with "smooth words." The English king was apparently so impressed that he proposed a marriage between his sister, Joan of Sicily, and Safadin: they could then jointly rule the Holy Land to the benefit of both Christian and Muslim. This went well until Richard added another stipulation: Safadin would first have to be baptized, for, as Joan had made abundantly clear, she would never "allow a Muslim to have carnal knowledge of her."[87]

Talks faltered, and, in late October 1191, the Crusaders finally decided to set off for Jerusalem. Everyone was overjoyed and "made great boasts and looked forward to completing their pilgrimage as they had previously vowed, whether the Saracens liked it or not."[88] Hailstorms and torrential rains—exacerbated by the ubiquitous Turkic arrow—poured on them

---

[*] According to Islamic teaching, in the year 610, Muhammad—flying atop a supernatural horse-like creature named al-Buraq—visited and prayed in Jerusalem, before flying into and touring the heavens, and finally returning to Mecca, all in the same night. This is one of Islam's primary claims to Jerusalem.

incessantly; they traveled in slippery, muddy conditions, and ate soggy food. "Pen cannot describe nor tongue tell their great adversities and misery" during their trek inland.[89] But they remained enthused nonetheless, and did sing: "God may we now our voices raise/In thanks, in worship and in praise!/Now we shall see Thy Holy Tomb!/ No man felt any grief or gloom/Or any sadness or distress/ For all was joy and happiness."[90]

By January 1192, they were twelve miles away from Jerusalem. A council was held between Richard and the leading barons and Crusaders. The wiser and more experienced military orders, the Templars and Hospitallers, argued that it was still too dangerous to assault the Holy City. Already the supply line back to Jaffa was under constant attack, and the consensus was that the army should return to and travel south along the coast to take and rebuild the port of Ascalon, thereby disrupting communications between Saladin's Syrian and Egyptian domains, and so compromising his ability to bring supplies and reinforcements from the latter. The logic was simple: Ascalon must first be placed, if Jerusalem was ever to remain, in Christian hands.

When Richard accepted and announced the military orders' counsel, the Crusader rank and file were outraged. They had gone through so much and were now so near to Jerusalem—only to retreat and go on what seemed to them yet another unnecessary adventure. Accordingly, much of the Crusader army—including all of the French—broke apart, returning either to Acre or Jaffa. Undaunted, Richard continued with the plan and was at and rebuilding Ascalon, a laborious project, on January 20, 1192.

After the "savage wintry months" had passed and Ascalon was rebuilt, "King Richard kept up untiring activity, pursuing the Turks tirelessly and persistently," writes the chronicler:

> [H]e attacked them so often, wearing them down without a break, frequently charging almost alone against many. Almost every day that he happened to run into the Turks he would carry perhaps ten, or twelve, or twenty, or thirty heads of his enemies. He also brought back [Christian] captives alive, whatever seemed best to him. Never in Christian times were so many Saracens destroyed by one person.[91]

Many indeed were the adventures Richard experienced during this phase of his sojourn. On one occasion, while "disguised as an Arab," he raided a well-armed caravan traveling from Egypt. "Borne on a high horse," the warrior-king "charged alone into the enemy—until his couched ashwood spear became weakened from piercing the enemy too many times with savage blows and shattered into many bloodstained splinters. Then he immediately brandished his drawn sword and bore down on the fugitives, seized them, threw them down, mowed down the hindmost and shaved off the last."[92] It was only "a brave and stout man who was able to mount his horse and save his life" during Richard's assault, which ended with much rich bounty falling to him: "It was a disastrous incident," concludes Baha' al-Din, "the like of which had not befallen Islam for a very long time."[93]

On another occasion, the Muslims, "thinking that they would capture or crush our people completely unawares," tried to ambush Richard while he slept in between travel with a small guard: "At the break of dawn Turks charged on them.... The king was the first to leap out from under his blanket. Seizing only a shield and sword, he advanced to meet the attackers, captured seven Turks and killed four. The rest fled before him."[94]

In yet another instance, while scouting "with an elite force of knights to see how the castle of Darum could be captured," Richard came across a Muslim contingent leading twelve hundred Christian captives to said castle. "When they realised from his approaching [lion] banner that the king was coming they were terrified...and rushed into the main tower of the castle, leaving their captives outside."[95]

When not fighting Muslims, Richard was dueling with nature, and the chronicler tells of a near fatal encounter with a wild boar, "foaming at the tusks" and "worked up to a fury." The beast ended up providing a rich banquet for the men.[96]

Time, however, was not on the Crusader-King's side. On April 15, 1192, Richard received word that his brother, John, was causing problems in England and Philip was conspiring to take over his lands in France. Richard had to act fast; he was soon back at and laying siege to the fortress of Darum, twenty miles south of Ascalon, another strategic step on the road to—because it would help sever Egypt from—Jerusalem. He worked with lightning speed and was seen carrying and running with heavy siege equipment brought from the shore "for the distance of almost a mile, going on foot and with much sweat."

Although the Muslims valiantly defended themselves, the "king kept the stonethrowers hurling by day and night, without a pause." Three days later "three Saracens came out and went to the king, seeking peace. They offered to surrender the castle on condition that every soul could depart in freedom, leaving behind everything which they possessed. The king did not agree. He told them to defend themselves as best they could." Per the usual custom of war, had they capitulated on his arrival, he would have let them go. But since they had opted to resist, and having put him to all this trouble, there would be no mercy.

The castle was taken on May 22, 1192—just four days after the siege began. Sixty Muslims were killed during its storming, while "forty [more] Christian captives were found in chains. They were released and restored to freedom." The remaining three hundred Muslims were themselves put in chains.[97]

One week later, on May 29, as Richard was preparing to move against Jerusalem, another messenger brought more troubling news from home: John and Philip had now openly allied against Richard. The king was faced with a terrible dilemma: considering that it had taken the messenger eight weeks to reach the Holy Land from England, what else had happened in the meantime? What would be happening two or three months from now?—which is how long it would take had Richard immediately set sail for his own lands. Worst of all, spending any more time marching against and besieging Jerusalem was far from guaranteed to restore it, though it would most likely lead to the loss of Richard's own kingdoms in Europe.

While weighing these matters, one of his chamberlains, William of Poitiers, encouraged the king to have faith and see his pilgrimage through, as captured in verse by Ambroise, a contemporary Norman poet: "Now it is said by great and small/Who wish you honor, one and all/How unto Christendom have you/A father been, and brother, too/And if you leave it without aid/'Twill surely perish, thus betrayed."[98]

Richard's problems home were hardly the only challenges confronting him. Although reunited under his leadership, the Crusaders continued to suffer from a scarcity of fighting men. As Richard of Devizes explained:

> The king of the English, Richard, had already completed two years in conquering the region around Jerusalem, and during all that time

there had no aid [neither in men nor money] been sent to him from any of his kingdoms.... The king's army was decreased daily in the land of promise, and besides those who were slain with the sword, many thousands of the people perished every month.... When it appeared that they would all have to die there, everyone had to choose whether he would die as a coward or in battle.[99]

Faced by these two options, the Crusaders again set off for Jerusalem under Richard's leadership on June 6. Making good progress—only two men died from snake bites—after five days, they again found themselves a few miles away from Jerusalem.[100] At one point, while galloping "through the mountains in hot pursuit of Saracens, slaying them as they fled," Richard reached a hilltop, believed to be Montjoie, the same hilltop Godfrey and the other First Crusaders got their first glimpse of Jerusalem.[101] On first seeing the Holy City from a distance, Richard, it is relayed, began to weep in anguish and begged God to shield it from his sight until and unless he liberated it.[102]

The Crusaders soon learned that they were in a worse predicament than before: Jerusalem's garrison was now swollen with Muslims—Saladin had mustered all his men around him; he had also poisoned all the surrounding wells. If, as seemed likely, Jerusalem did not fall fast, the Crusaders would be trapped in a waterless desert in the summer—sitting and dehydrated ducks for the hordes of roaming Turks that patrolled the region.

Another council was held. Although most of the French and his own men wanted to proceed, Richard argued that "we and our people are foreigners and know absolutely nothing about this region." As such, "we ought to follow whatever course of action the Templars and the Hospitallers honestly judge and decide that we should take."[103] After deliberating, the council of seasoned military order members concluded that, even if Jerusalem was captured, it could never be held onto without first subduing Egypt: Ascalon and Darum were not enough; the king agreed.

Once again, the rank and file howled in protestation: "They said that they had only wished to live [long enough] until the Christians gained Jerusalem."[104] The outraged French refused to take part in any Crusade against Egypt and instead took to mocking Richard in verse. Twice now Richard had led the Crusaders to the edge of Jerusalem and twice now he had failed to deliver. "You are rash in urging me into this venture," the frustrated king responded. "However, if you wish to head for Jerusalem now, I will not desert you. I will be your comrade, not your leader."[105] He was willing to join any assault and sacrifice his life; but he would not willingly lead his men on a doomed quest.

In fact, and as the sources attest, the welfare of his men was always of utmost importance for Richard. For example, during his first march onto Jerusalem in the winter of 1191, the Turks captured a band of Crusaders he had sent to forage. "You will not succeed in rescuing them," his advisors warned him. "It is better that they die alone than that you risk death in this attack, and so endanger the whole crusade." "The king changed colour as his blood boiled" and responded tersely: "I sent those men there. If they die without me, may I never again be called a king." "And without another word," the chronicler continues, "he put spur to horse and with indescribable rage—I might almost say madness—he charged the Turks" and made great slaughter among them, to the point that three Muslims, from awe or fear, "converted to the Christian faith and submitted to King Richard."[106]

The love he showed his men was reciprocated. Once, while out with "only a few of his household," many of his men were killed and he almost caught during another Muslim ambush—if not for the sacrifice of William of Preaux, who pretended he was the king, prompting the raiders to grab him and flee.[107] Even Muslim sources record Richard's knights sacrificing their lives by placing themselves in the line of fire for their king.[108]

On July 4, 1192—the fifth ominous anniversary of Hattin—the Crusader army, which had again splintered, began its long withdrawal back to the Christian-held coast; many returned to Europe. It was a black time for Richard. He had risked more than everyone else by going to and staying in the Holy Land and had nothing to show for it—except, maybe, contempt from his men and the loss of his own kingdoms in Europe. Now, as he rode back, "greatly enraged, or rather raving, and champing with his teeth the pine rod which he held in his hand," the king, according to Richard of Devizes, "at length unbridled his indignant lips as follows":

> O God! My God—why hast thou forsaken me? For whom have we foolish Christians, for whom have we English come hither from the furthest parts of the earth to bear our arms? Is it not for the God of

the Christians? O fie! How good art thou to us thy people, who now are for thy name given up to the sword; we shall become a portion for foxes. O how unwilling should I be to forsake thee in so forlorn and dreadful a position, were I thy lord and advocate as thou art mine! In sooth, my standards will in future be despised, not through my fault but through thine; in sooth, not through any cowardice of my warfare, art thou thyself, my King and my God, conquered this day, and not Richard thy vessel.[109]

He reached Acre and prepared to sail back home. Richard's Crusade was over.

The Battle of Jaffa

For Saladin, the time to strike and avenge himself on that English infidel who had repeatedly humiliated him had come at last. He set out of Jerusalem with "a countless horde"—twenty thousand horsemen and over one hundred "powerful emirs." They "covered the face of the earth like locusts" and galloped "as if they were driven by the Furies, and they swore that the Christians should be completely destroyed."[110] Tiny Jaffa—which the Crusaders sacrificed much to retake and which was pivotal to any plans for retaking Jerusalem—was their destination.

On July 27, swift messengers raced out of Jaffa to Acre; they arrived the next day, battered and bruised. Before they had finished delivering their message, "With God as my guide," Richard declared, "I will set out to do what I can," and instantly set sail on his fleet with some two thousand fighters. The military orders set off by land but were blockaded by Saladin's forces; the French in Acre "only repeated haughtily that they would go no further with him."[111]

Meanwhile, besieged Jaffa was fighting for its life. According to Baha' al-Din, after one of its walls collapsed, all the Muslims rushed into the city, "and there was not an enemy heart that did not tremble and shake." Even so, the Christians "were more fierce and determined in the fight and more eager for and devoted to death." When the main gate was finally battered down and an adjoining wall collapsed from the bombardment, a "cloud of dust and smoke went up and darkened the sky." Once it cleared, the Muslims saw that Christian "spear-points had replaced the walls and lances had blocked the breach."[112] Only death would release those Crusaders Richard had left of their charge to defend Jaffa.

Before long, and due to the great masses of rushing Muslims, the garrison was eventually driven to and holed up in the citadel, even as the sackers turned their attention to Jaffa's civilian populace: "Alas for the pitiful slaughter of the sick!" recalls the chronicler. "They lay weakly on couches everywhere in the houses of the city; the Turks tortured them to death in horrible ways." Even after an arrangement was made whereby the Christians would ransom their lives, "those despicable Turks who are more savage than beasts and lack all human feeling beheaded them as they were paying." Having "slaughtered countless numbers of the infirm," and, because "the Muhammad superstition" makes Muslims "detest pigs as unclean," the invaders slaughtered "also no few pigs." Then, "to insult the Christians," they intermingled the swinish carcasses with the Christian corpses.[113]

While Jaffa was being sacked, contrary winds delayed Richard's fleets—prompting him into another fit of anti-theodicy: "Lord God!" he burst, "why are You holding us back? Consider!—this is an emergency, and we are acting out of our devotion to You."[114] He finally arrived on the evening of July 31 but did not disembark. As Baha' al-Din explains, the Crusaders "saw the town crammed with the Muslims' banners and men and they feared that the citadel might have already been taken. The sea prevented their hearing the shouts that came from everywhere and the great commotion and cries of 'There is no god but Allah' and 'Allahu Akbar.'"[115] To make matters worse, "When the Turks saw the king's galleys and ships approaching, masses of them ran on to the shore," writes the chronicler, "raining down spears, javelins, darts and arrows densely so that they would have nowhere free to land. The shore was seething, so covered with crowds of the enemy that there was no empty space left."[116]

On the following morning of August 1, a fighting priest took his chances: he jumped out of the citadel's window, into the sea, and swam to the Christian fleets. On learning that, although the "Saracens had taken the castle and were rounding up the Christians as prisoners," a remnant of the garrison was still holding out, Richard exclaimed: "If it so please God…we should die here with our brothers." Without donning his full armor, and in the words of the chroniclers, the king "armed himself with his hauberk, hung his shield at his neck and took a Danish axe in his hand." With his crossbow in the other hand—and crying "death only to those who do not advance!"—he hurled himself into the waist-deep water "and forced himself powerfully on to dry land," all while firing his crossbow at the wild throng assembled along the shore and swiping incoming arrows away with his axe.[117]

Instantly, the rest of the Crusaders—fifty-four knights, a few hundred infantry, and some two thousand crossbowmen and archers—followed their king. To a loud battle cry, they plunged into the water and "boldly attacked the Turks who obstinately opposed them on the shore." Before long, and "at the sight of the king," the Muslims, none of whom "dare[d] approach him," were seen fleeing down the shore. The chronicle has the rest:

> Brandishing his bared sword, the king followed in such hot pursuit that none of them had time to defend themselves. They fled from his weighty blows. In the same way the king's comrades constantly assailed the fugitives, driving them on, crushing, rending, beheading and tossing them about until all the Turks had been violently expelled from the shore and left it empty.... The king fell on them with unsheathed sword, pursued them, beheaded and slew them. They fled before him, falling back in dense crowds to his right and left.[118]

Emboldened by Richard's sortie, Jaffa's holed up Christian defenders "mounted their horses and charged out from the citadel as one man," writes the Muslim historian, slaughtering many Muslims who were unaware of this recent turn of events. "Some of them, the dregs of the army," the somewhat abashed Baha' al-Din continues, "remained in one of the churches, busy doing unacceptable things.* The enemy pounced on them and slew them or took them prisoner."[119]

Once Richard, drenched in Muslim blood, became visible to Saladin's entourage, "a horrible howl went up," even as another hail of Turkic arrows rained towards his direction. Undeterred, the berserker king continued to "cut to pieces all he met without distinction" in his mad

---

* This cryptic reference may suggest that the jihadists were using Jaffa's churches as rape dungeons—which was not infrequently the fate of churches immediately following successful jihads. The sack of Constantinople in 1453—when Christian women were gang-raped in churches, often atop altars (see Chapter 6)—is just one of the most memorable. Hundreds of years earlier, during the ninth century siege of Salerno, and to quote Edward Gibbon, "a Musulman chief spread his couch on the communion table, and on that altar sacrificed each night the virginity of a Christian nun" (1952, 349). A century before that, during the initial Muslim invasion of Christian Spain, "many wild follies were committed on the altars" of churches, says a Visigothic dirge (O'Callaghan 2004, 204).

dash to Saladin, prompting the latter to flee "like a frightened hare." The sultan "put spur to horse and fled before King Richard, not wishing to be seen by him…. The king and his fellow-knights steadfastly pursued him, continually slaying and unhorsing…for more than two miles."[120] It was a disorderly retreat—everywhere plunder was seen hurled aside—and rout of the most ignoble kind, worse even than Arsuf.

Certainly it is easy to dismiss such accounts of Richard's prowess as legendary or exaggerated. The problem, however, is that the enemy confirms them. Here, for example, is how Saladin's own man, Baha' al-Din, who was present, records these events:

> [T]he king of England hastened to gain the shore [of Jaffa]. The first galley to deliver its men on land was his. He was red-haired, his tunic was red and his banner was red, as was his device. In only a short time all the men from the galleys [who were far outnumbered by the Muslims] had disembarked in the harbor. All this went on before my eyes. They then charged the Muslims, who withdrew before them and were cleared out of the harbor. I was on horseback so I galloped as far as the sultan and gave him this news…. Hardly a moment later the Muslims came fleeing towards the sultan [who ordered a general retreat].[121]

Although gloriously defended, Jaffa was also devastated. Countless Christian men, women, and children were butchered and mauled. As for those corpses the Muslims had intermingled with swinish carcasses, "At last," relays the chronicler, "the bodies of the Christians were buried in peace by the Christians, but they threw out the Turks' corpses to rot with those of the pigs."[122] Then they got to work on rebuilding the wall.

Not only was the battle of Jaffa one of the most heroic and critical defenses of the Third Crusade—had Richard arrived even hours later, Saladin would have taken that critically important coastal port to Jerusalem—it was also the last battle of the Third Crusade. By now, the Muslims had nothing but terror for Richard—this titan who had just defeated a force between five and ten times larger than his own. Peace talks—"or rather truce negotiations since for an orthodox Muslim [Saladin] there could be no peace to end the jihad"—resumed.[123]

Although welcoming of the Muslim delegations, Richard could not let down Saladin's ignoble behavior: "This sultan of yours is a great man," he scoffed. "Islam has no greater or mightier prince on earth than him. How is it he departed merely because I had arrived? By God, I had not put on my breastplate and was not ready for anything. On my feet I had only sea boots." Then, putting aside the bravado and turning serious, he said, "Greet the sultan for me and say, 'For God's sake grant me what I ask for to make peace. This is a matter that must have an end. My lands over the sea have been ruined. For this to go on is no good for us nor for you.'"[124]

Unwilling to meet Richard in battle, Saladin and his leading emirs—who deemed it a "disgrace for such a great horde to have abandoned Joppa before a few people who had no horses"—turned again to ambush tactics: they "made a mutual pact between themselves...that they would seize King Richard in his tent."[125] Thus, on learning from his spies that the king and a few of his men were encamped outside of Jaffa, Saladin and a group of Turks and Bedouins launched a surprise attack before the break of dawn on August 4.

Hearing the cries from his tent, "the king was roused and leapt in great alarm from his bed. Putting on his mailshirt of unbreakable mesh he ordered his knights to arise without delay"—even as the Muslims "rushed in with horrible shouts and then began to howl and fire javelins, darts and arrows very densely." Crying "everything is bearable for those of manly character," Richard, at the head of ten hurriedly horsed knights, "charged powerfully into the thick of the enemy...emptying saddles of their riders and transfixing some of them. Their initial impact was so great that their violent spirit carried them through all the Turkish lines as far as the last." Undeterred, the frustrated Muslims were determined to kill this vastly outnumbered Christian warlord and "kept charging up to the royal standard with the lion on it, seeking the king's life alone in preference to 1,000 others."[126] Once again, the chronicle has the rest:

> The King was a giant in the battle and was everywhere in the field, now here, now there, wherever the attacks of the Turks raged most fiercely. On that day his sword shone like lightning and many of the Turks felt its edge. Some were cloven in two from their helmet to their teeth; others lost their heads, arms and other limbs, lopped off at a single blow. He mowed down men as reapers mow down corn with their sickles.[127]

The carnage continued to the point that "the skin of his right hand tore because it was so damaged by the continual effort of brandishing his sword."[128]

Once again, Muslim contemporaries echo these near mythic accounts of superhuman valor. Recounting this same incident, Baha' al-Din writes that, while encroaching upon Richard's campground,

> [Saladin] found them to be few, about ten in number. The sultan was filled with eager anticipation and his men charged them as one man, but the enemy stood firm and did not move from their positions. Like dogs of war they snarled, willing to fight to the death. Our troops were frightened of them, dumbfounded by their steadfastness, and surrounded them in a single ring.... [T]he king of England took his lance that day and galloped from the far right to the far left and nobody challenged him. The sultan was enraged, and turned his back on the fighting [i.e., he fled in retreat].[129]

Such are a sampling of Richard's many exploits in the Holy Land. Although "King Richard had been hardened to battle from his tender years," it seems that his stay in Jerusalem—where faith and fury met—had fully unleashed the beast within him. "As he raged [in battles]," explains the chronicler, "it seemed as if his resolute courage was rejoicing that it had found a means of expression."[130]

As for Saladin, he continued to seethe with rage: "So," he taunted his emirs, "where are those who are bringing *Melech* [King] Richard as a prisoner [to me]?" And, once again, they gave answer that required all his powers of self-control to maintain his dignity: "Truly, lord, this *melech* of whom you ask is not like the rest of humanity.... We tried as best we could to capture him but without success. No one can withstand his sword or his terrible charge unharmed. It is death to encounter him. His exploits are superhuman."[131]

Finale

Then, two things showing just how human Richard was happened in quick succession. First, he fell "ill from the exhaustion of battle and the stink of corpses" that everywhere surrounded him.[132] Mere days after relieving Jaffa and defending himself against a variety of ambushes, the "king was extremely sick, and confined to his bed; his fever continued without intermission." It was kept secret, "for it was thoroughly under-stood that Saladin feared the charge of the whole [Crusader] army less than that of the king alone," writes Richard of Devizes.[133]

Adding to his sickbed miseries, Richard continued to receive dismal news from his lands in England and France. Philip—this onetime Cru-sader who had vowed to leave Richard's lands in peace—was now actively carving them up. While Saladin had a ready and endless supply of men and was on his own home territory, and therefore not pressured by time, the deathly ill Richard was grossly outnumbered, received no reserves, and had run out of time. "If it is easy for him to winter here and to be far from his family and homeland," Saladin once boasted, "how easy is it for me to spend a winter, a summer, then a winter and another summer in the middle of my own lands, surrounded by my sons and my family, when whatever and whoever I want can come to me."[134]

And so, in the end, it was not the Muslims who beat Richard but rather a fellow Crusader and his own brother who betrayed him. In the words of the chronicle, "After winning so many renowned and glorious triumphs over the Turks, King Richard was trapped by his brothers in faith, seized by those who were believed to share his Christian profes-sion—if only it were true!"[135] There was nothing left but to negotiate the best possible treaty with Saladin and return home—assuming he could still call it home.

After warning Saladin "not [to] be deceived by our withdrawal," for "the ram backs away to charge," and after much haggling, on Septem-ber 2, 1192, the king and sultan agreed to a three-year peace.[136] Saladin "granted free passage everywhere, and access to the Lord's Holy Sepul-chre without any exactions."[137] Additionally, he agreed to leave all of the Crusader holdings from Tyre to Jaffa in peace, though the latter espe-cially vexed the sultan. But he had little choice; the Muslims were beyond "exhausted" and much "discontent," his emirs warned Saladin, before rationalizing: "This Frank has asked for peace only so that he can sail away and return home. If acceptance is delayed until the onset of winter and the interruption of navigation, we shall need to remain here another year and then the hardship will be great[er] for the Muslims."[138] They were all eager to see Richard go.

For his part, the English king had to agree to the re-dismantling of Ascalon. As the chief port between the Holy Land and Egypt—which both he and Saladin knew was pivotal to whomever would permanently hold Jerusalem—Richard was loathe to agree to this stipulation, not least due to all the hard labor and resources he had spent rebuilding it. But in the end, he, too, had little choice.

Soon after the truce was ratified, many Europeans flocked to do what they had come to do—pilgrimage to Jerusalem—before returning home.[139] As might be imagined, and considering the Muslims had zealously guarded Jerusalem since cleansing it of the Christians five years earlier, this made for some rather awkward encounters. When the first unarmed group of Christian pilgrims arrived, "the Turks snarled at their arrival, watching them and grimacing with savage eyes as they went past. Their faces showed clearly the spiteful contempt which was going round in their thoughts; for attitude of mind is often revealed in facial expression. At this, even the more steadfast of our people were alarmed and full of uncertain trepidation.... The pilgrims spent the night in great fear...."[140]

Richard refused to join any pilgrimage: he had sworn to enter Jerusalem as its liberator or not at all. When some of his men returned from and sought to entice him to visit the Holy Sepulchre, he again refused, for he "could not consent to receive that from the courtesy of the Gentiles, which he could not obtain by the gift of God."[141] He finalized his affairs—including by ransoming William of Preaux, who had earlier saved Richard from an ambush by pretending to be the king—and, on October 9, 1192, was aboard his ship sailing home.

Five months later, the great Saladin—whose elation following his conquest of Jerusalem five years earlier had prompted him to vow to invade Europe "and pursue the Franks there, so as to free the earth of anyone who does not believe in Allah, or die in the attempt"—was dead at the age of fifty-five, in large measure due to the trauma of the Third Crusade.[142] More than one historian has surmised what might have been if only Richard had remained in the Holy Land for a few months longer until Saladin's death.

During his voyage home, the king went through more adventures, most notably by being shipwrecked and then imprisoned by Leopold, duke of Austria, who was at and bore a grudge against Richard after the conquest of Acre. Over a year later, and after the payment of a large ransom, Richard was released in February 1194.

On learning that the Lion was finally on his way, Philip sent a message to his co-conspirator, John: "Look to yourself; the devil is loose."[143] The French king made himself scarce, while Richard's brother "threw himself at the king's feet, seeking mercy for his crimes. The king immediately pardoned him," for he "did not deign to punish an inferior."[144] Before long, the warrior-king managed to undo all of John's and Philip's subversions. Over the next few years, Richard, moreover, strengthened his vast French holdings against the machinations of Philip, who remained intent on absorbing them.

Five years after the restoration of Richard, an incident occurred that would come to be known as "the ant that killed the elephant." In the spring of 1199, a horde of Roman coins was accidentally discovered by a peasant plowing the fields of Châlus. The lord of Châlus, Archard, claimed it. On learning of this, Richard—who was always raising and spending money, especially for the Crusades, which he planned on resuming—cited his status as Archard's overlord and demanded the treasure.[145] Archard refused and Richard besieged the castle of Châlus. A quick surrender was expected, and the English king, being accustomed to fighting Eastern hordes single-handedly, may have treated the whole affair nonchalantly, including by not fully arming himself; for, on March 26, a squalid defender atop the battlements—armed with a frying pan for a shield no less—fired his crossbow into the king's shoulder. Richard carelessly yanked the arrow out as he had done so many times in the Holy Land, where, in the words of the chronicle, "the king's body was [during battle] completely covered with darts, which stuck out like the spikes of a hedgehog."[146] This time, however, the shaft broke, leaving the metal head embedded. It turned gangrenous.

Such was the anticlimactic end of the Crusader-King of England who had survived countless Muslim swords, spears, arrows, and ambushes. As Richard lay in his deathbed, Châlus surrendered, and the guilty archer was brought before him. "Live on," he told him, "and by my bounty behold the light of day." In an act of penance and humility, the magnanimous king forgave the man, ordered him released and even given a hundred shillings. Alas for the archer, however; after Richard died, his enraged sister, Joan, had the man skinned alive and torn apart by wild horses.

Thus, King Richard I died on April 6, 1199, at the age of forty-two. In his brief life, he was the archetypal medieval warrior-king and chivalrous knight par excellence, evidenced in part by the fact that his moniker—"Lionheart"—lives on to this day. He sacrificed and risked much in his Crusade and went against the odds. At a time when the Crusader states were on the verge of collapsing, Richard cowed the forces of Islam, retook several cities and castles, and gave the Christians the much-needed breathing space to regroup and refortify. His capture of Cyprus was, moreover, a milestone for Crusading. So near to the Middle East, it became, for centuries, the chief base of resources to supply the coastal Crusader kingdoms; it was where every future Crusader stopped before entering into the lions' den of Islam.

On reflection, it seems likely that if he had reliable allies—Barbarossa fell and Philip betrayed—Jerusalem would have been liberated. For, whereas the First Crusade was a joint effort, with Duke Godfrey being one of several great lords committed to its success, the Third Crusade revolved almost exclusively around Richard, who, in the end, was still but a man. This fact must be accounted for when considering why the First Crusade accomplished its goal—the liberation of Jerusalem—whereas the Third did not. Decades later, even the French nobleman, Jean of Joinville (b. 1224), would criticize the French crown while immortalizing the Englishman's prowess:

> So soon as Acre was taken, King Philip returned to France, for which he was greatly blamed; but King Richard remained in the Holy Land, and did there such mighty deeds that the Saracens stood in great fear of him; so much so, as it is written in the book of the Holy Land, that when the Saracen children cried, their mothers called out, "Wisht! Here is King Richard," in order to keep them quiet. And when the horses of the Saracens and Bedouins started at tree or bush, their masters said to the horses, "Do you think that is King Richard?"[147]

Indeed, until this day, it is the name of Richard* that most personifies the archetypal Crusader enemy in the popular Muslim consciousness—a testimony to the havoc he wrought single-handedly.

---

* A personal though relevant anecdote is perhaps not inappropriate here: My parents, both of whose first names begin with an R, named all their children with names that begin with an R. When I was born, they had all but decided to name me Richard, but, in the last moment, decided against it on the off chance that our family might move back to Egypt, in which case, as they later told me, they feared I would be heavily discriminated against if not outright killed by some fanatic still smarting from the Crusades. That they went on to name me Raymond, also a popular Crusader name—though they never knew it—further underscores the singular weight the name of Richard continues to have in the Middle East.

CHAPTER 4

Saint Ferdinand: Savior of Spain

"On our side, Christ, God and Man. On the Moors', the faithless and damned apostate, Muhammad. What more is there to say?"

—FERDINAND[1]

"Would to Allah that the Moslems had then extinguished at once the sparkles of a fire that was destined to consume the whole dominions of Islam in those parts!"

—AHMAD BIN MUHAMMAD AL-MAQQARI[2]

After the Cid and his generation had passed, Emir Ali of the Almoravids (r.1106–1143)—"that murderer of the Christians," to quote from the *Chronicle of Alfonso the Emperor*[3]—saw his chance: "like a serpent thirsting in the summer heat," this son and successor of Yusuf bin Tashfin "raised his head [from across the straits in Africa] and… summoned all [his] princes, commanders, and soldiers…together with a great army of Arab mercenaries, and many thousands of horsemen, crossbowmen and great companies of foot-soldiers."[4] They invaded the Christian north of Spain, "attacking and devastating, massacring and slaughtering the Christians." Not content with the devastation he caused, Ali commanded his generals to send back to Africa "any of the Christian warriors, boys, virtuous women and girls whom you capture."[5]

130

Before dying and in the hopes of uniting León-Castile with Aragon, its eastern neighbor—thereby creating a solid front against this latest jihad—in 1109 Alfonso VI of León-Castile, then aged sixty-nine, married his widowed daughter and sole heir, Urraca, to his namesake, Alfonso I (1073–1134),* who succeeded his brother, Peter (the Cid's son-in-law), as king of Aragon and Navarre in 1104. The marriage was a bitter failure: "Urraca was vain and capricious, while Alfonso was brusque and impetuous and more inclined to think of himself as a knight in God's service than as a husband"—not least as he had been raised in a monastery.[6] So "she despised him," writes a Castilian chronicler, "and left him, turning to other affairs, unworthy of relation."[7]

In 1110, one year after they were wed and before hostilities had reached their desultory climax, the pope, thinking of the welfare of Spain, tried to annul their marriage on the pretext of consanguinity (the couple shared the same great-grandfather, Sancho III of Navarre). Although they increasingly hated each other, and were threatened with excommunication, they remained married for four more years—years which witnessed internecine warfare. At one point, the king of Aragon, being "inwardly touched by sorrow of soul," to quote from the contemporary *Latin Chronicle of the Kings of Castile*, "laid waste the kingdom of Castile."[8] It was a bad time for the Christians of northern Spain: the Muslims from Africa were encroaching on and terrorizing them, even as their sovereigns—a married couple no less—hated and warred on one another.

The Battler

In 1114, Alfonso finally conceded to a divorce and turned his "warlike and high-spirited" energy to reversing Emir Ali's recent gains, including by "inflicting many injuries upon the Saracens," says the *Latin*

---

* As the remainder of this chapter amply demonstrates, the name Alfonso/Alphonso was especially common to and ubiquitous among the Christian kings of Spain and Portugal—so much so that confusing them is commonplace. The name's meaning and lineage may explain its immense popularity. Based on the old Visigothic name, Adelfonsus, the name is made of two parts, *hathu* ("war") and *funs* ("ready"), that is, the "War Ready One"—a state the free Christians of northern Spain constantly needed to be in. The initial, inchoate phase of the Reconquista (the re-conquest of Galicia and León) was further spearheaded by the first Christian king of that name to arise after the Muslim conquest of Spain: Adelfonsus (Alfonso) I of Asturias (693–757). As such, the name denoted war and connoted war with Muslims, thereby invoking the Reconquista.

Chronicle—prompting Alfonso to be known to posterity as *El Batallador*, the "Battler."[9] Immediately he attacked and began to expand his small mountain fastness into the River Ebro Valley: "grievously afflicting the Moslems upon their north-eastern frontier," writes al-Maqqari, Alfonso subjected them to "his detestable rule."[10]

He put Zaragoza, which Ali had conquered in 1110, to a terrible siege, and reclaimed it in 1118. This permanent conquest of Islam's northern-most bastion—which the man the Battler looked up to in his youth, the Cid, had so long denied the Almoravids—was practically as significant as the conquest of Toledo thirty-three years earlier by his former father-in-law and namesake. "Thus," laments the Muslim historian, "was the mighty city of Saragossa, one of the vital members of the corrupted bodies of Islam, torn away, never to form again an integral part of it. There is no power but in Allah!"[11]

But Zaragoza was "not the only city which that accursed Christian reduced."[12] By 1120, Alfonso had doubled the size of his kingdom, at the expense of surrounding Muslims. Like the Cid and Alfonso VI before him, he was remarkably lenient to the Muslims—at least initially, before they gave him reason otherwise: those who wished to leave could leave in peace with their possessions; those who wished to stay could stay and live according to their customs and law, sharia.[13]

Described as a "quintessential crusader devoted to the destruction of Islam until his dying day," the Battler continued his relentless drive deep into Almoravid territory.[14] He "surprised several fortresses border-ing upon his domains, and carried fire and sword into the very heart of the Mohammedan territory," writes al-Maqqari.[15] Alfonso's ambitions against Islam seemed to know no bounds; he even founded a *militia Christi* "with the extraordinary goal of overcoming all the Muslims beyond the sea and opening a route to Jerusalem."[16]

One of his most notable Crusades occurred in 1125. Then, while car-rying with him "a cross made of the salvation-giving wood," he began his celebrated and destructive march throughout al-Andalus, Muslim Spain.[17] With great speed and ferocity, he ravaged virtually every Moor-ish kingdom, including the southernmost one, Granada, where the few remaining Christian dhimmis (or Mozarabs) were persecuted. Before leaving, he rescued twelve thousand of them; they joined his fiery trek, and many later helped repopulate the Ebro Valley along Zaragoza. In

1126 he granted a charter of liberties "to all you Mozarabic Christians whom I brought, with the help of God, out of the power of the Saracens and led into the lands of the Christians…. Because you left your homes and estates for the name of Christ and out of love for me and came with me to populate my lands, I grant you good customs throughout my realm."[18]

The Muslims of Granada responded by avenging themselves on the remaining Christian dhimmi population: "They were deprived of their property, imprisoned, or put to death. Many of them were deported to Africa"—interestingly, at the prompting of Averroes (Ibn Rushd), a man who remains highly celebrated in the West for his "progressive" insights—"where oppression of all kinds compelled them to embrace Islam.[19] Ten years later there was a fresh expulsion. The Christians were again deported to Morocco *en masse*."[20]

In 1134, Alfonso the Battler died, possibly in battle, though the *Latin Chronicle* cryptically states that it was "not by the power of the Saracens, but rather by their deceit" that the sixty-one-year-old king died.[21] The standard account is that he was grievously injured in a battle with the Almoravids and barely managed to reach the same Zaragoza-based abbey he had been raised in youth. Once there, and according to the *Chronicle of Alfonso the Emperor*, the Battler "went inside, ordered the doors to be closed and on account of his great sorrow he laid him down upon his bed. After a few days, grieved as his heart, he died in the monastery and was buried with his forefathers in the royal pantheon. After him,* or before, there was no one equal to him among the former kings of the Aragonese, nor as strong, nor as prudent, nor as warlike as he."[22]

Such an appraisal was shared, even if begrudgingly, by Muslims. From his first setting out against Islam, "until that of his death," writes al-Maqqari, "Allah permitted that this insolent Christian should always be victorious against the Moslems."[23]

When he died, and as happened with the Cid, Christians everywhere feared the future. In Zaragoza, men shaved their heads and rent their clothes; women scratched their faces bloody. All lamented: "O best defender, who have you named to defend us? For the Almoravids will

---

* As the *Chronicle of Alfonso the Emperor* was written sometime around 1150, this statement naturally does not take into account the other Aragonese kings of conquest that came after it was penned—most notably, James I the Conqueror.

now invade the kingdom that by royal power you ripped from the hands of the Saracens, and we will be captured without a defender."[24] Such fears were not unwarranted; due to Alfonso's failed marriage he had produced no heirs, leaving his kingdoms in limbo and leaderless at a critical time.

More Alfonsos Arise

The succession crisis was eventually averted; more importantly, as Alfonso I of Aragon had picked up the mantle of the Campeador, so too did a new generation of Christian leaders pick up the mantle of the Battler.

Prominent among these was Alfonso VII of León-Castile (1105–1157), the son of the Battler's ex-wife with her first husband, Count Raymond of Galicia (d. 1107). According to the *Chronicle of Alfonso the Emperor*, which was written during and mostly covers his life, in 1133, the seventh year of his reign, and the year before the Battler died, the twenty-eight-year-old "announced that his mind was wholly fixed upon the following: that he would invade the land of the Saracens [southern Spain, al-Andalus] in order to conquer them and to avenge himself" on their recent invasions, slaughters, and Christian expulsions to Africa.[25]

He and his men ravaged al-Andalus, including the famed cities of Córdoba and Seville. Unlike his predecessors—including his grandfather, Alfonso VI, the Cid, and his former stepfather, the Battler, all of whom, initially at least, had vouchsafed mosques to conquered Muslims—Alfonso VII and his men "destroyed all the mosques they came upon and when they encountered any priests and doctors of their religion"—a reference to Islam's assortment of sheikhs, ulema, fuqaha, muezzins, and clerics of all sorts—"they put them to the sword. They also burned all the books of their religion in the mosques."[26]

This does not appear to have been done in a fit of rage but rather as calculated policy. Thus, years later, while ravaging Jaen and other cities of al-Andalus in 1138, Alfonso's men again "destroyed their mosques and consigned to the flames the books of the law of Mohammed. They put to the sword all the doctors of that law they encountered."[27] Similarly, a church for John the Baptist was built "in the place where a mosque of Satan had previously been built."[28]

Why this sudden change? Certainly there was more resentment against Islam by the mid-twelfth century—thanks to the many atrocities committed in its name by the Almoravids—than there was during the Cid's generation, when a tamer, more dissipated, Islam prevailed. More significantly, however, Alfonso had learned from his predecessors' leniency: so long as the jihadist teachings of Islam—as contained in the Koran and hadith and recited by the ulema inside mosques and madrasas—were allowed to metastasize throughout the Islamic body politic, so long would Muslims be riled into becoming an existential threat devoted to the destruction of Christendom. Stripping them of the sources of their ideological antipathy was seen as a form of preemption in the long war against Islam.

But Christian motives were hardly limited to neutralizing their southern enemies. As the *Chronicle of Alfonso the Emperor* asserts, "the Christians were waging a campaign to reverse the wrongs that they had suffered at the hands of Muslims in times past, and above all to restore to Christian hands the territories that had been lost"—in a word, *Reconquista.*[29]

As such, in 1139, when Alfonso VII was ravishing central and eastern al-Andalus, Afonso Henriques, his then thirty-three-year-old cousin, was "committing great depredations in the western parts of Andalus," writes al-Maqqari, "and had even reduced some considerable towns," prompting the Almoravid emir, Abu Yaqub, personally to sail from Africa to Spain.[30] That same year, the forces of Afonso Henriques and Abu Yaqub met and clashed at Ourique. In one of the severest blows ever inflicted on the Muslims, the Christians triumphed and Afonso became the first king of the newborn nation of Portugal.

By 1146, the Christians were making unprecedented advances south, even taking Córdoba for a brief time. In 1147, with the aid of Second Crusaders—English, Scottish, Anglo-Norman, and Flemish men who were journeying to fight "the infidels and enemies of the cross of Christ"[31]— Afonso recaptured Almeria, Tortosa, and Lisbon from Islam, the latter being an event that "rivaled in importance the capture of Toledo in 1085 and Zaragoza in 1118."[32]

During these wars, invocations to Just War theory, and how the two religions figured in this construct, were regularly on display. Prior to the siege of Lisbon, the archbishop of Braga was sent to treat with the holed up Muslims; he charged them of having "held our cities and lands already for 358 years," and, as such, asked that they "return to the homeland of the Moors [North Africa], whence you came, leaving to us what is ours."[33] In response, Muslims displayed "with much derision the symbol of the cross. They spat upon it and wiped the feces from their posteriors with it. At last they urinated on it, as on some despicable thing, and threw our cross at us."[34]

One of the standard prayers Spaniards recited before battle suggests that such displays were not uncommon: "Grant by the power of your name and the most victorious Cross, the people of the Moors, who every-where always humiliate it, may powerfully be conquered." The Muslims "also continuously attacked Blessed Mary…with insults and with vile and abusive words, which infuriated us."[35]

The Almohads

Due to Christian advances against and triumphs over Islam, the Moors of al-Andalus began to rise against their onetime saviors, the Almoravids. Thus began another period of Muslim disunity (1144–1147) that would culminate with the overthrow of the North Africans. From the vantage point of the author of the *Chronicle of Alfonso the Emperor*, "There was great slaughter and confusion in all the land of the Hagarenes, such as there had not been since the day in which the Hagarenes crossed the Mediterranean to first take that land [of Spain]."[36]

History was repeating itself. Just as the Muslims of the Cid's time had accused their petty kings of being un-Islamic, too soft and overly given to pleasure—and hence invited the African Almoravids into Spain—so too were the people now accusing these selfsame Almoravids of the same corruption and calling on the aid of another pristine jihadist group to help overthrow them: the Almohads, who had arisen in North Africa on the general accusation that the Almoravids had strayed from true Islam, apparently evident in their loose morals, and therefore needed to be eliminated.

Interestingly, whereas the name Almoravid has a military meaning— from the Arabic *al-murabitun*, those jihadists who fight to expand or protect the frontier of Islam—the name Almohad has a doctrinal one. Coming from the Arabic *al-muwahhidun*, "they who profess the one-ness of Allah"—which in practical terms means they who believe in the totalitarianism of sharia—the term continues to be associated today with radical sects (such as the Islamic State ("ISIS"), whose gesture for such "oneness" notoriously consists of a raised index finger). As such, the Almohads were even more draconian than their Almoravid predecessors; for whereas "both believed in a puritanical Islam," only the Almohads "sought the foundations of Muslim law in Quran and Hadith alone, not in the writings of the jurists"—this being the hallmark of Islamic fundamentalism.[37]

Ibn al-Banna' al-Marrakushi ("the Moroccan," b. 1246), documented the wild fanaticism of the charismatic founder of the Almohads, Ibn Tumart (1077–1130)—who in his more ecstatic moments claimed to be the prophet Muhammad himself reincarnated—and the nature of his growing African following; an excerpt follows:

> Their enchantment with him grew, their respect for him was confirmed, so that at last they came to the point where if he ordered one of them to murder his own father or brother or son, he would have hastened to do so without the least hesitation. This would have been by the natural lightness with which these people shed blood; this is a thing which is one of the inborn traits of their nature, and to which the climate of their region predisposes them…. As to the alacrity with which they shed blood, I myself during my stay in the Sus [south of Morocco] saw some astonishing examples.[38]

Once they had overthrown the Almoravid base in North Africa in 1146, the Almohads—"the fiercest and most fanatical of all the Mahommedan hordes which had yet visited the country"—began pouring into Muslim Spain, where they proceeded to eliminate its onetime Almoravid saviors.[39] Once in control, the Almohads launched an intense persecution of all those dhimmis still living in al-Andalus; in the words of one contemporary chronicle, they slaughtered all "the Christians who are called Mozarabs, and the Jews, who had been there since ancient times, and they seized their wives, houses, and riches."[40]

Due to the heavy persecution, many Jews ostensibly converted, while others were required to wear a distinctive costume: "The Jews profess Islamism externally," observed al-Marrakushi; "they pray in the mosques and teach the Koran to their children." Familiar with the Muslim doctrine of *taqiyya*, "Allah alone knows what they hide in their hearts and what their houses conceal," he concluded.[41]

These two Islamic waves that struck Spain in the eleventh and twelfth centuries, first the Almoravids, then the Almohads, polarized Christian Spain from Muslim al-Andalus in ways that were irreversible. As historian Louis Bertrand writes:

> [A]ny hope of fusion between victors and vanquished…was henceforth made impossible of fulfilment…. Now, after so many massacres and expulsions, after this new flood of barbarous and fanatical invaders, understanding between Christian and Musulman became absolutely unrealisable. Religious passions and hatreds…acquired intensified vigour and virulence. Once more the fatal dilemma which had hung over Spain for more than four centuries presented itself to the Spaniards: expel the foreigner, or be expelled by him![42]

A Great Defeat; A Great Victory

Along with bringing the house of Islam in al-Andalus to "order," the Almohads further "inflicted great damage upon the Christian states and kept them almost continually on the defensive."[43] As an immediate response against this latest jihad, the Christian north expanded the roles of the military orders, including by establishing native ones to garrison strongholds and fortresses along the Christian-Muslim frontier. These warrior-monks became the first and sturdiest line of defense.

The ranks of the Orders of Santiago, Calatrava, Montesa, the Knights Templar, and the Hospitallers were augmented by the Almogavers: Christian volunteers (originally farmers, shepherds, and escaped or relocated dhimmis) clad in rough garments and armed with daggers who lived in the forests and wastelands along the frontier and made it their business to raid or repel Muslims—medieval Spain's "Robin Hoods."

The status quo remained largely unchanged for some decades—with the Christian kingdoms and the Almohad caliphate sometimes fighting, sometimes making peace treaties—until July 18–19, 1195, when things came to a head. The full might of the Almohads met and decisively crushed the full might of the Christians at the savage battle of Alarcos, just south of Toledo. "Never," writes al-Maqqari, "was there a more signal victory gained by the Moslems of Andalus." Indeed, Alarcos "became ever after celebrated for the complete defeat of the Christians, of whose number no less than thirty thousand perished by the swords of the

Moslems."[44] Due to this astounding victory, the Moors under the Almohads managed to capture several cities to the north, including Madrid, Ucles, and Guadalajara.

The Christian leader at the battle of Alarcos, King Alfonso VIII of Castile (1155–1214)—surnamed "the Noble" for his widely acknowledged just and pious rule—took the blame: he had rashly engaged the numerically superior Muslims instead of waiting for reinforcements. Even in the midst of battle had he acknowledged his mistake; then, "hoping to end his life with a glorious death rather than to withdraw from the battle in defeat," Alfonso had hurled himself among the Muslims, where the fighting was thickest. "His men, however," the *Latin Chronicle* continues, "realizing the danger threatening the whole of Spain [were he to get killed], led him unwillingly and involuntarily from the battle."[45] According to al-Maqqari, Alfonso retired to Toledo, where "he had his head and beard shaved, turned his cross upside down, and swore not to sleep in bed, approach a woman, or mount a horse or mule, until he had revenged his defeat."[46] (While the gist of this is true, diabolically positioned crucifixes and suggestions that Alfonso, a pious monogamist, otherwise normally "approached" women seem to be innocent projections on the part of the Muslim historian.)

Alfonso would brood for years to come—"the battle of Alarcos remained fixed deep in the king's mind," the chronicle states—until 1211, when the Almohads, under Caliph Muhammad al-Nasir, returned, intent on annihilating him, for Alfonso was still seen as the nearest and strongest infidel king.[47] In September they conquered a powerful fortress, which stood just eighteen miles south of and protected the road to Toledo, whence the king reigned. From their new stronghold, the now triumphant jihadists loudly pledged to behead him. Weeks later, Alfonso's eldest son and heir, Ferdinand, "the right hand of his father, was seized with an acute fever and gave up his life," says the chronicle:

> The king's heart broke…. Mourning was everywhere…the face of the land was changed deeply. The most noble queen Leonor, hearing of her son's death, wanted to die with him and got into the bed in which her son lay…and tried to revive him or to die with him. Those who saw it said that never was seen sorrow like unto hers.[48]

With the hordes of Islam fast approaching, and while mourning his beloved son, Alfonso made ready to defend Toledo—or, in his own words, made ready to "be counted among the martyrs." Seeing the dire straits Alfonso and Spain in general were in, Pope Innocent III called on Christians everywhere to rise up "against the enemies of the cross of the Lord who not only aspire to the destruction of the Spains, but also threatened to vent their rage on Christ's faithful in other lands." "Saladin took Jerusalem," troubadours everywhere sang in an effort to rile the Christians, and "now the king of Morocco announces that he will fight against all the kings of the Christians with his treacherous Andalusians and Arabs," who "in their pride think the world belongs to them."[49]

On July 16, 1212, the caliph and the king, with all the forces they could muster, met in battle at Las Navas de Tolosa, where the fate of Spain would be decided. Although Caliph Muhammad's army consisted of as many as "six hundred thousand warriors," to quote al-Maqqari— whatever its true number, it certainly dwarfed the Christian army—he "sustained one of the most complete defeats that ever disgraced the arms of Islam," and the ferocious jihadists "were put to flight with dreadful slaughter."[50] It was a resounding Christian victory of the highest order— the defining battle of the many centuries of Reconquista. Alfonso VIII of Castile, the same king who had led the Christians to their worst defeat (Alarcos, 1195), had now led them to their greatest victory (Las Navas de Tolosa, 1212).

Ferdinand III of Castile

It was between these two fateful battles that Ferdinand III of Castile—destined to be known by his peers as that "most brave knight of Christ" and "the Terror of the Saracen"—was born between 1199 and 1201 (henceforth and for computing's sake, the year 1200).[51] He was the eldest son of King Alfonso IX of León and Berenguela, daughter of King Alfonso VIII of Castile. That he was destined to play a major role in the Reconquista might have been surmised from his lineage: not only was he the maternal grandson of the hero of Las Navas de Tolosa, but both Alfonso VI, conqueror of Toledo, and the mighty Cid himself, were his fourth-great-grandfathers, while King Richard Lionheart was his granduncle (by marriage).

In 1204, the marriage of Alfonso IX and Berenguela was annulled on grounds of sanguinity, and the latter took her children and moved back home, to Castile. There, as a young boy raised at the feet of the veteran warrior-king, his grandfather, Alfonso VIII, Ferdinand was regularly regaled with stories of heroic exploits and tragic defeats against Muslims.

During these molding years, Berenguela would notice "her son tremble with enthusiasm to the depths of his soul." For, whenever he would "listen to his grandfather's stories…his eyes [became] intent and his face filled with excitement, his teeth gritted and his fists clenched, as if he were awaiting the order to jump over the Moors."[52]

Like many warrior-kings before him, as a youth, Ferdinand spent much of the day exercising and training with arms, which he showed an aptitude for. When not doing so, he would join great hunts for wild boar or bear. Even in the evening, when his body was at rest, his mind was preoccupied with the intricate stratagems of war, which he gave vent to by playing and eventually mastering the game of chess.

The young man's burgeoning militancy was tempered—one might say complemented—by his love for God; for Berenguela was a pious and loving mother, who, like Duke Godfrey of Bouillon's mother, devoted much of her time to the religious instruction of her children, particularly her eldest, whom she developed a strong bond with till her dying day. As a child, his mother would often see Ferdinand at mass, which "he attended every morning without fail," silently standing after receiving communion with his head bowed and eyes closed for a prolonged time. On once questioning him about it, he replied "I close my eyes to talk to Him better. I tell Him that He is my King and I am His knight, that I want to suffer great labors for Him in wars against the Moors, that I want to shed my blood for Him…."[53]

Sister Maria del Carmen, one of Ferdinand's chief modern biographers, sums up his early years as follows:

> [H]e combined asceticism with a practical sense of the realities of his position [among royalty], using the former as a training for his future crusade. Intimately convinced that Christ was calling him to spread the empire of the Holy Cross, he would practice long hours in the handling of weapons. And fully conscious of the responsibility of a king in whose hands God places the sword of justice, he would apply himself to the arid study of the laws and chronicles.[54]

His character is perhaps best captured by a conversation between two of his sisters: "I sometimes fear that he will leave the world and become a monk," said one, to which the other countered, "No, he derives great pleasure from weapons and is concerned about the reconquest of Spain from the Moors."[55] In this, there was no contradiction: as seen, medieval Christianity's muscular notions of right and wrong, truth and falsehood, only imbued his love for arms with a just cause.

In 1214, just two years after his victory at Las Navas de Tolosa, King Alfonso VIII of Castile, then aged fifty-eight, died following another expedition against the Almohads. The kingdom went to his sole surviving son, Enrique. When he too died in an accident three years later, the crown went to Enrique's eldest sister, Berenguela. According to the *Latin Chronicle*, however, because "all unanimously begged her"—and "because she was a woman and could not bear the burden of governing the kingdom"—she happily relinquished the crown to her eldest son, Ferdinand.[56]

No sooner was he proclaimed king of Castile in 1217 when Ferdinand encountered his first challenge—one that few newly made kings experienced: his own father, Alfonso IX, king of León, with ancient grievances and vague designs to take Castile for himself, declared war on his son in 1218, an event that traumatized the then eighteen-year-old king. "I cannot strike at you because you are my father and my lord," Ferdinand pled in letters after having mobilized his Castilian forces. "So, I am prepared to sit here and suffer with my troops until you come to your senses."[57] His father eventually relented and a treaty was made.

During his early years as king, Ferdinand's mother, Berenguela, a "woman of great prudence, wisdom, and energy," continued to influence the young monarch.[58] She arranged his marriage to Elizabeth (later renamed Beatrice) of Swabia—granddaughter of Holy Roman Emperor Frederick Barbarossa and granddaughter of Eastern Roman Emperor Isaac II Angelos—"a most noble girl of great beauty and honorable habits."[59] Between 1221 and 1234, she would give Ferdinand nine children, seven sons and two daughters.

In the same year he was married, on November 27, 1219, King Ferdinand knighted himself. He took "on his own authority," writes the chronicler, "the sword of war"—an ancient weapon kept in an old monastery—"as a sign of knighthood."[60] After kissing the sword's hilt, which in the medieval era was consciously fashioned after the Cross, he vowed to be the instrument of God's hand—"the same way this sword is in mine"—and did pray: "Show me, my King, what you want of this your knight."[61] (It is unclear if this is the same sword that he would later wield with great lethality and which in his portraits supplanted the more traditional staff held by kings, the sword Lobera, meaning, "Wolf-Slayer.")

Ferdinand quickly proved himself a formidable king, despite his youth. His decrees ended by asserting that whoever dared defy the king's words "shall unleash my wrath."[62] During these early years of consolidation, the Reconquista remained at the back of Ferdinand's head, and the young king "charged himself with the task of studying old chronicles, reading, reflecting upon and memorizing the histories of his royal ancestors," including "Alfonso VI who pushed the frontier as far as Toledo and the Cid, who conquered Valencia with a handful of men."[63]

When it came to Spain's history, Muslims, and war—or simply jihad and Reconquista—Archbishop Rodrigo (or Roderick) Jiménez de Rada of Toledo (1170–1247) was especially influential on Ferdinand. He had been his grandfather's best friend and counselor, and stood by Alfonso VIII at the battle of Las Navas de Tolosa. The archbishop soon became Ferdinand's principle advisor. An implacable but learned foe of Islam, Rodrigo had commissioned an early translation of the Koran into Latin—so that Christians might understand the "sacrilegious decrees and strange precepts" of the Moors—which was completed in 1210, two years before Las Navas. Further to "expose the secrets of the Moors," three years later, he commissioned a translation of an Arabic treatise by Ibn Tumart, the aforementioned founder of the Almohad sect.

Later in his life, and to "unravel that people's slyness and ferocity," Rodrigo personally wrote the *Historia Arabum* ("History of the Arabs"), based on and translated from "their" sources. It contains a biography of and shows "how, through false revelation the sly man Muhammad from his heart crafted a pestilential virus [Islam]."[64] Along with all this "intelligence" that he passed on to Ferdinand, he also had a special translation concerning Almanzor and his strategies made for the king in his youth from the original Arabic.[65]

As if any more Crusading inspiration was needed, in 1224, after his pilgrimage to Santiago de Compostela, John of Brienne, former king of Jerusalem, visited Ferdinand and married his sister in Toledo, where "a comparison of the oriental and occidental crusades surely must have taken place."[66]

That same year, in 1224, Almohad caliph Yusuf II died. Prior to this, and despite the Christians' decisive victory at Las Navas de Tolosa, which for various reasons could not be fully capitalized on, the status quo between Christian and Muslim Spain had largely remained the same. Now, with the caliph's death, Muslim unity in al-Andalus once again began to crumble: "so much discord broke out among the powerful men of that realm," wrote a contemporaneous Christian chronicler, wryly adding, "and it still goes on, and may it go on forever."[67]

Ferdinand's time had come at last. In 1224, "on a certain day" when the young king was feeling "inspired and aroused," he startled his mother and magnates at the royal court of Burgos by loudly announcing his intention "to serve God against the enemies of the Christian faith":[68]

> The gate is indeed open and the way is clear. There is peace in our kingdom while discord and capital hatreds, division, and quarrels are newly arisen among the Moors. Christ, God and man, is on our side, but on the side of the Moors is the unfaithful and damned apos-tate, Muhammad. What is there to do? I beseech you, most clement mother, to whom, after God, I hold whatever I have, that it may please you that I should go to war against the Moors.[69]

All present were "amazed" at "the king's passion." His mother asked him to step outside as she consulted with the magnates. Before long, "all agreed in this opinion: that the king should make war on the Saracens in every possible way."[70]

Word spread and soon the hardened warrior-monks of the military orders of Santiago, Calatrava, Montesa, the Temple and Hospital, as well as his old counselor, the archbishop of Toledo—all men who had, to quote the chronicler, "assumed the living cross" in an effort "to rip from the hand of the Muslims the land they held to the injury of the Christian name"—prepared for the great Crusade.[71]

Early Campaigns

Wasting no time, by the end of that same year of 1224, Ferdinand had hacked and slashed his way to—and was first to scale over the walls of—Quesada, a nearby Muslim fortress town. "Covered with Muslim blood from head to toe," he planted the Cross on the central mosque's highest minaret, saying he was doing so for "the Kingship of Christ on earth."[72]

The young king, who fought alongside and lived among his men, was finally living out the stories he was bred on: "Look, my friends, where God is giving us our meal for today," he would say whenever coming across a Muslim fortress. "It is the day to win our bread at a lance's thrust, like El Cid's knights used to do."[73]

But it was not all daring and bravado: "Ferdinand set his soldiers the most perfect example of devotion. He fasted rigorously, prayed much, wore a rough hair-shirt made in the shape of a cross, spent often whole nights in tears and prayers, especially before battles, and gave to God the whole glory of all his victories."[74] The Muslims fought back as best they could, but few could withstand the fast and furious assaults of the enthusiastic, youthful warrior-king of Castile.

After a brief respite, on the Feast of All Saints, November 1, 1225, the king—once again "stirred by the Spirit of God" and "holding firmly and irrevocably to the aim of destroying that cursed people"—returned to and again devastated the frontier, despite frigid cold and wet weather.[75]

Terrified at what the future might hold—namely, his head on a platter—Abdullah abu Muhammad, a regional ruler and the governor of Baeza, threw himself at Ferdinand's feet. He kissed his hand, paid tribute, swore fealty to and became his vassal, thereby ensuring his survival, including against other Muslims. For his part, and as his ancestors—including Ferdinand the Great, his son, Emperor Alfonso VI of Castile-León, and the Cid—had done before him, Ferdinand accepted such arrangements as alternative, nonviolent means of squeezing the Moors into defeat. There was also the added hope that such Muslim vassals and their subjects would eventually convert—and many in fact did (even if their sincerity remains unknown).

But alas for Abdullah; in 1227, the Muslims of Córdoba rose up against and beheaded the "apostate" ruler, "because he had made himself a vassal to a Christian king who was the sworn enemy of their religion."[76] As happened more than a century earlier, when the Valencians had slaughtered their king, a vassal of the Cid, Ferdinand was "heartily sorry" to hear of this development.[77] Perhaps disillusioned at the murder of his father by their coreligionists, his son Muhammad was baptized and took on the name of Ferdinand.[78]

Over the next few years, the Castilian king continued his assault along the frontier, reducing several more Muslim regions, some with blinding speed. During these times, and not unlike the Cid or Alfonso the Battler, Ferdinand went on to earn the love of those Christians living under Muslim domination. Thus, during another raid motivated by his "firm and irrevocable purpose of destroying that cursed race [the Muslims]," Ferdinand left a trail of devastation around Jaen on his way to Granada, and only relented on the condition that the Muslims of Granada release their Christian captives—thirteen-hundred of whom staggered to him "starved, dirty, covered with rags, their hair white from the dark dungeons, and exhausted by hard labor and hunger."[79] "The truth is," the king later explained, "those Moors from Granada could not have offered anything that I desire more since I esteem the life of one of my vassals more than the death of a thousand enemies."[80]

Although fierce in war, Ferdinand was merciful to those Muslims who surrendered. Far from giving them the three choices their ancestors had given his—conversion, tribute, or death—he allowed them to leave with their movable possessions and an escort. As al-Himyari, a Muslim jurist remarked, Ferdinand was "a mild man, one with political sense."[81] Even so, unlike—and perhaps because he had learned from the experiences of—the Cid and Alfonso VI, his "political sense" required subjugated Muslims to evacuate.

As repeatedly demonstrated during the Cid's conquest of Valencia, no matter how lenient a Christian ruler was with his Moorish subjects, and no matter how docile the latter appeared, whenever the opportunity arose, the Muslims immediately revolted—a fact regularly on display until, and the reason for, the final expulsion of the last vestiges of Islam from Spain in the early seventeenth century. The risk, at least for Ferdinand—who was always "severe in the administration of justice and the execution of the laws, but readily pardoned all personal injuries"[82]—was no longer worth it; expulsion was deemed the only sure way of maintaining peace in reconquered territories.[83]

Moreover, and like Alfonso VII of León-Castile and other Christian conquerors who arose during the Almoravid and Almohad eras—when the desecration of churches and their transformation into mosques became especially ubiquitous—Ferdinand was notorious for the elaborate (re)transformation of conquered mosques into churches. After he took Capilla in 1227, for example, the Archbishop of Toledo and others "cleansed the mosques of the Moors of all the filthiness of the Muhammadan superstition," to quote the *Latin Chronicle*, "and dedicated it as a church to the Lord Jesus Christ." The king attended its first mass.[84]

It bears emphasizing that such religious triumphalism was a sort of tit for tat. Every Spaniard was well aware that, centuries earlier and into Ferdinand's era, Muslims had regularly transformed conquered churches into mosques, right after they cleansed them "from the filth of idolatry and the stains of infidelity," to quote an early Muslim source.[85] Thus and in the words of his *Historia Arabum*, Archbishop Rodrigo describes the initial, eighth century invasion of Spain by the "vile African peoples who excelled neither through strength nor through goodness, but did all with trickery and cleverness":

> The sanctuaries were destroyed, the churches demolished, the places where God was praised with joy now blasphemed and mistreated [by the Muslims]. They expelled the crosses and altars from the churches. The chrism, the books, and all those things that were for the honor of Christianity were broken and trampled upon.... The honor of the saints and the beauty of the church were turned into ugliness and vileness. The churches and towers where they used to praise God, now in the same places they called upon Mahomat.[86]

An unprecedented level of Andalusian disunity culminated in 1228, with the rise of Ibn Hud of Zaragoza (1199–1238). Seeing how useless Islam's latest resuscitators had become against the Christian advance, he vehemently denounced the Almohads—whom he rather predictably accused of being lapsed Muslims and violators of sharia—before acclaiming and pledging his allegiance to the Abbasid caliph in Baghdad. Won over by Ibn Hud, most of al-Andalus—including the great cities of Seville, Córdoba, Jaen, and Granada—took him as their new master. Then he, "with an inexorable hatred," writes the Christian chronicler, and "to please" his new subjects, "viciously fell upon the Almohads, decapitating men, strangling them...cutting off the breasts of women, and extinguishing the life of children by a miserable death."[87]

It was déjà vu all over again: Just as the jihadist Almoravids had come as saviors and replaced the original Moorish kings of al-Andalus in the late eleventh century—only to be later accused of being insufficiently

Islamic and replaced by a new crop of jihadists, the Almohads, in the late twelfth century—so now the Almohads were accused of being insufficiently Islamic and eliminated in the thirteenth century. The only difference is that there were to be no more jihadist saviors from North Africa; the Moors, though unaware of it yet, were henceforth on their own.

Changes were also sweeping through the Christian kingdoms. In 1230, Ferdinand's father, Alfonso IX, king of León, died. Although Ferdinand had once been his designated heir, after the conflict that erupted between father and son on the latter's elevation to the crown of Castile in 1217, Alfonso IX had secretly designated his daughters from his first wife as his heirs.* A succession crisis erupted and Ferdinand was counseled to assert his right to León through arms. "I will not wage war against another Christian land," was his reply, "even if I were to gain the whole world."[88] The crisis was eventually averted by the political acumen of his mother and the goodwill of his half-sisters and their mother, who, during negotiations, agreed to cede the crown of León to Ferdinand.

Thus, in 1230, Castile and León were again united under King Ferdinand III, this time permanently. This was an especially ominous development for the Muslims: since León and Castile had split in 1157, the two kingdoms had been at odds, not infrequently allying with the Moors against one another (as Ferdinand's father had done against Ferdinand's maternal grandfather in the years before Las Navas de Tolosa, 1212). That they were now united under the rule of one man—one utterly committed to the re-conquest of Spain—boded ill for al-Andalus.

But first Ferdinand would need to consolidate his new kingdom of León, which required him to leave the Reconquista to others, including the military orders. On the western and eastern edges of Spain, Sancho

---

* Ferdinand's father, Alfonso IX of León (1171—1230), is an enigmatic and rather tragic figure. First feeling that he was slighted by the king of Castile, his cousin and future father-in-law, Alfonso VIII, and then feeling slighted by his own son's elevation to the crow of Castile, he was from the start a thorn in the side of the Reconquista. For a time he even allied with the Almohads against Alfonso VIII of Castile—to the point that the pope once called a Crusade against him—and he was the only Christian king not to participate in the epic confrontation at Las Navas de Tolosa. He did, however, atone for his behavior by spending the last fifteen years of his life Crusading against the Muslims. In 1230, the year he died, he conquered Merida and Badoz, and was even planning on besieging the great Seville, when he suddenly died at age fifty-nine, en route to Santiago de Compostela, where he was going to give thanks for his recent victories. There, he was given the honors of a Christian burial in the cathedral of Saint James the Moor-Slayer.

II of Portugal and James I of Aragon respectively made impressive gains, especially the latter, better known to history as "James the Conqueror." After wresting the Balearic Islands from Islam, in 1238 he reconquered Valencia, which had been under Muslim rule for 136 years, soon after its last Christian ruler, the Cid, had died. Not only was Roderick Díaz of Vivar also James's ancestor, but "the thought of the Cid stirred James I of Aragon when, in the final struggle for Valencia, he wielded Tizon, the sword the hero had won on those very same plains from the Almoravide leader Bucar."[89]

Despite such setbacks—and despite the effete reputation later Arab historians would ascribe to them, in part to explain Islam's eventual defeat—the Muslims of al-Andalus were far from defeated or overwhelmed; and the records tell of many jihadists, such as one Abu al-Rabi', who, according to al-Maqqari, "never ceased fighting in the foremost ranks, striking the infidels with his sword, encouraging the Moslems...and reminding them of the pleasures of paradise, until he himself was slain."[90]

In response to these bold Muslim advances, Ferdinand, still occupied with governing his new kingdom, entrusted his nine-year-old son and heir apparent, the future Alfonso X, to one of his generals, with the following instructions: "You see how the Moors have become quite proud and why it is necessary to lower their heads. Unfortunately, I cannot leave this [Leónese] kingdom of mine. I want them to receive an exemplary punishment by means of the Infante Don Alfonso, but because he is very young and not yet strong, I want you to go with him to protect him and to lead the army."[91]

The Great Campaigns: Córdoba and Jaen

In December of 1235, a daring band of Almogavars, led by a few knights, and aided by a few Muslim turncoats, stormed and with great violence took a portion of Córdoba's eastern quarter. Word reached Ferdinand in January of 1236, even as he was in mourning over the recent death of his thirty-year-old wife from childbirth complications. Through their envoy, the Almogavars "implored him to help them because they were placed in most grave peril." Against the Muslim "multitude of Córdoba, they were very few" and "separated from the Moors only by a certain wall running almost through the middle of the city."[92] Though at a standstill, time, the envoys made clear, was not on the Christians' side.

The king was heavily moved by such a heroic feat; and "the grief for the loss" of his wife "did not long suspend his warlike preparations."[93] On the same evening that the envoys arrived, Ferdinand's advisors strongly warned him against setting out immediately, during winter; they cited impassable roads due to snow, rain and floods, and possible ambushes from the "innumerable multitude of people in Córdoba"—to say nothing of Ibn Hud, now the de facto king of al-Andalus, who was even then headed to relieve the Muslim city.

But Ferdinand "placed his hope in the Lord Jesus Christ and closed his ears" to all such talk; he was resolved to "aid his vassals who had exposed themselves to such a great danger in his service and for the honor of the Christian faith."[94] After sending word to his magnates in Castile and León to muster their forces, he set off for Córdoba on the very next morning—with only one hundred knights.

Despite the terrible road conditions, he rode furiously through rain and sleet and reached the great Moorish city on February 7. Ibn Hud had arrived before him with a much greater force—reportedly thirty thousand infantry and five thousand horsemen—but, instead of awaiting and meeting the Castilians, and perhaps because they had soundly defeated him earlier at the battle of Jerez in 1231, he unexpectedly withdrew back to Seville.

As might be expected, the holed up Christians, "who were then placed in such great danger in Córdoba," burst in joy on seeing their king, this young man "who had exposed himself to much danger so that he could succor his people!" asserts the chronicler.[95] After rescuing the Almogavers, Ferdinand laid Córdoba to siege; as Christian fighters continued to pour in from León, Castile, and Galicia, the noose tightened around the Muslim city. Five months later, on June 29, 1236, Córdoba—for centuries, "the ornament of the world," the ancient seat of the Umayyad caliphs and al-Andalus's "most stalwart shield and bastion against the Christians"— surrendered to Ferdinand.[96]

Everyone had something to say about this grand event. Al-Maqqari, the normally and refreshingly objective Arab historian, captured Muslim sentiment by bemoaning how "that seat of the western khalifate, repository of the theological sciences, and abode of Islam, passed into the hands of the accursed Christians—may Allah destroy them all!"[97] For the indigenous Christians of Spain, however, the conquest—as with all conquests of the Reconquista—was the mere righting of a wrong. As the *Latin Chronicle* relays, the "famous city of Córdoba, endowed with certain splendor and rich soil, which had been held captive for such a long time, that is, from the time of Rodrigo, the king of the Goths [who was killed in 711, during the initial Islamic invasion of Spain], was restored to the Christian faith by the labor and valor of our King Lord Fernando."[98]

Ferdinand granted lenient terms: those Muslims who wanted to leave with all their movable possessions were granted safe passage; those who wished to remain and practice their religion could do so.[99] Either way, Ferdinand proceeded to repopulate it with "new inhabitants, followers of Christ."[100]

Before entering and claiming kingship of his hitherto greatest conquest, Ferdinand ordered that the standard of the Cross be carried before his own standard and placed on the highest minaret of the largest mosque—an event that "caused ineffable confusion and lamentation among the Saracens and, on the other hand, ineffable joy among the Christians."[101]

Next, the great mosque of Córdoba, which Abd al-Rahman I, a highly celebrated caliph among Western academics, built in the eighth century—after demolishing and cannibalizing the materials of Saint Vincent's, an important sixth century Visigothic church[102]—was "cleansed of all filthiness of Muhammad," the archbishop of Toledo wrote, and sprinkled with holy water and salt, so that "what had once been the devil's lair was made a church of Jesus Christ, named in honor of his glorious Mother."[103]

Finally, Ferdinand found the bells of Saint James Matamoros, "the Moor Slayer," which had been seized 250 years earlier by Almanzor and sent to Córdoba on the backs of Christian captives to adorn its great mosque as trophies of war.[104] Righting this ancient wrong, the king, who, as seen, was well acquainted with the details of Muslim-Christian history, had them returned to the shrine of Santiago—carried atop the backs of captive Muslims no less.

Following this latest victory and soon after returning to Toledo, the triumphant king—who during the long siege of Córdoba had deprived himself of all comfort and even slept in his armor, as "an example of suffering and mortification" to his men—collapsed and fell ill.[105] The truth is he had barely made it alive to the end of the siege and was now near the point of death, though this fact had been hidden from the rank and file.

Ferdinand remained convalescent and indoors for a season. He used this time to reflect, worship, and bond with his many now motherless children. Once, while listening to the recitation of the Poem of the Cid, the minstrel reached the part where the Campeador battled with the count of Barcelona, another Christian, which prompted a discussion with his children. "One thing is certain," Ferdinand concluded, "the Cid did not want this war with the count; it was forced on him. But I will tell you, my sons, that I am more pleased to see him make war on the Moors than on Christians; and I refuse to move against Christians unless absolutely forced to."[106]

Later that year, and thanks again to his mother's efforts, the widowed king took a new wife, Joan, Countess of Ponthieu, in 1237. She would go on to give him four more sons and a daughter.

As for Ferdinand's chief Muslim adversary, Ibn Hud lived on for about a year and a half following his failure to save Córdoba, at which point he was assassinated by one of his leading men in January 1238, apparently over a slave girl, "the daughter of a Christian chief taken in one of his [Ibn Hud's] campaigns," writes al-Maqqari: "she was one of the most beautiful creatures that ever lived, and Ibn Hud became deeply enamoured of her"—as did the envious general who would later kill him.[107]

Becoming fully cognizant of and desperate at their plight, a few Moorish cities called on and re-pledged their allegiance to the Almohads of Africa—if only they would return and help them against the Christian advance. The professional jihadists refused; they were quite done with Spain.

Because the Reconquista was not over, Ferdinand found himself on the warpath again. During the fall of 1245, he besieged, for the third time, the impregnable city of Jaen, east of Córdoba and just north of Granada. Although harsh weather soon prevailed, in order to boost morale, Ferdinand planted his tent in the middle of camp and announced it would remain there until he had "the unconquerable stronghold in his power."

When a large group of Muslims came sallying forth out of the city, "as was his custom," Ferdinand "was the first to take the spear and began to encourage his men with words of audacity." Then, after casting his sight up to heaven and saying "I seek Thy glory, Lord, not mine," he turned to his men and cried "Santiago and Castile!" before plunging into the fray.[108] While not in battle, he resumed his "harsh discipline," including by "placing close to his skin a terrible shirt of iron mail underlaid with points carved in the form of a cross which covered his chest and shoulders and part of his arms." Above this he wore his coat of mail.[109]

Before long, Muhammad I of Granada (Ibn al-Ahmar), the master of Jaen, soon found himself under assault—not by his Christian besiegers but by his own increasingly disgruntled coreligionists. His response was predictable: on February 28, 1246, he appeared before Ferdinand, threw himself at his feet, kissed his hands, and surrendered Jaen. Muslims were evacuated, the principal mosque was transformed into a church, and the king attended its first mass. Over the next eight months Jaen was repopulated with Christians.

Another brilliant conquest for Ferdinand, Jaen had revealed something else. The king's sickness had never fully healed. Although he tried to hide it, the harsh conditions of siege life, which he had again insisted on sharing with his men, had again taken their toll on Ferdinand, "his strength broken by years of austerities and physical toil."[110]

The Siege of Seville

Had Ferdinand permanently retired and withdrawn to his kingdoms, never again to set out against the Muslims of Spain, he and his conquests would be counted among the greatest of the Reconquista. Along with taking lesser cities, he had taken the kingdoms of Córdoba and Jaen—a scandal to Islam. Unswerving in his childhood goal of returning the whole of al-Andalus to Christian rule, however, a few months after the fall of Jaen, the indefatigable Crusader set his sights on the great Muslim kingdom of Seville, long known as "the jewel of Andalusia."

Not only was it the most opulent city of Muslim Spain, but, due to its strategic and well-fortified location—along the Guadalquivir River, with seaport access to the Mediterranean and Morocco—it had been the capital of a succession of Islamic dynasties, including the Almoravids and the Almohads, since the eighth century. Aside from Granada—which had submitted to becoming a vassal of and tributary to Ferdinand in 1246—Seville was now the only unconquered Muslim kingdom still to hold against the Christian advance. And it had good reason to be optimistic: it was virtually impregnable, had fortifications within fortifications and 166 watch towers; was protected by a ring of fortresses, and had sea access to North Africa. The city was further well-rationed, well-armed, including with formidable machines of war, and full of fanatical Muslim preachers who "spurred on the people to resist the infidels."[111]

It would, in short, be Ferdinand's most complex and formidable operation yet. As such, his son, the future Alfonso X, the warrior-monks of the military orders, his magnates, banner men, and vassals—including Ibn al-Ahmar of Granada (who years later would turn on and betray the Christians)—all joined in what promised to be an extremely long siege.[112]

In the fall of 1246 Ferdinand began by devastating much of the city's surrounding countryside and crops. He then methodically besieged and took, one by one, the ring of fortresses and towns leading to and within a twenty mile radius of Seville.

All this time jihadist sentiment ran high in the besieged city; the people were exhorted concerning the "paradise that Mohammad promises to those who die in the jihad and of the delights awaiting them there if they resisted Ferdinand the infidel."[113] A few "moderates" of Seville tried to follow Granada's lead and submit to being tribute-paying vassals of the king; but the majority were "opposed to any accommodation with the Christians, assassinated the moderate leader," and implored another group of North African Muslims stationed in Tunis to come to their aid, to no avail.[114]

Notwithstanding, in a few months, the siege had tightened like a noose around Seville, though the Moorish kingdom still had a steady supply of provisions flowing in from the countryside of Triana, which could still be accessed through a bridge that was well-guarded by a massive chain blocking passage to the Christians along that side of the Guadalquivir River. For months, the siege was dominated by skirmishes, duels, and battles, even as the Christian fleet tried unsuccessfully to cut off Seville's communications and supply routes.

As his was a sacred war, Ferdinand "spent much of his time in vigils of prayer and penance, and three times each week he would scourge himself until the ground was soaked with blood."[115] He was also mourning his beloved mother, Berenguela, who had died near Burgos sometime around the beginning of the siege, aged sixty-six.

Moreover, and once again, due to the privations he insisted on suffering alongside his men—including taking his turn at keeping night watch—Ferdinand fell ill. As might be imagined, if the besieged Muslim city suffered, so too did the Christian besiegers, including from bouts of pestilence. While in his sickbed, tragic news kept pouring in—including the death of his longtime mentor and friend, Rodrigo Jiménez de Rada, the archbishop of Toledo.

Despite it all, once he was barely able, Ferdinand mounted his horse and appeared before his men. Though they could see that he was "still pale and emaciated," his righteous exhortations and words of fury against centuries of Islamic abuses emboldened them to renew the siege with vigor.[116]

By the summer of 1248, heat and pestilence had reached awful new heights for both sides. Starvation set in; some were reduced to eating feces. As the Cid had done during his siege of Valencia, Ferdinand responded by enlarging and transforming his battlements and forti-fications into a city—complete with suburbs, churches, and eventually artisans and civilians—a "Christian Seville to accommodate a Christian population opposite Islamic Seville."[117]

Finally, the decisive event came. According to Prosper Guéranger's *Liturgical Days*, a chronicle, "The Mahometans had stretched an iron chain across the Guadalquiver, in order to block up the passage. Sud-denly there arose a violent wind, and one of the royal ships was, by the king's order, sent against the chain, which was thus broken, and with so much violence, that it was carried far beyond, and bore down [and broke through] the bridge of boats. The Moors lost all their hope, and the city surrendered."[118]

Before totally capitulating, however, Moorish elders repeatedly came to parley, each time stipulating fewer and fewer conditions to their advantage, none of which the implacable Christian monarch would accept—unconditional surrender being the price. Matters of religion were especially not open to debate. When one of the surrendering sheikhs lamented that Seville's "mosques will be changed into churches, and the crowns into crosses and bells," another Muslim present cried, "Not that! Before that happens, we will level the mosque and its mina-ret!" Because such grievance mongering would not do, the king's son, Alfonso, shot back—"I tell you that if even one tile is missing from its place, it will become possible to sail in the rivers of blood that will flow in the streets!"[119]

In the end, the Muslims had "no choice but to accept the iron will of that King Ferdinand, who, like a curse of Allah, crossed Andalusia exterminating Islam."[120] Thus, on November 23, 1248—after a sixteen month siege—Seville finally opened its gates; and with that, the Reconquista— the roots of which go back to around the year 720, when Pelagius and his Asturian "mustard seed" first defied the invading hordes of Islam— came to an effective close. Although Granada, the absolute last Muslim kingdom at the southernmost tip of Spain—in a hilly and remote region cut off from and therefore posing little danger to the rest of Christian Spain—remained Islamic for nearly 250 more years, it was also a tributary of Castile, thanks to Ferdinand.

In Seville, Muslims were permitted to sell their properties and leave with their movable goods, including wealth and weapons. The chronicles claim hundreds of thousands participated in this exodus, one of Islamic history's most tragic episodes. Most went to Granada; Christian ships ferried others to Africa. Al-Rundi, a poet born and raised in Seville well captures contemporary Muslim sentiment in verse:

> They weep over the remains of dwellings devoid of Muslims,
> Despoiled of Islam, now peopled by Infidels!
> The mosques have now been changed into churches,
> Where the bells are ringing and the crosses are standing....
> This misfortune has surpassed all that has preceded,
> And as long as Time lasts, it can never be forgotten....
> What an opprobrium, when once mighty people,
> Have been humbled to dust by tyrants and injustice!
> Yesterday they were kings in their own palaces,
> Today they are slaves in the land of the Infidels![121]

Naturally, Christians did not see it this way. They had merely liberated and restored what was Christian land centuries before Muslims had invaded and forcibly Islamized it.

On December 22, 1248, Ferdinand—"the tyrant, the accursed one," as Muslims were wont to describe their conqueror—made his procession into Seville, and worshipped in that city's principle mosque, now a cathedral. Such a splendid prize, he established his seat in and spent his energy on repopulating Seville, even as roaming bands of "moors were [forever] awaiting any opportunity to kill him."[122]

Finale

Now that virtually the whole of Spain was under Christian authority, the indefatigable Ferdinand began "making preparations to pass over to Africa, there to crush the Mahometan empire," in the context of joining the Crusade of his younger cousin, the king of France.[123] But by now, his already ailing body, ravaged by more than twenty years of privations, austerities, and warfare, would not allow for such a venture.

Right before commencing his African adventure, his old sickness struck him with extreme ferocity, and, on May 30, 1252, King Ferdinand III of Castile-León died, aged fifty-two. He was about four years younger than his ancestor, the Cid, who had also died from the ravages of a lifetime of nonstop warfare.

Although Ferdinand's career was not overly long—his Aragonese counterpart, James I, reigned for sixty-three years—much was accomplished in it. In the twenty years between 1228 and 1248 he spearheaded the Reconquista into central al-Andalus and ended up as undisputed lord and king of not only the northern Christian kingdoms of Castile, Toledo, León, and Galicia, but the great and southern Moorish kingdoms of Murica, Córdoba, Jaen, and Seville. The kingdom he bequeathed to his son, Alfonso X, was significantly larger than the one he inherited—due to the addition of Andalusian cities. As Ferdinand had from his deathbed explained to his successor:

> My lord, I leave you the whole realm from the sea hither that the Moors won from Roderick, king of Spain [541 years earlier]. All of it is in your dominion, part of it conquered, the other part tributary. If you know how to preserve in this state what I leave you, you will be as good a king as I; and if you win more for yourself, you will be better than I; but if you diminish it, you will not be as good as I.[124]

The dying king concluded by "bestow[ing] upon you my sword Lobera, that is of passing worth, and wherewith God has wrought much good to me."[125]

Ferdinand's accomplishments were such that they were celebrated far beyond the borders of Spain. The contemporary English historian Matthew Paris (c.1200–1259) went so far as to write that, in the sight of England, Ferdinand "alone has done more for the honor and profit of Christ's Church than the pope and all his crusaders...and all the

Templars and Hospitallers [had done in the Holy Land]." Writing some seven hundred years later, Reconquista historian Derek Lomax concurred: "At a time when the crusading efforts of the rest of Christendom hardly sufficed to maintain a foothold on the coast of the Holy Land, Fernando inflicted on medieval Islam its greatest defeat so far...."[126]

Why he targeted Islam and why he prosecuted the Reconquista with such vigor bears recalling, and is well documented in the encomium to Ferdinand recorded in the *Liturgical Days*:

> Thy ambition was to deliver thy people from an oppression, which had weighed heavily on them for long ages. Thy object was to save them from the danger of apostasy, which they incurred by being under the Moorish yoke. Champion of Christ!—it was for his dear sake thou didst lay siege to the Saracen cities.[127]

Indeed, for Ferdinand, the Crusade was always subservient to and an offshoot of his general relationship to God, which was on full display in his final days. As recorded by court insiders, this once glorious and victorious king took on, as he had done before, the guise of a sinful penitent. He cast away his crown and scepter, had a rope drawn around his neck to remind himself of his abject status, and spent his days and nights in deep prayer and confession. All his queen could do was weep from a distance.

Seen as a rare model of virtue—a "special athlete of Christ," to quote the pope of the time, Innocent IV—Ferdinand was canonized as a saint in 1671.[128] He remains the only Spanish king to receive that honor. And, even though some of his last words were "Naked I came out of my mother's womb which was the earth, and naked I offer myself," his reportedly uncorrupt body lies in a crystal case in the cathedral of Seville, which has been visited by countless pilgrims from the moment of his burial to the present.[129]

Despite all the well-deserved praise that surrounds his name—several cities the world over, including in California and Texas, are named after Saint Ferdinand, or "San Fernando"—his accomplishments must be seen within the context of all those other Christians, including the rank and file, who bled the plains of Spain red to liberate it. In fact, unlike heroes who were aided and empowered by their direct contemporaries, as Godfrey of Bouillon was by the other First Crusaders, and as the first part of this chapter has amply shown, Ferdinand stood on the shoulders of centuries' worth of "re-conquerors," all of whom paved the way for him.

This comes out clearly in al-Maqqari. After he records how the eighth century Muslim conquerors of Spain had dismissed Pelagius and his very few men as no threat to Islam—mockingly saying, "What are thirty barbarians, perched upon a rock [in the caves of Asturias]? They must inevitably die"—the Muslim historian, writing retrospectively, lamented: "Would to Allah that the Moslems had then extinguished at once the sparkles of a fire that was destined to consume the whole dominions of Islam in those parts!"[130]

Even so, in Reconquista lore, Ferdinand is accounted the greatest of them all.

Church of the Holy Sepulchre, Jerusalem.

Godfrey and other First Crusaders set off.

Above: A sketch of the Cid, "he of the flowing beard." **Right:** Godfrey statue, Brussels.

Below: Godfrey's sword, when it was still displayed in the Church of the Holy Sepulchre; photo from 1854. **Below right:** Godfrey breaks into Muslim-held Jerusalem.

Left: Pelagius (Pelayo) declared first Christian king of Spain following its fall to Islam in the eighth century.

Below: Cid compels Alfonso VI to swear on a Bible that he had nothing to do with the killing of his brother, Sancho II.

Above: Cid statue, Burgos.
Right: Saladin oversees the expulsion and enslavement of Christians from Jerusalem. *Below:* Richard Lionheart pulverizes Muslims at Arsuf.

Far left: Richard statue, Palace of Westminster.

Left: Painting of Richard I, 1841.

Below: Richard storms the shores of Jaffa.

Above: Painting of Ferdinand III, c. 1650.

Right: Painting of Santiago Matamoros, Saint James the Moor-Slayer, Cathedral of Seville.

Below: Muhammad I of Granada (Ibn al-Ahmar) surrenders Jaen to Ferdinand.

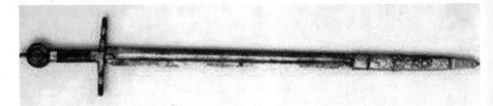

Above: *Ferdinand's sword, Lobera, Cathedral of Seville.*

Below: *The last days of Saint Ferdinand, 1887 painting.*

Bottom: *Captured Córdoban Muslims return bells of Saint James to his shrine, Santiago de Compostela, in Galicia.*

Above: Saint Ferdinand statue, Seville.

Right: Contemporary miniature of Saint Louis, thirteenth century.

Below: Louis IX in battle.

Left: Louis gives thanks for the relatively easy capture of Damietta.

Below: "Apotheosis of Saint Louis" statue, St. Louis, Missouri. BLM and Muslim activists attacked and are still trying to take it down due to Louis's alleged "Islamophobia."

Left: Louis captured in Egypt.

1840 painting of the siege of Acre, 1291, which ushered in the final expulsion of the Crusaders from the Holy Land.

Above: Ottoman Turks dragging away European slave-girls, woodcut, 1530.

Left: Near contemporary depiction of John Hunyadi, the "White Knight of Wallachia," c. 1488.

Battle of Varna: Moments before being beheaded, King Ladislaus (L) rushes into the Turkish ranks as Sultan Murad II (R) implores Allah.

Right: John Hunyadi statue, Buda.

Below: Battle of Belgrade: John Hunyadi and John Capistrano lead the final charge against the Turks.

Left: *Bust of George Kastrioti, Skanderbeg, Palace of the Nations, Geneva.*

Below: *Skanderbeg dueling with a Tatar at the Ottoman court, sixteenth century drawing.*

Top: Skanderbeg, "Lord Alexander."

Right: Monument to Skanderbeg, Croya.

Bottom: Final days of Skanderbeg, sixteenth century engraving.

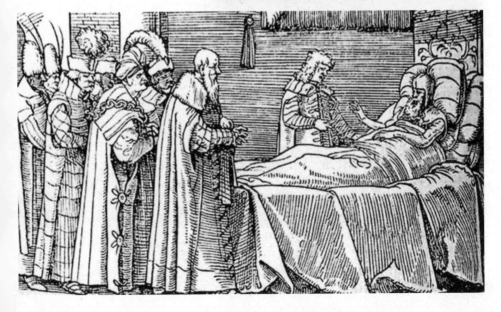

Top: Propagandistic German-language pamphlet, c. 1500, of Vlad dining in his Forest of the Impaled.

Left: Painting of Vlad, a copy of an original made during his lifetime, c. 1560, Ambras Castle.

Bottom: Remains of Vlad III Dracula's castle, Poenari, Romania.

Top: Painting of Vlad the Impaler, moments before nailing his Turkish envoys' turbans to their heads, c.1870.

Right: Bust of Vlad, Sighişoara, Romania.

Bottom: Painting of Dracula's "Night Attack," where he sought to assassinate Sultan Muhammad II, 1866.

CHAPTER 5

Saint Louis:
Christ's Tragic Hero

"A shield for the oppressed/For the wicked a hammer too/Your shoulders twice did bear the cross/And by this act you suffered loss/But zeal for Christ and ardor too/A holy martyr made of you."
—*LUDOVICUS DECUS REGNANTIUM*[1]

"This Raydafrans was one of the most important Frankish kings and the most powerful…. He was a devoted adherent of the Christian faith, and so his spirit told him that he should recover Jerusalem for the Franks, since it is, they claim, the dwelling-place of the one they revere."
—IBN WASIL[2]

Because King Richard's Third Crusade ultimately failed to wrest Jerusalem from Islamic control, three more Crusades were launched: the Fourth (1205–1204) was a total disaster; the Fifth (1217–1221) was a near success but ultimately failed. (In fact, due to the Franks' initial success, the Ayyubid sultan of Damascus took the desperate decision to raze Jerusalem's walls, since, "should the Franks take Jerusalem, they would rule over all of Syria."[3]) During the Sixth Crusade, in 1229, Holy Roman Emperor Frederick II made a ten-year treaty with the Ayyubid sultan of Egypt that temporarily restored many of Jerusalem's holy sites to Christian rule.

Soon thereafter, the Ayyubid dynasty fractured, as Saladin's descendants in Egypt and Syria jockeyed for power against one another. In exchange for their alliance against Egypt, the Syrians relinquished a much dilapidated Jerusalem to the Crusaders around 1240. Disaster struck a few years later. Egyptian sultan al-Salih Ayyub hired the Khwarazmians, a Muslim Turcoman tribe, to assault Jerusalem. Because the defenseless city was in no shape to withstand their attack, many of the Christians abandoned it and fled to the coast. The Turcomans easily captured Jerusalem on August 11, 1244.

In an effort to lure back their prey, which they were disappointed to see had fled, the Muslim tribesmen hung and displayed Christian banners found within the city. The ruse worked; rumor soon reached the fleeing Christians that the city had somehow been regained. Some, including many women and children who were unable to continue to the coast, returned to Jerusalem—only to get ambushed by the Muslims. Of seven thousand Christians, only three hundred escaped death or slavery. Some managed to flee to the caves and mountains of Syria, "only to be butchered miserably by the Moslem peasantry, nominally their allies."[4]

After writing that the Turcomans "advanced to Jerusalem, took it by storm, and put all the Christians to the sword," the Egyptian chronicler al-Maqrizi (b.1364) elaborates: "The women and girls, having suffered every insult from a brutal disorderly soldiery, were loaded with chains. They destroyed the church of the holy Sepulchre; and when they found nothing among the living, to glut their rage, they opened the tombs of the Christians, took out the bodies, and burnt them."[5] Finally, they broke and sent the marble pillars of the Sepulchre's entrance as trophies to adorn the tomb of Muhammad in Medina.

Now augmented by the Egyptian sultan's army, the Turcomans continued to the coast, where somewhere northeast of Gaza, around October 17, 1244, they encountered and fought an army of Crusaders and their Syrian Muslim allies. The latter only "faintly opposed" the first onslaught, writes al-Maqrizi, before they "instantly fled."[6] But "the Christians, who had been enraged to extremity by the savage excesses" of these new Muslim invaders, "fought with desperate valour," only to be "overwhelmed by tenfold numbers, and almost annihilated."[7] Thousands of dead Christians littered the battlefield of La Forbie, as it came to be known. All of Cairo celebrated, to the "sound of drums and trumpets," and the heads of the Christian slain were sent to adorn that city's gates.[8]

It was the worst blow meted out to the Crusaders in decades. The rest of the Christian forces holed themselves up in their fortresses along the coast and sent frantic letters to Europe begging for aid. In response, during the First Council of Lyon (1245), Pope Innocent IV proclaimed a new Crusade: Jerusalem, "in the wake of the grave disasters of frequent devastation and following her continuous laments for the frequent slaughter of her people," he declared, "now experiences the lash at enemy hands even more harshly."[9] After describing in a letter to King Henry III of England how the Muslims had "annihilated" the Christians—"all alike with the sword and spatter the fields with their blood"—Innocent highlighted their enemies' existential hatred for Christianity:

[T]heir fury extended to the…Sepulchre of the Savior. Laying sacrilegious hands on it, they…violated it, so that the frenzy of their minds, burning to heap abuse on Christ, might not even leave the undefiled places where He was bodily present, but after demolishing [these places] might extinguish all feelings of devotion for them in the minds of the faithful. And persisting in their savagery as far as the Temple of the Lord, they began to destroy it the more unrestrainedly, the more passionately they burn to undermine the principles of the Christian religion and to shatter the edifice of the orthodox faith.[10]

Despite Innocent IV's preparations, allotment of finances, and frantic calls for a Crusade, most of the major players were unresponsive. King Henry had his own problems with the nobles of England, and Emperor Frederick was in open conflict with the pope. Only one responded—and even before the pope had made his summons: Louis IX, the king of France.

Louis IX of France

King Louis IX was born on April 25, 1214. After his father's untimely death, the twelve-year-old prince was crowned king of France in 1226, with his mother acting as regent and counsellor. Louis came from a long line of Crusaders: his mother, Blanche, was the daughter of Alfonso VIII of Castile and younger sister of Berenguela, making Louis a grandson of the hero of the battle of Las Navas de Tolosa, and first cousin of

Ferdinand III, last chapter's hero. Richard Lionheart was his granduncle (by marriage).

Apparently even Louis's appearance suggested a Crusader lineage; for "he had the blue eyes, the fair complexion, and yellow hair which belonged to the House of Charlemagne"—one of the earliest Frankish Defenders against Islam—"from which he descended through his grand-mother, Isabel Hainault."[11] (One Muslim would later write that "He was of fine appearance.")[12]

His mother, Blanche, exercised an immense influence on his life and—as her elder sister, Berenguela, had done with Ferdinand III—carefully reared Louis. According to Geoffrey of Beaulieu (d.1274), a close confidant of the king, due to the "wise foresight of his mother," Louis "began to develop as a boy of outstanding talent and promise, and to grow day by day to perfected manhood, and to seek the Lord."[13]

Even so, and in keeping with the times, Blanche's concern for her son's soul overshadowed her concern for his life. "She used to say about me," Louis once reflected, "because she loved me above all other mortals, that if I were sick unto death and I were not able to get well except by committing a mortal sin, that she would prefer that I die than that I should offend the Creator."[14]

Louis attended mass daily, prayed punctually, and performed works of charity. He grew to be of courteous and gentle speech. In 1234, at age twenty, the king married Margaret of Provence, whose beauty and religious devotion were renowned. They raised their nine children (two others died in infancy) with pious discipline and severity. Like mother like son, Louis once said that he "would sooner wish that all [his] sons were dead than that they might offend God through mortal sin."[15]

From his earliest youth, Louis had a frail constitution and was prone to sickness. Soon after learning about the jihadist sack of Jerusalem, in late 1244, Louis fell severely ill with a high fever and dysentery. Week after week, his condition deteriorated until his family, leading barons and churchmen found themselves helplessly standing around their young king's deathbed. Finally, on a grey day he was pronounced dead; a sheet was pulled over him, and everyone in the chamber burst into tears—his mother hysterically so. Unwilling to give up on Louis, his brother Robert implored the corpse-king to return, at which point Louis, it is relayed, suddenly sat up and cried that he would take the cross—"For my spirit has long been overseas; and my body will go there, if it is God's will, and will wrest the land from the Saracens. Blessed is he who aids me in that!"[16]

So Louis took the Cross in December 1244, even before Innocent IV had formally called for a Crusade. Although ecstatic at his sudden recovery, both queens—his mother and wife—soon realized that he was deadly serious about Jerusalem and fell to their knees imploring him not to go. When his mother managed to have his vow commuted, he took it again.

Louis spent the following three years making preparations and setting his affairs in order. As one of Christendom's wealthiest kings, and with additional tithes raised from French churches, Louis's Crusade (accounted the Seventh by modern historians) was arguably the best funded and meticulously prepared of all Crusades. Other Christian kings, Henry III in England and Haakon of Norway, offered their encouragement but failed to contribute anything of consequence. Not only would Louis's Crusade be an overwhelmingly French affair, it would be a family one, too: his three younger brothers—and his wife, Margaret—would join him.

On June 12, 1448, Louis received his pilgrim's staff, heard mass at Notre Dame, and then left Paris, "not with military pomp, but barefooted, in pilgrim's habit." An eyewitness monk described him as "thin and haggard, rather tall, with the face of an angel. He seemed more like a monk than a soldier." The contrite king handed his scepter to his capable mother, who followed his procession as far as she could. When they parted she expressed a foreboding and lamented that they would never meet again.[17]

On September 17, Louis's fleets arrived in Cyprus, where he had sent many provisions in advance, and wintered there. During that time, as many as 260 Crusaders, including several notables, got sick and died.[18]

Mongolian Intermission

One of the more interesting episodes during Louis's Cyprus stay concerns the Mongols, who two decades earlier had burst onto the scene of world history, slaughtering and laying waste to everything on their westward path from Mongolia. The fact that most of the Mongols' victims were Muslim—ultimately a reflection of geography, nothing more—breathed life into the centuries-old European rumors of a magnificently powerful Christian king, a "priest king," aptly named Prester John. Reportedly living somewhere "in the East," it was believed that one day he would ride out at the head of a vast host and destroy the Muslims living between him and his Western coreligionists.

In late December 1248, a Mongol embassy arrived in Cyprus, seemingly confirming these rumors. They brought a letter to Louis from Eljigidei, a Christian Mongol commander operating in Persia. As opposed to the typical Mongol missive that was full of boasting, threats, and demands for submission and tribute—which Louis was familiar with, having received such an ultimatum in 1247—this letter opened with immense flattery, referring to Louis as "the great king of many territories, the mighty bulwark of the world, the sword of Christianity, the victor of the faith of baptism," and so on.[19]

The missive proposed an alliance between Louis and the Mongols against those "who despise the Cross"—a reference to the Muslims that lay between them. Güyük, the Great Khan, who was apparently very sympathetic to Christianity—some sources even say he was a convert—had reversed everything that the Christians in the East had suffered under Islam, so that they were all now "free from slavery and tribute," their properties safe and their destroyed churches rebuilt. The embassy carrying the letter added that, to avenge what Muslims had done to Christians, Güyük was about to invade the capital of the Abbasid caliphate, Baghdad, and, as such, desired the friendship of the French king.[20]

Another letter from the constable of Armenia to the king of Cyprus sent a few weeks before the Mongol embassy arrived—and saying, based on eyewitness testimony, that "the Saracens, who used to inspire them [Christians] with fear, now receive back [from the Mongols] what they did [then] twice over"—further heightened expectations among the Crusaders.[21] Louis responded by sending a gift-bearing embassy to open talks with the Khan and/or his viceroy.

The Battle of Damietta

In late May, 1249, Louis and his army, which now consisted of some twenty-five thousand Crusaders, including the knights of the Temple and Hospital, set sail from Cyprus. Their destination, based on the by now standard Crusader logic that Egypt must be neutralized before Jerusalem could be secured, was the Egyptian port of Damietta. Considering that Damietta was also the focus of the Fifth Crusade (1217-1221), none of this came as a surprise to Egyptian sultan al-Salih Ayyub. He sent men under Emir Fahreddin to refortify Damietta's garrison and hold the coast against any Crusader landing. The mastermind behind the Turcoman sack of Jerusalem in 1244 next sent a message warning Louis to forfend: "No one has ever attacked us without feeling our superiority," the sultan boasted. "Recollect the conquests we have made from the Christians; we have driven them from the lands they possessed;* their strongest towns have fallen under our blows."[22]

By June 4, the Christian fleet had anchored on the west bank of the Nile, across from Damietta. Between it and the city, legions of Muslims lined the shore and river bank, where they "made a loud and terrible noise with horns and cymbals."[23] A council was held in the king's ship. Although some said to wait for the other ships that had been delayed by a storm, Louis was set on taking the shore now. "Our men," wrote Gui, one of the knights present, "seeing the lord King's steadfastness and unwavering resolve, at his bidding made ready...to occupy the shore by force and go on land."[24] When his counsellors urged him not to join in the initial landing, due to the danger it posed to his person, Louis responded, "I am only one individual whose life, when God wills it, will be snuffed out like any other man's."[25]

And so, on June 6, to a loud battle cry, the Crusaders furiously paddled to the shore in smaller boats, and "in accordance with the lord King's strict and most urgent command, hastily leaped into the sea up to their loins." Clad in heavy iron and slowly plodding toward the coast, they were met by and fended off a hail of arrows. "Of all the ships, the lord King's put in first," continues Gui.[26] As his granduncle Richard Lionheart had done under similar circumstances nearly sixty years earlier at Jaffa, "Louis leapt into the water up to his armpits and waded ashore, shield round neck, helm on head, and sword in hand."[27]

Jean de Joinville (1224–1317), a close friend of Louis who participated in and is a chief source of the Seventh Crusade, continues: "So

---

* The heart of the Muslim world, the Middle East and North Africa—from Iraq in the east to Morocco in the west—later Turkey, and for centuries Spain and the Balkans, were originally inhabited by and conquered from Christians. Muslims, such as Sultan al-Salih Ayyub, were well aware of this fact.

soon as they [Muslims] saw us land, they came toward us, hotly spurring. We, when we saw them coming, fixed the points of our shields into the sand and the handles of our lances in the sand with the points set towards them." Confronted by this massive spike-studded shield wall, and seeing "the lances about to enter into their bellies," the Muslims "turned about and fled"—all except one, who, thinking his comrades were charging behind him, was instantly "cut down."[28]

Thereafter, the Crusaders "fell manfully upon the enemies of the Cross like strong athletes of the Lord," writes Gui: "The armed Saracens, stationed mounted on the shore, disputed the land with us…maintaining a dense fire of javelins and arrows against our men. And yet our men… pushed on and set foot on the land despite the Saracens."[29] The more the Muslims gave way, the more the Christians advanced onto dry ground. Before long, horses had been ferried over and mounted, leading to heavy, splashy cavalry charges, all under the cover of missile fire from the Christian fleet. Terrified by such daring, the Muslims tucked tail and ran.

Rather than falling back on and holding Damietta, Emir Fahreddin led his men some forty miles south of the Europeans. On seeing them flee, and not wanting to face, in the words of Muslim chroniclers, "the fury of the Christians," the garrison in Damietta, followed by its entire citizenry, fled the city under the cover of night in great disorder and panic—"barefoot and unclad, hungry and thirsty, in poverty and disarray, women and children" [30]—though not before cutting the throats or "dashing out the brains" of most of their Christian prisoners, many of whom were captured during the Fifth Crusade.[31] A few escaped captives and slaves, crying "Blessed is he that cometh in the name of the Lord," intercepted the Crusaders on their march to Damietta, which they were astonished to find completely deserted.[32]

On the morning following this spectacular start to his Crusade, Louis and his men went to Damietta's chief mosque. "Here, three days earlier," a shocked Gui wrote, "the prisoners categorically assured us, the most filthy Mahomet had been glorified with abominable sacrifices, cries from on high, and the blast of trumpets."[33] But because the mosque was formerly a church—"where Christians long ago had been in the habit of celebrating Mass and ringing their bells"[34]—like his cousin Ferdinand III, the king had the mosque purified with holy water and, "once it had been utterly purged of the pagans' filth," celebrated mass there.[35] In this manner, and as Blanche wrote to Henry III, "the site of the mosque, which some time ago—when the city was previously captured [by Muslims in the seventh century]—was the Church of the Blessed Virgin Mary, was reconciled and thanks were given there to God Most High."[36]

As these accounts make clear, thirteenth century European Christians were not oblivious to the fact that all of the Near East and North Africa—not just Jerusalem—were originally part of Christendom. This comes out especially in the Crusaders' talk concerning Egypt. For example, the foundation charter for the re-consecration of this church-turned-mosque-turned-church again, dated November 1249, makes the following assertions: "after this country [Egypt] is liberated from the hands of the infidels" and "when this land is liberated." Similarly, Guillaume de Sonnac, the Grand Master of the Templars, wrote about how "the Lord King plans…to return the entire country [of Egypt] to Christian worship."[37]

Elsewhere in Egypt, the Crusader takeover of Damietta was deemed a great and "terrible disaster, the like of which had never happened," writes Ibn Wasil (1208–1298), a Cairo-based contemporary of and chief Arabic source for the Seventh Crusade.[38] Fear gripped the Egyptian populace; the ease with which the Christians had conquered Damietta, the people lamented, may well result "in their conquest of Egypt and even (Allah forbid) of the whole of Islam."[39] They had reason to fear; it was well known that, with his conquest of Seville just one year earlier, Louis's own cousin, Ferdinand, had subdued all of al-Andalus, or Muslim Spain.

Because they had taken Damietta much sooner than anticipated—it had taken the Fifth Crusaders five months, not one day—Louis's schedule was disrupted. The flooding of the Nile was imminent and would make much of the land impassable. Accordingly, they would need to stay in Damietta for several months before continuing along the Nile to Mansoura. Queen Margaret and her ladies, with a guard of five hundred knights, resided inside the city, while the king and the bulk of his forces camped outside. All this time, local Muslims and roaming Bedouins continuously harassed, launched raids on, and skirmished with the Christians. "The Saracens," Joinville writes, "entered every night into the camp on foot and killed our people there where they found them sleeping." Most of them were decapitated, as Sultan al-Salih had offered "a besant of gold for every Christian man's head."[40]

The Battle of Mansoura

Knowing Mansoura was the Crusaders' next target, the sultan continued refortifying it, and proclaimed a jihad in its defense. As a result, "war galleys large and small arrived," writes Ibn Wasil, "complete with equipment and fighting men…while infantry, common folk and volunteers for the Holy War arrived at Mansura from every other region in a great throng that could not be counted."[41]

On November 20, the Christian army marched out south of Damietta for Mansoura along the Nile's eastern bank; a convoy of supply-carrying boats sailed alongside it. Due to the many watercourses and canals, which were often guarded by the enemy, the journey was fraught with difficulties. At one point, the Templars, who were always in the van, damned and charged over a waterway and annihilated five hundred Muslim horsemen, thereby clearing a path for and emboldening the rest.[42]

So it went for a month, until they reached the outskirts of Mansoura on December 21, 1249. There they found Emir Fahreddin's army—the same that had cravenly abandoned Damietta—encamped before the city, which was further blocked to the Crusaders by a tributary of the Nile. The Christian army camped across Fahreddin's camp, on a wedge of land between the Nile and said tributary. In a surviving letter, Louis explains what happened next:

> [W]e began to build over it [the tributary] a causeway, which would enable the Christian army to cross, and we devoted several days to this, with vast effort and at great risk and expense. The Saracens, resisting us with all their efforts, set up against the engines we had built there several machines of their own, and with these they shattered and broke with stones our wooden fortresses that we had placed over the crossing and utterly consumed them with Greek fire.[43]

Joinville described how this fiery bombardment, which sounded "like heaven's thunder," rained down on the Crusader camp for several nights. In the midst of this life-consuming inferno he would see Louis on his knees, his hands raised to and imploring God to protect his people.[44]

Matters remained at a standstill—with the Muslims torching every causeway the Christians built—until a Bedouin informant, in exchange for a rich reward, revealed a fordable area four miles downstream. Under the cover of darkness in the early morning of February 8, 1250, Louis dispatched the Templars, with his brother Robert of Artois and his men bringing the rear. Their mission was to ford and secure the landing for the main army, which would later follow with Louis.

It was a difficult and slippery crossing, and many knights drowned in the damp darkness; but the Templars and Robert managed to make it on the other side. Rather than wait for Louis, however, his younger brother decided to take the initiative and attack the unsuspecting Egyptian camp. The Muslims were so taken unawares that Emir Fahreddin was hewn down in his tent before he could even grab his sword.

Now in a battle-frenzy, Robert threw all caution to the wind and ordered the Crusaders to advance from Fahreddin's camp to Mansoura itself. Guillaume de Sonnac, the more experienced Templar Grand Master, begged him to stick to the plan and await Louis—only to be upbraided and labeled a coward by Robert. Continued goads and insults overcame Guillaume's wisdom until he cried, "Lift up our banner, then—let us go to our death!"[45] They charged into the city, hacking and hewing all and sundry, and even managed to reach Sultan al-Salih Ayyub's own palace.

There they were met by a different breed of Muslim warrior: the *Mamluks*—from an Arabic word meaning "owned"—slave-soldiers, at first of Turkic, later of Circassian, origin that the Ayyubids, especially under the current sultan, had been importing into Egypt in greater and greater numbers and increasingly relying on. From earliest youth, they were purchased or captured, converted to Islam and trained in a harsh and disciplinary environment for warfare. Although their piety was questionable—"Each one of them fornicates more than a monkey, steals more than a rat, and is more harmful than a wolf," observed al-Maqrizi—they excelled at holy war, jihad.[46]

Led by their leader, Rukn al-Din ("Cornerstone of Islam"), better known as Baibars (1223–1277), an especially ruthless slave-soldier, the Mamluks now violently engaged the Christians inside Mansoura. The narrow city streets made fighting and maneuvering especially difficult for the knights, many of whom were still mounted. Muslim citizens joined the fray by hurling missiles from the windows and porches of their homes. As a result, the Crusaders, including the king's brother, Robert—who had holed himself in and fought for hours from a house—were butchered to a man. Nearly three hundred battle-hardened Templars also fell on that day; only Grand Master Guillaume, who lost an eye, and four others managed to escape.

By now, Louis and the main army had crossed the ford and were nearing Fahreddin's camp. Instead of finding Robert and the Templars waiting there, the thundering sound of approaching hoof beats were heard, as the victorious Mamluks and now emboldened Muslims poured out of Mansoura to finish the rest of the Crusaders.

A fierce battle ensued and lasted all day. In the midst of the fray, Joinville espied his king: "Never have I seen so fair a knight!" he recalled. "For he seemed by the head and shoulders to tower above his people; and on his head was a gilded helm, and in his hand a German [large, double-handed] sword." With so many fighters on both sides, and on such a small strip of land, the fighting was very close and "no one drew bow or crossbow; it was a battle of mace and sword between the Turks and our people, all intermingled."[47] Along with the many slain on both sides, the sources tell of hacked limbs and noses, gouged eyes, and mangled faces. In the chaos, six Muslim fighters surrounded the king; they tried to grab his horse's bridle to lead him away. But "he alone delivered himself striking at them great strokes with his sword," says Joinville. "And when his people saw how he was defending himself, they took courage, and many of them abandoned thought of taking flight across the river, and drew to the king's side to help him."[48]

The day ended with the Muslims retreating back to Mansoura. The Christians had won the shore—though at great cost—secured Fahreddin's camp, and captured its war engines that had long harried them. Although casualties were high on both sides, it mattered less to the Muslims: being on their own home-base, they had an endless supply of men.

As the sun set, a bloodied and bruised Louis reclined in an enemy tent. Still unaware of the fate of his brother, Robert, when a Hospitaller passed by, Louis inquired if he knew aught of the count of Artois, to which he said, Yes: "of a certainty he was in paradise." "Ah, sire," continued the Hospitaller on seeing Louis's countenance disfigure, "be of good comfort herein, for never did King of France gain such honour as you have gained this day. For, in order to fight your enemies, you have passed over a river swimming, and you have discomfited them, and driven them from the field, and taken their engines, and also their tents, wherein you will sleep this night." Louis smiled and said, "Let God be worshipped for all He has given me." Even as he gave thanks, however, Joinville, who witnessed and recorded this exchange, espied tears streaking down the king's face.[49]

A bridge was quickly erected between the old and new Christian camps and fresh reserves crossed over—and not a moment too soon. For on Friday, February 11—after mosque prayers, when the sheikhs riled the Muslims of Mansoura to jihad—and in the words of a surviving Templar:

> [The Muslims] moved in from every side, that is, by land and water, launching horrific attacks on the Christian army. Advancing with lances, swords and various missiles, and shooting from virtually every direction a virtual hail of arrows from morning to evening, they did not cease to harass the resisting Christians, approaching in their audacity so close as to engage in hand-to-hand combat and attacking the king's own camp.[50]

After fighting them off, Louis learned that the camp of his other brother, Charles of Anjou, was being overwhelmed. Not about to lose another brother, "he rode spurring amidst his brother's men, with his sword in his fist, and dashed so far among the Turks that they burnt the crupper of his horse with Greek fire. And by this charge that the king made he succoured [Charles] and his men, and drove the Turks from the camp."[51] Even so, Louis sustained "not a few wounds that day," wrote the anonymous Templar; moreover, "the Sultan had gained heart and his men were rendered keener by their success and braver by their victory."[52]

As usual, the indigenous Christians, Egypt's Copts, were first to feel the brunt of this reborn sense of Islamic triumphalism over Christianity: "elated Muslims throughout the region precipitated popular actions against native Egyptian Christians, including the desecration of Christian holy space."[53] Such collective punishment was always par for the course. Earlier, the Fifth Crusade in Egypt "had roused all the Muslim fanaticism from which the Copts suffered." Then, the Muslim army marching to meet the Crusaders at Damietta "destroyed every [Coptic] church by which they passed; even the church of St. Mark in the suburbs of Alexandria was leveled to the ground."[54]

Now 'Everything Turned Contrary to Our Desires'

Back in November, when the Crusaders were still in Damietta, Sultan al-Salih Ayyub had died of illness. This was kept secret until February 28, when his son, al-Muazzam Turanshah, arrived in and became Egypt's latest Ayyubid master. Rather than war against the Crusaders, this wily sultan had dismantled ships surreptitiously carried past the Crusader camp in camel caravans and reassembled near—and thereby forcibly cutting off their supply line from—Damietta. Then, he handed the reins of war to nature and time. Louis later described these developments in a letter:

> When some days had elapsed...the Sultan's son reached Manssora from the East, and the Egyptians beat their drums and rejoiced at his arrival, and received him as their ruler. This gave no small boost to their morale, while on our side from that point onwards, by what judgement of God I know not, everything turned out contrary to our desires. A plague of different sicknesses broke out, and a general mortality among both men and horses, with the result that there were scarcely any in the army who did not mourn those who had died or were mortally ill. By this means the Christian army was reduced and the greater part had perished.... [M]any died of starvation.[55]

What happened is this: the Muslims had cast their many dead into the river and these now rotted corpses had resurfaced and congregated near the impassable makeshift bridge connecting the original Crusader camp with Fahreddin's captured camp, thereby polluting the water supply and spreading disease. It took eight days for a hundred laborers to clear the water of the bloated bodies, but by then the damage was done: the toxins in the air, water, and even food supply—for the fish the Christians ate had gorged on and been infected by the pestilent corpses—soon led to a plague that infected the entire camp.[56] "The ailment that had afflicted the Christian army in general was so severe that scarcely anyone avoided it," Charles of Anjou, the king's brother and future king of Sicily, said thirty-two years later in a deposition. "They suffered in their teeth and gums, and from dysentery, and the sick developed dark patches on their thighs or legs."[57]

The men's flesh, particularly around their legs, turned black and brittle, and dead flesh grew around and covered their gums. "Great pity it was to hear the cry throughout the camp of the people whose dead flesh was being cut away," Joinville recollected; "for they cried like women labouring of child." These horrors reached the point that a few Christians even deserted to their enemies, on condition of converting to Islam.[58]

For over a month, from mid-February to late March, Louis ordered his men to persevere as best they could. Because many sacrifices had been made to bring them to this point, the thought of abandoning the hard-won and strategically placed camp of Fahreddin across Mansoura was intolerable. But try as best they could, matters worsened. By the start of April, only one-sixth of the Crusader army was alive or in fighting condition.[*]

Even Louis, whose constitution was never hale, was now "suffering from the general plague and dysentery, so wasted that his bones seemed coming through the skin."[59] By April 3, "the King succumbed to this disease" and "was in complete distress," to quote his brother, Charles. "In informal moments he showed [his] brothers extensive dark patches on one of his legs. There was no physician."[60] It got to the point that Louis "fainted several times," writes Joinville, "and because of the sore dysentery from which he suffered, it was necessary to cut away the lower part of his drawers, so frequent were his necessities."[61]

There was nothing left for the Crusaders but to "entrust themselves all to the two-edged judgment of war or death," wrote the anonymous Templar. Under the cover of night on April 5,

> [The Crusaders] retreated along the [Nile] river towards Damietta, weakened and in no state to fight, and as the enemy, who were positioned as guardians of the banks, hurled missiles and Greek fire, they were pierced or set alight, or were slaughtered by the warriors, or drowned. The remainder engaged in close fighting with the enemy for as long as they were able. But what could a few achieve against such a great number of enemies, the hungry and starving against those who were alert and refreshed, those who did not know the terrain against natives? They stood their ground in the conflict, however, though the bloodshed was indescribable, until they were pitiably vanquished— alas! ....But almost all fought on until they breathed their last.[62]

---

[*] The *Gloriosissimi Regis*, which was compiled half a century later, gives more concrete numbers, saying that "bodily death" caused the army to be "reduced from thirty-two thousand in number to six thousand" (Gaposchkin, 69).

Although most Crusaders, including Louis, had taken the road to Damietta by land, their sick and dying were loaded in boats sailing on the Nile for the Crusader stronghold on the coast. On April 6, during the height of Muslim attacks—when the earth had become virtually invisible from countless protruding arrows—the ailing king "stood propped up against his saddle," as his chief counselors "urged him singly and in unison, to save himself by going on board ship." "But he would listen to none," writes Joinville, "and said he would never leave his people, and should make such an end as they made."[63] When his brother Charles rebuked him, saying, "you could be the cause of our deaths," the "King, agitated and with a fierce look," replied: "Count of Anjou, Count of Anjou! If you find me a burden, leave me behind, since I will not desert my people."[64] Barely managing to remount and spur his horse to the fighting, he cried back, "I have brought my people here, and I will take them back with me or die with them!"[65]

Louis's commitment to his men during this final act of the Seventh Crusade is widely attested. "The king," Joinville affirms, "who had upon him the sickness of the host and a very evil dysentery, could easily have got away on the galleys, if he had been so minded; but he said that, please God, he would never abandon his people."[66] Even Muslims, such as Sa'd al-Din ibn Hamawiya (d. 1276), an Egyptian contemporary, confirmed that "If the Frenchman had only wished to save himself, he could have taken refuge.... Yet he stayed in the thick of it to protect his followers."[67]

And so Louis's lot was theirs. So overwhelmed by the Muslim mass, and with thousands of Christian dead on the ground, the king, on bended knee, and in an effort to secure mercy for whatever of his men remained, offered the hilt of his sword to his enemies in surrender. Immediately he "was bound with a chain, and in this state conducted [back] to Mansoura," as were many other nobles, including his two brothers Alphonse and Charles—anyone who might fetch a high ransom.[68] No mercy, however, was shown to the rank and file.

Although countless were butchered—Templar Grand Master Guillaume de Sonnac lost his other eye and was burned with fire before being decapitated—the "number of slaves was so great, it was embarrassing," writes al-Maqrizi. So Sultan Turanshah ordered one of his henchmen "to put them to death.... Every night this cruel minister of the vengeance of his master had from three to four hundred of the prisoners brought from their places of confinement, and, after he had caused them to be beheaded, their bodies were thrown into the Nile."[69] Turanshah especially had no use for the many sick and dying found in the Christian boats and ordered them burned alive in their vessels.[70]

It was an Islamic victory of a magnitude unheard of. After describing the gory aftermath of seven thousand Christians slaughtered, burned, or drowned, Sa'd al-Din wrote, "I saw the dead, and they covered the earth in their profusion.... It was a day of the kind the Muslims had never seen before.... Of the Muslims, there were slain no more than a hundred."[71]

Hostage Crisis

Great now was the gloating; in the prisons the Muslims "blasphemed against Christ and ridiculed our men," who were "most vilely destroyed and treated with contempt," writes the anonymous Templar.[72] Mocking Louis, they said they would parade him in chains throughout Asia and present him as a gift to the caliph in Baghdad. As for the triumphant sultan, "being freed from a disagreeable war," Turanshah "gave himself up to all sorts of debauchery."[73]

It was a dark time. As so many Crusaders had done before—recall King Richard I's laments—the anonymous Templar questioned God's justice in a letter:

> O God, Whose "ways are past finding out" and Whose "judgments are unsearchable," did not Thy faithful come to repulse Thine enemies and to liberate from them the land of Thy birth, Thine own land, and to worship there Thy footprints? But in this affair Thou hast clearly shown mortal men how precarious is the joy of this world. Of a truth the whole of Christendom should duly bewail with bitter groans the terrible fate that befell the King of France and the Christian army as they fought against the infidel that pestilential day, the 6 April. Neither has to this day such an event been witnessed or reported.[*][74]

But if these were the understandable sentiments of a warrior-monk devoted to recovering Christ's Sepulchre, they were not, amazingly, shared by Louis himself—this man, this king, who had lost more than

---

* In fact, nearly two centuries earlier in 1071, the Eastern Roman Emperor, Romanos IV Diogenes, was also captured by the Turks after their decisive victory over the Christians at the battle of Manzikert.

everyone else. Based on extant eyewitness accounts from fellow prisoners, historian Frederick Perry writes the following of the king's captivity:

> Racked by illness and pain—though his life was saved through the skill of Saracen physicians—without attendants, clothes, or the common necessaries of life, threatened with torture or death, amid the overthrow of his hopes and the ruin of the holy cause to which he was vowed, he preserved an outward calm and a cheerful faith which were the marvel of all beholders. He was not heard to utter a single murmur against the decree of Providence, a single complaint or angry word at the great or petty misfortunes in which he was fallen; but divided his time between the assiduous practice of prayer and devotion, and the endeavour to secure tolerable terms for his army and himself without injury to the interests of Christendom.[75]

Again, Muslim accounts are in agreement. After describing his behavior during prison along similar lines, Sa'd al-Din adds, "He was a man of wisdom, constancy and faith (in their fashion), and they [other Christian captives] put their trust in him."[76]

Louis's disposition is all the more marvelous considering what he saw during his captivity, namely, the conversion to Islam or slaughter of his men, and constant blasphemy against Christianity, which, for someone like Louis, was insufferable. In his own words, "that most wicked race has offended the Creator by whipping the cross, spitting upon it, and finally trampling it underfoot."[77] Joinville, who was also present, offers a glimpse of the conversion process:

> Many of the knights and other people were kept by the Saracens in a court enclosed by mud walls. From this enclosed place they caused them to be taken, one after the other, and asked them, "Will you renounce your faith?" Those who would not renounce were set to one side, and their heads were cut off; and those who renounced were set on the other side.[78]

Because Louis, as one of the most powerful and influential European monarchs, had much to offer, conversion or death were not to be his lot. Damietta, moreover, still remained securely in Crusader hands, under the able leadership of his wife, Margaret. On learning of Louis's capture, the stoical woman had shown great determination to secure Damietta; she ordered more fortifications raised around it and commanded her husband's men to prepare to fight to the death—and to kill her and her newborn son, John, should the Muslims breach the city.

In other words, Damietta was a potential headache for the new sultan. Left in Christian hands and with access to the sea, it could become another coastal Crusader kingdom and base for ongoing operations and invasions against Egypt. To prevent this, Turanshah's men threatened Louis with menacing words and promises of a slow and agonizing death, to which the laconic king only replied, "God's will be done." Seeing he would not budge, and needing to conclude this Crusader affair soon to deal with other threats from the East, the Muslims became more reasonable.

In the end, a bargain was struck: Louis would relinquish Damietta, pay eight hundred thousand bezants, and release his Muslim captives; in exchange, the Muslims would release him and all Christian captives captured in the last two years.

A Mamluk Coup d'état

Soon after the bargain was struck, the Mamluks revolted against their sultan. They had always despised Turanshah; for he never missed the opportunity to remind them that, for all their valor, they were still his slaves. Moreover, according to Muslim accounts, "he engaged in acts of depravity with his father's Mamluks and concubines." Even after they had saved the day at Mansoura, he treated them with contempt and would "rehearse their execution, by slashing the heads off candles while drunk and calling out their names."[79] All during the war with the Christians, the Mamluks tolerated him; once it was over, they meted out their vengeance upon him.

A few days after striking the aforementioned bargain with Louis, as Turanshah sat at a victory banquet with his slave soldiers surrounding him, their leader, Baibars, "gave him the first blow with his sabre, and, though Turanshah parried it with his hand, he lost his fingers." Al-Maqrizi continues:

> He then fled to the tower which…was but a short distance from his tent. The conspirators followed him, and, finding he had closed the door, set fire to it. The whole army saw what was passing; but, as he was a prince universally detested, no one came forward in his

Church of the Holy Sepulchre, Jerusalem.

Godfrey and other First Crusaders set off.

*Above: A sketch of the Cid, "he of the flowing beard." **Right:** Godfrey statue, Brussels.*

*Below: Godfrey's sword, when it was still displayed in the Church of the Holy Sepulchre; photo from 1854. **Below right:** Godfrey breaks into Muslim-held Jerusalem.*

Left: Pelagius (Pelayo) declared first Christian king of Spain following its fall to Islam in the eighth century.

Below: Cid compels Alfonso VI to swear on a Bible that he had nothing to do with the killing of his brother, Sancho II.

Above: Cid statue, Burgos.
Right: Saladin oversees the expulsion and enslavement of Christians from Jerusalem. *Below:* Richard Lionheart pulverizes Muslims at Arsuf.

Far left: Richard statue, Palace of Westminster.

Left: Painting of Richard I, 1841.

Below: Richard storms the shores of Jaffa.

Above: Painting of Ferdinand III, c. 1650.

Right: Painting of Santiago Matamoros, Saint James the Moor-Slayer, Cathedral of Seville.

Below: Muhammad I of Granada (Ibn al-Ahmar) surrenders Jaen to Ferdinand.

Above: Ferdinand's sword, Lobera, Cathedral of Seville.

Below: The last days of Saint Ferdinand, 1887 painting.

Bottom: Captured Córdoban Muslims return bells of Saint James to his shrine, Santiago de Compostela, in Galicia.

Above: Saint Ferdinand statue, Seville.

Right: Contemporary miniature of Saint Louis, thirteenth century.

Below: Louis IX in battle.

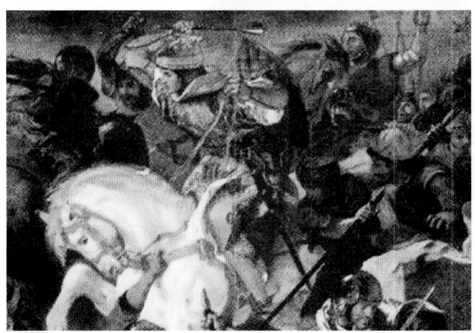

Left: Louis gives thanks for the relatively easy capture of Damietta.

Below: "Apotheosis of Saint Louis" statue, St. Louis, Missouri. BLM and Muslim activists attacked and are still trying to take it down due to Louis's alleged "Islamophobia."

Left: Louis captured in Egypt.

1840 painting of the siege of Acre, 1291, which ushered in the final expulsion of the Crusaders from the Holy Land.

Above: Ottoman Turks dragging away European slave-girls, woodcut, 1530.

Left: Near contemporary depiction of John Hunyadi, the "White Knight of Wallachia," c. 1488.

Battle of Varna: Moments before being beheaded, King Ladislaus (L) rushes into the Turkish ranks as Sultan Murad II (R) implores Allah.

Right: John Hunyadi statue, Buda.

Below: Battle of Belgrade: John Hunyadi and John Capistrano lead the final charge against the Turks.

Left: *Bust of George Kastrioti, Skanderbeg, Palace of the Nations, Geneva.*

Below: *Skanderbeg dueling with a Tatar at the Ottoman court, sixteenth century drawing.*

Top: Skanderbeg, "Lord Alexander."

Right: Monument to Skanderbeg, Croya.

Bottom: Final days of Skanderbeg, sixteenth century engraving.

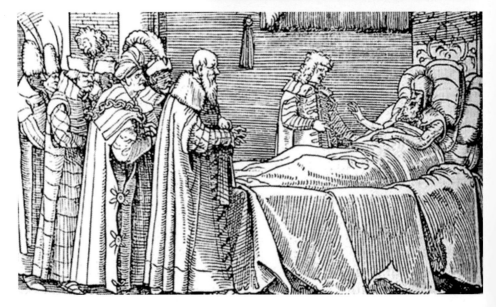

Top: *Propagandistic German-language pamphlet, c. 1500, of Vlad dining in his Forest of the Impaled.*

Left: *Painting of Vlad, a copy of an original made during his lifetime, c. 1560, Ambras Castle.*

Bottom: *Remains of Vlad III Dracula's castle, Poenari, Romania.*

Top: Painting of Vlad the Impaler, moments before nailing his Turkish envoys' turbans to their heads, c.1870.

Right: Bust of Vlad, Sighişoara, Romania.

Bottom: Painting of Dracula's "Night Attack," where he sought to assassinate Sultan Muhammad II, 1866.

defense. It was in vain he cried from the top of the tower, that he would abdicate his throne…; the assassins were inflexible. The flames at length gaining on the tower, he attempted to leap into the Nile; but his dress caught as he was falling, and he remained some time suspended in the air. In this state, he received many wounds from sabres, and then fell into the river, where he was drowned. Thus iron, fire, and water contributed to put an end to his life.[80]

Now crazed and in a blood-frenzy, the assassins continued by barging into Louis's cell, "in high fury, with bloody hands still steaming with hot gore and arms dripping with fresh-spilled blood," recalled William of Chartres, another close confidant of the king who was present.[81] Some, seething with rage, made as if to kill the king, while others pretended to be his friends—claiming they had killed Turanshah because he was about to betray and put to death all the Christians once Damietta had been surrendered.[82]

According to Joinville, one Mamluk even carved out and brought Turanshah's heart "to the king, his hand all reeking with blood, and said: 'What will you give me?—for I have slain your enemy, who, had he lived, would have slain you!' And the king answered him never a word."[83] This same Mamluk, apparently impressed but unfamiliar with the significance of Christian knighthood, demanded that Louis knight him then and there. The king refused, demands turned to threats, and Louis's companions advised compliance. He calmly replied that "neither for death nor for life would he honor an infidel with the belt of knighthood."[84]

After this rude intrusion, the Muslims withdrew and for the next three days discussed the Christians' fate. Some urged to slaughter them all and get it over with. In the end, and in what was later deemed a miracle, they decided to ratify Louis's treaty with Turanshah: the same terms were agreed upon, with a new addition.

Well aware of Louis's religious sincerity, they insisted that he take an oath that "if the king did not observe his covenants with the emirs, he should be as dishonoured as a Christian who denies God and His law, and who, in despite of God, spits upon the Cross, and tramples upon it."[85] Horrified, Louis refused to utter the words, despite a renewal of threats. When he still refused, the Muslims clearly articulated to a Christian familiar with Arabic the consequences of Louis's failure to take the oath. "Sire," he implored, "the emirs are greatly incensed…and be assured that if you do not swear this oath they will cause your head to be cut off, as well as the heads of all your people." "The king," continues Joinville, "replied that they could act in this matter as it seemed best to them; but that he liked better to die as a good Christian." The Muslims next took to torturing the aged patriarch of Jerusalem, who had come to negotiate on behalf of the Christians under the safe but now expired conduct of Turanshah, until he begged the king to take the oath, and he, the patriarch, would "take upon my own soul whatsoever there may be of sin in the oath that you take!" Joinville says "I know not how this matter of the oath was settled; but in the end the emirs held themselves satisfied," and the treaty was ratified.[86]

Inasmuch as Louis's unperturbed demeanor and unswerving disposition may seem exaggerated, belonging to the realm of hagiography, not history, the testimony of William of Chartres is worth quoting at length:

> Despite the fact that I was almost always with him at all times and places [during their Egyptian captivity], it is beyond my power to lay out just how wisely, how faithfully, and how constantly he bore himself in all things with respect to the Saracens, who came at him with frightening, overbearing threats and demands. This, however, I can assert in all truth and desire for brevity: that in everything he did he was utterly honest, shrewd in his answers, careful and true in his dealings, and fearless in his refusals. Under all pressure he always remained the soul of constancy, so that even the leading emirs marveled at him and said [as much] to the king, when he remained so unmoved in the face of unrelenting demands.... But he could not be swayed in the least by their fierce pressure and threats, or be made to promise anything, or concede or swear to anything that would result in harm to Christianity or burden his conscience. All who were there, even the higher Christian nobility, were amazed at how confident and unperturbed he was, while they themselves were quite afraid.[87]

Surprisingly, Louis even managed to keep his good humor. During a visit, the emir Husam al-Din, who found Louis to be "an extremely wise and intelligent man," questioned the king as to how he could ever think that he and a few thousand men could conquer Egypt. "The King laughed but did not reply," writes Ibn Wasil. The emir kept poking Louis and said that, according to Islamic law, the testimony of people who act as insanely as Louis had is inadmissible, to which "the King laughed and said: 'By God, whoever said that was right, and whoever made that ruling did not err.'"[88]

The dramatic events that transpired between Louis's first and second treaties were modestly set forth in the king's own letter to the French people dated August 1250:

> [The Mamluks] hacked him [Turanshah] to pieces with their swords before the eyes of almost all the amirs and a crowd of other Saracens. Immediately following this, many Saracens appeared at our tent, armed and inflamed with frenzy, as if they sought—so many feared—to vent their rage on us and other Christians.... Although they stormed and threatened, at length, as it pleased the Lord...we confirmed with them on oath the truce we had previously made with the Sultan; and we received from each and every one of them oaths, in accordance with their religion, regarding the observance of the truce.[89]

Denouement

On May 6, Damietta was surrendered to the Muslims. Immediately the flags of the prophet were "hoisted on the walls, and Islam was proclaimed there."[90] That same day the French also delivered the first half of the ransom, four hundred thousand bezants, which took two whole days to weigh out. Exuberant with their total victory, the Mamluks now contemplated doing what they had accused Turanshah of planning to do: betray and massacre all their Christian captives.

As Joinville later learned, a heated theological debate, largely based on the Prophet Muhammad's precedents, was taking place. The faction against treacherously murdering the Christians after making a pact with them argued that they had already killed their own sultan in cold blood, and, if anything, should be rebuilding rather than reconfirming their already murky credentials. The faction for killing the Christians cited the "commandments of Muhammad" to kill all enemies of Islam, which most definitely included Louis, "whatever promise of safety has been given to him, seeing that he is the most powerful enemy of the pagan [Christian] law."[91]

In the end, they decided not to betray the Christians: on May 8, Louis and his leading men were released. Contrary to the treaty, however, the

Muslims failed to release the more than twelve thousand Christian prisoners they had agreed to, only releasing four hundred. Moreover, they
"put to the sword many Christians who were left behind sick in Damietta, even though we have fully observed the terms of the agreement we
have with them and are [still] ready to observe them," a betrayed Louis
later wrote, adding:

> What is still more detestable…is that having made and sworn a
> truce they picked out young men from among the Christian captives
> and, leading them like sheep to a sacrifice, they did their utmost, by
> putting swords to their throats, to force them to apostatize from the
> Catholic faith and to proclaim the religion of the wicked Mahomet.
> Many of them, in their enfeebled and vulnerable state, turned away
> from the faith and professed this loathsome religion. But the rest, like
> strong athletes, rooted in the faith and persisting most steadfastly
> in their firm resolve, could in no way be overcome by the enemy's
> threats and blows, but put up a proper resistance and obtained the
> bloodied crown of martyrdom.[92]

Following their release, the surviving leaders of the Crusade sailed to
and met in council at Cyprus. As might be expected, the mood was grim,
and all were of one mind: the Crusade was over; it was time to go home.
Louis understood their sentiments, thanked them for their efforts, and
said each man was free to do as he would. The overwhelming majority
set sail for Europe, but the king chose to go to "the kingdom of Syria,
rather than leave the Business of Christ in a state of utter hopelessness
and our prisoners in such great peril." In his stead, he sent back to France
his brothers, Charles and Alphonse, "to be a comfort to our dearest lady
and mother and to the entire kingdom."[93] Only a thousand other Crusaders continued on with their king.

Before leaving, his brothers entreated that he return with them, but
Louis argued that, as king, and due to his influence, he had the best
chance to secure the release of the many Christian prisoners still rotting
in Egypt's dungeons. By going to the Holy Land, Louis also hoped to be
a magnet for other Crusaders to come to its aid. For their part, the pope
and Louis's mother continued to implore others to join and help him in
the Holy Land, to little avail. Blanche managed to get her nephew, Spain's
Crusading hero of last chapter, Ferdinand III, to take the Cross again and

come to his cousin's aid, but he died soon thereafter from a lifetime of war against and wounds from Muslims.

Crusade of the Shepherds

Meanwhile, news of the failure of Louis's Crusade—this Crusade that was meant to end all Crusades—rocked Christendom, especially Louis's kingdom of France. A flurry of letters and correspondences expressed extreme shock and confusion. Eudes de Châteauroux (b.1190), a scholastic philosopher, summarized the prevalent opinion:

> The aforesaid nobles were waging a Just War, with the aim of recovering the land which the ungodly Saracens had wrested from the Christians; while the Saracens were waging an Unjust War. How, then, did God permit that unrighteousness should conquer righteousness and impiety piety? Those nobles also fought with the intention of snatching the ungodly Saracens from an infidel death—and a death in Hell—and bringing them to salvation [a reference to the fact that Crusades always had a missionary element].[94]

In response to the Seventh Crusade's failure, "there arose evil deceivers of the people" in 1251. Known as the "Masters of the Shepherds," they "were violently stirred up by a demoniacal spirit," to quote from a contemporary account. Consisting primarily of rudely clad shepherds, they entered villages and cities while carrying "aloft swords, axes, and other weapons," all of which "inspired fear among the population and judicial authorities."[95] Their leader, a strange, wizened figure reportedly from Hungary insisted that Louis and his clergymen were corrupt hypocrites who had displeased God; only the common folk, who were pure of heart, could ever wrest Jerusalem from the pagans.

Due to a combination of fiery preaching and spellbinding theatrics, a great throng of peasants, many of whom were women and children, began to follow these renegades. Their ranks were augmented by thieves, cutthroats, and vagabonds, looking to prey on whomever they might. The more the people trusted the Hungarian enchanter, the more "he could no longer hold in the poison." He soon began to hurl the Christian sacraments on the ground and hacked off the eyes and noses of Christian statues, including the Virgin Mary—actions long reminiscent of Muslim behavior.[96] He and his men also called for the ransacking of villages that would not join their movement; many were killed, especially clergymen.

When the Shepherds entered Paris, they were especially intent on "annihilating the Jews, who were under the King's protection." In response, the people closed "the gates of the city, to avenge the injury done to the King through the Jews."[97] Enough was enough. As a contemporary chronicler explains,

[W]hen they had inflicted unspeakable injuries...a certain knight, surrounding himself with a band of warriors, fell on the aforesaid Hungarian and transfixed him with a lance; and the latter, who was heard by the bystanders to call upon Mahomet, forthwith expired. The rest scattered in flight.[98]

As this conjurer's final utterance suggests, it later came out that the Shepherds were agents of Islam, working to delude the "simpler folk," whom "they were trying to lead overseas and aiming to sell them to the [Muslim] peoples of those parts, just as we noticed earlier with the children,"* continues the chronicler.[99]

Although modern scholarship ignores or downplays this Islamic connection to the Crusade of the Shepherds, contemporary sources regularly emphasized it: the *Chronica Universalis Mettensis*, written just one year after the events it relates, says that "a certain apostate and magician, who had renounced the Christian faith and gone over to paganism [Islam], promised the King of the Saracens that he would bring him an infinite number of Christians on condition that he would receive from him for every Christian five besants."[100] Similarly, the English philosopher Roger Bacon (b.1220), a contemporary of Louis, described this incident as the work of Muslim agents and would-be slavers.[101]

In the Holy Land

Over in the Holy Land, Louis was biding his time. Since the death of Sultan al-Salih Ayyub in November 1249, three rulers had come and gone over the course of three months, and Egypt was in turmoil, thanks to the slave-soldiers. Accordingly, when war erupted between Egypt and

---

* Around 1203, a large group of French children were seduced into sailing to and fighting for Jerusalem by men claiming to be Crusaders, but who were clandestinely working for and sold the children to Muslims (Jackson, 193).

Syria in early 1252, each tried to curry the favor of Louis as a potential ally. The choice was easy: while both offered to restore Jerusalem after the war, only the Egyptians could offer the remaining Christian hostages. Louis further demanded "delivery of all prisoners and slaves, even of the [Christian] children who had been taken young and brought up in the Mussulman religion; [and] the giving up for burial of the heads of slain Christians which had been fixed round the walls of Cairo, some ever since the battle of Gaza [in 1239]."[102]

While the Mamluks were being accommodating, Louis further sent his men to find and purchase the freedom of any Christian captives or slaves they could find in Egypt. They would return with hundreds at a time.[103] In this, Louis's mission was a success; as his brother Charles of Anjou affirmed decades later, "This compassion for the captives was his major reason for wanting to stay, so that he could free them just as he did: had he returned, they would never have been released."[104]

In exchange, Louis allied himself with his former enemies, though he never really fought alongside them, as the Egyptians and Syrians made peace on April 1, 1253. The former rued having freed so many Christians.

As for the Mongols, their response to the mission Louis sent in early 1249 finally returned in 1251. During that time, Güyük, the Christian-friendly khan had died and was succeeded by Möngke Khan. Unlike the initial communiques sent to the French king, which were full of flattery and vows of good will, this one was typically Mongol. After boasting of putting numerous kings—bizarrely including Prester John—to the sword, the message ordered Louis to send annual tribute, otherwise, "we will destroy you and your people, as we have done to the kings already named." Although Joinville says "it repented the king sorely that he had ever sent envoys" to the Mongols, their response must not have been overly surprising. Sometime after the first, flattering mission arrived, and while contemplating if the Mongols would indeed form an alliance with the Christians against Islam, Gui the knight wrote from Damietta, "We have [still] heard nothing for certain, or worthy to pass on concerning the Tatars.[105] Nor do we hope for faith in the faithless, humanity in the inhuman, or charity in curs, unless God, for Whom nothing is impossible, brings about something unheard-of."[106]

Louis continued to do all that he could to help in the Holy Land, which ended up being minimal, considering that no other Christian leaders—and now neither Mongols—came to help. So he turned to building projects—fortifying the remaining Crusader kingdoms of Acre, Jaffa, Haifa, Caesarea, and Sidon with his own funds. It was during this downtime that his reputation for piety also began to grow. He spent much time fixing and building churches and monasteries, giving alms, and visiting the sick and dying.

One anecdote was ever after remembered. In Sidon he came across the putrid and mutilated remains of large numbers of Christians who had earlier been massacred by the Muslims of Damascus; he ordered them buried and given last rites. "Now," writes William of Chartres, "although all the others who were present reacted as though they had some sort of loathing and dread of picking up the bodies and gathering the now half-rotten, hacked-off limbs or touching the bones," the "king himself, as though having and sensing no repulsion, was there from morning even until noon…gathering up the limbs and entrails of these Christians." He did this for five days straight, to the amazement of all.[107]

After his mother's death in late 1252—news of which broke Louis's heart—the government of France fell to his brothers' hands, and he received letter after letter urging him to return. News of the Shepherds' Crusade and other mischief, as he later confided to a bishop, especially disturbed him: "If I alone bore the shame and calamity [of the Seventh Crusade], I could endure it; but alas! All Christendom has been brought to confusion because of me."[108] With nothing left to do, and with few men at his disposal, Louis finally left the Holy Land on April 24, 1254, nearly six years since he first left France.

Before returning, while at Jaffa, he was offered a chance to visit Jerusalem under the safe conduct of Aleppo's sultan; but, like his granduncle before him, Richard Lionheart, he would not enter what he could not liberate, as that might set a negative precedent.[109] Louis's final act before leaving was to establish a permanent garrison of one hundred knights at Acre, personally funded by and costing the French crown 4 percent of its annual revenue.[110]

A Saint Born of the Ashes of War

Despite his failed Crusade, on returning to France, Louis "was received with ineffable joy by all," says the *Beatus Ludovicus* (c.1300), which adds, "Although from boyhood he stood out for his saintly conduct, from this point forward he, like David, strove constantly to become even better."[111] Indeed, for the next sixteen years this veteran Crusader ruled as the model Christian king.

Much has been written about Louis's saintly conduct, and much of it might be dismissed by the modern, incredulous reader as mere hagiography, if not for the fact that it is well documented by reliable eyewitnesses and those who intimately knew him, including Jean de Joinville, William of Chartes, and Geoffrey of Beaulieu, Louis's confessor and confidant for the last two decades of his life. Nor can they be dismissed as mere sycophants: every king is surrounded by flatterers, yet none developed a reputation like Louis. Finally and as seen during his captivity, even those at the receiving end of his pious enterprises, "the Saracens themselves esteemed him to be a very holy, truthful, and wise person."[112]

This is not the place to detail the conduct that would later earn him sainthood—entire books have been allotted to that—and a brief summary must suffice: Every day, 120 poor people were fed from his own table; he often served them with his own hands, ate their leftovers rather than feast on a regal meal afterwards, and spent on their upkeep. "In short, whatever he gave to the poor he considered very well spent, and everything else he considered wasted."[113] He also spent liberally on churches, cathedrals, and monasteries. When some of his nobles complained, he retorted, "If I spent double as much in playing dice, or in hunting and fowling, nothing would be said of it."[114] He personally supported and found work for "a great number of wretched women who had prostituted themselves for lack of food."[115]

Louis washed the feet of beggars weekly and preferred to keep it secret—including from the beggars themselves, asking that blind ones be brought him.[116] When he asked Joinville if he washed the poor people's feet, the nobleman exclaimed, "Sire, it would make me sick! The feet of these villains will I not wash." "That was ill said," retorted the king, adding that if Christ did it so should Christians. "So I pray you, for the love of God first, and then for the love of me, that you accustom yourself to wash the feet of the poor."[117] (Joinville's uncharacteristic silence on his subsequent actions suggests a continued reluctance.)

The king regularly served those that others found repulsive. The following is a typical account:

Once, at dinner, Louis himself, on bended knee, ministered to a certain leprous monk who, because the corrosive disease had gnawed away his eyes and nose, was disgusting to everyone…. [Louis] placed food and drink directly into his mouth, believing that doing so would better please the leper, with the abbot [who was there] breaking out into groans and tears, greatly admiring the holy man for doing such things without being excessively horrified by such an abomination.[118]

When staying at monasteries, he would keep up with the monks in their tasks, punctual prayers, and biblical readings, "living and faring in all ways like the meanest brother of the order except that he showed more humility."[119] His children's upbringing was like his, Spartan: "Loathing and despising the vain songs of this world and the idle plays of actors, rejecting the attractions of musical instruments in which most nobility find enjoyment, he shielded his sons and his household from such folly."[120]

At one point he seriously considered retiring to a monastery and abdicating in favor of his eldest son. His wife, Margaret, would not hear of it. "But if he could not become a monk in name and profession he led a life as severe and self-denying, and almost as assiduous in prayer and fasting and penance, as if he had been immured in a cloister under the most rigid rule of austerity."[121] On holy days and to conquer the flesh (as 1 Cor. 9:26–27 was understood), "he wore a hair shirt on his body, in which there was an iron cross with four very sharp teeth that bit into him."[122] In time, such "austerities injured his feeble health, and after falling dangerously ill he was induced to relax them in some degree."[123]

Although such behavior might suggest a morose, puritanical personality, Louis was apparently so given over to gaiety that one of the penances he set on himself was "not to laugh on a Friday if he could help it." For the king "had a pleasant manner of speech seasoned with wit, and was very fond of conversation, saying that nothing was so good after a meal."[124] He frequently broke bread with theologians such as Thomas Aquinas, and was a lover of knowledge, building and maintaining great libraries.[125]

Despite—or perhaps because of—his zealous commitment to Christian mores, the French monarchy ironically reached its height of power and prestige, since the time of Charlemagne, under Louis's rule. As one chronicler remarked, "Many men wondered that one man, so meek, so gentle, not strong of body...could reign peacefully over so great a king-dom and so many powerful lords, especially as he was neither lavish in presents nor very complaisant to some of them."[126]

Muslim Persecution of Christians

Meanwhile, things did not fare so well for the few remaining Christian strongholds in the Holy Land. In 1260, Baibars, the same Mamluk slave-soldier who had defeated the Crusaders in Mansoura and assassinated Turanshah, beat the Mongols at Ain Jalut, and, after killing yet another sultan—so that the Mamluks now controlled Egypt and most of Syria—finally became sultan himself. Once he had consolidated his grip on power—no easy task considering that five Egyptian sultans had come and gone before him in just ten years, their exits and entrances often hastened by the sword—Baibars turned his zeal against the Christians, beginning with those living under his authority in Egypt, the indigenous Copts.[*]

An ardent Muslim,[†] the persecution Baibars inaugurated was one of the worst the Copts experienced since Islam's original invasion and con-quest of their country in the seventh century: churches and monasteries were desecrated, burned or transformed into mosques; Christians were randomly executed in brutal ways, including by being sawn in half or thrown into pits and burned alive; the Coptic Orthodox Church was reg-ularly extorted into paying exorbitant bribes. At one point, the Mamluk sultan decreed that all Christian and Jewish scribes—who then formed the majority of the government (or *diwan*), as literacy was then a mostly Christian and Jewish preserve—either convert to Islam or be beheaded. Some converted; others were martyred. After subduing the Christian

---

* The word "Copt" is an English transliteration of an Arabic transliteration of the Greek word for "Egyptian," Αἰγύπτιος (pronounced ai-gypt-ios). The Arabs took the middle of three syllables, *gypt*, and pronounced it *qibt* (قبط), hence the English "Copt." That Egypt's most indigenous popula-tion was (and remains) Christian is therefore even evident in the name the Arabs applied to them, which denotes *Egyptian* and connotes *Christianity*.

† Although modern academics regularly disassociate Baibars from Islam and present him as cynically exploiting jihadist rhetoric for purely political and propagandistic purposes, according to historian R. Stephen Humphreys, an expert on Baibars, "that terrifying man...was [in his own mind] purifying the lands of Islam from the pollution of unbelief.... [He] saw himself as a Muslim. We witness the public dimension of his commitment to the faith in his extensive program of public works and...in the quite puritanical morality which he demanded.... [A]ll the evidence indicates that Baibars was personally and deeply engaged with Islam, and this inevitably colored the way he envisioned his strategic policy" (Humphreys, 10, 13–14).

kingdoms of Nubia and Northern Sudan, Baibars even forcibly tried converting Christian Ethiopia to Islam.[127]

His Mamluk successors continued this policy of extreme persecution in Egypt, so that the sources are riddled with accounts of Christians being savaged, slaughtered, immolated, crucified, and their women and children raped and enslaved.[128] Always riding on the coattails of Mamluk savagery was Egypt's Muslim rabble, who took advantage of the anti-Christian climate by targeting and preying on the Copts with impunity. Noise of this severe persecution eventually reached and prompted the Catholic pope in Rome to send a delegation to Egypt in 1328 to plead for mercy on behalf of the Copts—even though the Christians of Rome and Egypt had not been in communion for nearly a millennium—to no avail.[129] Conversion increasingly became the only way for Egypt's Christians to evade persecution—though this decision was not taken lightly and often had traumatic effects.

> [Thus] in 1389, a great procession of Copts who had accepted Muhammad under fear of death, marched through Cairo. Repenting of their apostasy, they now wished to atone for it by the inevitable consequence of returning to Christianity. So as they marched, they announced that they believed in Christ and renounced Muhammad. They were seized and all the men were beheaded one after another in an open square before the women. But this did not terrify the women; so they, too, were all martyred.[130]

The same persecution, if to a lesser degree, prevailed in those regions of the Holy Land under Mamluk rule. As one example, in 1263, Baibars "gave orders," his biographer, Ibn Abdul Zahir (b.1223) approvingly writes, "that the church of Nazareth should be demolished, this being the most important place of worship for them; it is said that the religion of the Christians had its origin there."[131]

Having ravished the Christians under his authority, Baibars next turned to the coastal Crusader kingdoms. In 1265, he conquered Caesarea and Haifa and massacred every Christian who could not flee. He then besieged Arsuf, which was staunchly defended by 260 Knights Hospitaller. So outnumbered and eventually pushed to and holed in the city's citadel, they eventually accepted Baibars' terms of surrender, which included allowing them all to go free. Once they opened their gates, the

Muslim sultan reneged on his word and ordered them all shackled and enslaved and sent to march through the streets of Cairo—to jeers, slaps, and spits—wearing heavy wooden crosses around their necks. In 1266 he besieged the great Templar castle at Safed. When the Christian defenders had reached their final extremity, Baibars offered them surrender terms to withdraw unmolested to Acre. Unaware of his betrayal of the Hospitallers, they accepted, and again he broke his word, ordering them all beheaded. Then he turned to the undefended Christian village of Qara, massacring all the adults and enslaving their women and children.

All during this time and afterwards, he would march his troops to Acre, the best defended Crusader stronghold, which always beat him back. In 1267, Baibars scoured its countryside looking for Christians, beheaded them, and surrounded Acre's walls with their mutilated corpses. In 1268 he stormed Jaffa and slaughtered its Christians. Boasting of his jihad against the Holy Land's Christians in a letter, Baibars told of how "the churches themselves were razed from the faces of the earth, every house met with disaster, the dead were piled up on the seashore like islands of corpses, the men were murdered, the children enslaved, the free women reduced to captivity."[132]

Next to fall in May 1268—and great was its fall—was the ancient Christian city of Antioch, one of the oldest and best fortified Crusader kingdoms. After his men had breached the city, which was swollen with Christian fugitives, especially women and children, Baibars ordered its gates shut behind them. An orgiastic bloodbath—also known as the "single greatest massacre of the entire crusading era"—followed.[133] In a letter to Bohemond VI, lord of Antioch, who was not present at the time of its fall, Baibars gloated over what took place in explicitly jihadist terms:

> You would have seen your knights prostrated beneath the horses' hooves, your houses stormed by pillagers and ransacked by looters… your women sold four at a time and bought for a *dinar* of your [own] money! You would have seen the crosses in your churches smashed, the pages of the false Testaments scattered, the Patriarchs' tombs overturned. You would have seen your Muslim enemy trampling on the place where you celebrate the mass, cutting the throats of monks, priests, and deacons upon the altars, bringing sudden death to the Patriarchs and slavery to the royal princes. You would have seen fire

running through your palaces, your dead burned,...your palace lying unrecognizable, the church of St. Paul and that of Qusyan [Cathedral of Saint Peter] pulled down and destroyed.[134]

A Second Crusade

Even before Antioch fell, on March 24, 1267, Louis—to everyone's shock and consternation—took the Cross again to provide succor to the Christians of the Holy Land. In the words of Geoffrey of Beaulieu, Louis, "hearing about so many disasters...and so many repeated perils threatening the Holy Land, yearned at the end of his days to attempt some lofty work for God, and it was not easy to stop him." He therefore vowed to organize, fund, and launch another Crusade in an effort to counter the "dangers to the Holy Land that seemed so imminent."[135]

This second venture—accounted in the histories as the Eighth Crusade—was even better funded and organized than his first Crusade, which is saying much. Even so, the royal court was against Louis's undertaking, and few others were willing to join him—not even his faithful Joinville; the pope himself, the traditional caller for Crusades, was initially reluctant. For all his zeal, Louis was now fifty-three and worn down, including from the religious austerities he had imposed on himself; his was not a figure to inspire hope for victory in arms. The Crusade would again take on the seeming of a family affair, led by Louis, his brothers, Charles and Alphonse, his three sons, Philip, Peter, and John, and his son-in-law, Theobald II, king of Navarre.

Their immediate target was Tunis. By creating a secure base in North Africa (as the Fatimids had done in 969), the logic was that the Crusaders could then turn east to Egypt. Moreover, Muhammad I al-Mustansir, the emir of Tunis, formerly a vassal of Sicily, had been for years sending embassies to Louis claiming that he was eager to become a Christian, if not for the fear of his own people. As Geoffrey of Beaulieu explains, Louis was further "led to believe by trustworthy men that this king of Tunis had great good will toward the Christian faith, and that he might quite easily become a Christian...if he were able to do it while maintaining his honor and without fear of his own Saracens."[136]

Louis was always interested in Muslim conversions, as it offered both religious and practical benefits. As with Egypt, Louis "desired that the Christian faith, which had flourished so gracefully of old in Africa and especially in Carthage [Tunis] in the days of the blessed Augustine and other orthodox doctors, should spring into blossom in our day and should spread abroad to the honor and glory of Jesus Christ."[137] Louis also expressed a sincere interest in saving lost Muslim souls and often spent liberally on the upkeep of Muslim converts.[138] More practically speaking and based on precedent, it was thought that the Tunisian king's conversion might precipitate the conversion of all his people.* A Christian Tunis would be a loss for the jihad—Muhammad I was sending large revenues and men to Mamluk Egypt—and a gain for the Crusade.[139]

Before they embarked for Tunisia, Louis, standing aboard his ship, harangued his sons below with words of encouragement:

> Consider sons that I, now aged, have crossed other seas before for Christ, and that your mother the queen is far advanced in years. We have possessed our kingdom in peace…enjoyed temporal riches, honors, and pleasures as was good and right…. [Now] see that for faith in Christ and his church I neither spare my old age, nor do I take pity on your forsaken mother. I relinquish delights [and] honors, and, for Christ, I offer my wealth, and I lead you [Louis's eldest and future king, Philip III], who are about to reign, and your brothers, and your first born sister, with me, and I would even have led my fourth son if he were of age.

The king closed his appeal with an ominous look to the near future:

> And therefore I wish that you listen and consider well in your own minds, so that after my death, when you attain the kingdom, you spare nothing for the preservation and defense of the church of God and the faith—neither yourself, nor what belongs to you—not your kingdom, not your wife, not even your children. I give this example to you and your brothers so that you will all do the same.[140]

Louis arrived in Tunisia on July 18, 1270, with, if al-Maqrizi is correct, thirty-six thousand Crusaders.[141] He quickly learned that Muhammad I

---

* For example, once the barbarian kings that overran the Roman Empire converted to Christianity, all their people followed suit. Something similar happened after the Christian conquest of Toledo in 1085, and, later, in Valencia, during Louis IX's own lifetime and youth. Moreover, Tunisia was separated by vast deserts from the Eastern sultanates and close to the Christian Mediterranean, further suggesting that conversion and cooperation were not implausible (see Jordan, 22).

al-Mustansir had lied*—or else was still too afraid to convert.[142] So the king turned to and easily captured a fortress near the ancient remnants of Carthage, where he established camp. Although Muhammad sent his men to skirmish in an effort to draw the Crusaders out, Louis ignored the bait, remembering the lessons of Mansoura. He waited for the rest of the fleets to arrive, including those of his brother Charles, now king of Sicily, his Aragonese son-in-law, and the English, under Prince Edward—England's future "Longshanks"—who took the Cross at the last minute.

While waiting for reinforcements, history repeated itself: a pestilence borne of the African desert heat swept through the Crusader camp, plaguing all and sundry with dysentery and fever. Anguished men slowly died—including Louis's twenty-year-old son, John, who was born in Damietta, Egypt, and was now dead amid the ruins of ancient Carthage. This was too much for the wearied king, who himself soon fell deathly ill, "tired out by continuous fever."[143]

On the night of August 24, Louis had himself laid in a bed of penitential ashes spread in the shape of a cross; there he received the sacraments and recited the Psalms. Some two decades earlier, he had told Joinville that "the Enemy [Satan] is so subtle that, when people are dying, he labors all he can to make them die doubting as to some points of faith." Therefore, when that hour comes, those dying must cry "Away! Thou shalt not tempt me so that I cease to believe…. Even if thou didst cause all my members to be cut off, yet would I live and die in the faith."[144]

According to William of Chartres and Geoffrey of Beaulieu, who were both with him in his final moments, the king lived up to his own exhortation when the time came. "Not wanting to hear a word about anything of this world or of the flesh," William writes, "he concentrated instead only on spiritual things." Then, continues Geoffrey, "when he could speak only softly and with difficulty," he encouraged his men to restore North Africa to Christianity and urged them to become acquainted with the Koran, in an effort to win Muslim souls.[145]

Finally, he was heard to repeat a prayer, over and over, in a continuously fading voice: "Grant us, we ask, for the sake of your love, that we

---

* Louis is today often accused of naivety concerning the emir's potential conversion. However, such criticism fails to take into account the many anecdotes of Muslim leaders claiming to want to convert but fearing their own people—as Ayyubid sultan al-Kamil reportedly told Saint Francis of Assisi—to say nothing of the very real punishments, including death, that continue to be meted out to Muslims who apostatize to Christianity till this very day.

may despise worldly success and fear none of its misfortunes." When his voice had been reduced to a whisper, he faintly uttered, "Father, into your hands I commend my spirit," and closed his weary eyes as if to sleep.[146]

Before the sun arose on August 25, 1270, Louis IX of France—that Most Christian King, as he later came to be known—was dead, aged fifty-six.

With his death, so the Eighth Crusade came to a quick close. When Louis's brother Charles finally arrived, he opened talks with Muhammad, who offered many concessions to Charles's kingdom of Sicily and paid a large war indemnity. Thus Charles was the only one to profit from the Crusade, even though he did little—and, according to many a bitter Crusader, was, because of his delay, partially responsible for Louis's death.

When Prince Edward arrived from England, he was stunned to see the French packing and leaving. Edward would continue on to Acre— history's Ninth Crusade—which he highly fortified, making it virtually impregnable. In response, Baibars agreed to a ten-year peace treaty, and then died on July 1, 1277—apparently by accidentally drinking a beverage that he had poisoned for an Ayyubid prince.[147]

The Sunset of Crusading

But Baibars was only the first of an array of brutal Mamluk sultans. Before long, Muslim sieges on the remaining Crusader holdings in the Holy Land resumed. In 1285, the powerful Hospitaller castle at Marqab, which had long thwarted Baibars, was taken, and "the call to prayer resounded with praise and thanks to Allah," to quote a contemporary Muslim, "for having cast down the adorers of the Messiah and freed our land of them."[148] In 1289, after Tripoli fell,

> a great many Franks fled with their women to the island and the church [of Saint Thomas, a short distance by sea]. The Muslim troops flung themselves into the sea and swam with their horses to the island, where they killed all the men and took the women, children and possessions. After the looting I [Abu al-Fida, the Muslim narrator] went by boat to this island, and found it heaped with putrefying corpses; it was impossible to land there because of the stench.[149]

Meanwhile, back in Tripoli, it was more of the usual: "Muslims put holy pictures [icons] to an insulting use, subjected images to various insults and dragged a crucifix through the streets at the tail of an ass.... Christian children who were captured...were made Muslim and taught to spit on the crucifixes."[150]

Finally, in 1291, tens if not hundreds of thousands of Muslims surrounded Acre, where the Templars and Hospitallers had congregated for the final showdown. Massive siege engines pounded the wall day and night, and "the battle raged furiously," wrote a Muslim participant. In an act of desperate valor, the "Franks did not close most of the gates; in fact, they left them wide open and fought in front of them in defense." But no matter how many Muslims they killed, countless took their place. The city was finally captured on May 18, 1291; thousands of men were ritually beheaded.[151]

Afterwards, a Dominican monk present at Acre's fall "was forced to see [thousands of] Christian women and children sold into slavery after being paraded through streets, watch nuns become concubines, hear the Christians being taunted that their Jesus could not help them against Muhammad."[152]

In response, the few Crusader holdings left—Beirut, Sidon, Tyre—surrendered. "Thus the whole of Syria and the coastal zones were purified of the Franks," wrote Abu al-Fida, "who had once been on the point of conquering Egypt and subduing Damascus and other cities. Praise be Allah!"[153] All that remained to the Crusaders was Cyprus, captured by Richard Lionheart over a century earlier.

Although many smaller Crusades were forthcoming, Louis's experiences boded ill for the movement in its entirety; for here was a wealthy and wise king, who had given it his all—twice—with nothing to show for it but suffering and death, and not even at the hands of Muslims but rather nature. Was God *not* on their side? In a letter from 1250, during Louis's first Crusade, Innocent IV ominously wrote that if Jerusalem is not "delivered from the hands of the pagans by the energy and power of our dearest son in Christ, the illustrious King of France, there can scarcely be any hope of its subsequent recovery."[154] This would prove to be true.

Even so, rather than being seen as a failure, posterity—including that of Islam*—would remember Louis as one of France's greatest and most

---

* Centuries after the 1270 Crusade, North Africans refashioned the original Arab chronicles concerning Louis's "reputed goodness, recognizing it as a kind of sanctity, even though inferior by being Christian in nature." In these later retellings, "Louis IX emerges as a sublimely righteous man,

just of kings. In 1297, the Catholic Church canonized him as a saint—the only king in over a millennium of French history to receive that honor—due to his well-documented pious and charitable character. Till this day he continues to rank as one of the greatest kings among the people of otherwise staunchly secular France.

That said, of all the Defenders in this book, Louis's failures are the greatest. As Guéranger observed when comparing the two canonized cousins, whereas the life of Ferdinand III of Castile "was a series of happiness and success," the "life of that other admirable King, Saint Louis of France, was one of almost uninterrupted misfortune."[155]

Yet if a hero is judged by his commitment and self-sacrifice, as opposed to actual results and success, Louis may well be accounted the greatest of them all.

---

full of virtues and of profound faith, moved to risk his life to save his enemies and bring them to his faith"—a motive which Muslims of all people could appreciate. In these later retellings, however, Louis receives a revelation that Islam is the true religion, quietly slips out of his pestilent camp, converts to Islam, and becomes a Muslim sage wandering the wastelands of North Africa. As William C. Jordan concludes, "Wishful thinking, to be sure, but the legend, a parodic fantasy of retribution, does suggest that Muslims retained the memory of precisely what their crusader opponents—especially Louis IX—had been up to. To this extent, they have been more perceptive than many modern students of his reign" (Jordan, 146–147).

CHAPTER 6

John Hunyadi:
The White Knight of Wallachia

"We have had enough of our men enslaved, our women raped,
wagons loaded with the severed heads of our people, the sale of
chained captives, the mockery of our religion.... [W]e shall not
stop until we succeed in expelling the enemy from Europe."

—JOHN HUNYADI[1]

"Tis John, called Hunyadi, who is to be the salvation of
Christendom."

—JOHN CAPISTRANO[2]

The final expulsion of the Crusaders from the Holy Land in 1291
coincided with the rise of a new Islamic power—one that would
require every ounce of Crusading zeal to be redirected from offensive
warfare (trying to reconquer Jerusalem) to defensive warfare (trying to
protect Europe).

In the late thirteenth century, a Turkish chieftain by the name of
Osman (1258–1326) began laying the foundations of and eventually
imparted his name to what would become the Ottoman (from Osman)
Empire. After purging northwest Anatolia of its ancient Christian character—sources speak of churches aflame and Christians massacred,
enslaved, or fleeing—Osman's successors entered the easternmost strip
of Europe and took the old fortress town of Gallipoli in 1354.[3] There,

198

"where there were bells," an Ottoman chronicler wrote, Suleiman, a grandson of Osman "broke them up and cast them into fires. Where there were churches he destroyed them or converted them to mosques. Thus, in place of bells there were now muezzins."[4] Cleansed of all Christian "filth," Gallipoli became the first jihadist base whence the terrorization of the Balkans began; or, as Mustafa, an Ottoman emir later boasted, Gallipoli became "the Muslim throat that gulps down every Christian nation, that chokes and destroys the Christians."[5]

Despite European resistance, by 1371 Thrace and large swathes of Bulgaria and Macedonia were overrun and devastated. Traveling through them later that same year, Issaye, a Mount Athos monk, recorded his impression: "The Ishmaelites," he wrote, conflating Turks with Arabs— both Muslims—"massacred one part of the Christians with the sword, and led off others into slavery; the rest were carried off by a premature death." He described how nature—in the guise of a terrible famine and ravenous wolves—"decimated" the rest: "Alas, what a sorrowful picture to behold! The land is left devoid of all goods, men, livestock, and other produce." The devastation and desolation was so horrific that those who remained alive "truly envied the dead," concluded Issaye.[6] (Such accounts underscore the fact that, as historian Dimitar Angelov writes, "the conquest by the Turks had disastrous consequences for the Balkan peoples and for centuries trammeled their normal economic and social development."[7])

In an effort to drive their Islamic tormentors out, on June 15, 1389, a large coalition of Christians—Serbians, Albanians, Bosnians, Bulgarians, Greeks, Hungarians, and Wallachians—fought but lost to the Turks at Kosovo. On September 25, 1396, an even larger coalition of Balkan Christians—this time augmented by Western, primarily French, forces— tried again and lost again to the Turks at the battle of Nicopolis. A new wave of terror and slave raids ensued, as Ottoman suzerainty extended deeper into the Balkans.

The victor at Nicopolis, Bayezid I, one of Ottoman history's many depraved sultans, especially relished the human booty. Describing his palace, the Greek historian Doukas (1400–1462) wrote:

[T]here one could find carefully selected boys and girls, with beautiful faces, sweet young boys and girls who shone more brightly than the sun. To what nations did they belong? They were Greeks, Serbs, Wallachians, Albanians, Hungarians, Saxons, Bulgarians, and Latins. Each of them sang songs in his native language, although reluctantly. He himself [Sultan Bayezid] unceasingly gave himself over to pleasure [another translation more forthrightly says "lascivious sexual acts"], to the point of exhaustion, by indulging in debauchery with these boys and girls.[8]

If this was the fate of the great sultan's slaves, who were considered "lucky," one can only surmise the fate of the average Turk's Christian slaves—and these were many, often selling as cheaply as animals.

At the turn of the fifteenth century, even impregnable Constantinople itself, which Bayezid had sporadically laid to siege, was on the verge of collapsing, when a "savior" came from the East—another wolf in Prester John's clothing—the Mongol warlord, Timur. Although both were Muslims, he and Bayezid had fallen afoul of one another, and gone to war at Ankara, in 1402. Not only was it a Mongol victory—culminating with Bayezid spending his last days in a cage—but it caused a civil war to erupt in and partially incapacitate the Ottoman Empire.

Turkish authority correspondingly waned and in some cases was overthrown in the Balkans, prompting some Christians to think, to dream, that complete freedom from the Muslim yoke was only a matter of time. Wishful thinking; by 1430, the jihadist nightmare was back—and with a vengeance. Along with conquering Thessaloniki, the Turks relaunched systematic and even more devastating raids into Serbia, Albania, Romania, and Hungary.

Jihadist War Machine Par Excellence

Part of the reason for Turkish tenacity and success lay in the fact that, of all its Islamic predecessors, the Ottoman war-machine was fanatically committed to the concept of jihad (which is saying much). What came naturally to the pre-Islamic, tribal Turk—warfare on and plunder/ enslavement of tribal outsiders—was now imbued with a pious rationale. What Christians were taught was sin—murder and rapine—took on a holy and sacred character for the Turks, so long as their victims were non-Muslims, which by default made them enemies, infidels, whom sharia requires to be killed, subjugated, or enslaved.

As Gregory Palamas, a clergyman who was taken captive by the Turks when they landed in Gallipoli in 1354, wrote, "They live by the bow, the sword, and debauchery, finding pleasure in taking slaves, devoting themselves to murder, pillage, spoil...and not only do they commit these crimes, but even—what an aberration—they believe that God approves them!"[9]

Further inspiring the Muslim holy warrior, or *mujahid*, was that Islam guaranteed him paradise if he died during the jihad. It was, in fact, this win-win scenario that made Islam immensely appealing to the tribal peoples—Arabs, Berbers, Turks, and Tatars—who converted to it in droves: not only were they validated in living as they always had—by preying on "the other"—but now they were guaranteed success one way or the other: if their jihad succeeded, plunder and slaves in the now; if their jihad failed—if they died—eternal pleasure with the *houris*, "wide-eyed" and "big bosomed" concubines in paradise, as well as "eternally young boys," to quote the Koran.[10]

Such a "theology" did much for Muslim morale, so that, whereas in Europe, warriors were just one of several professional classes, among the Turks, every capable man was expected to participate in the holy war—hence the legendary sizes of the armies regularly mustered by the Ottoman Empire, history's jihadist state par excellence. Its continued existence depended on continuously expanding into infidel—primarily European—territories and exploiting their resources, primarily their people.

In other words, the Ottoman Empire's economy consisted of plunder, its labor force of slaves. Without either it would collapse. All that the Turks knew—and excelled at—was warfare. It was their conquered Christian population that would sustain them: the poor masses were either enslaved or made to pay exorbitant tributes (jizya); the skilled and talented among them were enslaved and made to serve or fight for the Ottomans.

As devastating as Ottoman raids were in the fourteenth century, they were arguably worse, particularly the slave-raids, when the Turks remerged from their Mongol-induced hiatus. Thus, after the aforementioned sack of Thessaloniki in 1430, seven thousand Christian women and children were sexually savaged and hauled away "like senseless animals." Such "was the evil and ill-fated firstfruits of future calamities," Doukas wrote in retrospect.[11]

Indeed, eight years later, on December 12, 1438, Bartolomeo de Giano, an Italian Franciscan holed up in Constantinople, detailed in a letter the "calamitous and lamentable slaughter that we see in these days." Raiding every corner of the Balkans, the Muslims were erecting "great mountains of [Christian] heads," wrote the eyewitness. Others were either enslaved to "serve their wicked and filthy pleasures" and/or made into "Saracens who will later be enemies of the Christians," that is, forced to convert to and later wage jihad for Islam. He saw the young and old "led away in iron fetters tied to the backs of horses.... [W]omen and children were herded by dogs without any mercy or piety. If one of them slowed down, unable to walk further because of thirst or pain, O Good Jesus! she immediately ended her life there in torment, cut in half [by the Turks]."[12]

From Hungary, three hundred thousand Christians were "carried off in just a few days"; from Serbia and Transylvania, one hundred thousand were hauled off. Less dramatic numbers—thousands or tens of thousands of Christians being enslaved from here or there—seem to have been regular occurrences. As one scholar correctly observes, "The massive enslavement of Slavic populations during this period gave rise, in fact, to our word 'slave': in Bartolomeo's time, to be a slave was to be a Slav."[13]

"[S]trengthened by their victories and afire with such a great lust for gain," the Muslim invaders, Bartolomeo continues, "believe without doubt that they are going to destroy the entirety of Christendom in a short time." Every day in formerly Christian territories under Turkish rule, the Franciscan fumed, "the most holy name of Christ is denied and Muhammad, the son of the devil, exalted." Everywhere churches, crosses, and Bibles were "cast down and trampled underfoot!"[14]

The Balkans was experiencing the same transformation that the Christian Near East did under the Arab invaders of the seventh century. "It was only eighty years ago or so that not a single Turk was found in Greece," Bartolomeo observed, before adding, "unless it is provided with some swift remedy, Greece shall soon become like Arabia or Egypt."[15]

Most disturbing of all, these travesties, lamented Bartolomeo, were happening because there were no more Defenders against Islam:

Where is the glorious kingdom of the Franks now, which in ancient times drove the Saracens from Hispania? Where is the great power of the English?... Where now is the king of Aragon, terror of the infidel? Where are the other powers and Christian princes?... O where now is...Godfrey, Bohemond, Baldwin, and the rest of the princes who... liberated the sepulcher of Jesus Christ from the hands of the infidel?[16]

It was in this backdrop that John Hunyadi—destined to be "the most outstanding fighter against the Ottomans in the first half of the fifteenth century"—rose to prominence and rocked the Turks to their core.[17]

John Hunyadi

John Hunyadi was born in Transylvania, in modern day Romania, around 1406. His Wallachian family was relatively unknown until they were elevated by their great feats of arms. King Sigismund of Hungary conferred Hunedoara Castle in Transylvania—hence the Hunyadi surname—and the thirty-five villages attached to it to John's father and uncles. Young John was likely raised there, where "the idea of a common struggle of the Romanian and Hungarian peoples against the Ottoman invasion became deeply rooted in his mind."[18]

As a young man, he went into the military service of George Branković, the Serbian despot. After saying that "He displayed a remarkable daring and zeal on whatever mission he was sent by this ruler," Laonikos Chalkokondyles (1423–1470), a contemporary Greek chronicler, offers the following anecdote of the young man's relentless drive:

> While the ruler of the Serbs was out hunting, a wolf appeared before him, and he challenged Janko [John] to go after the wolf. Janko gave chase and pursued his prey with all his might. When his prey fell into a river and began to swim, he too jumped into the river and swam across on his horse. After he crossed the river, he did not let up at all in his pursuit until he finally caught up with the wolf and killed it; then he removed its skin and turned back toward the ruler. He crossed the river again, presented the wolf's skin to the ruler, and said, "Lord, what you ordered has been done. I have killed the wolf, and here is its skin for you to use in whatever way you require." It is reported that the ruler of the Serbs was amazed at this feat, and said that there was no way this man would not rise to great power.

Thus he spoke, and henceforth he courted him with gifts of money. Hunyadi spent a long time there and then went to the Hungarians.[19]

By 1430, and like his father before him, Hunyadi, now twenty-four, entered into the direct service of Sigismund, king of Hungary. Two years later, he married Erzsébet Szilágyi, a Hungarian noblewoman, who gave him two sons. Chronicles from that era describe Hunyadi as "a man of medium height, large eyes, red cheeks, and with a serious countenance. He liked arms more than anything else." Indeed, for him warfare was "what water means for fish, or what the shady woods mean for swift stags."[20]

Hunyadi's first serious military actions were south of the Danube, along the inconstant borders with the Turks. A consummate soldier, he was constantly studying the art of war and was especially fond of Caesar's military journal. As he explained to his peers, "the profession of the arms is not as easy as some might think; one must acquire a great deal of knowledge and experience."[21] And he most certainly did, for his early exploits won him such fame that he came to be known as the "White Knight of Wallachia."

"Greatly impressed" by Hunyadi, in 1441, Ladislaus III, the young king of Hungary and Poland appointed him *voivode*, or "warlord," of Transylvania; he also made him "commander of the army fighting the Turks and put him in charge of all the castles adjacent to Turkish territory."[22] Considering that Ottoman Sultan Murad II (r.1421–1444; 1446–1451) had vowed not to rest "unless he hears the praises of Muhammad sung in all of Hungary as soon as possible," such a promotion is indicative of the king's great confidence in Hunyadi, now aged thirty-five.[23]

The voivode immediately began to overhaul the military. Although cavalry continued to dominate the army, Hunyadi "was one of the first in Eastern Europe to attach importance to the infantry, introducing it to firearms, which were still a novelty."[24] Because the higher nobles were notoriously unreliable—"they care only about their bellies, they will not go to war where the Ottomans are threatening, they do not defend their people," a contemporary observed—Hunyadi increasingly relied on mercenaries, mostly Hungarians, Poles, Germans, and Czechs.[25]

So committed to the defense of the frontier, the voivode often paid them from his own pocket, including through those revenues raised on his vast estates, which in a few years' time consisted of a few million acres that greatly funded the anti-Ottoman struggle.[26] The men, in their turn, came to respect and admire Hunyadi's commitment, not least because he fought side-by-side with them. In years to come, inspired men from as far as Switzerland, France, and even Spain would come to fight under his banner.

Early Campaigns

No sooner did Hunyadi overhaul the military than he did the unthinkable: he took the offensive against the Turks, traditionally the Muslims' prerogative. From his headquarters in Belgrade, he crossed the Danube and crushed a large Ottoman force in 1441—the very same year he became voivode of Transylvania. Thereafter he began to lead successful raids so deep into subject Ottoman territory that it took his men several days to traverse.

Such impertinence could not go unpunished. A large Ottoman army, under the leadership of Mesed Bey—one of Sultan Murad's favorites, who had earlier terrorized Hunyadi's Transylvanian homeland and was even then preparing for another invasion—was mobilized and sent to annihilate the insolent infidel. Before the two forces collided on March 22, 1442, Mesed Bey gave instructions "to try to kill Hunyadi at any cost."[27] To that end, the Turks were given detailed descriptions of the White Knight's armor and appearance. When this became known in the Christian camp, a lesser noble, Simion Kamonyai, offered to exchange armor with his lord. This supreme sacrifice was accepted.

Once Hunyadi's shining armor appeared on horseback, all the Turks converged on its bearer and slaughtered him; but, even as they let their guard down in celebration, the real Hunyadi was leading a successful charge elsewhere. Before long, the "battlefield was strewn with Turkish corpses." Even the elderly Mesed Bey was killed, his head thrust atop a spear. With that, "news of Hunyadi's brilliant victory spread far and wide."[28]

Outraged, Sultan Murad next dispatched Sihabeddin Pasha, governor of Rumelia. Swearing vengeance, he appeared at the head of a mighty host—as many as eighty thousand Ottomans—and boasted that the Christians would flee "hundreds of miles at the mere sight of his turban." Although vastly outnumbered, Hunyadi gave battle on

September 2, 1442, and Sihabeddin "incurred a defeat far more disastrous than that of Mesed Bey which he had hoped to avenge." Thousands of Muslims were killed.[29]

Christendom continued to marvel at Hunyadi's exploits (which, nonetheless, often came with a stiff price, including the death of his younger brother and "faithful companion since their youth").[30] Historian Patrick Balfour (Lord Kinross) summarizes the atmosphere of these times:

> To the Hungarians and Serbs he became the romantic "White Knight," leading his cavalry charges in shining silver armour, whose heroic feats of arms offered a timely hope for Eastern Christendom, promising to liberate it once and for all from the infidel Turks and restore it to unity. Defending some two hundred miles of the southern Hungarian frontier, he won several signal victories against the Ottoman forces, inflicting severe casualties upon them and stimulating the zeal of Christians....[31]

Both Christians and Muslims were especially impressed that, instead of taking a defensive position, Hunyadi was actually taking the offensive—crossing rivers and mountains to confront the Turks in their own domains. There was, in fact, a method to this madness; as Romanian historian Camil Mureșanu explains,

> He was aware of the plans of conquest of the Ottomans and understood that limiting himself to defense meant to expose the country to constant incursions and plunders and to harassment that would eventually lead to exhaustion. That is why he preferred to take the offensive, involving deep penetration into enemy territory, to defeat the adversary decisively on his own territory, thus putting an end to the war that had been going on, with interruptions, for more than half a century. His preference for the offensive was also justified by the support that he was certain he would find in Ottoman lands from the subject [Christian] populations: Romanians, Serbians, Bulgarians, who were waiting for help to come from the north for their liberation.[32]

The Long Campaign

By the end of 1442, "everyone spoke of making war on the infidels and driving them out of Europe"—and it was entirely due to the martial exploits of John Hunyadi, who "was honored as the national hero and savior." The Islamic banners and insignia of the Ottomans, captured on Hunyadi's campaigns, "were distributed among the churches of the land. Here Christians gathered in prayer and thanksgiving, from which they drew strength for their great undertaking."[33]

The time was ripe, a hero found. On January 1, 1443, Pope Eugenius IV issued an encyclical calling for a Crusader coalition to drive the Turks out of Europe, relieve Constantinople—which, for the last eight months, since April 1442, had again been under siege by the Muslims—and secure the Mediterranean, which was then "infested by the piracy of the Moors of North Africa."[34]

Despite all the enthusiasm surrounding Hunyadi's victories, no real help came from the West. The voivode did, however, manage to convince his lord, Ladislaus III, then eighteen-years-old, to take on the role of *defensor christianitatis*, or Defender of Christendom, and spearhead the Crusade without Western aid.[35] The young king of Hungary and Poland agreed.

George Branković, the Serbian despot, a complex figure who played a delicate balancing game between the Turks and his Christian neighbors during his nearly thirty-year reign—now submitting to, now resisting Ottoman suzerainty—was by now also an ardent supporter of the Crusade. He had tried to appease the Turks, and had even given his daughter to the sultan, "but the result of this policy were the loss of his country, the occupation of Semendria, and the capturing and blinding of his two sons."[36] Branković joined the Crusade with six thousand Serbian fighters.

In the end, about twenty-five thousand fighters from Hungary, Poland, Wallachia, Moldavia, and Serbia were raised for the Crusade, many paid and directly supported by Hunyadi. He used the element of surprise by leading this army into Islamic territory only at the end of September 1442—when campaigning season was supposed to end, not begin. Hunyadi was always in the vanguard, a day ahead of the main army and King Ladislaus, its formal leader.

The Christian army marched south, scourging the Turks in every encounter and liberating Serbian town after town. The deeper the Christians penetrated into subject Ottoman territory, the larger their army became, as overjoyed Christian subjects, casting off the yoke of their Muslim masters, rushed to join and augment the ranks of their saviors.

After Hunyadi took Nish (now Niš) in early November, three different Muslim armies converged on the town, in an attempt to trap and annihilate the Christians. With lightning speed, Hunyadi defeated all three, one by one, before they could unite.

By late November, they had reached Sophia in Bulgaria—more than 450 miles whence the Crusaders had first started marching. Considering that Sophia had been under Islamic rule for more than half a century, since 1382, the long oppressed "Bulgarians went wild with joy."[37] Liberator and liberated reconverted the mosques back into churches and gave thanks in them.[38] The long cherished dream of freedom from Islamic domination was becoming palpable:

> The Balkan peoples became excited by the hope of their liberation which appeared close.... [T]he local population welcomed them everywhere with gifts and food, so that the soldiers hardly used the supplies they had brought along. The camp of the king became filled with Bulgarians, Bosnians, Serbians, and Albanians.... According to the sources from that time, the population was very much set against its [Turkish] oppressors.[39]

The victorious Crusaders next set their sights on Adrianople (Edirne)—the very capital of the Ottoman Empire, and the sultan's own seat of power, situated 150 miles west of Constantinople. Once a beautiful Greek city, Adrianople was now a major center of the Muslim slave trade. Its markets were so inundated with Christian flesh that children sold for pennies, "a very beautiful slave woman was exchanged for a pair of boots, and four Serbian slaves were traded for a horse."[40] Outside the Ottoman capital often lay the remains of the unwanted or undesirable; as Bartolomeo de Giano observed four years earlier, "so great a quantity of [European] bodies lay consumed, partially rotted, partially devoured by dogs, that it would seem unbelievable to anyone who had not seen it with their own eyes."[41]

Between the marching Christian army and the Thracian plain leading to Adrianople stood the vast and snow covered mountains of the Balkan range. Although it was by now December—when no one campaigned—Hunyadi forced the march through the frigid cold and harsh terrain, even as panicked Turks did everything to stall him, including blocking the already narrow passes with stones and felled trees and creating walls and narrow paths of slippery ice. Still Hunyadi came on; before long, the sultan was advised to retreat from his capital—so terrified were the Turks.

On December 12, 1443, Hunyadi and his advance cavalry got entrapped at the Zlatitsa Pass; many perished of cold and starvation. On arriving to ambush them, the grand vizier remarked with contempt that he owned more cows than the Christian army had men. After haranguing his exhausted and frozen men with words of violence and hope, "Hunyadi again led that battle himself, and, despite being outnumbered, drove the Turks back to their fortifications in the mountains."[42]

The final battle came on Christmas Eve. Jan Długosz, a contemporary Polish historian (1450–1480), offers a snapshot, one naturally centered around his king, Ladislaus III, who was just behind Hunyadi:

> The Turks withdraw to their camps in the mountains, but Wlady-slaw does not leave them in peace. He launches a fierce attack on Christmas Eve. The Turks shower the Poles with arrows to which the King replies with bullets, crossbow bolts and other missiles. The King himself is hit in the chest with several arrows, but his armor prevents them wounding him. It is long since his men have eaten and the King, afraid to let them fight on, withdraws. The Turks think the withdrawal is flight and attack, but the King turns back and routs them.[43]

Due to the fierce and unrelenting winter, and with their supply lines stretched thin, Hunyadi finally ordered a withdrawal—and not a moment too soon. Many men had died of starvation, and many more would die on the long trek back home. Sources record the emaciated men "staggering from side to side as though about to fall; with their pallid faces and sunken eyes, they are more like skeletons than humans." To make the march easier, all worn down horses were killed and eaten, and all heavy weapons and non-essential equipment were buried or burned, lest the Turks get them.[44]

The skeleton army finally arrived in Buda, led by their king—bare-footed, singing Christian hymns, and brandishing more captured Islamic banners. After receiving a hero's welcome, they fell to their knees and gave thanks for their victories in the main cathedral.

"This march of the crusaders," Balfour correctly observes, "was a military feat seldom paralleled in history."[45] It is now known as "the Long

Campaign," as the Christian army was in nonstop action for more than six months—most of which was in winter and hundreds of miles deep into enemy territory—at a time when campaigns usually lasted no more than two months and rarely past fall. It consisted of seven major battles, all Christian victories.

"[N]ever had the Muslims suffered so much from the cunning and malice of the *gâvur* [infidels]," wrote a Turkish chronicler concerning this Crusade.[46] Not only was "the Ottoman world terrified"—with Muslim cities everywhere hunkering down and refortifying themselves—but even the Mamluk sultan in distant Egypt across the Mediterranean made preparations "to defend Cairo if they heard that John Hunyadi entered Asia Minor."[47]

The Battle of Varna

As happened with King Richard Lionheart two and a half centuries earlier, now Hunyadi's "name struck such fear into the enemy that, when their children cried, [Turkish] mothers made them be quiet by threatening that John would come," to quote Aeneas Piccolomini (1405–1464), the future Pope Pius II, and a contemporary of Hunyadi.[48] Indeed, so "dismayed and stricken with fear"—in a word, traumatized—at what they had just experienced, and so convinced that "the military strength of not only Hungary but also Germany had been mobilized against them"—that "the whole West had formed a league"—the Turks, rather uncharacteristically, "sued for peace."[49] King Ladislaus agreed and a ten-year truce was declared.

Rome was outraged that a peace had been made just when the Ottomans' overthrow seemed imminent. Pope Eugene IV implored Ladislaus to maintain the Crusade and "hurl back the infidel sect of Muhammad overseas," whence it could no longer terrorize the Christian West.[50] Others, including Hunyadi himself, were not so sure; he was concerned at how utterly exhausted Hungary was, how costly the last battles were, and how difficult it was to obtain outside help. But he resigned himself by saying, "I listen to the ruler, I do not rule."[51]

For long Ladislaus deliberated; although he did not want "to abandon his defense of Christendom," he also did not want to renege on the peace treaty he had made with Murad.[52] During that time, John Palaeologus, the emperor of perennially besieged Constantinople—who knew the Turks better than most—sent a message warning the Hungarian king "against false, deceitful peace treaties" from the Ottomans (a sentiment echoed by many contemporary Christians*). When soon thereafter the Turks refused to surrender several castles they had agreed to in keeping with the treaty, Ladislaus finally decided to resume the war.[53]

He managed to put together an army of some twenty thousand fighters drawn primarily from Hungary, Poland, and Wallachia. The Serbian despot—having achieved an advantageous peace with his Ottoman neighbor following the Long Campaign—did not participate and likely exposed the Christians' plans to Murad. In response, the sultan himself led the Muslim army, which at the very least outnumbered the Crusaders by four-to-one (though several sources put the Ottoman army at one hundred and twenty thousand men). Such swollen numbers could mobilize so quickly only because Murad had proclaimed a *defensive* jihad,[†] prompting his chief ulema to issue a fatwa, "in accordance with sharia law," saying that, "because the infidels who are as low as the dust are attacking us, it is an obligation on all of us to join the jihad."[54]

Being so outnumbered, Hunyadi's plan was to shock and awe the enemy—"to attack them violently, to strike terror amidst them" with "vigour and quickness."[55] The opposing forces finally met at Varna by the Black Sea. There, on November 10, 1444, in the midst of a massive sea-storm and driving wind, the Christians and Muslims collided in one of history's most dramatic battles. In the words of an Ottoman chronicler: "They shot each other with cannons, muskets, and crossbows, like a rain of death. The accursed king [Ladislaus] stood in the middle, the accursed Yanko [Hunyadi] on one side…and attacked Sultan Murad and overwhelmed him, carried both his wings away, and grappled with the Anatolian troops. It was a very great battle."[56]

---

* As the contemporary, Konstantin Mihailović (b. 1430), a former Ottoman soldier, wrote, "If the emperor [Turkish sultan] makes peace and an armistice with someone, even as he makes peace, he seeks again to deceive him" (Mihailović, 15).

† According to Islamic jurisprudence, whereas offensive jihad (*jihad al-talab*)—when Muslims invade and seek to conquer non-Muslim territories—is a communal duty (*fard kifaya*) on the Muslim polity (*umma*), meaning as long as some Muslims are committed to it, the rest are exonerated, defensive jihad (*jihad al-difaʾ*)—when Muslims defend their territories against infidel encroachment—is an individual duty (*fard ʿayn*), meaning every capable Muslim is obligated to participate.

So overwhelmed by the fiery onslaught of this Christian blitzkrieg, the much larger Turkish lines began to break; terrified Muslims "fled before the infidels had even attacked them," continues the Turkish chronicler. "No one remained; they ran away without looking behind them." On seeing this, Murad cried, "O Allah, give the religion of Islam strength and bestow victory on the religion of Islam out of respect for the light of Muhammad."[57] Instantly, Allah reportedly "caused temptations to enter the heart of the accursed king [Ladislaus] so that he became overweening and attacked Sultan Murad. In his pride he thought himself a mighty hero...and hurled himself against Sultan Murad's people. Through Allah's grace the king's horse stumbled and he himself fell head over heels on his face." Two giant Muslims instantly pounced on and beheaded him. Concludes the Ottoman chronicler:

> When Sultan Murad saw it, he thanked Allah greatly and had the head stuck on a spear and held aloft. Criers cried in all four directions, saying "The king's head has been cut off and stuck on a spear!" The whole scattered army reformed around Sultan Murad.... When the accursed Yanko [Hunyadi] saw that the [Christian] armies were beginning to scatter [on news of the king's slaughter], he said to the infidels, "We came here for the sake of our religion, not for the sake of the king!" and thus he brought the army to order again. Then he turned and made two or three attacks. He saw that the Muslims had increased in numbers [because those who had fled were returning] and thought it best to flee without further ado. When the army of Islam saw this, they pursued the infidels on every side. The soldiers of Islam had beaten the soldiers of the infidels and began to kill them.[58]

While the above Muslim account is permeated with hagiographical elements, its general outline is confirmed by Christian sources. Greek historian Doukas succinctly summarizes the battle as follows:

> A terrific and frightful battle was fought from early morning until the ninth hour [3 p.m.], and the Christians butchered the Turks mercilessly. At about the tenth hour the Saxon king [Ladislaus], accompanied by about five hundred troops, turned his cavalry toward the enemy. Janos [Hunyadi] attempted to stop him but could not. And as the Saxon king drew near, his horse was struck a mortal blow, throwing its rider headlong. The Turks decapitated him on the

spot. Janos became aware of what had happened when he saw the head hoisted on a lance. There were cries and shouts, such as, "Let him flee who can!" The Turks slaughtered most of the Christians. As night fell, Janos barely escaped by crossing the Danube.[59]

Turkish casualties were so high, and mangled bodies were so widely scattered, that it took the sultan three days before he could confirm his victory.[60] Aside from those few who managed to escape, the Christians were utterly annihilated. There and then, "in accordance with a barbarous custom, the Sultan ordered tables to be set and held a feast among the corpses of the vanquished."[61] As for Ladislaus's head, Murad "had it flayed and the skin stuffed with various roots and cotton so that it would not spoil; and he had the hair combed and prepared with sulfide, so that it would be made up as if it were alive. And he ordered that this head be stuck on a pike and carried about all his cities," as proof that Allah "had let him vanquish his enemy."[62]

Because Varna was arguably the greatest victory of Murad's career, he decreed that "all the community of Muhammad should be informed [of it]. Let there be great illuminations and celebrations so that all the community of Muhammad can rejoice, and the infidel[s]…suffer grief and foreboding when they hear of it."[63] In a letter to the sultan of Tabriz, Murad boasted of how Allah had made him victorious "in scattering and confounding the infidels who are as low as the earth," adding "may Allah exterminate and destroy them and may He not leave a trace of them on the face of the earth." Especially invective words were directed against the "the ill-omened Hungarians, who are worshippers of idols…enemies of the religion of the Prophet and deniers of Muhammad's message."[64]

A dynastic crisis followed the untimely death of Ladislaus III, this twenty-year-old Crusader who was killed before marrying and producing an heir; and a period of great turmoil followed in Hungary, as the higher nobles and barons jockeyed for power. John of Zrenda, Hunyadi's comrade, described the situation in a letter dated April 24, 1445: "The truth is kept quiet, the barriers of common sense are broken, the reins of law have loosened…. The iron, arbitrary, unrestrained violence destroys and does not respect anyone's rights: hate, treason, and the most impudent oppression are free to rule."[65] During this time, Hunyadi's "advice was always the same: that the discords should be brought to an end…

and that they should keep in view, above all else, the cloudy southern horizons," whence the Turks would eventually reappear.[66]

Due to the prestige surrounding his many victories against the Turks—in 1445 he destroyed yet another Ottoman army encroaching near Belgrade—and because he was the most able man for the job, on June 5, 1446, Hunyadi was elected governor of Hungary and regent of the new king, Ladislaus V, then just six-years-old.

The Battle of Kosovo II

Although busy ruling Hungary "with an iron rod," Hunyadi "could not forget the shame he had incurred at Varna and pondered day and night on how to erase the infamy and repair his losses," writes Aeneas.[67] His disgrace was compounded by the fact that the emboldened Turks had again begun to raid, slaughter, and enslave all along the border. Thus, in 1447, less than a year after being appointed regent, Hunyadi began contemplating a new offensive.

A year later, none of those solicited were willing to join or aid the Hungarian governor's new war effort, including Hungary's higher noblemen and barons—the elites—theoretically Hunyadi's closest and most reliable allies. Due to his relatively modest and "self-made" background, they had "never recognized him as one of their own: they regarded him with contempt, considering him an upstart."[68] They were further "upset by his energetic rule" and, as such, offered him the most limited of aid; indeed, not a few of them "were secretly hoping that he would be defeated and not return [from battle] or have his prestige weakened to such an extent that he could be removed from power."[69]

King Casimir IV of Poland, citing ongoing Muslim raids—by Tatars not Turks—was also only able to offer a thousand mounted fighters. Even the new pope, Nicholas V, who was supposed to raise troops and money for this new Crusade, excused himself, telling Hunyadi to postpone the campaign for another year. The governor of Hungary responded with frustration—but also resolution—in a letter dated September 8, 1448:

> We have addressed Your Holiness with complete faith, with the conviction that we shall obtain not only promises, but real help. Your holiness, however, encouraging us rather than giving us support, wishes the postponement of the campaign and anticipates a delay in

the assistance. But when our old enemy has gained new powers as a result of its latest victories over Christianity and is gathering great forces at our borders, it is useful for us to take up arms, so that an attack does not find us unprepared.... The war has been decided, the army has been gathered, the orders have been given. Power is always greater when used in attack rather than in defense, and the outcome of the war smiles more favorably upon the one who pursues the enemy in its own land. Besides, it is not certain that next year we will be able to gather the same army and that it will be as enthusiastic. We are prepared to do everything to defend our country from impending danger. Our descendants will glorify our victory, as well as our death in battle. We and our brave comrades have endangered our lives for the well-being of Christianity, and it would be appropriate for the Holy Father to offer financial help for the gathering of a supporting army.[70]

In the end, Hunyadi managed to raise some twenty-four thousand soldiers—most of them on his payroll. While marching with them into enemy territory, where they witnessed much suffering and destruction, Hunyadi received another irresolute message from Pope Nicholas. This was too much. After explaining that he was advancing against the Turks "not only to fight the war, but to end it,"[71] the warlord unburdened his soul in another letter dated September 17:

[T]he enemy attacks our neighbors [the Serbs], incites [them] to war against us. We have decided to attack him instead of waiting for him to attack us. We have had enough of our men enslaved, our women raped, wagons loaded with the severed heads of our people, the sale of chained captives, the mockery of our religion.... [W]e shall not stop until we succeed in expelling the enemy from Europe.[72]

Hunyadi was counting on meeting up with the distant Albanians, but the Serbian despot—casting his lot with the Ottomans once again—prevented their passage. Frustration turned to rage when Hunyadi and his men learned that the Serbs had betrayed them, including by "refusing to take up arms against the Turks, though the war was started to right their wrongs and recover their possessions now in Turkish hands," writes the Polish chronicler.[73]

At the fields of Kosovo—where, nearly sixty years earlier, and rather ominously, the Turks had first crushed a Christian coalition in

1389—Murad, with as many as sixty thousand Ottomans, surprised Hunyadi. The latter defiantly harangued his outnumbered men to fight with all their might and either "win a good and secure life for our country, forever," or "die with glory, and eternal life is waiting for us on the other side."[74] For his part, the ever pious Muslim sultan dismounted, fell to the floor facing Mecca, performed two prostrations, and implored Allah to empower the "community of Muhammad."[75]

The battle lasted a full three days, from October 17–20, with many reverses and shedding of blood. Aeneas's account follows:

> Hunyadi did not wait to be challenged but initiated the fight himself. When battle was commenced, the outcome of the struggle long remained uncertain. Where Hunyadi fought, the enemy was routed and turned tail, and a great slaughter was carried out. In the same way, Murad was victorious on his own wing, where he overwhelmed and routed the Hungarians. Finally, when the two victors came head to head, the Christians were unable to withstand the onslaught of the Turks. Although they were superior in courage, they were surpassed in numbers and compelled to give way out of exhaustion rather than defeat.[76]

Despite Hunyadi's "threats and pleas," the outnumbered Christian army began to crumble; before long its "rank and file was massacred." Fifteen thousand Christians lay dead; not content, Murad ordered them all decapitated, their heads placed on spears.[77]

During the carnage and chaos, three Muslims captured Hunyadi, without knowing who he was, for he was often fighting at the front alongside his men. Jan Długosz has the rest:

> One of them goes off to hunt other fugitives, leaving the others to guard Hunyadi. These now quarrel over a golden crucifix he wore under his shirt, which they had not previously noticed. As they are squabbling, Hunyadi picks up a sword and kills one of them and wounds the other, and so recovers his possessions. He wanders for several days and eventually reaches Serbian territory and, trustingly, goes to a castle, where he is seized and kept prisoner for three months....[78]

Clearly, the significance of the word "Balkanization" is much older than commonly assumed.

At any rate, Hungary's elites got what they wanted—the disgrace of Hunyadi. He remained governor, though his prestige tanked; no one especially wanted to hear any more talk of Crusades. Considering that the army he had spent two years rebuilding had been annihilated at Kosovo, the upper nobles became increasingly aggressive and defiant. Rather than fold and capitulate, however, Hunyadi revealed that there was more to him than battle and bloodshed, and the next few years saw him transformed into an adroit politician and diplomat.

Muhammad the Conqueror

In 1451, Murad II died and was succeeded by Muhammad II* (b. 1432), one of his many sons, known to history as "the Conqueror." The first thing this nineteen-year-old sultan did was profess his desire for peace with his Christian neighbors—a claim that appeared all the more sincere due to his notoriously libertine lifestyle. The "evil one," wrote a bitter Doukas retrospectively, repeatedly professed that "he was a genuine friend of Christians, and that the Christians...had a trusted friend in him."[79] The war-weary Europeans took him at his word, and on November 20, 1451, a three-year armistice was declared.

In fact, Muhammad needed and asked for peace with the Christians in order to focus on and quell a Turkish rebellion in Karaman. After he had consolidated his rule, the sultan—who "deceived under truce whenever he could"—reneged on all vows of peace and put Constantinople to siege in April 1453.[80] Hunyadi immediately wrote him citing their armistice and calling on him to lift the siege; it fell on deaf ears. Weeks later, on May 29, Constantinople—that ancient Christian bastion that was first targeted for conquest and besieged by Islam eight centuries earlier—finally fell to Muhammad.

The well-documented atrocities that followed remain mind boggling: Christian women, children, and even men were herded, sexually abused or raped, and sadistically mutilated. "There were lamentations and weeping in every house, screaming in the crossroads, and sorrow in all churches," wrote George Sphrantzes, an eyewitness; "the groaning of grown men and the shrieking of women accompanied looting,

---

* Although his name is spelled in Old Turkish (which uses the Arabic script) as *Muhammad* (محمد), it is pronounced by modern day Turks and often transliterated in English as "Mehmet."

enslavement, separation, and rape."[81] Even inside the Hagia Sophia, one of Christendom's greatest and oldest basilicas, the Muslim conquerors "engaged in every kind of vileness within it, making of it a public brothel."[82] On "its holy altars" they enacted "perversions with our women, virgins, and children," including "the Grand Duke's daughter who was quite beautiful."[83] She was forced to "lie on the great altar of Hagia Sophia with a crucifix under her head and then raped."[84]

Everywhere churches were desecrated, their crosses and Bibles spat on and consigned to the flames. To cap off his triumph, Muhammad the Conqueror had the "wretched citizens of Constantinople" dragged before his men during evening festivities and "ordered many of them to be hacked to pieces, for the sake of entertainment."[85] Muhammad then retired to a night of debauchery with young captive boys;[86] and his fighters retired to their tents—and "every tent was filled with handsome boys and beautiful girls," to quote Tursun Beg, a leading Turk who was present.[87] The rest of the city's Christians—as many as sixty thousand—were hauled off in chains to be sold as slaves.[88]

Consternation, fear, and terror spread throughout Europe following this traumatic event. Not only did the fall of this ancient city founded by the first Christian Roman emperor have symbolic dimensions; but if its legendary walls could be breached by the hordes of Islam, whose walls could long withstand them? In short, "from the moment when the crescent supplanted the cross on the dome of St. Sophia the whole situation completely changed. It was now no longer a part but the whole of Christendom that was in immediate danger."[89]

Such concerns worked to Hunyadi's favor, in that more and more Christians began to appreciate "the specter of the Ottoman danger": "It was clear that the Ottomans could no longer be driven from Europe. On the contrary, new and powerful attacks from them were to be expected. The Hungarian nobles, who neither wanted to defend their country, nor to lose it completely, ceased their open actions against John Hunyadi, realizing that they would need him again."[90]

Plans for a new Crusade were discussed at the imperial diet held in April 1454 in Regensburg. Many noble and heroic words of Christian solidarity were proclaimed, but in the end nothing came of them. At first, the Holy Roman Emperor, Frederick III, known as "the Peaceful," showed interest in participating, but then backed out. Nearly a year later, in February 1455, at another conference in Neustradt, Hunyadi stormed in and barked at the emperor: "enough words, show us facts if you are a true Christian and a true emperor!"[91] But Frederick kept vacillating.

Rumors of Wars

For Sultan Muhammad's part, far from being sated by accomplishing what Muslims had been trying to accomplish for over eight hundred years—that is, the conquest of Constantinople, a fond dream of the Prophet Muhammad[*]—his Ottoman namesake continued saber-rattling and swore to be master of Europe in his lifetime. Considering that he was only twenty-one when he conquered the city of the Christian Caesars, this was not an inconceivable dream. All that stood between him and the West was the natural barrier of the Danube River, which tended to demarcate the extent of Ottoman suzerainty. It was mostly guarded by the Hungarians, whom Muhammad especially sought to subjugate and disgrace for their long years of defiance; or, in the terse words of a Turkish chronicle, Muhammad sought to "humble the pride of the enemy of the faith [Islam]."[92]

In response, once the aged Alfonso Borgia became Pope Callixtus III on April 8, 1455, he vowed to "sacrifice all the treasures of the church—nay, life itself—for the holy cause [of securing Christendom against Islam]."[93] A bull preaching a new Crusade was issued and legates sent to all the courts of Europe.

But this was not 1095; Crusading zeal had long since diminished among the heads of Europe. "The spirits of our princes waver," explained Aeneas: "the kings slumber."[94] Hungary continued to suffer from dynastic disputes and internal discord, which worked to the favor of and greatly empowered the nobles and elites. They, as usual, thought first and

---

[*] As attested to by several early hadiths, including one which has Muhammad say, "Surely, Constantinople will be conquered [by my umma/community]; how blessed the commander who will conquer it, and how blessed his army" (Gullen, 192). According to a later Turkish account, "[A Muslim youth said:] 'Apostle of Allah, I have traveled far and wide…but of all the places I have seen, I never saw a place like the land of the Rum [Anatolia, modern-day Turkey, for centuries the heart of the Eastern Roman Empire]. Its towns are close to each other, its rivers are full of water, its springs are gushing…and its people are extremely friendly—except that they are all infidels.' And he described it at such great length that the blessed mind of the Apostle became very fond of Rum indeed. [So Allah declared:] 'My blessed apostle has taken a liking to Rum, so I on my part must grant that province to his umma. May they pull down its monasteries and set up mosques and madrasas in their places'" (Hillenbrand 2007, 159).

foremost of their own interests. Even the now fifteen-year-old king himself, Ladislaus V, "a trivial and cowardly boy, was entirely in the hands of evil and alien counsellors, who taught him to hate his fatherland and endeavored to govern in his name."[95] Five months after his pontificate began, Callixtus III had lost heart, writing on September 5, 1455,

> We learn with heartfelt grief that our glorious Hungary, so full of good works and good-will, so long the shield and buckler of Christendom, lies in confusion and disorder, head and limbs alike being crazy and feeble. Thus our faith will be deprived of its surest prop unless her leaders give each other the right hand of fellowship and return to the paths of true peace and charity.[96]

In an effort to ameliorate the situation, the pope summoned Cardinal Juan de Carvajal, a Spaniard, ceremoniously adorned his chest with a red Cross on white background—the symbol of the new Crusade—and sent him off to preach in Hungary, Poland, and Germany, "to rouse" Christians "to arms and stem the power of the Turks"[97]

During this time, one man did not need any prodding to take up the Cross. Even as the Turkish war drums were beating, Hunyadi was acting fast. He again wrote to and implored Emperor Frederick to rise up in defense of the faith while he still could. If the whole of Christendom could raise just one hundred thousand men—a trifle compared to the countless legions ever ready at the sultan's beck and call—he would personally donate one hundred thousand ducats to the war effort, lead it, and annihilate the Turks once and for all. When, on November 22, Cardinal Carvajal reached Austria and added to Hunyadi's appeal, Frederick accepted the Cross from his hands and swore to participate in the Crusade (little would come of it).

Carvajal next arrived in Buda, where the young Hungarian king summoned a diet on February 6, 1456. An animated Hunyadi was there, swearing to raise as many as ten thousand fighters at his own expense and to shed every last drop of blood in defense of Christendom. The White Knight's inspiring harangue and bold words prompted Carvajal to refer to him in a letter as the "Macchabeaus of our times." Another papal representative confidently wrote back to Callixtus: "'Tis John, called Hunyadi, who is to be the salvation of Christendom."[98]

The enthusiasm became contagious at Buda: Ladislaus offered to raise twenty thousand men, if Italy, Aragon, and Burgundy would contribute a total of thirty-two thousand men. At even this prospect, Hunyadi "confidently promised that with such a host behind him he would not leave the Turk a spot in Europe whereon to lay his head—nay, that the recapture of Constantinople would only be the first step towards the recovery of the holy sepulcher at Jerusalem."[99] Crusading zeal had returned—or had it?

The very day after the diet convened, news reached Buda that Muhammad, at the head of a mammoth army, was finally on the war path. The sultan, who "was itching with impatience to begin the campaign," was not just coming to conquer; he was coming to punish and humiliate.[100] As such, he would take no chances. Since 1455 and all throughout the beginning of 1456, he had been assembling an army the size of which was beyond "the bounds of computation."[101] Chroniclers place its number between one hundred fifty thousand to as many as four hundred thousand (though the smaller number is more realistic). With this war machine came much heavy artillery, including twenty cannons, each nearly thirty feet long. To add insult to injury, some of these monstrous destroyers of Christian cities had been forged from melted church bells seized from Constantinople.[102]

A veritable zoo consisting of camels, oxen, buffaloes, and whatever else could be harnessed, dragged all this heavy equipment and provisions for hundreds of miles from Adrianople: "Of mills for grinding corn, ovens for baking bread, and vessels for divers uses there was no end," wrote a contemporary: "[T]hey were also bringing with them legions of dogs to eat the corpses of the Christians. They came, we are told, not as if to besiege a fortress, but to conquer a kingdom."[103]

Muhammad's destination, it soon became clear, was the ancient fortress of Belgrade along the Danube, the key to Hungary and beyond. To say that he was—and had good reason to be—confident in his latest jihadist undertaking is an understatement. According to Aeneas,

> As he drew closer, Muhammad was full of hope and swollen with incredible pride, thinking that neither mountains nor rivers stood in his way. Bragging to his men, he claimed that Hungary was already all but conquered. The [Holy Roman] emperor of the Latins, he said, was close at hand, and, now that the [Eastern Roman] empire of the

Greeks had been destroyed, the end was near for that of the Latins, too; the whole world would be subject to the Turks. He promised them large spoils and offered up Germany and Italy for his soldiers to pillage. He boasted that every place lay open to Turkish arms.[104]

Cognizant of all the death, destruction, and atrocities this massive Muslim march presaged—memory of the sack of Constantinople was still fresh—a great panic swept along the Danube. The rulers of Wallachia and Serbia fled to Hungary with their wives and children; the ruler of Moldavia sent salt to the sultan and promised an annual tribute of two thousand ducats. Most ignominious of all, Ladislaus V, the young Hungarian king, immediately reneged on all his bold words at the diet of Buda and fled his capital to Vienna under the cover of darkness (on the pretext that he was going "hunting").

In so doing, he set the example: every man for himself. The nobles took provisions and shut themselves up in their castles and fortresses. Great demoralization and despair set in among the populace. Even Carvajal, the legate, who only yesterday was satisfied with his efforts to raise a Crusade, lost hope, writing to the pope:

> This kingdom [of Hungary] is on the eve of a terrible disaster, for neither with its own resources nor yet with the aid of the [Holy Roman] empire can it bring together forces sufficient to cope with the Turk. Our only hope is that God will listen to the prayers of your holiness and move the hearts of the princes to send their fleets. So pressing is the peril that the delay of a day or even of an hour may bring about such a defeat as shall make all Christendom weep for evermore.[105]

Only one stood his ground and kept his word—only Hunyadi. Even as the king fled west, Hunyadi raced to the eastern frontier—towards, not away, from the Turkish army that, like an overwhelming morass, was swallowing everything in its way. His actions are all the more remarkable considering that his regency and governorship of Hungary had ended a year earlier—meaning he had every right to behave like the other nobles, that is, selfishly. He immediately manned the fortress of Belgrade with six thousand veteran fighters under the command of his brother-in-law Mihály Szilágyi and Hunyadi's eldest son László.

He then desperately called on the nobles of Hungary and Wallachia to supply him with more men; it fell on deaf ears. In the end, "of the thousands of gentlemen who held their lands by military tenure, and were bound by honour and duty alike to defend their country by force of arms, only some half-dozen of his personal friends, with a handful of horsemen, appeared at his summons."[106]

Unable to rely on the men of state, Hunyadi turned to a man of God, the seventy-year-old Franciscan, John Capistrano, "a wise man held in great religious esteem by the western peoples," to quote Chalkokon-dyles.[107] Capistrano and Hunyadi shared more than name: for "the desire to rescue Christendom from the infidel was the ruling passion of them both." "Come hither to me," Hunyadi wrote to the friar, "that the power of God may sustain the efforts of man."[108]

Capistrano went to southern Hungary with a small band of veteran Crusaders, calling on the people to take the Cross and defend their nation against Islam. His "burning zeal, soul-piercing eloquence, and heroic austerities" set tens of thousands of the lower classes aflame.[109] They had had enough of their impotent betters and "were not content contributing money for the crusade, nor did they care any longer what their feudal lords thought about their taking the cross and leaving. It was time, they argued, to take matters into their own hands."[110]

Before long the old Franciscan had assembled and was followed by a massive throng of would-be Crusaders, composed "not from the rich or the nobly born but the penurious and simple common people," observed Aeneas: "Over forty thousand received the sign of the cross—an army protected more by faith than the sword."[111] But their quantity could not conceal their quality. According to historian Nisbet Bain,

A sorrier band of warriors surely never came together. We are told by one who saw these crusaders that they were all men of low degree, or rather no degree—rustics, beggars, mendicant friars, hermits, day labourers, and such like. Not a sword or a lance was to be seen in the hands of any of them. Slings, cudgels, pitchforks, hatchets, and axes were their only weapons. Yet this motley throng, fired by the zeal and enthusiasm of Capistran, was animated by the spirit of martyrs and heroes, and was ready to follow to the death the withered little old man whose frail body was worn to a skeleton by ceaseless fastings, watchings, and journeyings, and whose feeble arms leaned heavily on the tough oaken staff on which he had carved the name of the Redeemer.[112]

The world had turned upside down. "Where is the Roman Empire which has always fought the barbarians?" a contemporary document inquires: "Where is the French king, who wants to call himself the Christian king? Where are the kings of England, Denmark, Norway, Sweden, Poland...? Unarmed peasants, blacksmiths, tailors, tradesmen are walking in front of the armies; it seems that they alone have been granted by God faith in great deeds!"[113]

During those same few weeks, and after much exertion—pleading, praying, paying—Hunyadi had finally managed to raise a regular army consisting of some twelve thousand infantry and a thousand cavalry; they all mobilized at his camp along the Danube. Hurriedly, day and night, many of these new recruits were drilled in the arts of war, even as Hunyadi had all the riverine crafts he could appropriate, some two hundred, converted into vessels of war.

The Siege of Belgrade

By late June 1456, Muhammad's vast forces had reached the old and strategically situated fortress of Belgrade. Twenty-three years earlier a French visitor described it as follows:

> Belgrade is surrounded by high walls. Along the walls on one side flows the Sava River, and on the other side is the city, on the bank of the Danube. The fortress is, therefore, located in a triangle formed by the two rivers. The land is high on all sides except on the land-side where it is so flat that one can walk all the way up to the moat.... The fortress, which is very strong on account of its location, is surrounded by a moat and a double wall.[114]

Both Christians and Muslims knew that if Belgrade could not resist the Ottomans, the rest of Hungary and further west would be exposed to and eventually inundated by the hordes of Asia.

On arriving, Muhammad set to surrounding it, both by land and water. He set his camp on the neck of the headland, so that the land side of the fortress also resembled a sea—a sea of Turkish tents, which is all that the Christian defenders atop Belgrade's walls could see for miles around. By water, sixty galleys and 150 smaller vessels of war choked the fortress. Many of them were chained together to serve as a blockade against any would-be relief.

Once everything was ready, Muhammad ordered the heavy bombardment to begin on July 4 (the anniversary of another important Islamic victory over the Cross, at Hattin in 1187). The crashing and careening cannon fire was so thunderously loud that it could be heard for a hundred miles around. Twelve days later, on July 16, massive breaches punctuated this once formidable fortress. Everything was so going according to plan that Muhammad reaffirmed his oath that, not only would he take Belgrade, but soon Buda and the whole of Hungary.[115]

Two days earlier, on July 14, as Hunyadi was still outfitting his fleet, a messenger from Belgrade arrived and reported that the fortress was on its final leg. But Hunyadi was far from ready: his professional army was barely as large as Muhammad's personal guard; and, while "the sight," writes Chalkokondyles, of the forty thousand or so peasant Crusaders following Capistrano "inspired confidence everywhere," Hunyadi remained doubtful—not of their commitment but because he was well-acquainted with the enemy. Either way, the time was now or never; they must all set out for Belgrade's relief or die trying.[116]

Thus, hours after the messenger arrived on July 14, in the pitch blackness of a moonless night, the Christian relief force set out on and along the Danube. Hunyadi rode aboard the largest vessel in his makeshift fleet, a flagship bringing the rear, full of provisions and weapons. Most of the smaller ships in the van were manned by the zealous Crusaders. The bulk followed on foot along the riverbank behind Capistrano.

On seeing the puny Christian fleet nearing their professional galleons, many of which were fettered together by chains and formed a huge damn across the water, the Turks scoffed, even as they braced for the inevitable crash. On the signal—loud cries of "Jesus! Jesus!"—the Christian flotilla smashed into the chained Muslim ships.[117] Simultaneously, Belgrade's defenders, who were closely watching, sent out their forty ships to aid their would-be rescuers. They were manned "mainly with Serbians…people who despised the Ottomans and were ready to do anything to resist them."[118]

The Danube flowed with hot blood as a savage river battle took place for five hours. All that time, Capistrano, with Cross held aloft and imploring heaven, ran about the riverbank, "with all the vigour of a robust youth."[119] His prayers were answered: The massive linked chains of the Ottoman boats eventually burst asunder, and the Christian fleet made it to and reinforced Belgrade, which was at its final extremity.

Three or four of the largest Ottoman galleons—and the thousand fighters aboard them—sunk in this river war; another four galleons were captured. The rest were in such disarray, full of dead and dying, that, once they reached land, Muhammad ordered the vessels burnt—lest they too fall into Christian hands.[120] "From that point on," affirms Chalkokondyles, "the Hungarians held the river and were able to make conveyances from the opposite shore to the city, to strengthen its defenses. Present were Hunyadi and his men as well as the monk Capistrano."[121]

A spectacular start for the relief force, it was but a scratch to the Turks: their fleet was always an added measure, nothing indispensable. Worse, on that same day, Ottoman cannons—now living instruments of the sultan's wrath—exploded in a barrage of fire that rocked Belgrade to its very foundation. Unsurprisingly, and despite his heroic splash, Hunyadi found its garrison in a fatalistic mood. As always he harangued them with bold and pious words:

> What fear you? Is this the first time you have seen the Turks? Are not these the very same we have so often put to flight, and who have sometimes put us to flight also? Why should their familiar aspect disturb you now? Surely you know by this time what manner of men they are! Be of a stout heart, then, my dear sons. Put your trust in Christ. Did He not die for us? And should we, then, account it a hardship to die for Him? Be valiant, then, and strive manfully. If God be with us the foe will prove a coward. What more need I say to you when you have already proved the truth of my words so many times beneath my banner?[122]

For another week, the cannons continued to thunder. By now, and despite the energetic and renewed repairs made possible by the relief force, Belgrade's ramparts were on a level with the ground, though a few towers and bastions partially stood. Even the moat was now filled with massive logs hauled a great distance by the Turks' beasts-of-burden for the purpose of bridging the city.[123]

Finally, at the crack of dawn on July 21, for miles around, "one could hear the ceaseless beat of the drums that announced the attack."[124] The time had come; now it was Muhammad's turn to harangue his men, which he did to great effect—including by again promising them victory one way or another: wealth and women either in the here or hereafter. Then, "the sultan gave the signal, and the janissaries [elite shock troops of the Ottomans], drowning with their shouts of 'Allah! Allah!' the din of the horns and kettledrums, rushed headlong into the city through the three great breaches which yawned open before them."[125]

Expecting to slay or be slayed and either way gain an earthly or heavenly paradise (in keeping with Koran 9:111), the Muslims were shocked to find the walls undefended, the citadel deserted. Convinced that the Christians had tucked tail and run, the raiders instantly set to plundering. But it was all a ruse: Hunyadi had earlier told the Christians to hide in every nook and cranny, among crumbled stone and in hidden passage, to prompt the invaders to let their guard down; only when the trumpet blast was heard were the defenders to emerge and ambush their besiegers. Accordingly, once thousands of Turks had crowded in between the walls and the citadel, the signal was given: to the piercing sound of blasting horns, the "hellish Janko," to quote a Turkish chronicler, came charging out of the citadel, even as throngs of peasant Crusaders appeared above the walls and behind the Turks.[126] The janissaries were trapped between a rock and a hard place:

> A terrible struggle ensued. The Turks, though taken at an advantage, were as ten to one and armed to the teeth, whilst most of their antagonists were scarcely armed at all. A hand-to-hand melee went on in every street, but the fight was fiercest on the narrow bridge leading from the citadel to the town, where Hunyadi commanded in person, and on the bastions, which were defended by crusaders hastily brought across the river on rafts.[127]

In this manner, "the battle continued by day and night," writes Aeneas: "At one moment, the enemy seemed vanquished, at another victorious."[128] Despite being so wildly disadvantaged in numbers and arms, the Christians—including Hunyadi, who fought in their midst like a common foot-soldier—held their own and managed to kill many.

For their part, the Turks, who fought "like ravening beasts," to quote Ottoman chronicler, S'ad al-Din, "poured out their life's blood like water in the place of death, and countless heroes tasted the pure honey of a martyr's death and were caught up into the arms of the *houris* of paradise."[129] Still, for every one Muslim martyred, a dozen fresh jihadists appeared—even as hails of Turkic arrows turned the ground into a spike-studded field.

Unable to withstand this Muslim press, the Christian ranks began to break and retreat; some leapt off the wall into the river far below. "But John Hunyadi remained firm in the middle of his troops, as did the crusaders, among whom women were seen fighting as well."[130] When a Turk tried to place the flag of the Islamic crescent on the highest wall, one Titus Dugovich rushed to him and, embracing him tightly during their bitter struggle, hurled both himself and his foe—and the Islamic standard—from off the high tower to their deaths.[131]

It was now just before dawn, July 22; the battle had raged for a day and night, and it was clear that the Christians—having reached the limits of human capacity and endurance—were on the verge of collapsing under the sheer numbers of their foes who continued to pour in. High up on a watch tower, the seventy-year-old Capistrano was seen waving the banner of the Cross and imploring Heaven: "Oh Jesus, where are Thy tender mercies which Thou hast shown to us of old? Oh, come and aid us, and tarry not. Save, oh, save Thy redeemed, lest the heathen say, 'Where is now their God ?'"[132]

At that point, the Christians, pushed back to the citadel and high places, began to rain down fire on the votaries of Islam. With all the combustibles they could gather—wood, dried branches, anything that would burn—"and with one accord setting fire thereto," the defenders "cast them down, mingled with burning pitch and sulphur, both upon the Turks who were in the ditches and upon those who were scaling the walls," writes one Tagliacotius, who participated in the battle, before continuing:

> None could flee from the face of the fire. All who were in the ditches, the multitude whereof no man can number, were consumed by the fire; not one of them remained alive. Those who were about to descend into the ditches fell back in terror, and those who were in the camp and strove, furiously fighting, to occupy the bridge, seeing themselves every way encompassed by the flames of an exceeding great fire, gave up fighting, and loudly shouting, strove to escape, who, smitten with blind terror and full of confusion, and thinking to

escape by leaping from the walls, plunged again into the fire and were there consumed. But they who feared to take the leap were cut down by the crusaders in the open space within the outer wall.[133]

After all the shrieks had died out and the smoke cleared, the rising sun slowly revealed the gory aftermath. All around Belgrade, inside and out, were the dead and dying bodies of countless Turks—charred beyond all recognition:

> [T]he ditches and the whole space between the outer walls and the citadel were filled with their scorched and bleeding corpses. Thousands of them had perished there. The janissaries in particular had suffered so terribly that the survivors of them were thoroughly cowed, while the sultan's body-guard, which had led the attack, was well-nigh annihilated. So, after a twenty-hours' combat, the Christian host was able to breathe freely once more.[134]

And yet, in terms of actual casualties—in terms of numbers—this was but a scratch to the gargantuan Ottoman army that still surrounded Belgrade. Another assault was expected; and Hunyadi—who "well knew that the Turk is never so dangerous as when he is in difficulties," a lesson he had well learned at Varna and Kosovo—proclaimed that everyone was to remain on guard and at his post, on pain of death, "lest the glory of the day be turned into confusion."[135]

By late noon on July 22, however, a handful of the thousands of Crusaders stationed outside Belgrade were ambushed by the Turks. On seeing this, other groups of peasant Crusaders rushed out from behind the walls or off the islets to their brethren's aid—despite even Capistrano's remonstrances. Indeed, before long, the ancient Crusader himself got carried away—literally, being caught up with another large outpouring of Crusaders, and figuratively, as his harangue turned from words of defense to offense: "The Lord who made the beginning will take care of the finish!" he cried in the stampede. Seeing that the die had been cast, Hunyadi and his professional men-at-arms rushed to their aid. By 6 pm, the entire Christian army was fighting outside the ruined walls Belgrade.[136]

In this bedlam, even Muhammad was espied fighting "with no other helmet and cuirass than belief in Allah and confidence in the ascendency of the star of Islam," to quote S'ad al-Din's hagiographical account; he illuminated "the dark day with the flashes of his dazzling scimitar."[137] Although he decapitated a Crusader with a swing of his jewel encrusted sabre, it was too late. The masses of Turks making up his army, who had set off expecting a relatively easy victory, had had enough. When the fiery Christians managed to capture and turn the blasts of several Ottoman cannons on their former besiegers, demoralization turned into panic. When even the ranks of the mighty janissaries, who had more reason than most to be demoralized, began to crumble, the enraged sultan cried that he "would tear their eyes out" and accused their leader, Hassan Beg, of cowardice, threatening to impale him if he survived.

"O sultan!" Muhammad's terrified servant cried, "most of the janis-saries are wounded, while the rest are unwilling to obey. But I am here at your disposal. Instead of being angry at me, watch me now fight-ing in the midst of the Hungarians and dying on your behalf."[138] And with that, Hassan rushed in to the thick of battle where he was swiftly chopped down.

On seeing the janissary leader hewn to pieces, the Muslim army came undone: "Muhammad, unsupported, bewildered, severely wounded [in the thigh by an arrow]…and foaming at the mouth with impotent rage, yielded to the tearful entreaties of his staff." He "turned his stately steed into the path of safety," writes the Turkish chronicler, adding that "his hand never let go the bridle."[139]

It was a complete rout;* for eight miles and all through the night, the Crusaders chased the fleeing sultan and his crumbling army—they who only days earlier were confident of conquering the whole of Hungary. Muhammad would not rest until he reached his capital, Adrianople— where, in a rage, he ordered the massacre of those contingents that were first to flee at Belgrade. In total, his losses were immense: some fifty

---

* Doukas characteristically offers a very succinct and handy summary of the siege of Belgrade: "He [Muhammad] marched against Belgrade with a huge force and a large number of siege engines. Upon his arrival, he demolished the walls with his cannon…. [T]he outcome of the battle was so obvious that the Turks were soon pillaging inside the city. Janos [Hunyadi] arrived that same day. He crossed the river, entered the city, and routed the Turks. He slaughtered some and wounded others, driving them out of the city. He then sallied forth through the gate with a large contingent of troops, and seized all their war engines. Many Turks were killed—even the tyrant was wounded in the thigh—before Janos finally returned to the city and put the Turkish ships to the torch. The tyrant, returning to Adrianople in disgrace, threatened to march against Belgrade the following year" (Doukas, 255–256).

thousand of his men were killed; three hundred cannons and twenty-seven war vessels were captured.[140]

Finale

"Never before," Hunyadi observed in a letter written three days later to his absentee king of Hungary, "has a Turkish sultan been so ruinously defeated, and never have the chroniclers recorded a deeper humiliation."[141] It was, indeed, a glorious day for Christendom: "Europe celebrated the victory like never before. Processions took place at the German imperial court in Venice, and in remote England, at Oxford. Pope Callixtus III praised 'to the sky' the name of the illustrious voivode, as that of one of the most glorious men that had ever lived."[142]

Callixtus even established a new religious holiday to mark the Christian victory: church bell ringing every day at noon—a tradition that continues to this day, including in older Protestant churches (even if both Protestants and Catholics have forgotten or been shielded from its origin and significance).

As for the sultan—"the braggadocio" of whose arrival at Belgrade "was equaled by the shame and dishonor of his retreat"—he "never recalled that defeat without stroking his chin and his beard, shaking his head, and cursing the day on which he had joined battle at Belgrade," writes Aeneas.[143]

Despite being so thoroughly spent from the anxieties, privations, exertions, and sheer warfare of the past six weeks, the relentless Hunyadi renewed his calls to strike now, while the iron was still hot. If only enough men could be marshalled, he reasserted, Europe could be rid of the Muslim menace—and Constantinople restored—once and for all.

But it would not be; twenty days after this crowning victory of his career—while "all Europe was ringing with his name and bonfires in his honour were blazing in every city in Hungary"—John Hunyadi breathed his last.[144] As often happened to besieged cities, a plague had broken out at Belgrade, and the fifty-year-old warrior-general had at last contracted it.

He was initially sent to recover in nearby Semlin (now Zemun, a municipality of Belgrade). When Hunyadi felt his demise draw nigh, he begged his old comrade, Capistrano, who had accompanied him to Semlin, to transport him to the local church for his final communion.

The Franciscan told him to rest; the Eucharist would be brought to him. "Not so," retorted the savior of Belgrade. "It is not meet that the Master should come to his servant. It is for the servant to go and seek his Lord."[145] Then, "although his strength was failing," writes Aeneas, "he ordered himself to be carried into church, where he made his confession in the Christian way, received the divine Eucharist, and surrendered his soul to God in the arms of the priests."[146]

Thus died John Hunyadi on August 11, 1456 and was buried in his hometown of Transylvania. Ten weeks later, Capistrano also died.

And so, in the midst of celebrations came mourning: "The whole world was deeply disturbed by the death of the one upon whom the hopes of freedom and peace of the peoples of south eastern Europe had rested. The pope, the kings, the scholars of the time, all…grieved over his death."[147] Even the contemporary Polish chronicler Długosz, who for political reasons often portrayed Hunyadi in an unfavorable light, conceded that "His death was detrimental not only to Hungary, but to the entire Christian world, because there was no one else among the Hungarian princes and noblemen to lead the struggle against the Ottomans with the same enthusiasm."[148]

Hunyadi was so mourned because, unlike most of the other noblemen of power and influence—who always evaluated the Ottoman threat in the context of their own positions and possessions, a fact the wily Turks always knew how to manipulate and exploit—Hunyadi was a true patriot who thought of his countrymen and Christendom before himself. As a modern day biographer writes, "The difference between him and other noblemen was that he put his personal power in the service of his country. Relying on the militant spirit of the people and on the use of mercenary troops, John Hunyadi was able to take the offensive against the Ottomans," as opposed to passively waiting around to fight on the Turks' timetable.[149]

He was always with his army, at the front lines, winning his men's favor and trust. During the Long Campaign, he always rode in the van and on the return the rear. At both Varna and Kosovo he fought by his men's side as long as they could resist; and though brave and warlike, "His correspondence reveals a moderate man, for whom war and victory were not an aim but a means. His great goal was to end the war, to secure peace for his people."[150]

On reflection, Hunyadi's life is reminiscent of the Cid's: both were born of lesser nobility and were resented by the elites; both fought alongside and were loved by their men; and both—due to their great resistance against the forces of Islam—rose to great heights in their own lifetimes and went on to become national heroes of Spain and Hungary. And whereas the bloodline of the Cid would generations later flow in the veins of kings, such as Ferdinand III, Hunyadi's own son, Matthias Corvinus (b. 1443; r.1458–1490), was elected king of Hungary two years after Belgrade—the first such king not to be born of royalty.

Hunyadi further left an infrastructure and reformed military that kept the Turks at bay for decades after his death. As historian Camil Mureşanu writes, "He left to the peoples, with whose destiny he had identified himself in the great battles of defense against Ottoman domination, a heritage of which the successors to the leadership of the country did not prove themselves worthy for long: freedom, a firmer will to fight for it, a spirit of solidarity, and a vast military experience." Although the Turks eventually subjugated Hungary, it managed to resist for some seventy more years after Belgrade—and "these seven decades were largely the result of John Hunyadi's efforts and the continuation of his policies."[151]

Even so, in 1456, Sultan Muhammad II still had much time: Hunyadi, the *Athleta Christi*, or "Champion of Christ," as Pope Pius II dubbed him, was dead; so was Capistrano, who became a "Soldier Saint," his coat of arms consisting of an Islamic crescent being pierced by a sword; even George Branković, the mercurial Serbian despot, died that same year. But in 1456, the young and ambitious conqueror of Constantinople was only twenty-four-years-old.

Muhammad II would soon, however, confront another man of Hunyadi's cast and temperament—indeed, a man who was directly enabled and inspired by the White Knight of Wallachia—the subject of next chapter.

CHAPTER 7

Skanderbeg:
The Albanian Braveheart

"As we view it, he is the only great bulwark withstanding the fury of the savage Turk and blocking his way to the rest of the Christian countries. We well know how many disasters he and his people have suffered."

—POPE CALLIXTUS III[1]

"I will judge your merits, when I see your swords smoking with the blood of the Turks.... Let Muhammad, as long as he will, seek peace. As for us, we will purchase our peace with the sword."

—SKANDERBEG[2]

As seen in the previous chapter, "the single most important institution of the 15th century Ottoman state, as well as its neighbor Mameluke Egypt, was that of slavery."[3] During its lifetime, the Ottoman Empire enslaved several million Europeans—far "surpass[ing] the transatlantic trade in black slaves."[4] Christian slaves served two purposes for the Turks: the first and more obvious function was simply that—to be their slaves; to serve, please, and do forced labor for their Muslim masters. The great mass of Christian slaves—certainly all of the females—served in this capacity.

A second function of slavery revolved around empowering the Ottoman state. Any Christian exhibiting any ostensible talent—physical or mental, strong body or mind—was enslaved and made use of, usually as an Ottoman soldier or administrator. Not only was this strategy meant to profit and strengthen the Turks; by continuously robbing them of their best and brightest, it was also meant to weaken and bleed dry the Christians.

Janissaries: Islam's Christian Slave Soldiers

The Greek historian Doukas sheds light on why the Turks needed to "draft" strong European men into their army. First, he describes the "ancient" strategy and initial invasions of Turkish hordes into the Balkans in the mid- and late-fourteenth century, the success of which was built atop sheer numbers:

> The nation of the Turks, more than any other, is a lover of rapine and injustice. This is true even against their own kinsmen; if their attacks are aimed at Christians, what more need be said? If they hear the herald's voice summoning them to the attack...they descend like a flooding river, uninvited, the majority without purse and foot pouch and without spears and swords. Countless others come running, swelling the number of troops, the majority of them carrying nothing but a club in their hands. They rush against the Christians and seize them like sheep.... They continue to do so to this very day.[5]

In time, however, such unsophisticated, tribal warfare proved less effective against the Christians. In order to systematize their ranks to fight decisive battles, the Turks appropriated what historian Victor Davis Hanson calls the "Western way of war." They created an Ottoman military division entirely staffed by the most physically superior European men they could enslave and train as boys. These would become the janissaries—from the Turkish word *yeniçeri*, "new soldier"—the most feared element of the Ottoman army. Unlike most native Turks, who continued to serve as light cavalry and mounted archers, these Europeans-turned-Turks served as infantry shock troops and were dedicated to bringing military encounters to a decisive end.

Thus, from the late fourteenth century on, all subject Christian families from the Balkan region—Albanians, Bulgarians, Greeks, Macedonians, Romanians, Serbs—were compelled, on pain of death, to make an annual "blood tribute" (*devshirme*) payable in their own flesh, that is, their own sons, some as young as eight. After the boys were examined, the very best—the handsomest and halest—were hauled off, often torn from the grips of their hysterical mothers. Any father who dared offer resistance was executed on the spot.

These children were then marched to the Ottoman heartland, forcibly converted to Islam, indoctrinated in the teachings of jihad, trained to be—and rewarded for being—warriors par excellence, and then set loose on their former Christian kin, thereby perpetuating the cycle of conquest, enslavement, and conversion, always to Islam's demographic gain and Christendom's demographic loss.* (One historian estimates that "hundreds of thousands" of Christian families were "ruined" by this system.[6]) Writing in the mid-fifteenth century, Doukas continues:

> This army of "new troops," moreover, increases every year and now numbers ten thousand. The slaves acquire slaves, and the slaves of the slaves acquire slaves, and all are called slaves of the [Ottoman] ruler. Among them could be found neither Turk nor Arab, but all of them without exception were Christians—Romans [Greeks], Serbs, Albanians, Bulgarians, Vlachs, and Hungarians. Now that they have abjured their faith and delight in the pleasures of the present as swine relish their greens, like rabid dogs they bear an implacable and mortal hatred against our [Christian] compatriots.[7]

Despite Doukas's natural vexation, it must be remembered that most janissaries had no choice in the matter: after being forced to recant Christ and embrace Muhammad as children, they were indoctrinated into hating and waging war on their former kin, now "infidels." That they were, to quote Vasiliki Papouli, "degraded to the level of animals" and

---

* Gianfrancesco Morosini, a sixteenth-century Italian diplomat and eyewitness, left behind a detailed account of the Janissary institute. First, the Turks found, herded, and marched off the most physically promising Christian boys, "just as if they were so many sheep." On reaching their new barracks, the boys were "either persuaded or forced to be circumcised and made Muslim." Nor were these merely symbolic or superficial acts: "The first thing they are made to learn is the Turks' false religion, which they know so well as to put us [Christians] to shame." Next, "They make them drudge day and night, and they give them no bed to sleep on and very little food." They were allowed to "speak to each other only when it is urgently necessary" and were made to "pray together without fail at four prescribed times every day." As "for any little offense, they beat them cruelly with sticks, rarely hitting them less than a hundred times, and often as much as a thousand. After punishments the boys have to come to them and kiss their clothing and thank them for the cudgelings they have received. You can see, then," concluded the Italian observer, "that moral degradation and humiliation are part of the training system" (Allen, 405–406).

exhibited a "dog-like devotion to the sultan"—the man responsible for abducting them from their families and faith—is further proof that they are among recorded history's earliest victims of Stockholm Syndrome, defined by Merriam-Webster as "the psychological tendency of a hostage to bond with, identify with, or sympathize with his or her captor."[8]

Not all, of course, were so easily brainwashed and manipulated, particularly not those who were snatched later in life. As one sixteenth-century European observed: "They gather together and one tells another of his native land and of what he heard in church or learned in school there, and they agree among themselves that Muhammad is no prophet and that the Turkish religion [Islam] is false. If there is one among them who has some little [Christian] book or can teach them in some other manner something of God's word, they hear him as diligently as if he were their preacher."[9] No fools, the Turks were aware of this and ever watchful for any hints of disloyalty.

As with all unflattering Islamic phenomena, it bears mentioning that even this abduction, forced conversion, and jihadist indoctrination and transformation of Christian children into Islamic terrorists—long "considered one of the most devilish, and perhaps unique, methods of world conquest among all those yet devised by humankind"[10]—has been whitewashed and portrayed by Western academics "as the equivalent of sending a child away for a prestigious education and training for a lucra-tive career."[11] Such a characterization flies in the face of the evidence. One sixteenth-century testimonial tells of the "sorrow" of "the fathers and mothers who are separated from their children at the prime of life":

> Think ye of the heart-rending sorrow! How many mothers scratch out their cheeks! How many fathers beat their breasts with stones! What grief these Christians experience on account of their children who are separated from them while alive and how many mothers say, "It would be better to see them dead and buried in our church, rather than to take them alive in order to become Turks and abjure our faith. Better that you had died!"[12]

Similarly, in his memoir, Konstantin Mihailović (1430–1501), a Ser-bian who was abducted in his youth and marched away by the Turks, saw nothing "prestigious" or "lucrative" about becoming a janissary. "We always thought about killing the Turks and running away by ourselves among the mountains," he writes, "but our youth did not permit us to do that." Once when he and a group of other boys broke free and escaped, "the whole region pursued us, and having caught and bound us, they beat us and tortured us and dragged us behind horses."[13]

Even those personally chosen by the sultan found nothing admirable about their lot. After Ottoman Sultan Murad II took eight Christian youths into his service, they made a pact to assassinate him by night, saying "If we kill this Turkish dog, then all of Christendom will be freed [from Ottoman tyranny]; but if we are caught, then we will become martyrs before God with the others." When their plot was exposed, and Murad inquired what caused them to "dare attempt this," they responded, "None other than our great sorrow for our fathers and dear friends."[14] He had them slowly tortured over the course of a year before beheading them.

George Kastrioti

From the very start of Ottoman aggression in the Balkans, Albania was, like its other Christian neighbors, a prime target of the jihad; "handsome youths and pretty girls," to quote an Ottoman chronicler, were regularly seized from this rugged and mountainous nation bordering the Adriatic Sea. In one Ottoman campaign from as early as 1375, there was such a surplus of slaves that, atop their regular booty, the sultan gifted every Turkish soldier with an Albanian slave (after he had taken his fifth, as mandated by the Koran and in emulation of the prophet).[15]

After various raids and military clashes, the Ottomans finally subjugated the Albanians in 1415. In order to ensure the nobles' good behavior, Sultan Murad II took their sons as hostages. One of these leading Albanian noblemen, John Kastrioti, had nine children, four of whom were boys. The sultan demanded all four to be sent to Adrianople, and John obliged. For whatever reason, three of his sons were eventually killed by their Turkish masters; only the youngest, ten-year-old George (b. 1405), survived.

Although modern academics argue over whether George Kastrioti was formally trained as a janissary, or whether his noble background precluded him, the fact is he underwent what all janissaries did, making such arguments moot: he was circumcised and converted to Islam in his childhood and put through all of the grueling training at, and eventually graduated from, the janissary boarding school of Enderun. Konstantin Mihailović, the aforementioned Serbian janissary and contemporary of George, further asserts that the Albanian was trained as a janissary.[16]

Rather than challenge or break him, the severe Turkish training young George was subjected to only complemented what was already in his soul: a penchant for war. Before being taken hostage, in his earliest youth as an adolescent, he used to "vigorously train himself on the crest of Mount Croya or elsewhere. Come blizzard or frozen hell, he would then choose to sleep over improvised beds of snow. In the scorching heat of summer, he would again and again keep hardening himself like an invincible guerilla [fighter]."[17] Unsurprisingly, George quickly rose to the highest echelons of the Ottoman military, fought on various fronts— where he never lost a battle—and eventually became a highly decorated Ottoman general.

His warrior spirit was complemented by a suitable figure. Sources describe him as something of a physical specimen: he was "tall and slender with a prominent chest, wide shoulders, long neck, and high forehead. He had black hair, fiery eyes, and a powerful voice."[18] Contemporaneous accounts of his legendary strength state that his sword swing could, like Godfrey of Bouillon, cleave a man or animal in twain.[19]

Marin Barletius (1450–1513), a young contemporary and chief biographer of George, who collated many of the Albanian's orations as recorded by earwitnesses and found in archives, provides one of the earliest descriptions of him. After a Tatar who was envious of young George's growing reputation at the Ottoman court challenged him to a duel to the death, the Albanian stripped to his waist and warned his boastful contender not to violate the rules of honor:

> Scanderbeg, both by voice and countenance, betrayed a wonderful resolution and assurance. And the [Ottoman] audience was impressed with his manly perfection. His arms looked as if nothing like them had ever been seen. His neck was strong and somewhat bending, such as possessed by wrestlers. His shoulders were big and marvelously spread. The color of his visage was fair and white.... And the cast of his eyes was straight and pleasant, without any blemish or imperfection.... Like Alexander the Great, he was built like a giant. Physically he was invincible.[20]

The Tatar did not stand a chance: during their match, George struck his head off with a sword swing and held aloft the severed trophy before Murad, thereby winning the sultan's favor.[21] It was, in fact, during this time, when George was in his early twenties, that the impressed Ottomans began to call him Skanderbeg—"Lord Alexander"—after Alexander the Great of Macedon.[22] (Albanians and Macedonians were/are believed to share similar ancestors.)

Seeing him as one of his finest bred studs, Murad lavished Skanderbeg with fine presents and privileges, and, due to his military genius, command of a five thousand cavalry regiment. Some years later, an army of janissaries was placed under his command.

Ottoman Years

In 1428, war broke out between Venice and the Ottoman Empire. Skanderbeg's father, John Kastrioti, and the rest of the Albanians immediately allied with Venice in an effort to overthrow the Muslim yoke. An Ottoman chronicler explains what happened next:

> [Sultan Murad] gathered heavily armed soldiers and attacked the fortress of Salonika [along the Adriatic coast], saying that this was a holy war. They made a great war and with the help of cannons destroyed the city's walls, yet the Infidels [Christians] were not subdued. The Padishah, in the name of Allah, ordered that they begin to pillage. The fortress was then taken…. The lands of John Kastrioti were also taken, and many other fortresses were conquered.[23]

Thereafter, and because they could, the Turks increased their insatiable demand for tribute—in both coin and flesh. By 1431–1432, countless more Albanians were enslaved and hauled away, many to be transformed into future enemies. One year later, at the start of 1433 during a council at Basel (in Florence), Cardinal Julian Cesarini (1398–1444) chastised the rest of Christendom's factious nature and indifference to the jihad being waged against their Eastern coreligionists in a speech worth quoting at length:

> Look all around you, and see how the people of Christ are trodden upon and devoured by Turks, Saracens and Tartars. Why do you not commiserate with the many thousands of your brothers, who year after year are reduced to the harsh servitude of the infidel? O

if you would but listen, when the brigands divide up the spoils of Christendom, how great are their sighs and laments, when the wife is allotted to one person, the husband to another; the father to one, and the son to another; one brother to one, and the other to another. How numerous are their cries, how numerous the whimpering gasps of these, my miserable children, when they are separated from one another, never to see each other again. Who, then, can restrain you from tears? Will you not perhaps desist from fighting each other? But what is more pitiful, is that many of those who are led into captivity, and who are not able to bear such a hard servitude, deny the Catholic faith, and are led to the abhorrent sect of Mohammed. How many kingdoms, provinces, cities, towns are daily seized and depopulated? They have now cornered you in a small area in the west. Little remains, but for them to dispel you from the ends of the earth. By thunder! Why do you not reflect upon the suffering of your mother and your brothers? Why, upon hearing such things, do you wage such cruel war against your own, and spill the blood of your Christian brothers freely and without mercy? Discord among Christians is the cause of all these calamities. If they would only grow wise and harbor love, this sort of persecution would soon end.[24]

Although the speech brought many in attendance to tears, little came of it by way of succor to the persecuted Christians of the Balkans. Not ones to wait for rescue, and because they "were determined to be autonomous and free in every way," to quote chronicler Michael Kritoboulos (1410–1470), the Albanians soon rebelled again, for a time successfully.[25] Then, in 1436, the Turks came with a fury; in the words of Oruç Bey, a contemporary Ottoman, the Muslims "pillaged and destroyed the lands of John Kastrioti, the men were put to the sword, while the women were made slaves…. They conquered…and returned with great plunder." Before leaving, the Turks erected large pyramids of Albanian heads.[26]

In an effort to maintain his lands and power, John Kastrioti had given away his four sons, and now had nothing to show for it. Skanderbeg's father died a few months later, a broken man.

While his Albanian homeland was being ravaged, Skanderbeg was elsewhere scoring triumphs for his Ottoman masters. After the death of his father in 1437, several Albanians secretly traveled to and begged George to return and, as John Kastrioti's only living son—and, as they learned, a natural born leader—take his place. He curtly dismissed them for daring to utter such treason. In time, however, Murad, seeing Skanderbeg as best suited for the job, appointed him governor of Croya—a highly strategic fortress in central Albania that had been part of his father's lands and, therefore, his inheritance—"a duty he took on willingly and thus was sent to his land," writes an Ottoman chronicler.[27] During this time, Skanderbeg became closely acquainted with the locals. Two years later, in 1440, he was removed from Croya and sent to govern Dibra, another important fortress that also happened to be on his father's land and inheritance.

For Freedom's Sake

Everything changed once John Hunyadi and the Hungarians crashed onto the Ottoman scene with their Long Campaign. On November 3, 1443, the Transylvanian voivode and the Turks clashed at Nish in Serbia. Skanderbeg was also there, commanding a large contingent of Ottoman troops. Suddenly, and to the shock of his men, he ordered a retreat in the midst of battle. Seeing their fearless champion tuck tail and run created panic among the Turks. But it was all a ruse: during the chaos, Skanderbeg absconded from the Ottoman camp with three hundred Albanian fighters loyal to him.

Before leaving, he "seized the Ottoman imperial secretary and forced him to issue, in the name of the Sultan, an order for the Governor of Croya to surrender the fortress and its lands to him," writes John Muzaka, a contemporary Albanian nobleman.[28] The terrified clerk did as he was bid. As he pondered the secretary's fate, Skanderbeg concluded that he would most certainly inform the sultan once released, and so put him—and the secret he knew—to death.

Highly fortified, rich in resources, and situated in central Albania, Croya was key to any meaningful resistance against the Ottomans, which is precisely what Skanderbeg had just initiated. Before reaching it, he had organized local support in Dibra, which now joined and marched alongside him. On November 28, 1443 he arrived before the walls of Croya's White Castle and sent his trusted nephew Hamza with the decree to the unsuspecting Ottoman governor, who, thinking he was obeying the sultan, relinquished control of Croya that same night.

Once the governor departed for Adrianople, Skanderbeg's motley crew of Albanian fighters, like their distant ancestors before the walls of Troy, slipped into Croya in the dead of night and massacred the remaining Turkish garrison, thereby freeing this strategically important fortress town from Islam's grip. Skanderbeg cast down the Ottoman standards and raised his family's banner again—a black double-headed eagle against red background. "Thus, he became lord of Croya," writes Muzaka, "a powerful land."[29] The nineteenth century American poet, Henry Wadsworth Longfellow, immortalized this episode with the following stanzas:

The crescent banner falls/and the crowd beholds instead/like a portent in the sky/Iskander's banner fly/the Black Eagle with double head; And shouts ascend on high/for men's souls are tired of the Turks/and their wicked ways and works/that have made of Ak-Hissar [the White Castle]/ a city of the plague; and the loud exultant cry that echoes wide and far is: "Long live Scanderbeg!"[30]

On the next day in Croya's packed cathedral, Skanderbeg "dropped the mask of dissimulation, abjured the prophet and the sultan, and proclaimed himself the avenger of his family and country"—all to wild cheers.[31] Everything finally came out into the open. Hitherto, only a handful of Albanian confidants had known his mind; now all learned that he had always remained loyal to his country and faith—that his alleged allegiance to the Turks was a necessary evil to safeguard his life until the right opportunity presented itself.

During his speech, Skanderbeg explained how dangerous it was for someone in his high-ranking and sensitive position to let even mere thoughts of breaking free from his Muslim masters enter his head: "I hardly dared to trust myself with my own conception of my plans. Neither could I think myself assured that I had communicated it to my own thoughts. I mistrusted even my tongue, impatient as it were of a matter so important, lest it should impart it to the very walls of my private chamber."

As a witness, he cited his nephew, Hamza, who was also converted to Islam in his youth, fought for the Ottomans, and escaped and reconverted with his uncle after the battle of Nish. Only "few others besides him" understood their chief's mind. As an indication of how watchfully suffocating the Ottoman atmosphere was—Murad II "distrusts no one so much as the Janissaries" wrote ex-janissary Mihailović, and always planted spies among them—even among these, his most trusted men, Skanderbeg never risked uttering a word that might betray him:[32]

> Although we lived together as a family, as it were, in one and the same course of life, although we ate at one and the same table and though we did in a manner breathe jointly with one and the same soul, nevertheless, neither they [Hamza and other Albanian confidants] nor any man alive ever heard me mention my country—except during the war with Hungary. Neither was there any man that heard me use any speech, or utter any word at any time, which might reveal me to be a Christian or a free man, until such time as I saw and perceived that I might freely do so and without fear of danger.... [Even so] I still lived in the hope that you should one day see me as I am now.

Even after Skanderbeg had, as it were, "crossed the Rubicon" into Albania, he was not sure what he would find or if his countrymen would be supportive of a rebellion. To his great relief, he discovered that

> It was not I that put arms in your hands. I found you ready in arms. I found you everywhere bearing the signs of liberty in your hearts, in your faces, in your swords, and in your lances. And, as most loyal teachers and guardians ordained by my father, you have put the scepter in my hands with no less faith and diligence than as if you had kept and preserved it especially for me even unto this day. And you have brought me by your effort and careful care into my ancestral possession [of Croya] without shedding any [Albanian] blood.

Not only had Croya been recovered, but "the Dibrans [Albanians] and all the people are now united with us," Skanderbeg continued, as his liberation speech turned into a harangue. As such, now—when the Turks were preoccupied with Hunyadi—was the time for "the recovery of the rest of our country." But as this could only be done by taking several fortresses garrisoned by Turks—no easy task—"Let us try," counseled Skanderbeg, "by all means: by art, cunning and strategy, by pains and toil, by patience and the sword to achieve our first victory."[33]

And so it was. Despite the severe winter that had set in, Skanderbeg led his men to besiege several Turkish-held fortresses in Albania. Because it was winter and all of the Ottomans' resources were needed to respond to Hunyadi's Long Campaign, no aid was sent to these castles, five of which fell to Skanderbeg.[34]

The Mustering of Albania

While discussing the failed Albanian uprisings of the 1430s, which led to the dispossession (and eventual death) of Skanderbeg's father, Konstantin Mihailović concluded that "The reason he [Murad] defeated them [Albanians] so easily was that one looked on while he was defeating another."[35] In an effort to overcome such chronic disunity, where each noble considered only his own interests—a reality the Turks regularly manipulated to their advantage—on March 2, 1444, Skanderbeg summoned a meeting of Albania's feudal lords and nobles at Saint Nicholas Cathedral in Alessio (now Lezhë).

There, the lord of Croya made clear that they must, once and for all, either accept war against or slavery under the Turks, who are "accustomed only to rape, theft and robbery" and who live on "deceit and fraud," emphasized Skanderbeg. Due to his deep acquaintance with the Muslims—he had spent the last three decades of his life surrounded by them—Skanderbeg further bemoaned Turkish guile and Christian gullibility: "I would to God…that the credulity and light beliefs of us Christians would at once come to an end and that we would at once wax weary of the treachery of the Ottomans."

He asked God to forgive his father, John Kastrioti, for giving "too much credit to the fair words and speeches" of Sultan Murad II, who "under the pretense of a deadly peace" seized John's "own proper children in bondage…. But why do I complain of my father? This error and this destiny is common unto all Christian princes. What shall I say of the Greeks, the Serbians, and others of our faith and profession [whose children are regularly taken by the Turks]?"

In calling them to outright war against their suzerain—many of these Albanian nobles were still vassals of the sultan—Skanderbeg realized what he was plunging his country into: "All men generally will call me cruel and will detest me, and, I cannot think without horror, as a new author of wars and perils and of bloodshed and murder. Whereas they ought rather, be it said without boasting, to call me the preserver of their liberty."

"Up then," he concluded. "Let us levy and muster our soldiers. And let us make known unto all ages to come that we are men worthy of a Christian Nation."[36]

To loud cries of freedom, Albania's aristocracy then and there formed an alliance—the "League of Alessio"—in an effort to overthrow the Turkish yoke. Skanderbeg, now seen as the first among equals, "was unanimously chosen the commander-in-chief of the armies, and to his sole direction was committed the conduct of the war. He was esteemed most worthy of the honor bestowed upon him on account of his skill and science in military affairs, his great prudence and deliberation, [and] his long acquaintance with the manners and customs of the barbarians...."[37]

Now with the combined nobles' support, Skanderbeg rushed from village to village rallying the countryside to the cause of freedom. Inspired by his formidable persona and commanding voice, his love of God and country, the people responded in droves. His inchoate but growing army was composed of "peasants, farmers, highlanders, shepherds, cowpokes." Every man was "selected on the basis of his physical stamina, mental alertness, family background, deep religious belief, and love of freedom." This new Albanian army had three branches: cavalry, infantry, and guerilla. The latter "were carefully trained how to attack, confuse, ambush, encircle, terrify, and annihilate a numerically superior army of the enemy."[38]

Before long, the land was ablaze with enthusiasm: "Blacksmiths and craftsmen, like their predecessors of biblical times, literally began beating plowshares into swords. Almost overnight, they most excitedly produced bows, steel nosed arrows, lances, halberds, arquebuses, pikes, and axes. The very sharp swords and daggers, which they created with loving care, would still be hot when thrust into the eagerly awaiting hands of Scanderbeg's puny army."[39]

By May 1444 he had a standing army of eight thousand men and a reserve of nearly ten thousand—most of which were light cavalry, armed with swords, spears, bows and arrows. An impressively large army for hitherto factious Albania, it was still beyond puny compared to the hundreds of thousands of fully equipped, professional soldiers the Ottomans could regularly muster. But what they lacked in numbers these Albanians made up for in spirit—for they would now be fighting side-by-side with their fellow countrymen against their common oppressor in the name of freedom. Most heartening of all, their captain, Skanderbeg, whom the peasants came to love, dressed and ate plainly, and worked and sweated alongside them—behaving in every way like an "Albanian Braveheart."

First Fruits

No sooner did Sultan Murad II make a truce with Hungary's King Ladislaus III following the Long Campaign than he turned his attention to Skanderbeg's Albanian uprising. As many as forty thousand Ottomans under Ali Pasha were dispatched near Dibra. The Albanians' first test had come, and Skanderbeg exhorted them "to take up arms, to break the chains of so long a servitude and bondage, and to drive the enemy from our soil...."[40] With nearly his entire army and reserves—fifteen thousand men, cavalry, infantry, and guerilla—he went to give battle to the Turks.

On seeing that they were outnumbered, many of his men—who, unlike their Muslim foe, were not professional soldiers—cowered. Mounted atop his warhorse and brandishing his sword, Skanderbeg responded by announcing that whoever was afraid should "leave at once for his home"—since such a one was "unworthy both of the name and the sword he bears," indeed, "unworthy of the air he breathes." Nor did those who stood their ground win the fierce war-veteran's instant approval: "I will judge your merits," he informed them, "when I see your swords smoking with the blood of the Turks."[41]

The battle took place near the Vale of Torvioll (in modern Debar), a densely wooded and mountainous region. Days before it, Skanderbeg had ordered his men to light fewer and fewer campfires and speak only in hushed voices—to give the Turks the illusion that the Albanian army was even smaller than it actually was. Accordingly, on June 29, 1444, Ali ordered his men to charge at the Christians, who quickly began to break and run to the hills.

The overconfident Turks followed in close pursuit, only to discover that Skanderbeg had lured them into a trap: three thousand Albanian horsemen, led by his nephew, Hamza, emerged from the defiles; they surrounded and slaughtered the startled Muslims. The more confident the long oppressed Albanians became, the more they gave vent to their rage in battle. The bloodbath ended with twenty-two thousand dead Turks; reportedly only 120 Albanians died.

News of this remarkable Albanian victory reached Europe and got the attention of Pope Eugene IV, who saw in Skanderbeg a potential magnet for Christian resistance. The Crusader-king of Hungary, Ladislaus III, congratulated the Albanian warlord in a letter: "For to say nothing of those things which, even from your childhood have continually made you envied" and "gained you an immortal fame and glory even amongst the barbarians themselves"—a reference to Skanderbeg's "valor, so well known"—"What can be more glorious than this victory...?"[42]

Skanderbeg thanked him, extolled their joint "defense of the Christian religion," and condemned European disunity, which left those who most defied the Turks—in this case, Ladislaus's Hungarians and Skandebeg's Albanians—to bleed: "Both [our] Nations, as it were, have become the expiatory sacrifices of the sins and offenses of others. We all now by turns perish, while every man thinks himself born but for himself alone."[43]

Skanderbeg was supposed to join with Ladislaus and Hunyadi at Varna, but the Serbian despot, George Branković, wary of jeopardizing the advantageous peace he had made with Murad following the Long Campaign, prevented the Albanians' passage through his land—one more cause that led to the Christian defeat at Varna on November 10, 1444 and the decapitation of Ladislaus III. By way of retribution, and to avenge the death of the young Hungarian king, Skanderbeg ravaged and devastated Branković's lands.

Over the following year, he continued to make inroads against Ottoman strongholds in and around Albania, so it was soon said that "the possessions of the Sultan were the revenues of Scanderbeg."[44] In late 1445, he ambushed in the mountains and routed another Turkish army four times larger than his small force of thirty-five hundred men. During the fierce fighting, the Ottoman commander, Firuz Pasha, and fifteen hundred other Turks, were slain. Skanderbeg faced and defeated the Turks two more times in the following months.

In short, the Albanian warlord was spoiling Murad's great victory at Varna. This even comes out in the sultan's letters boasting of his jihadist bona fides. In one, after saying Allah had made him victorious "in scattering and confounding the infidels who are as low as the earth [at Varna]," Murad begrudgingly admitted that, even so, "in every year and in every circumstance, the victorious armies of Islam have encountered" those not so easily "scattered and confounded"—especially "the pig-headed Albanians."[45]

A War of Words

Sultan Murad II eventually turned his attention to Lord Alexander—this man who remained defiant when the rest of the Balkans was either subdued or licking its wounds from Varna. He began with words.

Referring to Skanderbeg as a "serpent" raised "in my own bosom," in a letter dated June 15, 1445, Murad, still drunk over his victory, called on the Albanian to learn from those Christians who dared defy him and were slaughtered: "[M]end your ways, you graceless man, and expect not further whether my indignation will break out. Let not these trifling allurements of your good fortune [at defeating the Turks] so puff up your foolish desires and sharpen your conceits."

Then the sultan got personal: "I would you at least remember my courtesies," he wrote in reference to how he had elevated Skanderbeg within the Ottoman ranks, "if any spark of humanity remains in your savage nature." He even expressed concern for the Albanian's soul, now that he had renounced Islam—"not to speak of the laws of Muhammad which you despise, and the holy Prophet you condemn, for the zeal you have for the Christian Superstition."

Having chastised his former ward, Murad turned on the notorious guile of the Turk; he acknowledged that "the love of your Country did move you," even so, "I now pardon you for all that you have offended me." Skanderbeg could even keep Croya on condition that he return the other Ottoman-held towns and fortresses he had since taken:

> Otherwise you had rather cry in vain for mercy, when your furious outrage will have me in person be an implacable avenger. You know your own Forces. You know the strength of my arms. You have before your eyes the fresh example of the Hungarian fortune [at Varna], so that you need no further admonitions.... Farewell—if you be wise.[46]

The wily sultan was relying on his usual game of divide and conquer. As the former janissary Konstantin Mihailović once explained, "if the emperor [sultan] makes peace and an armistice with someone, even while he makes peace he seeks again to deceive him. And when he makes peace with someone, he wages war with another; and when he subjugates him, he lays blame on him also, and straightaway the cunning one always goes as if in a circle so that the Christians are always tormented.... Whoever has taken soup with them [Turks] has had to repay them in meat."[47] Murad knew that most nobles would have accepted his terms—keeping their own territories unmolested in exchange for abandoning their neighbors' to the sultan. In so doing, however, they would also have been allowing themselves to be surrounded, singled out, and, in time, subjugated by the Turks.

The former Ottoman general, Skanderbeg, knew all this as well: "I have with patience received and seen both your letter and your messenger," the Albanian responded in a letter dated July 12, 1445. "And they have caused me greater occasion for smile than anger."

> Truly, Murad, although your immoderate railing might move a man of greatest patience to intemperate speech, yet I impute it to your advanced age and partly to the waywardness of your nature, and the rest of your conceived grief, which I know you can hardly moderate. And rather for that reason I have not set down myself to contend with you in foul and unbecoming language, but with arms and the just fury of war.

Murad's concern for Skanderbeg's soul was especially ironic, responded the Albanian, "being ignorant of your own estate as a studious defender of a most damnable error [Islam]." As for Murad's supposed shock at Skanderbeg's disaffection, the latter expressed even more shock:

> You took away my father's kingdom by force. You did murder my brothers, and myself you did most wickedly vow to death when I little feared any such cruelty. And does it now seem strange to you, O Murad, that an invincible mind desirous of liberty, should seek to break out of the bonds of so great and insolent a slavery?

Concerning the bulk of Murad's letter—that Skanderbeg was a treacherous ingrate—George Kastrioti unburdened his soul:

> Charge me with such crimes forever, I care not. The long catalog of your kindnesses toward me, which you rehearse, I could willingly remember, if it did not draw with it the woeful remembrance of my greater miseries which, if they were to be compared together, the greatness of your good deeds would be overwhelmed by the

multitude of your greater tyrannies. These I would rather you should count by yourself, then blush while I repeat them. Every man who knows them may marvel how I had the power to endure them, or how you were not weary at last of your cruelty and secret hatred.[48]

Whatever humiliations, degradations, and machinations Skanderbeg had in mind, no doubt chief among them was that Murad had, as he had with so many other male slaves, sexually defiled him, as Chalkokondyles's contemporary chronicle clearly attests: "Skanderbeg, the son of John Kastrioti, as a child, had attended the sultan's Porte, had been the sultan's young lover,* and fled back to his native land."[49]

Although forgotten today, the Turks' notorious penchant for pederasty used to scandalize Christians to no end. As M. J. Akbar writes, Christians were "particularly aghast at the open homosexuality....Venice forbade lads under fourteen from visiting Constantinople [then Istanbul] for fear that they would be afflicted with the 'Turk disease.'"[50] It was, in fact, a chief reason that parents so dreaded the *devshirme*—the "blood tax"—some to the point of mutilating their sons to disqualify them from induction into the janissary corps.

At any rate, not one to succumb to childhood trauma, Skanderbeg closed his letter as follows:

> Therefore, hereafter, cease your angry threats, and tell not us of the Hungarian fortune [at Varna]. Every man has his own resolution, and every man a particular providence of his own actions. And so will we with patience endure such fortune as it shall please God to appoint us. Meanwhile, for direction of our affairs, we will not request counsel of our enemies, nor peace from you, but victory by the help of God! Farewell.[51]

Betrayal

Despite his insolent reply, Murad did not immediately move against Skanderbeg, whose star had greatly risen—ironically to the Albanian's own detriment. The more his fame grew, the more men from everywhere acclaimed and joined his army, the more Albania centralized around his

---

* *Paidika* (παιδικά) the Greek word rendered here as "young lover," is more accurately and colloquially translated as "young sex-slave" and "young plaything," respectively.

person, the more the other nobles of the League of Alessio—theoretically his equals except in command—became disempowered and disaffected.

Similarly, the "patrician" Venetian Senate, which for long had great influence on Albania's political and economic order, grew bitter against this "upstart"—to the point of offering in May 1447 a one hundred thousand ducat pension to an unnamed Albanian noble to assassinate Skanderbeg. The attempt failed; war erupted over the following year. This all worked perfectly for the Ottomans, as now the Venetians themselves called on the Turks to help crush Skanderbeg between them.

The time for Murad's vengeance had finally arrived; the sultan personally led a massive Ottoman army of some eighty thousand men straight for Sfetigrad, eastern Albania's most important fortress. Before their arrival, Skanderbeg exhorted the Albanian garrison to hold fast against the "violence of his fury," and reminded them that the moment of truth was here at last: "All men have fixed their eyes upon you, either to commend or to condemn you or else to follow and imitate your virtue."[52]

And with that, he left the reins of war with his loyal nephew Hamza and quickly rode off to intercept the Venetians, who were making inroads from the west. By May 1448, Murad had put Sfetigrad to siege, while Skanderbeg, with the much welcomed aid of Venice's rival, Alfonso V, king of Aragon and Naples, fought back the treacherous Venetians (who not infrequently allied with Christendom's archenemy for their own mercantile interests).

Like other Christian fighters before him—recall the words of Duke Godfrey or Ferdinand III—Skanderbeg took no delight in fighting his coreligionists: "Let no man marvel at seeing me in arms against Christians, against Venetians," he explained to his men, "since they themselves have given me such a just occasion and have put the sword into my hands."[53] Such was Just War theory in action—war against those who break the rules of justice, be they Christian or not:

> Nevertheless [Skanderbeg continued], I would rather that you did not conduct yourselves toward these as against other enemies: But I would rather that you use better moderation and less fury and, being inclined to mercy and clemency, try to have them as prisoners than to have them slaughtered in the field of battle.... For it is not with barbarous, fierce and savage nations that we have now to deal but

with Christians, against whom we are to contend according to the rights and laws of arms, with equity and justice, and only to repulse injustice as well as to live in peace and freedom.[54]

On July 23, 1448 near the Drin River, Skanderbeg defeated the Venetians. Without a moment to lose, the indefatigable warrior rushed to Sfetigrad's aid with twelve thousand men. Vastly outnumbered by the Turks, Skanderbeg's men were limited to skirmishing and guerilla tactics.[55] Although heavy losses were inflicted on the Turks, the Albanians could not break the siege.

As was not uncommon in those days, Ali Ferez Pasha, a highly decorated Ottoman commander, challenged Skanderbeg to a duel to the death before the walls of Sfetigrad. When his lieutenants begged him not to take the challenge, the forty-five-year-old Albanian rebuked them:

> God forbid, my good soldiers, that as long as this hand of mine can handle the sword and as long as this body of mine retains its accustomed strength and vigor…I shall refer to Him who is the giver of all victory. Reserve, therefore, your good reasons for some other season when you shall see me aged and stricken in years, when my limbs begin to fail….[56]

Besides, while this Ali was a "cruel beast," so too was he "a man of sufficient worth to feel the weight of my sword."[57] The Ottoman and former-Ottoman clashed on horseback and Skanderbeg, as he had done all those years back before Murad's eyes, again swiftly slew his challenger. Even so, this delay tactic worked: unbeknownst to most, a Turk had poisoned the wells with a carcass, prompting Sfetigrad to capitulate on July 31, 1448, after a grueling ten-week-long siege.

The Turks—who lost thousands of men—were unable to capitalize on their new acquisition by recuperating in it and then marching westward into central Albania, according to the original plan: John Hunyadi was just then marching towards Kosovo. Murad quickly garrisoned the fortress and went to face his other archenemy. Once again and as he had done before at Varna, the Serbian despot prevented the Albanians from reaching the field of Kosovo, where Murad scored his second great victory over the Hungarians on October 20, 1448: Skanderbeg was just thirty miles from Kosovo when the sultan decimated Hunyadi's army.

The Siege of Croya

With Hunyadi finally neutralized, Murad was prepared to exercise his full wrath on Skanderbeg. In what was meant to be the campaign to end all campaigns, in the spring of 1450 the sultan led a gargantuan army of as many as one hundred sixty thousand men into Albania—straight for Skanderbeg's stronghold, the White Castle. Underscoring the epic nature of the forthcoming siege, accompanying Murad was his young son, the future Muhammad II, and several leading Ottoman beys, including Evrenoz Pasha Sebalia, the governor Skanderbeg had tricked out of Croya back in 1443.

Against this mammoth Muslim army, and due to the recent wars he had fought and the defection of nobles, Skanderbeg could only raise some eighteen thousand Christian defenders. Many of these were adventurous foreigners—Germans, Frenchmen, Italians, and Slavs—who had been inspired by and therefore joined the Albanian freedom fighter.

Skanderbeg evacuated all of the women and children from Croya, garrisoned it with fifteen hundred men, and took the rest into the nearby mountains, whence they would harass the besiegers and try to undermine their supply trains with guerilla tactics. Meanwhile, all along their route to Croya, the Turks left a trail of devastation; countless Albanians were enslaved. Local peasants resorted to heroic but futile ambush tactics and a scorched earth policy, before also retreating into the mountains.

Murad finally arrived and put Croya to siege on May 14, 1450. Day after day, Ottoman cannons rocked the White Castle with projectiles weighing as much as four hundred pounds.[58] As Chalkokondyles writes, the sultan "bombarded the walls with cannons and brought down a large section of them…. But Skanderbeg lit fires from the mountain signaling to those in the city that when there was need, he would be there to assist them. He attacked some of the sultan's men who went up the mountain and fought against them, performing remarkable deeds."[59]

Meanwhile, the janissaries—"traitors to God and their country, the worms whose conscience is ever tormenting their souls," to quote the former janissary, Skanderbeg—terrorized and devastated the land of their former brother-in-arms, burning homes and grain fields.[60] Several Albanian nobles individually surrendered in the hopes of retaining their lands and titles; others actively welcomed the Turks in the hopes of breaking Skanderbeg's influence and regaining their privileges. The League of Alessio was no more; and Venice, once again, supplied the Islamic invader.

Despite such odds, a Venetian report complained that "Skanderbeg is defending himself heroically"—so much so that, if not for Venetian provisions, the Turks "would have pulled up their tents" and retreated: "for this reason, it is feared that Skanderbeg, the moment he frees himself [of the Turks] will attack the lands of the Republic [of Venice in vengeance]."[61]

Similarly, after stating that Murad "attempts with all his might and vigorous battle to crush him [Skanderbeg]," a pessimistic letter from the senate of Ragusa to John Hunyadi offered a glimmer of hope: "the brave men inside are bound by honor to defend it to the death. Skanderbeg himself is not far from the Turkish tents and daily inflicts heavy losses on the enemy because he takes advantage of the nature of the country and the nearby mountains where he hides without being discovered."[62]

In short and by all accounts, Skanderbeg and his men, inside and outside of Croya, fought tooth and nail, and managed to inflict heavy casualties on their much larger enemy. In the words of a nineteenth century historian:

> With matchless strategy he contrived to keep the myriads of his opponents from the walls. With energy almost superhuman, he swept unexpectedly, now here and now there, by night and by day, into the midst of the foe; every swordsman of his band hewed down scores, and his own blade flashed as the lightning and caused Moslem heads to fall like snowflakes where he passed. Thousands of the bravest warriors of Amurath [Murad] were thus swept away continuously. His hosts were diminishing to the point of danger to his very person.[63]

At one point, Murad espied Skanderbeg and his men on a reconnaissance mission high up in a mountain overlooking Croya. Shaking his head, the sultan was heard to mutter that perhaps "the best way was to let alone that furious and untamed lion"—to stop "feed[ing] that unhappy beast" with the blood of his men.[64]

Murad persevered, however, as the breaching of Croya seemed imminent, the cannons having leveled so many of its ramparts. Thus, on an appointed day, after "the sultan had demolished a large part of the walls, he engaged his entire army in the battle," writes Chalkokondyles." To a loud cry, the janissaries violently hurled themselves into and "attempted to seize the city at the place where the walls had collapsed to the ground. But they did not overcome those in the city, who were fighting beyond hope. He then decided to starve the city into surrender and made a second, most ferocious attack," but that too failed.[65] Countless more Ottomans lay dead and dying.

By now Murad was at his wit's end: he "retired to his pavilion, overcome with grief and rage...tearing his hair and his beard, and pouring out blasphemous speeches against the majesty of heaven, seeming to call the Almighty in question for suffering his gray hairs and his former glory, and the Ottoman name, to be disgraced and humbled for the sake of a paltry castle in Epire [Albania]."[66] As might be expected, contemporary Ottoman chronicles are succinctly more sparing: Murad and his army "struck Croya with cannons and turned it into a graveyard. He hoped that they would surrender but they did not. Winter then arrived."[67]

And that was that: having marched one of the largest armies he had ever mustered, and having invested Croya for eight months, Murad resigned and lifted the siege on October 26, 1450. Some twenty thousand Turks had been killed for nothing—including, arguably, the sultan himself.

Although the official history states that Murad II died three months later, on February 3, 1451 in Adrianople, according to the usually reliable Marin Barletius, Murad died in Albania, right before the siege was lifted and because his proud spirit could not tolerate yet another defeat—an especially humiliating one—at the hands of Skanderbeg. According to this version, the future Sultan Muhammad II, who was also at the siege, wisely kept news of his father's death secret till he could arrive at Adrianople and secure his succession—which even then he did with some difficulty—hence the official version that Murad died in Adrianople.[68]

Although Albania was by now devastated and plagued by starvation, "That Christmas was the happiest the people had enjoyed since his return to Croya seven years earlier."[69] Moreover, if Skanderbeg's victories over the Turks in the late 1440s had first caught Europe's attention, his epic defense of Croya against everything the proud sultan and victor of Varna and Kosovo could hurl against him caused an explosion of euphoria throughout the West—not least as Murad, who had long terrorized southeastern Europe, had died soon thereafter. Pope Nicholas V hailed Skanderbeg a "Champion of Christendom"; more Western European adventurers and would-be Crusaders came and joined his legendary army. King Alfonso V of Aragon and Naples—who had aspirations of spearheading a great Crusade against the Turks—made a formal alliance with him on March 26, 1451.

Skanderbeg, meanwhile, worked to refortify and barricade Albania, being under no illusions concerning the future. He also confiscated various estates from those nobles who had betrayed him during the siege, and they "could do nothing," writes John Muzaka "for he had the army in his hands and they had perpetually the Turks at their back."[70] In further centralizing his authority, Skanderbeg also better improved Albania's chances against the Turks. Cementing it all, in April 1451, he married Donika, the daughter of George Arianiti, an especially powerful Albanian noble and early freedom-fighter against the Ottomans.

Thus, one year after the siege of Croya, which was meant to annihilate him, Skanderbeg emerged more powerful than ever. As for Muhammad II, the new sultan was busy quelling rebellions and consolidating his power; but he did not forget the humiliation of Albania and "spoke openly of his purpose, ere long, to convert the happiness and joy of Skanderbeg's marriage into tears and lamentations."[71]

Skanderbeg did not need to hear this to know it. Soon after his nuptials, he warned his countrymen that they were getting "soft and slothful"; having had a well-deserved reprieve at "ease and liberty, we no longer," said he, "have any reason to abandon our arms and let our wonted virtue, as it were, lay asleep and forgotten." In short, this was hardly the time for them to "stay indoors" and "dwell in pleasures and grow corrupt and effeminate."[72] Under his Spartan leadership, they resumed their military training and war preparations.

In 1452, one year after becoming Ottoman sultan, Muhammad II dispatched two armies, for a combined total of twenty-five thousand men, to terrorize Albania. Skanderbeg and his men rushed to intercept them before they could merge, and defeated them both, singly, on the same day, July 21. Skanderbeg ransomed one of the pashas—the other was killed during the fighting—back to Muhammad for thirteen thousand ducats, which were distributed among his grateful men.

Then again, on April 22, 1453, Muhammad, who was then besieging Constantinople, dispatched another expedition under Ibrahim Pasha. In the midst of severe thunderstorms, Skanderbeg and his men charged into the unsuspecting Muslim camp; three thousand Turks were butchered, the rest fled in chaos. Skanderbeg personally slew and placed Ibrahim's severed head on a pike—in conscious emulation of the Turks' treatment of Hungarian king Ladislaus III at Varna.

A Season of Treason

It was, in short, more of the usual, even under the new sultan and conqueror of Constantinople. "The time has now come," Skanderbeg declared when Muhammad was preoccupied with Serbia in 1455, "when we must employ our whole power and endeavors to dislodge the Infidels and to expel them altogether from our country."[73] He accordingly led a large force in July, augmented by Alfonso V's men, to reclaim the fortress of Berat, which was still held by the Ottomans. Once the fortress was on the verge of capitulating, Skanderbeg left the siege to his generals and departed for other urgent matters.

Suddenly, forty thousand Turks appeared out of nowhere—led by one of Skanderbeg's own generals no less! Moisi Golemi had become the latest Albanian noble to sellout. In exchange for allowing this massive Ottoman force to enter Albania secretly, Sultan Muhammad, ever the poisoner of friendship, had promised Moisi a large annual pension and the right to rule his lands. On hearing of this betrayal, Skanderbeg rushed back to Berat, but it was too late: not only did the fortress remain in Ottoman hands; some five thousand Christians lay butchered. It was a bitter and unexpected blow.

In the following year, 1456, while Muhammad was besieging Belgrade, he dispatched fifteen thousand Ottomans into Albania under his new vassal, Moisi, who knew the lay of the land. Skanderbeg, more defiant than ever, met and defeated the traitor head on. The latter begged forgiveness and was, amazingly, granted it—along with all his confiscated lands back.

Although Moisi remained loyal thereafter—until he was captured and executed by the Ottomans eight years later—he would not be the only of Skanderbeg's confidants to defect, a fact underscoring the envy more and more nobles bore against their increasingly celebrated chief.

Indeed, one year later, in 1457, the worst of all betrayals came: Skanderbeg's nephew, Hamza Kastrioti—whom Skanderbeg once characterized as "my chiefest friend and counsellor and the faithful companion of my travels"—turned on his uncle.[74] His grievance was born on the same day that Skanderbeg's only son, John, was born, in late 1456. Up until then, it was assumed that Hamza, whom Skanderbeg had adopted after his father (Skanderbeg's elder brother) died, was heir to Croya, which he had helped liberate and defend. Now that no longer seemed to be the case.

Although men betray for any number of reasons—envy, greed, cowardice—the Turkish sultans were always careful to exploit them. Muhammad II was especially intent on defeating Skanderbeg "by any possible subterfuge, bribery and corruption."[75] Accordingly, once the sultan learned of Hamza's disaffection, he offered to give him every-thing—even governorship of all Albania—if he would but submit to Muhammad and lead the Ottomans to victory against the hated Skanderbeg. Hamza accepted the offer.

That same year, in 1457, yet another of Skanderbeg's nephews, George Strez Balšić, also betrayed his leader by selling the fortress of Modritza to the Turks.

On learning of all these defections, Pope Callixtus III wrote to Skanderbeg. After likening the "terrible Turks" to a "serpent which now hides and now emerges to do damage to the Christian people and breaks forth and tortures them," he implored him to persevere so that,

> Christians will see that in the midst of the greatest furor and onslaught of the most powerful enemy, Your Lordship did not waver but with presence of mind you kept your fortitude and manly strength. All know what you performed and with the greatest praise extol you to heaven and speak of you as the true knight and defender of Christianity.[76]

Callixtus's only lament—now that John Hunyadi had just died—was that there were no more Skanderbegs: "We thank God that, had the perfidious enemy managed to overrun your country, had you not withstood as a strong bulwark against him, he would have found his way into the Christian world.... If the other Christian princes had your courage, we would not be worried and tormented over the safety of our faith."

Nor was this mere flattery; Callixtus conveyed the same sentiments to others. "As we view it," he confided in a letter to Alfonso V, "he is the only great bulwark withstanding the fury of the savage Turk and blocking his way to the rest of the Christian countries. We well know how many disasters he and his people have suffered."[77]

The Battle of Albulena

The betrayals finally came to roost in late May 1457: eighty thousand Turks under the joint command of Hamza and Isak bey Evrenos marched through and devastated the Mat River valley in north central Albania. Because Hamza was well acquainted with his uncle's guerilla tactics, Skanderbeg had to improvise. Instead of hiding his vastly outnumbered army—by now barely one-tenth the size of the Muslim army—in the mountains and awaiting the opportune moment to strike, he divided them into many smaller units and dispersed them in the valleys and woods. For three months, all the Turks saw were tiny roving bands of Albanians, none of which dared leave the mountains and engage them.

As a result, by late August, the Ottomans concluded that Skanderbeg had become a moot point—that he was "done up with," that his men had "deserted" him, and that he himself had quit to "the mountain fastness in order to save his skin."[78] But just when the Turks were most convinced that the Albanians had lost both their leader and their nerve, on September 2, 1457, Skanderbeg, having reunited his eight thousand men, launched a swift strike.

Under Mount Tumenishta, to loud cries and the braying instruments of war, he and his cavalry and guerilla fighters suddenly burst into the Turkish camp in a frenzy of war. The trapped Turks were terrified—despite assurances from Hamza that the Albanian army was much smaller than it seemed. Panic spread, and the Muslim army was routed on the plains of Albulena: as many as thirty thousand Turks were either butchered or captured in the bloody onslaught; the remainder fled back east in great disarray under Isak bey Evrenos.

In a victory to top all victories, the Master of Albania had yet again outdone himself—which is saying much—and in the process left the same amount of dirt on Sultan Muhammad's face as on his father's before him. As historian Kristo Frashëri writes,

Albulena was a brilliant fresh military victory on the Turks many times superior in numbers. It was at the same time a victory over the wavering treacherous feudal chieftains. It was moreover a victory over the misgiving that had arisen as to the future destiny of the rule of Skanderbeg. Together with the valorous Albanian fighters the hero had come off victorious through incomparable difficulties. They won the unbounded admiration of the entire world. The victory at Albulena raised the prestige of the Albanians and their chief in the international arena more than at any time before.[79]

In thirty-three different written appeals to various European kings and princes, Callixtus "urged them to become Skanderbegs." On December 23, 1457, the pope declared Skanderbeg Captain-General of the Curia (Holy See) in the Crusade against the Muslims and dubbed him an *Athleta Christi*, "Champion of Christ," an honorific he shared with the late Hunyadi.[80]

Because many of his leading generals had been captured at Albulena, Muhammad sent a delegation to ransom them—and to offer "peace and perpetual friendship" with Skanderbeg. Not one to be fooled, the Albanian berated the Turkish generals before releasing them. After informing them that he was always amenable to a *true* peace, he insisted that they, the Ottomans, would not "alter our mind on any point or detract anything from our resolution." Moreover, "We deem any kind of amity with you most infamous, as long as we see so many outrages and injuries everywhere to the Christians." "Let Muhammad," Skanderbeg continued, "as long as he will, seek peace. As for us, we will purchase our peace with the sword. And, having once gotten and attained it, we will likewise by the sword seek to maintain it."[81]

With that, he sent his ransomed prisoners on their way. As for Hamza, who was also captured, he was sent to detention in Naples. Although his generous uncle later forgave his betrayal and reinstated him, in 1460 Hamza was captured and slowly tortured to death by the Turks in Constantinople.

The Congress of Mantua

Although Callixtus III died a few months after calling on Christendom to emulate Skanderbeg, his successor was every bit as wary of Islamic encroachments. Months after becoming pope, in 1459, Pius II—who "saw the Ottoman menace not merely as a danger for eastern Europe but for Christianity itself"—convened the Council of Mantua, where he passionately called for a concerted Crusade against the Turks:[82]

> [For] can we expect peace from a nation which thirsts for our blood...? Lay aside these infatuated hopes. Mahomet will never lay down his arms until he is either wholly victorious or completely vanquished. Each success will be only a stepping-stone to the next until he has mastered all the Western Monarchs, overthrown the Christian Faith, and imposed the law of his false prophet on the whole world.[83]

During the congress, all mentioned Skanderbeg with great praise and it was assumed that he would be the supreme general of an army led by the Hungarians.

But if Christians could be mobilized into marching thousands of miles into hostile territory in 1095, in 1459, they could not even be mobilized into defending or liberating their own territories. Despite Pius's repeated appeals for the Christian powers to join in a common Crusade, which he had raised funds to help subsidize, few now were willing to confront the Turks, a fact that Pius lamented in his address: "Oh, that Godfrey, Baldwin, Eustace, Hugh, Bohemond, Tancred, and those other brave men who re-conquered Jerusalem were here! Truly they would not need so many words to persuade them."[84]

Nonetheless, wary of the sword rattling emanating from Europe, and in order to quell uprisings elsewhere, in 1460, Muhammad turned to guile. Because Albania had been thoroughly ravaged for two decades and desperate for a respite, he sent a cloying letter to Croya, referring to Skanderbeg as his "beloved friend," citing their "youthful years" together, and professing his "singular zeal and affection" for this rebel who had otherwise repeatedly humiliated him and his father.[85] Muhammad concluded by offering a lasting peace on favorable conditions to Skanderbeg—except for one.

In what was no doubt meant to sting, Muhammad required Skanderbeg to send his one and only son, three-year-old John, to be the sultan's "guest" (that is, hostage). Skanderbeg—well acquainted with Muhammad's penchant for pedophilia—responded with diplomacy, saying he would do so "if fatherly love would permit it.[86] But since I have but him, and he is yet a tender child, it is neither for his good nor for ours to have him now taken from us, now that he ought to be most tenderly cherished and carefully educated."[87] No doubt Skanderbeg had his own traumatic experiences in mind, when, more than five decades earlier, his own father, John Kastrioti, had delivered him up as a hostage to Muhammad's father, Murad. Although the Albanian would not budge on this condition, the sultan conceded and agreed that "I will as long as I live—Allah be my witness—observe and keep a sincere and inviolable Peace with you forever, except that you first give me just cause for violating it."[88]

Naturally, and as Edward Gibbon once remarked, "Peace was on his [Muhammad II] lips while war was in his heart," before long the sultan violated the treaty.[89] In 1461, Skanderbeg left to aid his Neapolitan allies against their rivals; on returning to Albania, he found three Turkish armies inside and terrorizing his country. Once again, the exasperated but indefatigable warrior-general rallied his people and led them to victories against all three expeditions—all within the same month—"in the ruthless battles of Mokra, of Pollogu, and of Livadi."[90]

As an indication of just how much Muhammad had come to despise the Master of Albania, when Skanderbeg's top generals, including the aforementioned Moisi Golemi and Muzaka, another of Skanderbeg's nephews, were captured, instead of ransoming them, a courtesy Skanderbeg had often granted him, the sultan had them skinned alive over the course of fifteen days before feeding their mutilated remains to hungry dogs.[91]

Months after that, in early 1465, Muhammad resorted to tactics unbecoming of the "Great Conqueror of Constantinople": he sent two assassins into Albania to eliminate his nemesis; they were exposed and executed.

The Second Siege of Croya

Although the Master of Albania continued to defy the Ottoman Empire, by the winter of 1465, his land was in utter ruins. Two decades of continuous Turkish invasions and atrocities had devastated Albania. Famine was widespread—and, because of it, population decline, as many emaciated Albanians had fled to Italy. Few fit men remained to fight, and even fewer came from abroad. Nor was papal or any other kind of support forthcoming, considering that Pius II, who appreciated and was supportive of Skanderbeg's struggle, had died a year earlier. To top it all off, Skanderbeg's scar-riddled and battle-weary body was now over sixty-years-old.

Aware of all this—and "having vowed by the head of Allah to defeat Scanderbeg"—Muhammad, at the head of another gargantuan army of one hundred thousand men, marched into Albania in the summer of 1466.[92] Despite the nation's wretched condition, once the Muslims entered it, "There followed a great hand to hand battle," to quote Kritoboulos, "with attack and counter-attack, a terrible struggle, for the Illyrians [Albanians] resisted stoutly and fought bravely. But he [Muhammad] routed them and took the passes by force, and drove them out with great slaughter."[93] All "mature males among the prisoners," adds Tursun Beg (b.1420), Muhammad's contemporary biographer, "were brought by the Sultan's order in his presence whereupon he mercilessly ordered their execution."[94]

Unable to prevent the massive Muslim army from invading their land, the few remaining Albanians "took their wives, flocks, and every other moveable up into the high and inaccessible mountain fortresses," scorching the land behind them as they had done in 1450.[95] So committed to freedom or death, "When they were pursued by the Turkish soldiers, and finding no way out, the Albanians threw themselves down the cliffs and perished," adds Kritoboulos.[96]

Muhammad soon reached and surrounded the White Castle of Croya. As in 1450, the fortress was garrisoned by a small force while Skanderbeg, ensconced in the mountains, made desperate sorties against the Turks whenever possible. "The enemy was holding out stubbornly in towers and passes in the steep mountainous regions," observed Tursun Beg, "but the Sultan's troops were spurred to great efforts by thoughts of Holy War (ghaza) and booty (ghanima)."[97]

Two months later, Muhammad left half of the army to continue the siege under Ballaban Pasha Badera—a master strategist and expert in guerilla warfare who had helped the sultan breach the cyclopean walls of Constantinople—and took the other half to ravage and plunder the countryside. Some Albanian nobles took the knee to him, while others fled.

On reaching the center of Albania, Muhammad ordered the construction of a fortress—subsequently named Elbassan, possibly a corruption of "the smiling one" (el-bassam) in Arabic—with materials that had been brought for that purpose. He garrisoned it with fighters who continued to raid and devastate the land all around—preventing the already starved and bedraggled Albanian freedom fighters from "coming down from the mountains during the winter to till the land or to pasture or care for their flocks, or do anything else," writes Kritoboulos.[98] It was a crafty move. Rather than try to take an Albanian fortress, Muhammad simply built his own, so that the Albanians "would be continuously so confined and undergoing hardships, they would one day be compelled to submit to the Sultan."[99]

Then the gloating sultan, at the head of a vast train of twenty thousand Albanian slaves—including "a great number of children"—retired to Constantinople, whence he expected to receive word of Croya's capitulation.[100] But the White Castle remained a tough nut to crack; and the siege dragged on into winter, which the Turks did not expect. As for Skanderbeg, he had been remarkably quiet, and rumor had it that the old man had finally succumbed, either to the Turks or death.

In fact, in late 1466, he had absconded to Rome across the Adriatic. Dressed as a poor wayfarer, he appeared before Pope Paul II. "The lord Scanderbeg arrived here Friday [December 12, 1466], and the households of the cardinals were sent out to meet him," wrote an ambassador who was present: "He is a man of advanced age, past sixty; he has come with few horses, a poor man. I understand he will seek aid."[101]

In a lengthy and moving speech before the pope and his advisors, Skanderbeg expressed how "both I and my people are plunged and drowned in blood more than any other nation in Christendom," as the "Turkish Prince, following in the footsteps of his ancestors," terrorizes Albania:

> Every day he does invade your flock, does dismember and persecute your people. Not being satisfied with so many murders, rapines and atrocities which he has committed in Asia and Europe, he now strives with all his overwhelming power to suppress and destroy me and my people, with our poor realm being left as the last objective of his cruelty. The long continuous wars and the many battles, which we have had, have worn out and have eaten up and consumed our forces. We are now in our last cast, so much that not any part of our body is left whole and sound enough to receive any more new wounds. Neither have we any blood left to us which we may shed and bestow

for the commonweal of Christendom. ....The enemy is even now at my door. He has not only destroyed and laid desolate my nation but as well has murdered and holds captive my people. He holds Croya, the key and bulwark of my realm, in a tight siege and has resolved never to depart from there until it becomes Turkish.[102]

"While there is time left," Skanderbeg continued, "provide me in the swiftest time possible, I beseech you, with the most urgently needed aid so that we may repress his violence and stem his fury, which has grown so mighty that it threatens and menaces not only the existence of Christendom but also the Church of God and even our faith as well." He closed his appeal with an ominous warning: "If the private miseries of your soldier do not move you, then at least let the common necessity, the imminent peril to your flock and the future devastation of the realm of Christendom stir you up and persuade you."[103]

Unfortunately for Skanderbeg, Paul II was no Crusading pope like his predecessors. After honoring the Albanian with "a sword of heraldic significance," a "robe of a crusader," and a five thousand ducat donation, the pope sent Skanderbeg on his way.[104] He stopped by his Neapolitan allies, who gave him another one thousand ducats, as well as weapons and supplies for his war effort.

Skanderbeg returned to his beleaguered castle in early spring and, with no saner options left, made preparations for an all-out attack—once again, while vastly outnumbered, with a paltry fifteen hundred men under his command. Thus, sometime in April he launched another legendary charge against the Muslims. According to a curt letter written soon thereafter, and as Skanderbeg had done so many times before, "he killed many of the Turks"—even their formidable commander, Ballaban Pasha, was killed in the charge—"and won a great victory."[105]

And so, on April 23, 1467, nearly eleven months after the siege first started, a tattered and haggard Skanderbeg limped into his dilapidated White Castle, where his skeleton-like crew of defenders acclaimed him their savior.

Yet even now, there was no time to rest, much less celebrate. Skanderbeg and his men, cognizant of the dangers it posed, rushed to lay siege to Elbassan, the newly constructed Ottoman stronghold. Because it was built on a navigable outlet to the Adriatic Sea—and therefore posed a direct threat to the eastern seaboard of Italy—even the vacillating Venetians helped.

But before they could take the Muslim stronghold, Muhammad—who on learning of defeat at Croya had flown into a rage—sped back to Albania at the head of another one hundred thousand man army and lifted the siege of Elbassan in July 1467. According to Kritoboulos, he again "pursued their prince, Alexander, who took refuge in the inaccessible fortresses of the mountains, in his customary retreats and abodes in the hills."[106] Muhammad proceeded to lay Croya to siege again—only for Skanderbeg to appear out of nowhere again, slaughtering Turks left and right. Rather anticlimactically, the sultan ended up withdrawing, though, and in order to console himself, only after first taking "a vengeful toll of lives in the lesser defended provinces."[107]

By the fall of 1467, not only had Skanderbeg liberated Croya, but he had miraculously reclaimed most of his former territories from the Turks. Although another Albanian triumph, the country was by now unrecognizable. Historian A.K. Brackob summarizes:

> Mehmet's determined efforts [like his father's before him] had met with failure. Albania had proved to be a costly battleground for the Ottomans, but its inhabitants also paid a high price for their resistance. The economy was devastated. Large numbers of Albanians had been killed in battle during the Ottoman invasions, while others had fled to southern Italy. Despite this, the Albanians, using every resource at their disposal, continued their struggle to maintain their independence from the Islamic Empire.[108]

Finale

During the winter of 1467, the tireless Skanderbeg traveled to and summoned a meeting of the remaining nobles at Saint Nicholas Cathedral, where the now defunct League of Alessio was founded twenty-three years earlier. The order of business was how best to deal with the new threat of Elbassan, which remained a thorn in Albania's side—or, more literally, its center.

Days later, in January, Skanderbeg was "suddenly stricken with a strong and violent fever."[109] Like Hunyadi before him, the sixty-three-year-old Skanderbeg had contracted the plague—ever the companion of war and pestilence—and was slowly dying.

As his comrades-in-arms surrounded his deathbed, the Master of Albania waxed philosophical. The two most important things in a man's life, he offered, are first to "adore God" by faithfully serving him, and second, "to give our lives and to shed our blood for our country's preservation and safety." As such, they had had a good run against the Turks—"according to our heart's desire."

> But now, my dear friends, in the ordinary course of human events, when I have reached threescore and three years of my age, seized by a grievous sickness and shorn of my accustomed strength, I begin to wax feeble. And, little by little I go by the way of all flesh.... [The time is come] for me to lay aside this mortal and frail burden of my body.... [Even so] I have run the race which it pleased God to appoint me.[110]

The erstwhile warlord and terror of the Turk, now in the seeming of a wise patriarch, proceeded to give them the best advice he could think of—advice based on a lifetime of experience fighting for and against the Turks. Snippets follow:

> [B]efore my soul departs from my body and before I leave you, there is one thing of which I find it necessary to admonish you and to plead with you: until now, during my lifetime, you have endured all suffering for the safety and dignity of our Christian religion and our country. By these means you have won the favor, honor and admiration of all the princes of Christendom. Even hereafter, when I am dead and gone, let that be the only and the whole desire of your hearts. All things, I can assure you, will fall out happily for you as long as you continue steadfastly united and as long as you put the public and common good above personal interest.... But have no doubt whatsoever that the Ottoman tyrant will seek to cause disunity among you, to divide your forces. He will use many plots and devices to turn you one against the other. And when he sees you are at variance with each other, he will in the long run oppress you one by one and utterly consume and destroy all of you.... As soon as he hears of my death, this enemy will endeavor ceaselessly to reach that very goal.[111]

And with that, George Kastrioti—the great Skanderbeg, Lord Alexander, the Albanian Braveheart—died on January 17, 1468, to the great consternation of Christendom. He was laid to rest in Saint Nicholas Cathedral.

As Skanderbeg had correctly predicted, on learning of his nemesis' demise, Muhammad was heard to proclaim that "Asia and Europe are mine at last. Woe to Christendom! She has lost her sword and her shield!"[112] Without wasting a moment, he again put Croya to siege and, on June 16, 1468—just five months after the death of its lord, who had rebuffed three titanic Turkish sieges—the White Castle surrendered. Muhammad had given his word that its defenders could leave unmolested; but once they emerged, the treacherous Turk ordered every man slaughtered and every woman and child enslaved.

Over the years, other Albanian fortresses and cities fell like dominos; in a few decades, the whole of Albania, or what was left of it, was finally absorbed into the Ottoman Empire. Even before then, as many as another two hundred thousand Albanians—including Skanderbeg's wife and young son—had fled to Italy, itself the next and long awaited target of Muhammad's jihad, now that he finally possessed Albania, which is all that had stood in his way. Indeed, as far back as 1454, a Venetian diplomat had warned that "the conqueror of Constantinople had resolved to make himself the master of Rome and all Italy; just as he had taken possession of the daughter, Byzantium, so he would also conqueror Rome, the mother."[113]

Accordingly, on July 28, 1480, a fleet of Turks landed in and captured Otranto, located in the heel of the Italian boot, causing mass panic throughout the peninsula. More than half of Otranto's twenty-two thousand Italian inhabitants were massacred, five thousand led away in chains. On a hilltop (subsequently named "Martyr's Hill") another eight hundred were ritually beheaded for refusing to recant Christ for Muhammad; their archbishop was sawn in half. Local churches were ritually desecrated and converted into mosques.[114]

In short, the Ottoman jihad had finally reached the heart of Europe. Fortunately for it, Muhammad II, the conquering sultan, died less than a year later, aged forty-nine, likely poisoned by his son and successor, Bayezid II. On the very next day, Pope Sixtus "ordered processions in Rome to celebrate the death of the great enemy of Christendom and conqueror of Constantinople."[115] Such prescient celebrations were warranted; for a few months later, the Ottomans withdrew from Italy in September 1481.

As for Albania, in retribution for its long years of defiance, it was so thoroughly Islamized over the following centuries that it remains today one of a very few Muslim-majority nations in Europe. Even so, and as a reflection of the high esteem and great honor the Muslim-majority populace of Albania have for Skanderbeg—this man who must otherwise be seen as a "traitor" to and avowed enemy of Islam*—they adopted his standard, a black double-headed eagle against red background, for their own national flag following independence from the Ottomans in 1912.

Legacy

Of the eight Defenders in this book, Skanderbeg has arguably been the most celebrated throughout Europe. In the centuries following his death, more than one thousand books in over twenty different languages, and any number of operas and plays, were written about him.[116] In a letter dated 1756, Major General James Wolfe of Britain wrote that Skanderbeg "excels all the officers, ancient and modern, in the conduct of a small defensive army."[117] In 1905, historian William J. Armstrong went so far as to write that "the exploits even of the renowned paladins of the crusades, whether Godfrey or Tancred or Richard or Raymond, pale to insignificance by similar comparison.† Only the legendary feats of King Arthur and his knights...suggest a parallel of wondrous achievement."[118]

Such unequivocal praise is not unwarranted. From late 1443 to early 1468—nearly twenty-five years—Skanderbeg committed his life to the successful defense of his tiny homeland against the world's most powerful empire. He renounced a life of wealth, honor, and prestige among the Ottomans and willingly embraced a life of nonstop war among and

---

* In fact, to avoid this conundrum—how can Muslims praise and take for a national hero a Christian enemy of and apostate from Islam?—the Christian background and zeal of Skanderbeg and his generation has largely been scrubbed and suppressed, first by Albanian and later by Western historians. In reality, "Scanderbeg possessed deeply rooted spiritual qualities. Before each major battle, for example, he would kneel and devoutly pray to God for guidance to victory" (Drizari, 92). Even so and to this day, Skanderbeg and the Albanian people's struggle against the Ottoman Turks is largely presented as one of nationalism, never religion, for obvious reasons.

† To be fair, one of the overlooked reasons Skanderbeg is more popular than, say, Godfrey, is because the former is also much closer to us in time—which naturally means there is a larger and richer literary and historiographic tradition surrounding him than for those men who thrived centuries earlier, the colorful details of whose lives and speeches are largely lost, if ever recorded.

on behalf of his own people—not infrequently living in mountains and caves as a fugitive, though always living in freedom. His "ingratitude" naturally provoked the Turks to no end and led to wave after wave of jihadist invasions, each larger and crueler than its predecessor. Yet, in a total of twenty-four battles and sieges, he beat them all back, even as a battle-scarred and war-weary veteran of sixty-three years.[119] In the end, the only thing that could defeat Skanderbeg was his own mortality.

His great victories are attributed to an indomitable spirit; a swift mind—he was reportedly fluent in Albanian, Arabic, Bulgarian, Greek, Italian, Latin, Serbian, and Turkish;[120] a powerful body—he reportedly slew three thousand Muslims with his own hands;[121] and something else: having spent some three decades among the Turks, he could do what few other Christians could: think—arguably act—like a Turk. As Konstantin Mihailović, after describing Turkish machinations and perfidy, wrote, "it is far easier for one to defend himself against the Turks who is familiar with them than for one who does not know their custom."[122]

Not only Albania but all of Europe benefited from Skanderbeg's stalwart defense and perseverance. Had the Ottomans managed to transform Albania into a launching pad into Italy in 1450 instead of 1480, Muhammad II, the Conqueror, would have had thirty years, not just one, to pursue his long cherished goal of conquering Rome and, from there, inundating Western Europe with his Eastern hordes. That Skanderbeg was a quintessential Defender of the West was even acknowledged by the United States Congress, in a 2005 resolution titled, "Honoring the 600th anniversary of the birth of Gjergj Kastrioti (Scanderbeg), statesman, diplomat, and military genius, for his role in saving Western Europe from Ottoman occupation."[123]

Perhaps the greatest—if most indirect—praise comes from Skanderbeg's arch enemies, the Turks (who ironically, and like the Cid's enemies, further dubbed him with the name posterity knows him by). When the Muslims conquered Croya a few months after he died in 1468, they located and exhumed his body—less, however, to desecrate and more as a reflection of the legendary status he held even among them: for the Turks carefully divided and transformed his bones into talismans and distributed them among themselves, convinced that whoever wore these amulets near his heart would be transformed into a mighty warrior—into a Skanderbeg.[124]

CHAPTER 8

Vlad Dracula:
The Dread Lord Impaler

"[W]e will not flee before their savagery, but stand by all of the Christians...[and] by all means we will fight them."

—VLAD DRACULA[1]

"[T]he Gaiours [Infidels] are incapable of united action against us. The Christian potentates will never unite against us.... No doubt they think much, speak much, and explain much, but after all they do very little."

—OTTOMAN GENERAL[2]

As discussed in Chapter 6, after the first battle of Kosovo, 1389, the Turks dominated the lands south of the Danube. Directly north of that river—and next on the Ottomans' picking list—lay Wallachia, modern day Romania. The Turks tried to conquer it several times over the following decades but were repeatedly repulsed by Mircea I (b.1355; r.1386–1418), voivode of Wallachia—"the bravest and cleverest among the Christian princes"—to quote an impressed Turkish chronicler.[3]

In 1431, during a grand ceremony in Nuremberg, Sigismund, king of Hungary, inducted one of Mircea's sons, Vlad (1395–1447), into the Order of the Dragon, dedicated to defending Christendom against the Turks. Henceforth he would be known as Vlad Dracul—the "Dragon"—in reference to his order. That same year Sigismund also recognized Vlad's claim to the throne of Wallachia.

It would, however, take another five years before Dracul could become Vlad II, warlord of Wallachia, in 1436. The reasons for this are instructive: the Wallachians did not recognize the rights of primogeniture; all sons of a voivode could make a claim to his throne. The result was brutal infighting and constant instability—so that there were twenty-nine different voivode reins during the fifty-eight years between 1418, when Mircea I died, and 1476. During that time frame, voivodes ruled an average of two years before being ousted or killed.[4]

This hopeless situation was exacerbated by the fact that the two opposing powers surrounding Wallachia, the Kingdom of Hungary and the Ottoman Empire, treated it as their chessboard—the former supporting whichever claimant could help defend Christendom, the latter whichever claimant could help further Islamic encroachment. And behind it all, in the shadows, were the boyars—the nobles—who regularly conspired against whichever voivode did not further their own limited and often mercantile interests (as seen during John Hunyadi's career).

In this context of instability, and especially after his sponsor, Sigismund, died in 1437, Vlad II Dracul fell under the Ottoman sphere of influence—becoming the first of the Wallachian voivodes to accept vassalage, meaning submission, to the Turks, even as he "wait[ed] for a more favorable moment to reveal his feelings of hostility toward them."[5] Wasting no time, on the following year, in 1438, Sultan Murad II raided Transylvania—with the aid of his new and now somewhat remorseful vassal.[6] Aside from the death and devastation they caused, the Turks enslaved and hauled off forty thousand Transylvanians.[7]

After 1440, when Crusading efforts were rekindled under the leadership of John Hunyadi, Dracul, whose heart was always with the Christian cause, became cooperative. The suspicious sultan ordered him to appear in Adrianople. On arriving in early 1442, Murad had Vlad shackled and thrown in a dungeon on "trumped-up charges."[8]

When Hunyadi installed his own man in Wallachia, Murad thought better of it and decided to release Vlad later that year. Before doing so, however, and as a guarantee of his loyalty, Murad, as was his custom, demanded that Dracul offer up his two youngest sons as hostages in his place, and the voivode complied: "he sent for them and when they arrived," writes Doukas, "he delivered them [to the sultan] even though they were still adolescents."[9] The two young brothers, Vlad, named after his father, and Radu, were immediately sent to and imprisoned in a remote Anatolian fortress.

Like Skanderbeg, who was also delivered up by his father under similar circumstances nearly three decades earlier—to Murad's later regret—one of these brothers, popularly known today as "Count Dracula," would go on to terrorize the Turks in ways no vampire could.

Vlad III Dracula

Vlad, the second of Vlad II Dracul's three sons, was born sometime between 1428 and 1431 (henceforth and for computing's sake, 1430). He received a typical European education for nobles, with the added benefit of a fierce upbringing. According to Vlad's modern biographers, historians Radu R. Florescu and Raymond T. McNally,

> From the tenderest age, a great deal of emphasis was placed on physical fitness [in Wallachia]—even at court, children were exposed to the elements on stormy nights in true Spartan tradition; should they survive the chills and fevers of the accompanying colds, they were considered to have strong physical and moral character, essential traits of good warriors. For physical exercise, even a five-year-old tot had to be able to ride an unsaddled horse at a gallop.[10]

As the coming pages will show, Vlad was a top graduate of this school of hard knocks.

Concerning his appearance on reaching manhood, along with the well-known painting made during his lifetime (a copy of which is at Ambras Castle in Austria), Niccolò Modrussa, an Italian, left the following description:

> He was not very tall, but very stocky and strong, with a cold and terrible appearance, a strong aquiline nose, swollen nostrils, a thin and reddish face in which the very long eyelashes framed large wide-open green eyes; the bushy black eyebrows made them appear threatening. His face and chin were shaven, but for a mustache. The swollen temples increase the bulk of his head. A bull's neck connected his head from which black curly locks hung on his wide shouldered person.[11]

Although history remembers him as Vlad Țepeș (pronounced *Tspesh*), that is, "Vlad the Impaler"—due to his penchant for that form of execution—his actual name, as evidenced by his extant signature, was "Vlad III Dracula," meaning "son of the dragon," a reference to his father, Vlad II of the Order of the Dragon. As his reputation blackened over the years, this patronymic increasingly came to connote and eventually denote "son of the Devil." Although contemporary Turkish sources have various sobriquets for him—including "the merciless infidel," the "wicked horseman," and the "Devilish Impaler"—to most Turks, he came to be known as Kaziklu Bey: the "Lord Impaler."[12]

In 1442, however, when his Ottoman captivity began, Vlad was "a gaunt and rather ungainly youth" of about twelve; and his younger brother and fellow hostage, Radu, was only six.[13] For the next six years, they lived without father, mother, or kin, surrounded by jailers of strange tongue and religion. Concerning these early molding years, French historian Matei Cazacu writes:

> The circumstances affecting the two hostages were precarious in the extreme; their lives were in constant danger in the case of any tergiversation or change in the relationship between Vlad Dracul [their father] and the Turks. Dracul was not a man to keep a pledge to the infidel. Raised and educated at the court of Emperor Sigismund of Luxemburg (who was also king of Hungary), he knew that any method, fair or foul, could be legitimately used in the crucial struggle against the Turks.[14]

Indeed, two years after committing his sons to the sultan as a sign of fidelity, in 1444, Vlad II sent four thousand Wallachians to participate in the failed Crusade of Varna—thereby all but guaranteeing his sons' execution. As he wrote to the governor of Brașov in 1445, after learning that there were doubts concerning his loyalty to the Christian cause, "Please understand, that I have allowed my little children to be butchered for the sake of Christian peace, in order that both I and my country might continue to be vassals to the Holy Roman Emperor."[15]

Neither of his two sons was killed—or even blinded with hot irons, as the hostage sons of the Serbian despot, George Branković, were in 1441. Murad likely kept the two youths alive as bargaining chips for Vlad's neutrality, which he again gained in 1446. Having had enough of

Vlad II and his vacillations, John Hunyadi instigated an uprising of the boyars in Târgovişte, the Wallachian capital. In 1447, they overthrew and beheaded Vlad on the accusation that he was too fickle and friendly with the Turks. (In reality, he, like the Serbian despot, was always trying to walk a fine line between the menacing Muslim empire and the Christian kingdom of Hungary.) The sadistic Wallachians also tortured and buried Vlad's eldest son, Mircea, alive.

Fearing Wallachia under Hunyadi's control, Murad turned to his young hostage, Vlad. Unlike his younger brother and fellow captive, now known as "Radu the Handsome," Vlad had displayed a promising militancy—he was prone to fierce temper bouts and regularly whipped into submission, all of which "toughened his character to a diamond-like hardness"—and therefore could make for an effective voivode.[16] In 1448 Murad sent young Vlad with an Ottoman force to reclaim his slain father's throne, though only "with the understanding that he would come to him each year to pay homage and to bring tribute," writes the contemporary, Konstantin Mihailović, "just as his father had done."[17]

In circumstances that are unclear, Vlad, then aged eighteen, succeeded and took the throne of Wallachia—but only for two short months before another claimant drove him out. From that point in 1448 to 1454, Vlad disappears from the histories.

Voivode of Wallachia

Suddenly, even as John Hunyadi lay dying of plague in Belgrade—and in part thanks to the White Knight's direct support—Vlad Dracula reappears, sometime between July and August 1456.[18] After invading Wallachia and killing Vladislav II, its voivode, in single combat—this being the same man who led the overthrow and murder of his father in 1447—Vlad reclaimed the throne for a second time, aged twenty-six. Immediately he set about consolidating his grip on power. Dracula had been ejected before—and his father and elder brother killed by their own subjects—and was now determined to stay. He began by creating a personal guard of loyal warriors closely attached to his person.[19]

Next, he inaugurated a brutal purge of the ever scheming boyars. After inviting all those "distinguished men of the realm" whom he suspected of treachery to a banquet, he lightheartedly asked them how many voivodes had come and gone before him in recent times. When they laughingly responded "many," he, more seriously, asked why that was—before telling the now alert nobles exactly why: because of them and their conniving ways. Having previously locked the great doors of the banquet hall from the outside, he and his men then fell on and butchered the boyars.[20]

Dracula then exacted vengeance on those mobs that had buried his older brother alive—though only after he had exhumed Mircea's body and confirmed the truth of it: the men were impaled, and the women and children put to forced labor on his castle of Poenari, high atop the Carpathian Mountains. Not only were such brutal measures revenge against the boyars and the people for their role against his father, brother, and his own first overthrow; it was, as shall be more closely examined, the use of calculated terror—terrifying anyone from daring to scheme against him.

Finally, Dracula radically transformed the military: "he surrounded himself with a number of distinguished and devoted soldiers and servants to whom he gave the money, wealth, and social positions of those [boyars] he killed," writes Chalkokondyles, "so that, in a short time, he brought about a radical change, and this man completely altered the organization of Dacia [Wallachia]."[21]

But was Vlad, like his father, still a vassal of the Ottomans? He quickly answered this question by formally pledging his allegiance to the Turks' archrival, Hungary, and concluding a convention with his Saxon neighbors in the Transylvanian cities of Braşov and Ţara Bârsei on September 6, 1456: "under oath and with faith in God," the joint statement read, "we have decided and agreed that whenever, over the course of time, because of fear of the Turks or a coup by our enemies...[that we will come to the aid of one another, etc.]."[22]

Soon thereafter, Vlad sent a letter to his "brethren, friends and neighbors" in Braşov:

Now the time and appointed hour about which we spoke before has arrived: the Turks intend to put great burdens, almost impossible to bear, upon our shoulders, forcing us to bow down before them. It is not for us or ours that they put such a great burden but for you and yours; the Turks do this to humiliate us. As far as we ourselves are concerned, we could have made peace, but on account of you and yours we cannot make peace with the Turks because they wish to pass through our country to attack and plunder you.

In other words, the Turks, still thinking they could rely on Wallachian compliance, were heavily pressuring Vlad to cooperate and open the way to Transylvania (as his father had done in 1438). As such, "for our good and for yours," he requested that the Transylvanians send two hundred, or even just fifty, "chosen men" to stand by him during his next meeting—for "when the Turks see the power of the Hungarians, they will soften, and we will tell them more men will come."[23]

Not only did nothing come of this plea, but three months later, the Hungarian governor sent a letter to these same nobles of Braşov asking them to help oust Dracula and install another pretender, Dan. The Saxons were only too happy to comply: they were already monopolizing and therefore violating the free trade agreement they had recently ratified with Vlad, and abusing their privileges in Wallachia. Meanwhile, the Saxons of Sibiu were supporting yet another claimant to the Wallachian throne.[24]

As seen, such casual treachery was not new for the time and place; but Vlad meant not to play along. On learning of these plots, his retribution was swift and terrible: he went to and devastated the Saxon cities—reportedly impaling thousands. As for the pretender, Dan, Dracula easily repulsed his Braşov-sponsored invasion in April 1460. "And then," to quote from an early German source, Vlad forced Dan "to dig his own grave and ordered that the funeral service be read according to the Christian rite, and then he had him beheaded next to his tomb."[25]

Ironically, while these accounts would later be sensationalized to cast Vlad as a psychotic terrorist (on which more below), often left out is the pivotal role the Turks—and their religion*—played in his childhood. "Undoubtedly," write his modern biographers, his "six-year period of Turkish captivity, at an age when character is molded...is relevant

---

* Islamic scriptures are full of calls to terrorize, mutilate, and massacre infidels (non-Muslims). After declaring "I will cast terror into the hearts of infidels," Allah calls on Muslims to "strike off their heads and strike off their every fingertip" (Koran 8:12). Similarly, "It is not for a prophet to have captives [of war] until he inflicts a massacre in the land" (Koran 8:67). Other penalties for infidels who "spread mischief in the land is death, crucifixion, cutting off their hands and feet on opposite sides, or exile from the land" (Koran 5:33). "I have been made victorious with terror," the Prophet Muhammad further declares in a canonical hadith. Ottoman psychological warfare was very much informed by such scriptures. Similarly, concerning their Arab predecessors of the seventh to ninth centuries, Ibn Khaldun (b.1332) asserts that "Terror in the hearts of their enemies was why there were so many routs during the Muslim conquests [of the Middle East, North Africa, and Spain] (Ibrahim 2018, 41)."

in accounting for Dracula's cold and sadistic personality." During this time he also "learned the effectiveness of the Ottomans' use of terror tactics"[26]—most notably impalement, an especial favorite of the Turks.* (As one example, during his siege of Constantinople in 1453, after beheading all the sailors of a Venetian ship, Sultan Muhammad II ordered the life of its captain "to be taken by a stake through the anus," writes Doukas.[27])

In reality, even the most perverse deeds that would later be attributed to Vlad—such as dining in the midst of his impaled Saxon victims—were all but Turkish customs. After the carnage at Varna, for example, Murad II held a "feast among the corpses of vanquished Christians."[28] (Even so, according to mainstream news sources such as CNN, the Islamic State ("ISIS") learned its sadistic methods of torture and execution, not from its Islamic heritage, which is replete with examples stretching back to Islam's prophet, but rather from Vlad III Dracula.[29])

As for the notorious anecdote at hand, Vlad's reprisals against Transylvania, according to historian Anton Balotă,

> Careful historical and economic research has pointed out that Dracula's invasions of the Transylvanian lands of the Saxons was not the product of an evil policy of a voivode bent on massacres, but the result of a deliberate and conscious policy, applied with a cruelty which was characteristic of the time. The policy of Dracula toward the Saxons was guided by the need for a strong resistance against the Turks.[30]

Indeed, even the Saxons' own liege lord, the Hungarian king, blamed them: "You yourselves," Matthias Corvinus wrote to Sibiu, "through your greed, gave him [Vlad] reason to come against you causing great damage. For this, you must bear most of the guilt."[31]

At any rate, by 1460, Vlad III Dracula had established himself as unquestioned warlord of Wallachia. Moreover, and "in contrast to the disloyal boyars, the peasantry as a whole looked favorably upon Dracula

---

* Jacopo de Campi, a Genoese merchant and longtime trader with the Ottomans, left the following description of the procedure: "The Grand Turk [makes] the man he wishes to punish lie down on the ground; a sharp long pole is placed in the rectum; with a big mallet held in both hands the executioner strikes it with all his might, so that the pole, known as a *palo*, enters the human body, and according to its path, the unfortunate lingers on or dies at once; then he raises the pole and plants it in the ground; thus the unfortunate is left in extremis; he does not live long" (Ibrahim 2018, 231).

and rallied to his cause"—not least as he "defended the peasants from Turkish demands by refusing to pay the tribute (from 1459 onward) in both money and kind (grain, horse, et cetera)" and "also steadfastly opposed all Turkish endeavors to enroll Wallachian children in the janissary corps."[32] Topping it all off, and better to solidify their alliance against the Turks, Vlad married an anonymous blood relative of the Ottomans' arch-nemesis, Hungarian king Matthias Corvinus (r. 1458–1490)—Hunyadi's boy.

To Bow or Not to Bow to Muhammad?

Now when "it was reported to the sultan that Vlad was planning a rebellion"—Sultan Muhammad II, a master of the divide-and-conquer strategy, was always kept informed by his vast network of spies—"and that he [Vlad] had turned to the Hungarians, [and] had come to an agreement with them," the "sultan took this matter most seriously," writes Chalkokondyles.[33]

So Muhammad decided to put matters to the test. He sent emissaries to Târgoviște demanding that Vlad send, not just the three years' worth of tribute he had failed to deliver, but an additional tribute of five hundred children for the janissary corps (that is and as seen, five hundred Wallachian boys who were to be forcibly ripped from their parents' arms, indoctrinated in Islam, raised to be future jihadists, and, when the time was right, released back to terrorize and conquer their former kin).

On that fateful day, sometime around 1461, three Ottoman diplomats, having climbed fifteen hundred concrete steps to reach Dracula's castle high atop a misty mountain, approached the throne of the Wallachian warlord. At one point during their audience, Vlad inquired—although he knew full well—why they had failed to remove their turbans in his presence. They replied that it was their "custom and law" to keep their heads wrapped—to which Dracula retorted, "And I shall uphold your law, so that you adhere to it firmly." Then, according to the Old Russian Chronicle, one of the very earliest sources on Vlad, he "ordered that their turbans be fastened to their heads with little iron nails."[34] Before dismissing the brain-hemorrhaged emissaries, he commanded them to tell their master not to "send his customs to other lords, who don't want them, but let him keep them [to] himself."

On learning that his diplomatic mission had failed, abysmally, the sultan next turned to trickery. Sometime in the Fall of 1461, Muhammad sent a high-ranking Ottoman, Yunus Bey, a Greek convert to Islam (formerly Thomas Katabolinos), to win over the voivode, including with smiles and professions of peace; simultaneously, another of the sultan's servants, Hamza, the bey of Nicopolis, just south of Wallachia, was notified that "the sultan would be personally gratified if, by guile or whatever other means, he would capture" Dracula once he crossed the Danube into Ottoman territory.[35]

After Yunus Bey arrived and left, Vlad described the essential portion of their meeting in a letter to Hungarian king Matthias:

> [T]he Turks, the cruelest enemies of the Cross of Christ, have sent their highest-ranking messengers to convince us not to keep the peace and the agreements we made with Your Majesty, and not to celebrate the wedding [between Vlad and Matthias's relative], and to join with them alone, and to go to the Porte of the Turkish Sultan, that is to say to his Court. And if we fail to give up the peace, the agreements, and the wedding with your Majesty, the Turks will not keep the peace with us either.[36]

Even before he sent this letter, however, Vlad had conceded to Yunus's firm but honeyed words of reconciliation and agreed to go and pay homage to Muhammad. Thus, sometime in the winter of 1461/1462, he crossed the Danube into Nicopolis with fifty Wallachian children—an initial portion of his tribute to Muhammad.

But it was all a ruse; the man who was to be deceived was himself deceiving his would-be deceivers: Vlad's personal guard was fully armed and prepared for war; others were hiding in the mountains; the children were a false token of submission. As Dracula later wrote to Matthias, "by the grace of God...we found out about their deceit and trickery, and it was us who captured Hamza-beg."[37] Or, in the more outraged words of Ottoman chronicler Aşıkpaşazade (b.1400):

> The bey of Wallachia, that damned son of a bitch, attacked Hamza bey about midnight. He killed many Turks and took Hamza bey prisoner. The Infidels crossed the Danube at several places and made an incursion into the regions neighboring Wallachia and plundered, causing much damage in that vilayet [Ottoman province].[38]

In fact, Vlad had captured both Hamza and Yunus, took them back to Târgoviște and, in "honor" of their "high" positions, placed them on very high stakes in his "Forest of the Impaled," which surrounded his castle for six miles in circumference (and on which more later).

"Immediately after that," writes Chalkokondyles, "he prepared as large an army as he could"—which amounted to two thousand Wallachians—and marched directly back to and again crossed over the Danube.[39] Further demonstrating that, when it came to ruses, he could give as good as he could take from the Turks, he approached the fortress of Giurgiu in Nicopolis. Although his celebrated grandfather, Mircea I, had built it to defend Târgoviște from the Turks, it was now in Ottoman hands. Pretending to be one of their own and speaking in fluent Turkish, Dracula fooled the garrison into dropping the drawbridge, at which point he and his men stormed the fortress and adjoining lands, massacring, according to Vlad's own computation in his letter to King Matthias, "23,884 Turks"—"not including those who were burned in their houses and whose heads were not presented to our officials [for the count]."[40]

In this manner he passed through "the land that belonged to the sultan, killing everyone, women and children included. He burned the houses, setting fire wherever he moved. Having worked this great slaughter, he returned back to Wallachia."[41] The Old Russian Chronicle confirms that, after Dracula had rampaged "for about five days in the sultan's land.... Nothing remained, the whole land was made empty, and Dracula drove others, who were Christian, onto his land and settled them there. And having taken a vast multitude of conquests, he returned."[42]

As material proof of his triumph, "he had the noses cut off all those living and dead, male and female," writes Konstantin Mihailović, and "sent these noses to Hungary," saying that "as many Turks had been defeated and killed as there were of these noses."[43]

Finally and to underscore that this was the only sort of "obeisance" Muhammad could ever expect from him, Vlad released some leading Turkish officers with the following instructions: "Go, you will tell your sultan what you have seen; I have served him, as far as I was able. And if my service is pleasing to him, I will serve him still, as much as is in my power."[44]

In response, Turks everywhere were "so terror stricken," writes a contemporary chronicler, "that those who could [flee the Balkans and] cross to Anatolia considered themselves fortunate."[45] Even at the sultan's court in "Constantinople itself, there was an atmosphere of consternation, gloom, and fear...by the awesome reputation of the Lord Impaler ('Kaziglu Bey'), as they began to call him."[46]

War

So war it would be. The outraged sultan ordered Ottomans from all around the empire to mobilize and prepare for another great jihad. Vlad clearly no longer feared and had dared show his true face to the Muslims—and as such needed disciplining, Tursun Beg explained (without, of course, mentioning Muhammad's own treacherous designs that preceded and prompted Dracula's rampage):

> [V]ictory [over boyars, Transylvanians, etc.] made him too confident of his own power and when the Sultan was away on the long expedition in Trebizond, driven by his arrogance and inclination to quarrel, he planned to cause damage to the Ottoman countries. As he had reached the throne with the help of the Sublime Porte, this deed could not go unpunished.... He neither came nor paid the tribute. Then he had to be punished and destroyed.[47]

For his part, Vlad knew well the repercussions of his brazen raids—and meant for there to be no turning back. Even contemporary Turkish chroniclers understood that Dracula was signaling to his Christian coreligionists that, as Skanderbeg had done in 1444, he too had crossed the Rubicon. After describing the havoc he caused south of the Danube, Aşıkpaşazade continued his chronicle by saying that Vlad "cut off the head of Hamza bey, which he sent, together with the heads of other Muslims, to the Hungarian king with the message: 'I am now an enemy of the Turk.' All the Infidel rulers heard this and believed that this Infidel had indeed become an enemy of the Sultan."[48]

Indeed, in an urgent letter to the Hungarian king dated February 11, 1462, Dracula explained how he had declared war on the Turks, rather than betray him, Matthias, and Christendom. Less than three years earlier, at the Council of Mantua, Pope Pius II had called for a great Crusade against the Ottomans—with all eyes on Hungary to take the lead—and the time to act was now, Vlad implored:

> [K]now that we have done all that we could, for the time being, to harm those who kept urging us to leave the Christians and to take their side;…. that we have broken our peace with them, not for our own benefit, but for the honor of…the Holy Crown of Your Majesty, and for the preservation of Christianity…

Vlad did in fact have a loose treaty of sorts in place with Muhammad around 1459, when both men, especially the latter, were busy responding to local rebellions or intrigues. It was remarkably lenient on Wallachia.* In other words, by ravaging the sultan's lands, Dracula truly seems to have been acting on religious rather than realpolitik considerations— meaning there is no reason to doubt his claim that "we have broken our peace with them, not for our own benefit [as there was none], but for… the preservation of Christianity." Vlad continued in his letter to Matthias:

> Seeing what we did to them [Turks], they left the quarrels and fights they had up to now in other places, including in the country and Holy Crown of Your Majesty [of Hungary]…and they threw all their strength against us. When weather permits, that is to say in the spring, they will come with evil intentions and with all their power…. Therefore…if it is Your Majesty's desire to fight against them, then gather all of your country and all of the fighting men, both cavalry and infantry, and bring them to our Wallachia, and be so kind as to fight against them here.

If Matthias preferred not to come himself, then "send your whole army," Dracula continued; and if that was still too much, "then send only what you desire, at least from Transylvania and the Saxons…. [P]lease do not delay but tell us truly the thoughts of Your Majesty." Vlad closed by making unequivocally clear that he, at least, was personally determined to overthrow the Turkish yoke, once and for all:

---

* In exchange for paying nominal tribute (no mention is made of a "blood-tax" in boys for the janissary corps), "The Turks shall not interfere in the affairs of the country, nor rule over it, nor enter the country, except for a single Imperial emissary who shall come with the permission of the Prince…. Wallachia shall govern itself according to its own laws…and the Prince [as opposed to the Sultan] shall have the power of life and death over his subjects" (Treptow 2020, 137–138.)

Because by no means do we want to leave unfinished what we began, but to follow this through to the end. Because we will not flee before their savagery, but stand by all of the Christians, and if he will kindly lend his ear to the prayers of his poor subjects and grants us victory over the Infidels, the Enemies of the Cross of Christ, it will be the greatest honor, benefit, and spiritual help for Your Majesty…and for all true Christians. Because we will not flee before their savagery, but by all means we will fight them. And if, God forbid, it ends badly for us, and our little country is lost, Your Majesty will not benefit from this either, because it will be a loss for all Christianity.[49]

As Vlad had predicted, by spring of 1462, Muhammad's vast army, made of various contingents from all around the Ottoman Empire, assembled in Constantinople. Contemporary sources place its number between one hundred fifty thousand to three hundred thousand men, and describe it "as vast as the sea."[50] Vlad also feverishly worked to raise the "largest army of the country" he could—but that consisted of no more than thirty thousand Wallachians.[51] Moreover, and as with Skanderbeg's men, the "bulk of Dracula's army was composed of peasants." Their "armor" consisted of sheep's wool or other, thick animal skins; their weapons of "axes, scythes, hammers, or scimitars," though the better off had proper swords and bows and arrows.[52]

Aware of the terrible odds confronting them, the Wallachians hid their women and children in the local mountains and oak forests before going to and submitting themselves to Vlad's command. He himself, knowing their desperate plight and not wanting any weak links among his men, made clear that "Whoever is afraid of death, he will not go with me, but will remain here."[53]

Finally, on April 26, 1462, the vast Ottoman forces—which included twenty-five triremes and one hundred and fifty boats sailing across the Danube—set off for Wallachia. Vlad was not hard to find; he and his men were arrayed along the river's northern bank. The mighty janissaries tried to force a landing but were hewn down by the desperate Christians; before long, 250 of the sultan's finest slave-soldiers lay dead on the shore. Muhammad, "greatly afraid, fearing that all his Janissaries would be killed, seeing that so many of us were dying," writes former janissary Konstantin Mihailović, who was present, "quickly prepared, and having one hundred twenty cannon, immediately began to fire them heavily and

thus we drove all the army from the battlefield and established and fortified ourselves…. And Dracula, seeing that he could not prevent the
crossing, moved away from us."[54]

Thereafter, the mammoth Muslim army began its northward march
through Wallachia, leaving much death and destruction in its wake, as
recorded by several contemporary sources. "Shouting 'Allah, lead us to
victory!' the soldiers passed through many places," writes chronicler Sa'd
al-Din; "they inflicted such a merciless punishment on Wallachia that it
seemed as if the end of the world had come, shedding much blood with
their terrifying swords."[55]

Chalkokondyles says the Muslims sought for and "marched directly"
to wherever "the Wallachians had placed their women and children for
safety"—their hiding places that were betrayed by Radu, Vlad's own
brother turned Turk who accompanied the sultan (and about whom
more anon).[56] According to Ottoman chronicler Aşıkpaşazade, having
been so terrorized, "All the inhabitants of Wallachia came and surrendered to the Sultan—only Kaziklu voivode [Lord Impaler] did not."[57]

Because he was vastly outnumbered and could not risk a head-
on clash with the Turks, "the Vlach," writes Doukas, "deploying all
his troops along mountain defiles and wooded areas, left the plains
deserted"—though only after scorching the land and poisoning the wells
along the Turks' route.[58] Thus, for seven days, as the Muslims marched
for Târgovişte, "not a drop of water [was found] to quench their thirst,"
writes Tursun Beg. "All the carts and animals stopped…. The heat of the
sun was so great that one could cook kebabs on the mail shirts of the
gazis." The "angry Sultan" upbraided his generals and "the scouts were
scolded and punished."[59]

Meanwhile, from his mountain fastness, Vlad resorted to ambush
tactics and guerilla warfare—the only way outnumbered Christians
could fight the countless hordes of Islam, as Skanderbeg had long known.
Dracula's army "remained in the woods, always close to the Emperor,"
writes Chalkokondyles; "and if a detachment [of the Turkish army] happened to go astray, it was immediately destroyed by them."[60]

All this time, Hungarian king Matthias Corvinus—this son of John
Hunyadi who was most expected by pope and peasant to spearhead the
Crusade against the Turks—failed to appear, even though the Turks were
perilously close to his domains. Convinced that if the Hungarians had

only augmented his vastly outnumbered forces, he would have been able to affix every last invading Muslim on a stake, Vlad was beyond vexed with Matthias. In desperation, he sent messengers to the Hungarians themselves, once again stressing that Wallachia's loss would be their loss:

> Hungarians, you know that we are your neighbors and that both our countries are next to the Danube. You have probably heard by now that the Emperor of the Turks is waging a terrible war against us, with a large army. And if he conquers Dacia [Wallachia], you know very well that he will not sit still, but he will wage war against you, and your countrymen will suffer greatly at his hands. So, it is time now that you should give us assistance and defend yourselves as well by keeping their army as far as possible from your country; please don't let them spoil our country and ruin and conquer our people.[61]

Not only was Vlad denied Hungarian aid; before long he found himself fighting on two fronts, against the Ottomans *and* fellow Romanians: having "fallen out with Vlad," Stephen of Moldavia—his own cousin whom Dracula had helped elevate to the throne five years earlier—took advantage of the Ottoman assault on Wallachia and laid siege to Chilia (a contested region then held by Vlad).[62] Denouncing such disastrous Christian infighting which, as ever, only placed a smile on Muslim faces, the governor of Caffa lamented in a letter to King Casimir of Poland, dated April 2, 1462:

> I understand that Stephen, prince of Moldavia or Wallachia Minor, is fighting with Vlad voievod who makes happy war with the Turks. This quarrel not only helps the Sultan but what is more dangerous, if the Turks enter these two Wallachias, it will represent a great danger for us and for other neighboring countries.[63]

Terror in the Night

It was in this context of utter despair that the voivode of Wallachia launched one of history's most daring assaults. Knowing that his small force could never defeat the invading Muslims, who were "as numerous as the stars in the sky," he decided to do the next best thing—decapitate the head of this vast Islamic snake ravaging his country: in an effort to demoralize and disband the Turks, Vlad decided to assassinate the sultan.[64] Thus, on the pitch black night of June 16/17, 1462, somewhere near the foothills of the Carpathian mountains, where Muhammad and his vast Turkish host were encamped and asleep, Dracula, with anywhere between two thousand and seven thousand horsemen, violently blitzed into the lion's den in search of the sultan's head.[65]

According to the testimony of one of his riders, "moving as quick as lightning in all directions," the Impaler "butchered large numbers of Turks" during his mad hunt for Muhammad. In the darkness and din of war, the sultan, startled and confused like the rest, "fled from the camp" in a panic. The same source says this midnight visitation of horror lasted for six hours, ending just before dawn. It was only then, when Vlad had retreated to his mountain stronghold, that the sultan was "brought back almost by force."[66] As for Dracula, "No one dared pursue him, since he had caused such terror and turmoil."[67]

Due to its spectacular and unprecedented nature, contemporaries wrote a fair bit about this daring run, known in the sources only as Dracula's "Night Attack." "At first," writes Chalkokondyles, who offers the most comprehensive account, "there was great terror in the camp, as the sultan's men believed that some large foreign army had attacked them, coming from abroad; they believed that they were utterly doomed, and were reduced to great fear and trembling." He explains how Vlad appeared to them as one with great authority, riding in tight, phalanx formation "with torches and horns, to signal the attack."

> [Thus] the Turks became very terrified and were paralyzed, each staying where his tent was pitched.... He charged first against the sultan's Porte [personal encampment]. But they missed [it] and fell instead upon the tents of the viziers, namely of Mahmud and Ishak. A great battle was fought there and they killed camels, mules, and pack animals [to immobilize the Ottomans]. As they were fighting in an orderly and compact group, they suffered no losses worth mentioning; but if any group broke away, they would immediately fall on the spot at the hands of the Turks.... Then they turned and charged [again] against the sultan's Porte, but they found the sultan's men deployed outside [it]. They fought there briefly, then turned to the camp's market, plundered it, and killed anyone who stood in their way. With the approach of dawn, Vlad withdrew from the camp, having lost very few men that night.[68]

Konstantin Mihailović, who was in the Ottoman camp, further underscores the overall paranoia that plagued the Turks even before this night raid:

> Although the Romanian prince had a small army, we always advanced with great caution and fear and spent nights sleeping in ditches [that were surrounded with stakes]. But even in this manner we were not safe; for during one night the Romanians struck at us. They massacred…several thousand Turks…. [T]he sultan incurred great losses.[69]

Although Ottoman sources predictably exaggerate Turkish valor and Wallachian losses, they all, nonetheless, affirm the daring activity and dread name of Dracula—including by using language and imagery that Hollywood would later capitalize on. Thus, in the words of the chronicler Sa'd al-Din,

> On a dark night, his heart full of wickedness and accompanied by his Infidel army, he flew like a black cloud toward the army of the wise Sultan, attacking him…. At midnight, the army of Wallachia started like a torrent toward the Imperial camp and made their way on horseback into the middle of the triumphant army. The Turkish soldiers thrust their fiery swords deep into their black hearts. The heaps of corpses which poisoned [the earth] were so high that the victims of the slaughter could be easily seen even on such a dark night. With Allah's help, the lives of the Turkish soldiers were protected from the numerous attacks of the abject enemy. The soldiers gathered their courage and were quick in stabbing and cutting off the hands of the enemies.[*] They surrounded the vile troops, attacking them from one side and killed numerous Infidels with their sword. They surrounded them in the middle of the battlefield, leaving no escape for the Infidels…. Although Kaziklu [the Impaler] fought bravely, he decided to run away with a few of his men, for he was no longer as powerful as he had been before. An ocean of blood had covered the earth in those places so that no matter what direction his horse took he had to walk in blood and on wounded bodies.[70]

---

[*] In reference to and keeping with Koran verses such as 5:33: "The penalty for those who wage war against Allah and His Messenger and spread mischief in the land is death, crucifixion, cutting off their hands and feet on opposite sides, or exile from the land."

As might be expected, with the passage of time, later Ottoman chroniclers all but reversed the facts of this event. Writing more than half a century later, Muhammad Nesri suggests that the Muslims were aware of and allowed Vlad to fall into *their* trap:

> When they realized that Kaziklu voivode was attacking them at night, they [Turks] remained silent, until his soldiers scattered among them. The Turkish soldiers then shouted Allah's name ["Allahu akbar," the *takbir*] and fought against the infidels. They slaughtered so many of them that not even half of the Infidels survived. Kaziklu barely escaped with [his] life…. The remainder of Kaziklu's army surrendered and knelt before the Sultan, accepting slavery.[71]

At any rate, Vlad's gambit failed; for no matter how well planned* or executed, his violent rampage among the Muslims was, in the words of Tursun Beg, "as if a drop of water fell into the ocean," so vast was the Muslim army.[72] It remains, nonetheless, one of the most desperate and heroic "military episodes in the history of the Ottomans," writes historian Nicolae Iorga, for "until then there did not occur in Turkish history so bold an attack against the person of the sultan himself"—not even at the hands of Hunyadi or Skanderbeg.[73]

Back in his mountain hideout following the Night Attack, "Dracula himself began to look over those who had returned with him from that battle," says the Old Russian Chronicle, adding: "to the man who was wounded in the chest he would give great honor and accolades, but the man who was wounded in the back, that man he would have impaled on a stake through the anus, saying, 'You're not a man, but a woman.'"[74]

As for Muhammad, to save face and sate his rage, with the crack of dawn the sultan ordered his men to hunt down as many Wallachians as possible. Thousands of destitute men were hauled before him and ritually slaughtered.[75] Their heads were "cut off to nourish swords," writes Tursun Beg, with the following explanation: "This is why, as the Koran says, the powerful sword must fall upon them and split them in two: 3,700 Infidels were brought to the Sultan alive and then cut in two."[76] In response, terrified boyars, Wallachia's noblemen, "all gathered and went

---

* According to Chalkokondyles, before the Night Attack, "it is said that" Vlad, under disguise, "entered the Emperor's camp as a spy, and that, going around, he found out how the camp was set up. But I myself cannot believe that Vlad himself would take such a risk…." (Treptow 2019, 434).

to beg of the Sultan," writes one Ottoman chronicler, "kneeling down in front of him and submitting themselves to him."[77]

Even so—even in the midst of Muhammad's bloody vengeance and assertion of dominance—a cold chill continued to run up his back, as captured by the following account: A Wallachian taken captive during the Night Attack was brought before and questioned by the sultan. He responded forthrightly to everything—until, that is, Muhammad inquired if he knew "where Vlad, the ruler of Wallachia, happened to be?" The man replied that he "knew exactly" where the voivode was, "but would tell them nothing whatsoever, because he feared Vlad." Even after the Turks politely reminded him that "they would kill him if he did not tell," their captive replied that "he was more than ready to die, and would not dare to reveal anything about that man." Seeing that the Wallachian preferred to be tortured to death by his Turks rather than risk the wrath of the Lord Impaler, a thrilling spasm of terror—and not a little admiration—shook Muhammad. As he casually watched and listened to the death throes of the Wallachian's execution, the sultan was heard to remark that, "with such fear surrounding him," Dracula could become unstoppable.[78]

The Forest of the Impaled

Soon after the Night Attack, Muhammad set off for Târgoviște, the seat of the Wallachian throne. The march was slow; having learned from and apparently still traumatized by Dracula's nightmarish raid, "every night that he halted he dug a ditch all around the camp, which he reinforced on the inside by blocking it with barriers; he also increased the number of sentries and ordered that his armies should be under arms day and night."[79]

Finally, on approaching their destination, the Turks espied from afar and in the dimming light of sunset what appeared to be countless fuzzy and crooked looking objects jutting from the earth—a sort of defensive measure, perhaps? On getting closer, they realized that they had come upon what they had thought or hoped was mere legend or rumor—the Forest of the Impaled, which surrounded Dracula's castle for six miles in circumference[80]:

> [There] thousands of stakes of various heights held the remaining carcasses of some 20,000 Turkish captives; their bodies were in a state of complete decomposition, due to the heat of the summer and

the ravages of ravens and other Carpathian birds of prey, many of which had made their nest within the skulls and skeletal remains of the victims. Barely recognizable because of the higher stakes used in deference to their position, were the remains of the Greek Katabolinos [Yunus Beg] and Hamza Pasha, who had been impaled months before. The tattered remains of their gaudy vestments fluttered against the evening sky. The entire area reeked with the stench of death— the smell of rotting flesh. Dracula had deliberately stage-managed this sinister spectacle as part of his terror tactics to destroy whatever spirit was still left in Muhammad after the unsuccessful assassination attempt a few days before. Indeed, the "forest of impaled" was horrible enough to discourage the most stout-hearted officers who witnessed the scene.[81]

While discussing this nightmarish incident, Chalkokondyles says that "the Turks, seeing so many people impaled, were scared out of their wits. There were babies clinging to their mothers on the stakes, and birds had made nests in their breasts." Worse, even now, "Vlad stayed close to the sultan's armies, killing anyone who dared go astray...."[82]

Rather unsurprisingly, and because, according to Doukas, "When the tyrant beheld this terrible portent, he was panic-stricken," that same night Muhammad ordered an especially deep trench dug around his encampment, along with other safeguards designed to keep out the Impaler. His efforts were futile. During that same night, Vlad, "arising in the half-light of dawn," continues Doukas, "descended" from his high places and made another "sudden charge" wherein he "cut down countless" Turks.[83]

And with that and the break of dawn, "Muhammad gave orders for the retreat. In his eyes, Dracula's country was not worth the price of victory."[84] Even after having reached a largely abandoned Târgoviște in the heart of Wallachia, Muhammad and his hordes "were scared, truth to say, of the Dacians [Wallachians]," continues Chalkokondyles, "who were by no means less courageous than before and continued to harass them on and off, so the Turks crossed the Danube [on June 29] in a great hurry."[85] It was a most ignominious retreat, according to a Venetian report based on the eyewitness testimony of an Albanian runaway slave: "the Sultan arrived in Adrianople [on July 11] with his army in great disorder and without any sign of victory"; the bulk of his forces arrived by land two weeks later and were "weakened by starvation and illness."[86]

Contrary to all expectations, the sultan and his gargantuan Muslim army had been repulsed by the Lord Impaler and his vastly outnumbered Wallachians. Due to "the lofty courage" of Dracula and his men, they were able "to carry the war against the Turks without foreign aid," wrote Niccolò Modrussa, the shocked Florentine secretary of King Matthias, even though "it was everybody's opinion that such a war could only have been sustained by the united forces of all Christians."[87]

The outcome "was considered as a great victory for Vlad the Impaler by Christian Europe and was announced so everywhere." Even in the distant island of Rhodes, where the Knights of Saint John (formerly the Hospitallers) reigned, monks "tolled the bells and have sung Te Deum to worship the glory of the Romanian prince."[88] In short, and in the words of historian Mircea Iogaru, "The Ottoman invasion of 1462 ended in a complete military disaster. Mehmed II did not succeed—because of the heroic resistance of the Romanian people led by Prince Vlad Țepeș—to transform Wallachia into a pashalik and to include Romanian territory below the Carpathians within the borders of the Ottoman Empire."[89]

Betrayal after Betrayal after Betrayal

The sultan and his men did, however—and as usual—have one consolation: countless Christian women and children were enslaved and hauled back to Ottoman territory during the Muslim army's invasion—thanks, as seen, to Muhammad's minion, Vlad's own younger brother, Radu, who had accompanied the sultan and, being familiar with the lay of the land, had betrayed the Wallachians' hiding places in the forests and mountains.[90]

Perhaps as a reward—and as one last shot for himself—before retreating, Muhammad left this same Radu "inside the country to make a deal with the Dacians and bring the country under his control," writes Chalkokondyles; "and he ordered the governor of the land [a neighboring Turkish beg] to be of assistance [to Radu]."[91]

Radu's background story is somewhat tragic. Since he and his brother Vlad were delivered up to the Turks two decades earlier, Muhammad had transformed "Radu the Handsome"—so-called for his widely acknowledged fine looks—into his personal catamite. Although the young Wallachian had initially resisted Muhammad's sexual advances, in the end—and because he was no Vlad, nor even a Skanderbeg, who had learned to rise above his molestation at the hands of Muhammad's father, Murad II—Radu succumbed, further becoming utterly "faithful and loyal" to his master, to quote Sa'd al-Din.[92] After explaining how Muhammad "kept him [Radu] as his lover and maintained him," Chalkokondyles offers the sordid details behind this development:

> It happened that the sultan was almost killed by the boy [Radu] when he had wanted to have sex with him. This was when he [Muhammad] had first gained the throne [in 1451].... He was in love with the boy [then aged 15] and invited him for conversation, and then as a sign of his respect he invited him for drinks to his bedchamber. The boy did not expect to suffer such a thing from the sultan, and when he saw the sultan approaching him with that intention, he fought him off and refused to consent to intercourse with him. The sultan kissed the unwilling boy, who drew a dagger and struck the sultan on his thigh. He then fled in whatever direction he could find. The doctors were able to treat the sultan's wound. The boy had climbed up a tree there and was hiding. When the sultan packed up and left, the boy came down from the tree, began his journey, and, shortly afterward, arrived at the Porte and became the sultan's lover.[93]

Twenty years later, not only was Radu Muhammad's creature, but he had a claim to the Wallachian throne no less than his brother and could promise the boyars what Vlad would—and now could—not: peace with the Turks. If Wallachia would merely acknowledge the suzerainty of Muhammad and deliver the usual jizya/tribute that Vlad had ceased—that is, pay a little lip service and a little coin, for the blood-tax in Wallachian boys was now wisely omitted—the Turks would leave them in peace.[94] In short, all that required changing was the person of the voivode—from the Impaler to the Handsome One.

To better help him woo the nobles, Muhammad had left Radu with "high honors and money and many fine clothes."[95] Arrayed in glory, Radu then "called each and every one [of the boyars] to him" and, with "sweet reasonableness," explained the benefits that they—which the Wallachian Ottoman cleverly articulated as "*we*"—would reap by merely taking him, instead of his brother, for voivode:

> I am aware of the mighty forces that the sultan controls, which sooner or later he will use to lay waste what remains of your country. If we

continue to oppose him, we shall be despoiled of all that is left to us. Why do you not reach an agreement with Sultan Muhammad? Only then will you have peace in the land and in your homes. Are you aware that there are no cattle, no horses, no farm animals, no food left in this country? [Before retreating, the Turks "drove away more than two hundred thousand pack animals, horses, and cattle" from Wallachia.[96]] Surely you have borne such sufferings long enough because of my brother, because you were loyal to this man who was responsible for more suffering than any other prince.[97]

It bears mentioning that, due to the brothers' "differences of character, temperament, and physique," Vlad and Radu had "developed for each other an intense hatred" over the years. This went back to and was in part "exacerbated by the associated differences in treatment they received" during their imprisonment as children under Murad and Muhammad— both of whom no doubt played it to great effect precisely to place a wedge between and manipulate the brothers.[98]

Now, in envious vengeance against the brother that rose above the physical and psychological abuses he had succumbed to, Radu promised the world to the war weary Wallachians. Even those boyars who approached him merely "to pay ransom for their relatives who were now slaves, he enticed and urged them to pass the word to others to come to him and to trust him." Discussing their options—hold out and suffer with Dracula or submit to and prosper with Radu—the nobles "crossed over to him little by little. And the other Dacians, as soon as they realized it, deserted Vlad and sided with his brother."[99]

They either did not realize or chose to forget that the only reason the Turks in the person of Radu were being lenient—the only reason the Wallachians were not all in chains—was precisely because Vlad had repulsed them, and this—enticement and accommodation—was all that was left to the Ottomans. As Romanian historian Ştefan Andreescu asserts, "the boyars chose to take advantage of the Turkish failure by making peace on favorable terms (and in so doing by sacrificing Vlad the Impaler)."[100]

For his part, since Muhammad had withdrawn, between July and October 1462, the relentless Vlad—outnumbered, ensconced in the mountains bordering Transylvania, and still hoping for aid to arrive— continued to attack and harass the Turks under his brother. Although the Impaler made some advances, by September 8, when the boyars formally acknowledged Radu's authority, Vlad "realized that his killings were of no avail and he left for the Hungarians," to quote Chalkokondyles, sometime in early October.[101] And so, what Muhammad "had failed to do with military force, Radu and the boyars eventually succeeded in achieving with diplomacy—though the freedom of Wallachia had in essence been ensured by Dracula's stubborn resistance."[102]

Not, of course, that the indefatigable Impaler thought he was through. In the fall of 1462 he still harbored hopes that the Hungarian king, Matthias Corvinus—this defender of Christendom and son of John Hunyadi—would be true to his position and help spear a counterattack to oust the Turkish puppet Radu from Wallachia. Even the pope expected this; following the aforementioned Council of Mantua in 1459, Pius II had given Matthias much of the funds raised for Crusading to liberate the Balkans from—not sit idly by and cede more territory to—the Turks.

But now, as Muhammad no longer posed a threat to Transylvania or Hungary—thanks entirely to Vlad—and as Matthias had already spent the money allotted for Crusading, the Hungarian king was reluctant to move, finally doing so well after the sultan had retreated and apparently for show. Even worse, when his relief army finally arrived in Braşov in November, and Dracula galloped out from his hiding place to hail his "saviors," Matthias ordered him arrested and thrown in a dungeon: It turned out that Vlad was a traitor to Christendom—or so Matthias claimed, citing letters he had just intercepted. In one, dated November 7, 1462, Vlad had reportedly written to Muhammad proposing to help the Turks conquer Transylvania and Hungary in exchange for the crown of Wallachia.

In fact, the letters were forgeries produced by the Saxons of Braşov to avenge themselves against Vlad's reprisals of 1459–1460.[103] Even the Hungarian king's own court chronicler doubted the official story: "On his way there, I do not know the reason why because this was never understood clearly by anyone," Antonius Bonfinius diplomatically wrote, "he [Matthias] captured Dracula in Transylvania, but the other Dracula [Radu], whom the Turks had appointed prince of that province [Wallachia], he approved of, against all expectations."[104]

Few could believe that the only man who had sacrificed everything to defy and beat the Turks would now betray, and in such an uncharacteristically abject manner, the Christian cause—and all to receive what was already always available to him, vassalage to the Ottomans. The contemporary Polish chronicler, Jan Długosz, went so far as to remark that the Hungarian king's imprisonment of Vlad suggested that he was "in league with the Turks."[105]

'A Wicked Blood-Drinking Tyrant Called Prince Dracula'

By the end of November, and because the "intercepted letters" story was not enough, Matthias had to explain himself more fully to Pope Pius II and several regional magnates who had sent vast sums of money for him to support Vlad's war effort. And so began one of history's earliest propaganda campaigns—or, in modern parlance, "fake news": from the court of Matthias Corvinus, and with the aid of his Transylvanian Saxons, the first set of "stories" against Vlad, detailing his diabolical cruelties and clandestine aid to the Muslims, appeared in December 1462, complete with fantastical and lurid engravings. Thanks to the new movable-type printing press invented a few years earlier by Johannes Gutenberg, these tracts were quickly disseminated all over Europe.

Appearing under titles such as *The Frightening and Truly Extraordinary Story of a Wicked Blood-Drinking Tyrant Called Prince Dracula*, these pamphlets became instant best sellers.[106] No depravity was spared Vlad; the stories discussed in graphic detail how he boiled people alive, shredded others "like cabbage," forced "parents to eat their children impaled and broiled, husbands to eat their wives' breasts," forced Tatars to swallow their own semen, and built secret trapdoors to drop his victims "on cunningly located stakes below."[107]

Most historians dismiss these early stories to emanate from Matthias's court as obvious propaganda. Reading the first German set, one can see why: from beginning to end, line after line, the entirety of the text depicts Dracula engaging in one vile or bizarre act after another—hacking peoples' ears, noses, limbs, and genitals; blinding, strangling, boiling, skinning, roasting, and feeding people to wild animals—with nary a word of explanation or context.[108] He supposedly did it all because he was a sadist, an immoral monster—in short, "the Devil's Son," as the name Dracula (originally "the Dragon's Son") came to mean following publication of these stories.

Obviously, if these accounts were true, Vlad would have had zero support from the populace, though, as seen, he had tremendous support, including during his war with the Turks, being betrayed only towards the end by the easily bought nobles. Vlad did, of course, inflict barbaric punishments on his enemies—not, however, because he was diabolically insane, but as a matter of carefully crafted state policy. As seen, and as well captured by a Bulgarian poem composed years before Vlad's first rein, there was little law and order in the land:

> Wallachia is split apart, the people run to the mountains, to the valleys, away from the cruel Turks, away from Hungarian barbarians. The old men they [Turks] cut down, the young ones they enslave, the girls they rape, the youth they capture and enroll in their armies…. Wherever they pass they burn the villages.[109]

Such a situation was only exacerbated by the noble class, the boyars, who, as seen, made and unmade voivodes based on their limited self-interest. In this context of chaos, nothing less than sheer terror would keep both domestic and foreign enemies in check. Anyone daring to break Dracula's rules risked—and *knew* he risked, which was the whole point—an excruciating death. Such terrifying governance instilled obedience and an unshakeable centralization of authority around the ruler, both of which were wanting since Mircea I. Vlad the Impaler lived up to the prudent maxim that it is better to be feared than loved decades before Machiavelli penned it. As Romanian historian Anton Balotă writes,

> Dracula's policies introduced order in the country, and this helps explain his sudden resistance to the Turks which he could not have organized previously without the help of his people…. Dracula attained his political goals…by using strong, sometimes especially cruel and harsh methods. His goal was the reestablishment of the prestige and authority of the ruler.[110]

Even his contemporaries agreed that Vlad was "very cruel, but extremely just," to quote Antonius Bonfinius: "He behaved with such harshness in this barbarous country that everyone might have their things in safety, even in the middle of the forest.[111] Such assertions invoke the well-known legend of the "golden goblet": Dracula reportedly left a magnificent, jewel-encrusted cup unattended near a well for passersby to draw water—a thing that shocked strangers, "for however long it was there, no one dared to take that goblet."[112]

One view adds that such terror was not simply a matter of state policy, undertaken, perhaps begrudgingly, by the voivode. His severe personality—as moral as it was monstrous, as just as it was tyrannical—naturally inclined Dracula to mete out the most terrifying punishments for those who dared transgress the law. This is the interpretation of the earliest Slavic text concerning the Impaler, the aforementioned Old Russian Chronicle of Efrosin, which appeared less than a decade after Dracula's death. According to it, "he hated stealing so violently in his country that anyone who caused any evil or robbery, or a lie or an injustice, did not live long. Be he an important boyar, priest, or monk, or an ordinary person, be he the richest man, he would not escape death. So feared he was..."[113] As for women, any caught in the act of adultery—or just being lazy—could expect the stake or worse.[114]

Vlad was even ruthless with those who would or could not carry their own weight—"vagabonds," in his own words: "These men live off the sweat of others, so they are useless to humanity. It is a form of thievery. In fact, the masked robber in the forest demands your purse, but if you are quicker with your hand and more vigorous than he you can escape from him. However, these vagabonds take your belongings gradually by begging—but they still take it. They are worse than robbers. May such men be eradicated from my land!"[115] (As he was voivode, such wishes tended to be realized.)

Dracula's reputation as a no-nonsense despot with a hyperactive sense of justice is such that, till now, whenever there is talk of corruption or immorality, it is common for Romanians to resignedly end the conversation by quoting the following lines of an old poem, "Where art thou, old prince, Vlad Tzepesh, on them all to lay thy hands."[116]

In short, Dracula did resort to cruel punishments—though the lurid descriptions contained in the early German stories are largely fictitious. More importantly, there was a method behind the madness (which the propaganda completely ignored): to keep a historically volatile environment in order through fear. Nor can it be emphasized enough that, although impalement has now become synonymous with Vlad III Dracula, most of his contemporaries—not just the Turks—practiced it: Stephen of Moldavia—now "Stephen the Great," one of Romania's most celebrated heroes—once had twenty-three hundred Wallachians impaled; and in the written legal codes of the Saxons of Transylvania—they who first cried foul—impalement was prescribed as a suitable punishment for a variety of crimes.[117]

But whereas the quality of punishment was similar across the board, clearly the quantity meted out by Vlad the Impaler was unique. That coupled with Dracula's severe and unbendable persona—which further plunged Wallachia into a brutal war with the largest empire of the time—made him a polarizing figure: some—especially the peasants who had little to lose and whose social mores were receptive to draconian laws—rallied to him; others—nobles, princes, and even kings who had much to lose and thrived on diplomacy—turned against him.

Dracula Resurrected

The anti-Ottoman Crusade came to an end with Radu the Handsome's ascension to the throne of Wallachia and Matthias's imprisonment of Vlad in late 1462. He was sent to the fortress of Visegrad on the Danube above Buda, where he would remain until 1475. Thus, for thirteen long years, the Romanian scourge of Turkic Islam spent much of his prime, from the age of thirty-two to forty-five, behind bars. During these long years of solitude—and if the gossipy stories, which would continue to spread, be true—he roamed his small cell like a caged animal looking to capture and impale any unwary vermin—rats and birds, insects when neither could be caught—daring to enter his domain.

Then, in the summer of 1475, Dracula's two former allies that had betrayed him—his cousin, Stephen of Moldavia, who had warred against him during the Ottoman invasion, and King Matthias, who had framed and imprisoned him—concluded that the Lord Impaler was needed again. Two years earlier, Stephen's protégé, Basarab Laiotă, another contender for the Wallachian throne, had seized it from and killed Radu—only to turn against Stephen and help the Turks invade Moldavia. In a letter to Matthias, Stephen "requested the removal of Basarab from the Wallachian throne and the enthroning of a Christian prince, I mean Dracula, with whom we can both collaborate."[118]

Matthias agreed and released Vlad; as further proof of his sincere intentions and to formalize relations with his former captive, Matthias had his own first cousin, Jusztina Szilágyi, married to Vlad (his mysterious first wife had died earlier under equally mysterious circumstances). He then relocated the Impaler to a home in Pest, apparently so the former outcast could have time to readjust to society and rejuvenate his princely bearing. This proved unnecessary: Dracula was as Dracula always had been. Thus, when an officer barged into his Pest home in search of a runaway criminal believed to be hiding in his courtyard, Vlad instantly decapitated the official with a swing of his sword. The other officers fled to Matthias, who sternly questioned Dracula—"Why have you committed such a crime?"—only to receive the following, far from contrite, reply:

> I did not commit any crime. It is the police official who committed suicide. Anyone will perish in this way, should he, like a thief, invade the house of a great ruler such as myself. If this man had come to me first and had explained the situation to me, and if then the criminal had been found in my own home, I myself would have delivered the criminal over to him and would have pardoned him.[119]

Matthias appears to have been amused by his implacable, far from broken vassal and his undiminished insistence on protocol. Indeed, before releasing Vlad, the Hungarian king seems to have enjoyed keeping him visible at court so that visitors might be awed by the terrifying man Matthias had helped transform into a bestial legend. Thus, on one occasion, "the king received Turkish diplomats in the presence of Dracula. He knew of the psychological impact that this confrontation would entail—the awesome 'Lord Impaler,' even as captive, had the power of sending shivers down the spines of the Turkish delegates."[120]

Before he could try to reclaim his Wallachian throne, however, Vlad would first have to earn the right. Matthias made him a captain of his Hungarian army and sent him to fight the Turks alongside Stephen Bathory of Transylvania. Once unleashed on the Turks, and true to form, Dracula obtained several notable victories against them, particularly in Bosnia and Serbia in early 1476. In June, Vlad and Bathory, according to a contemporary document, urged Stephen of Moldavia "not [to] fight the Turks, but wait until they joined him with all their troops," each of which would "carry an axe...so as to be able to prevent the usage of roads by blocking them with tree trunks and wood in preventing a retreat from the Turks." The plan worked, followed by a wholesale slaughter of the Muslims. As Ștefan Andreescu remarks, "Without any doubt, this was another innovative idea coming from the prince [Vlad] who was always trying to find the most radical solutions to crush the power of the Crescent." By August, Vlad had helped drive the Turks out of Moldavia.

In short, "the study of the itinerary he followed in 1476, and the military activities in which he participated during the same year, show him, more than ever, to be a hero in the struggle to free the whole of southeastern Europe from Ottoman domination." [121]

Even Matthias, this one time jailer of Vlad, found himself boasting in a letter to the duke of Saxony that "as soon as he [Sultan Muhammad] learned of the approaching of Stephen Bathory and Vlad the Impaler, he lifted the siege [of the city of Neamt] abandoning the cannons. He took flight and never stopped until three days later when he arrived at the Danube, when the original journey had taken several weeks."[122]

Concerning one of Vlad's final conquests during this time, that of Zvornik—where "neither village nor house" was spared—the bishop of Agria wrote a report that blends the real Dracula, a fierce and implacable foe of everything Turkish who relied on psychological warfare, with the sadistic Dracula of legend that he, the bishop, and almost all of Europe, had long imbibed:

> But I shall not fail to mention the cruelty of Dracula. No one should ignore it. With his own hands, he tore apart the bodies of captured Turks and had them impaled, saying "When the Turks see them, they will be stricken with terror and flee." He is the one who erected forests of impaled people.... [H]e killed more than 100,000 men, condemning them to impalement or some other terrible torture. This explains why the king kept him in jail for fifteen years [sic]. But, there too, unable to control his brutality, he would catch rats, crush them and run pieces of wood through their bodies, inflicting on them the same treatment he inflicted on men. However, the king released him during the last year from his confinement and sent him to fight the Turks who lived in great fear of him. [123]

It did not occur to the good bishop to wonder why Christian leaders such as Matthias and Stephen, both highly regarded in their nations then and now, would be seeking to reinstall Vlad as ruler of a neighboring kingdom if he were truly an unbalanced lunatic.

Having defeated the Ottomans south of the Danube and driven them out of Moldavia, Vlad was finally able to turn his efforts to regaining the throne of Wallachia. With the aid of a grateful Stephen of Moldavia, he drove out Basarab Laiotă from Târgoviște sometime around November 8, 1476; by November 16, the nobles had (re)given him their oath of allegiance; and on November 26, in front of a great assembly, Dracula was crowned—for the third time—as warlord of Wallachia. Vlad and Stephen swore "love and support for each other, so that the whole country [of Romania] was sure that the Turks would not bother them anymore."[124] Next Dracula wrote to and restored trade with the Transylvanian officials of Brașov and Tara Barsei: "God has opened the roads to you everywhere," the Impaler informed them. "Therefore, go now freely where you like and feed yourselves. And God will be pleased."[125]

Christian solidarity, which the Turks most feared, was returning between Hungary, Transylvania, Wallachia, and Moldavia, as intimated by the words of King Matthias in a December 8, 1476 letter to the pope: "Vlad Dracula, my captain, a fierce warrior...in accordance with my wishes and desire was received as prince by the inhabitants of the country."[126]

Dracula Impaled

Alas for Vlad, his third rein was destined to be like his first—short. Worse, just one month after his enthronement, sometime in late December 1476 or early January 1477, "the Turks entered Wallachia and again conquered the country and cut to pieces Dracula, the captain of the king of Hungary, with approximately 4,000 of his men," a letter written to the duke of Milan by his ambassador to Buda tersely relayed on February 1, 1477.[127]

Accounts as to what exactly happened differ. In a letter to the Venetian senate dated May 8, 1478, Stephen of Moldavia wrote that after his coronation, Vlad "asked me to leave some of our men for his protection, as he did not have too much trust of the Wallachians [boyars]. And so, I left him 200 men from my personal guard.... [A] very short time after, the unfaithful Basarab returned [with his Turkish allies] and found him [Dracula] alone and killed him; all of my men were killed together with him, except for ten."[128]

Another account states that, while Vlad was successfully driving off Basarab and his Turkish sponsors, the nobles, in Ides-of-March style, treacherously fell on and stabbed him to death with their daggers—though not before he killed five of them with his sword. In fact, and rather tellingly, most accounts highlight treachery. After all, many had tried to kill Dracula over the years, all unsuccessfully: he was untrusting—paranoid even—always kept a personal guard around him and, in short, rarely let his guard down. As such, the following account of his death by the contemporary Austrian chronicler Jakob Unrest (b.1430), which suggests an elaborate deception, may strike closest to the truth:

> Dracula was killed with great cunning, because the Turks wished to avenge the great enmity which he had borne against them for so long and also the great damages [he] inflicted upon them. They hired a Turk [or an Ottoman servant to act] as one of his servants with the mission of killing him while he served him. The Turk was apparently instructed to attack Dracula from the back. He was then to cut off his head and bring it back on horseback to the sultan.[129]

That much was certainly true: Vlad's head was sent to and thrust atop the highest stake in Constantinople—proof that the Dread Lord Impaler was finally dead, forty-seven years after he first entered the world.[130] And so ended one of history's most fascinating figures—a man who had become a terrible legend in his own lifetime.

Legacy

What is the judgement of history concerning Vlad III Dracula? Kurt W. Treptow, author of the newest biography on the Impaler, offers the following:

> Vlad was both a heroic and tragic figure. A man who tried to shape history, but also one shaped by it.... Vlad's greatness lies in the fact that he sought to rise above the limits placed upon him by time and place. It is natural to root for the underdog, the one who stands up to fight for what he believes is right against all the odds. This is one of the reasons Vlad has captured the imagination of countless generations and why so many sought to denigrate him during his lifetime. His heroic...defiance of the most powerful Empire of his day, is, above all, what secured his place in the history of Europe....[131]

The voivode of Wallachia was first and foremost an implacable, arguably existential, foe of the Turks, even though he, like his father and especially brother Radu, could have submitted to and benefitted from them. He spit in their face the first chance he got and was willing to do anything to keep them out of his Wallachian kingdom. He learned to fight fire with fire and employed the same terror tactics he had learned under his Muslim tutors. Like Skanderbeg before him, his success was in large measure due to the fact that he too had involuntarily become intimately acquainted with the Turks in his youth, an experience that left an indelible mark on him—as did the long periods of captivity he experienced. As Florescu and McNally write,

> Dracula's whole life must be viewed across prison bars—he actually spent twice as many years in jail as he did on the throne, and during any one of these moments his own life was threatened. This fact assuredly provides the historian with a pertinent clue as to why Dracula held life in such low esteem. One may add to these explanations that as a child he had virtually no family existence. When a young boy, he was sent off to a distant alien court as a hostage, knowing that his father was pursuing policies incompatible with promises made; he witnessed the sexual abuse of his younger brother, Radu, and the blinding of other hostages. Later in life he learned that his father had been assassinated; his elder brother was buried alive; ....[He] faced mass defection of the boyars and conspiracies by members of his family, including Stephen. Finally, the Hungarian king Matthias, upon whom he had placed his trust, betrayed him.[132]

Despite it all, Vlad always managed to rise again and defy the Turks in ways few others could. Regardless, following his death, Wallachia—like Albania and Hungary following the deaths of Skanderbeg and Hunyadi, respectively—was quickly subjugated by the Turks, and would remain under Ottoman rule (effects of which are still apparent) for nearly half a millennium. Without men such as the Lord Impaler, the Albanian Braveheart, and the White Knight to guide and inspire—and through sheer acts of will to defeat the Muslims in several encounters despite outrageous odds—it was inevitable that the entire Balkans region would eventually succumb to the Ottomans, thanks to selfish, cowardly, or opportunistic rulers and nobles, but even more so, to Christendom's fractious nature, exacerbated by the Catholic/Orthodox and later Protestant divide.

In fact, the Turks themselves always relied on Christian disunity to further their jihad. Back on May 27, 1453, Muhammad II was debating whether or not he should order an all-out assault on the walls of Constantinople, since failure could dramatically weaken his forces against a potential Christian counter emanating from Europe. Ottoman general Zagan Pasha—originally an Albanian seized in his youth, converted to Islam and trained as a janissary—counseled the sultan to go ahead and order the assault. His logic was hard to counter:

> Thou, O Padishah, knowest full well the great dissensions that are raging in Italy, especially, and in all Frankistan [Christian Europe] generally. In consequence of these dissensions, the Gaiours [Infidels] are incapable of united action against us. The Christian potentates will never unite against us. When, after protracted efforts, they conclude something like a peace among themselves, it never lasts long.... No doubt they think much, speak much, and explain much, but after all they do very little. When they decide to do anything, they waste much time before they begin to act. Suppose they have even commenced something. They cannot progress very far with it because they are sure to disagree amongst themselves how to proceed....[133]

Muhammad ordered the assault; two days later Constantinople fell. Zagan Pasha was rewarded by being elevated to the office of Ottoman Grand Vizier.

Speaking of Constantinople, and returning to Vlad, there is another often forgotten, ignored, or underplayed motivation concerning his resistance to the Turks:

> Following the fall of Constantinople, he [Dracula], like many of his successors, considered himself the only truly independent patron and defender of Eastern Orthodoxy, centuries before Russia assumed this traditional mantle.... Beyond his country, however, was the much broader concept of a fatherland of European civilization that had to be defended from an alien creed. This mission he inherited from his mentor Hunyadi and the crusaders of old.[134]

In fact, like the rest of the Defenders of this book—and despite his singularly diabolical reputation—Christianity figured prominently in Vlad's calculus against his Muslim enemies. This is evident, for example, in the treaty he made with Muhammad around 1459; it was very zealous over guarding Wallachia's Christian prerogative as seen in some of its terms:

> If any Christians shall adopt Islam when they are outside of the country [in Ottoman territories], upon their return they shall once again return to Christianity.... When a Mohammedan shall have

a dispute with a Wallachian, the case shall be judged by the royal council, according to the traditions of the land [that is, according to Christian not Muslim notions of justice].... Turkish merchants shall not have the right to take with them Wallachian servants of either sex, nor shall they be allowed a special place for their prayers.[135]

Moreover, and contrary to the perverse portrayals that later defined him, "Dracula was often seen in the company of Romanian Orthodox monks. He was known to be particularly fond of the monasteries of Tismana and of Snagov, both of which he often visited.... Even when he imposed the death penalty, he insisted upon proper ceremony for his victims and a Christian burial.... Dracula was also enough of a Medievalist to take his Dragon oath seriously, seeing himself as a Christian crusader against the Infidel."[136]

He also founded the monastery of Comana, sent donations to Mount Athos, and even "created a sovereign Church in his country, essentially laying the groundwork for a Romanian Orthodox Church. This should be recognized as one of his greatest achievements as prince of Wallachia."[137] Additionally, according to a contemporary document, Vlad built "a fortress at Bucharest," meaning he laid the foundations of the modern state of Romania.[138]

Just like Skanderbeg, Vlad would not only go on to be honored in his native homeland (of Romania) but his fame would spread around the world—indeed, much more so than the Albanian warlord. But that is where their similarities end; for if whatever fame Skanderbeg currently enjoys in the West still revolves around his heroic resistance against the Turks, today Dracula is best remembered as an undead blood sucker. With the publication of Bram Stoker's novel, *Dracula* (1897), it was déjà vu all over again for the hapless voivode; for if the fifteenth century Saxons had transformed Vlad into a maniacal—but still human—sadist, the twentieth century Irish novelist transformed him into a vampire—a denizen of the night, fluttering about in the darkness in search of his latest victim (before "retiring" for the day into a coffin).

As is well accepted, Stoker knew little of premodern Romania, and even less of the historic Dracula. Accepting the aforementioned Saxon propaganda at face value—particularly Vlad's alleged penchant for drinking his enemies' blood—Stoker essentially found a suitable name to slap onto the bloodsucking antagonist of his novel, thereby providing it with a historic veneer. *Dracula* became an iconic bestseller, subsequently inspiring countless books, novels, Hollywood movies, and television series revolving around vampirism—none of which say anything about and all of which distort the true Vlad III Dracula of history.

Nor was the enigmatic voivode's reputation helped in 1933, when excavations were dug in an unmarked grave at Snagov monastery, long believed to be where Romanian monks ceremoniously buried the headless body of their patron. The finding was something straight out of a horror film: "Under the tombstone attributed to Vlad," reported the head excavator, "there was no tomb. Only many bones and jaws of horses."[139]

Conclusion

"Christianity was saved in Europe solely because the peoples of Europe fought. If the peoples of Europe in the seventh and eighth centuries, and on up to and including the seventeenth century, had not possessed a military equality with, and gradually a growing superiority over the Mohammedans who invaded Europe, Europe would at this moment be Mohammedan and the Christian religion would be exterminated. Wherever the Mohammedans have had complete sway, wherever the Christians have been unable to resist them by the sword, Christianity has ultimately disappeared."

—U.S. PRESIDENT THEODORE ROOSEVELT[1]

"Mrs. President [Angela Merkel], ladies and gentlemen: Our society will change. Our city [Berlin] will change radically. I hold that in 20, 30 years there will no longer be a [German but rather a Muslim] majority in our city. …And I want to make it very clear, especially towards those right wingers: *This is a good thing!*"

—DR. STEFANIE VON BERG,

SPEAKING BEFORE THE GERMAN PARLIAMENT (BUNDESTAG), 2017[2]

In a development that speaks more about us than them, yesterday's heroes are become today's villains. Although venerated as heroic Defenders of the West by their contemporaries and centuries' worth of posterity, all eight men profiled in the preceding pages are now explicitly or implicitly seen as the "bad guys" by many of their civilizational heirs.

Why? For starters, they *defended* the lands and cause of Christendom and actually *stood against* the conquering armies of Islam. This is a big no-no for that overwhelming force—generically known as "the Left"—that currently dominates mainstream thought and discourse, particularly through those two institutions that have had a profound impact on shaping Western society's epistemology: media (social and otherwise—news, films, comedies, documentaries, and, of course, Hollywood) and academia (from kindergarten to postgraduate studies).

According to these molders of thought, Islam was and is a peaceful religion, and all past and present quarrels between it and the West were, if not based on "misunderstandings," squarely the latter's fault (via Crusades, religious bigotry, colonialism, racism, *ad nauseam*). As such, far from "standing against Islam," good and enlightened Westerners should appease and acquiesce—in a word, *submit*—to it.

Aside from the many fashionable ways of doing this—from never voicing any criticism against Islam (defined as "Islamophobia"), to turning a blind eye to and being "patient" with Islamic intolerance and aggression, to opening Western borders to millions of Muslim migrants, many of whom are violent lawbreakers—consider one especially apropos example. To mark the nine hundredth anniversary of the Crusader conquest of Jerusalem, in 1999, hundreds of self-identified Christians participated in a "reconciliation walk" that began in Germany and ended in Jerusalem. Along the way, they wore T-shirts with the words "I apologize"—in Arabic, no less. According to their official statement:

> Nine hundred years ago, our forefathers carried the name of Jesus Christ in battle across the Middle East. Fueled by fear, greed and hatred...the Crusaders lifted the banner of the Cross above your people.... On the anniversary of the First Crusade, we...wish to retrace the footsteps of the Crusaders in apology for their deeds.... We deeply regret the atrocities committed in the name of Christ by our predecessors. We renounce greed, hatred and fear, and condemn all violence done in the name of Jesus Christ. Where they were motivated by hatred and prejudice, we offer love and brotherhood.[3]

Fine sentiments, no doubt. That said, the writers of this statement make no mention—and apparently had no idea—that Duke Godfrey and the other First Crusaders traveled to the Holy Land only because

Muslims had been slaughtering and enslaving literally hundreds of thousands of Christians in the region over the preceding years and decades;[4] or that Muslims had violently conquered that city most holy to Christians—Jerusalem, repeatedly defiling and torching Christ's Sepulchre therein—to say nothing of the Islamic conquest of two-thirds of the Christian world in the preceding centuries, all of which gave Europe's Christians little choice but to fight fire with fire. As Bernard Lewis famously observed, "The Crusades could more accurately be described as a limited, belated and, in the last analysis, ineffectual response to the jihad—a failed attempt to recover by a Christian holy war what had been lost to a Muslim holy war."[5]

At any rate, being enemies of Islam is just the tip of the iceberg as to why the men profiled in the preceding pages are now so abhorred. They are, after all, guilty of far greater "sins": every one of them was the living embodiment of what is today condemned as "toxic masculinity" and "the patriarchy." Worse, not only were they all white, male, and Christian, but—far from being ashamed or apologetic over these now "troubling" attributes—two of these identity markers, their masculinity and religious faith, are precisely what animated them to act.

From here one may understand why hostility continues to spark out against these otherwise long dead men from a forgotten age. Thus, in June 2020 in St. Louis, Missouri, throngs of "progressives"—led by Black Lives Matter and Muslim activists—violently targeted for destruction the forty-foot iconic statue of King Louis IX, erected over a century earlier in honor of that city's namesake. It mattered little that the saint-king had spent much of his life and wealth in pious works of charity to better the lot of his fellow man; he was, they decried, a Christian "Islamophobe" who waged "two brutal crusades against Muslims in Egypt and Tunisia," and hence had to be torn down.[6] Once again, left unsaid was what Muslims had done to Christians in the preceding years, including if not especially in Egypt and Tunisia during and after the Islamic conquests of those formerly Christian nations.

When American patriots came to that statue's defense, including Catholics who held prayer vigils around the saintly effigy, BLM and its Muslim allies violently attacked them, including by trying to set an elderly man on fire.[7] "We allowed them to spit on us, call us names, put their fingers in our faces, push us, and antagonize," said one of the defenders present (sounding not unlike—but certainly much more passive than—Saint Louis before his abusive jailers in Egypt). "But we did not retaliate. We continued to peacefully pray."[8] Last reported, BLM and others are still trying, not only to have the statue removed, but to rename the city of St. Louis altogether.

Of course, poor Louis's "sins" are hardly limited to his stance against Islam; the attack on his statue is part of a much larger assault—the demonization of Western history in its entirety—as seen in the fact that countless other statues of what were once deemed heroes of Western civilization were vandalized and/or torn down throughout the United States during the summer of 2020, ostensibly in response to the inadvertent death of George Floyd, a black man. This incident has apparently led to the eye-opening revelation if not epiphany that *everything* about America—beginning, of course, with its history and heritage—is "racist" and in need of purging, or, as they say, "canceling."

In such a climate, contemporary Americans whose ancestors immigrated from Europe, whence this book's Defenders hailed—from Britain, France, and Spain in the west, to Hungary, Romania, and Albania in the east—are expected to be remorseful for *who they are*. If their living descendants are supposed to be so cowed, it needs no great expounding to see why the West's heroic ancestors—whose confidence in their religion and culture was beyond unshakeable—are now so despised.

Nor is such an anti-Western outlook limited to, say, wayward or aggrieved "youth groups," influenced by "popular culture." The seeds of even the most radical Leftist views tend to trace back to academia, which provides groups like BLM and Antifa with a veneer of intellectual legitimacy. While so-called "critical race theory" more than sufficiently validates this charge, within the context of this book, consider how academics have systematically degraded its heroes in recent years, and for the very same reason—because they *must be inherently bad*.

As discussed in the Cid's chapter, the authoritative writings concerning Roderick Diaz of Vivar—from the primary sources of his own eleventh century to the scholarly ones of the early twentieth century—portray him as a Christian hero of Spain who long defied and defeated the Almoravids, the eleventh century's version of "ISIS." Today, however, the mainstream academic view concerning the Cid is that he was a callous mercenary who cared little about Christianity or Spain. Modern historians are even quick to dismiss the Campeador's definitive biography, written by a professor who "devoted over twenty years to the study of the Cid," was widely acknowledged as "the authority on the mediaeval history and literature of Spain," and received the most Nobel Prize nominations (twenty-three) in history: Ramón Menéndez Pidal (1869–1968). (In reality and if anything, Pidal appears to have *downplayed* the cultural clash between Christians and Muslims in Spain, though apparently not enough for his postmodern critics.[9])

It is, moreover, rather ironic that, while many contemporary academics are nuanced enough to cast a historiographical context for Pidal—saying that he was writing through a nationalistic prism, elements of which may be true—they habitually fail to appreciate that they, too, are most certainly writing from within a very obvious historiographical tradition—a Leftist one, dedicated to demonizing anything and everything of Western history, in this case, its heroes.

Or consider the prevailing characterization of King Richard I of England. Although the original and contemporary sources present him as a fearless warrior-king who sacrificed much to recover the Holy Land, he is today best remembered as "a bad son, a bad husband, a selfish ruler, and a vicious man"—to quote influential English historian William Stubbs—not to mention a closet homosexual.[10] After positing that "there can be no doubt that in some ways the real Richard was very like the figure of romance"—that is to say, chivalrous, heroic, and self-sacrificing, in a word, *Lionheart*—John Gillingham, a more objective historian and biographer of Richard, wrote in 1978:

> It is only in the last thirty years that the story has gone around that Richard was a homosexual. Although this is now generally accepted as the "plain, unvarnished" truth about Richard, repeated in works as staid as the *Encyclopaedia Britannica*, it is in fact no more than a highly coloured assertion which cannot be substantiated—in other words a new legend which tells us more about our own times than it does about the character of the man whom it ostensibly concerns.[11]

Indeed, first made in 1948—eight centuries after Richard's era—the homosexual claim is, on close inspection, startlingly weak.[12] It hinges on arguments such as, despite being married for eight years, Richard produced no heirs. Not only is the absurdity of this supposed "deduction" self-evident—is every childless man a homosexual, then?—it ignores that he did have at least one illegitimate son. Another argument is that a contemporary source wrote that, in their youth, Richard and King Philip II of France sometimes shared a bed, even though "It was common for people of the same sex to share a bed," as Gillingham explains, adding:

> The *jongleur* who reported this had no fears that his audience would misunderstand him. He meant to imply that…they were close politically, not sexually. If men exchanged a kiss it was a gesture of friendship or peace, not of erotic passion. It is an elementary mistake to take it for granted that an act which has one symbolic meaning for us today possessed that same meaning eight hundred years ago. When Richard and Philip rode to Paris together, it was an act not of sex but of political defiance…. [In fact] Thirteenth-century opinion was in no doubt that his interests were heterosexual…. Richard's need for women was such that even on his deathbed he had them brought to him in defiance of his doctor's advice.[13]

At this point it becomes difficult to tell if the academics who are determined to downgrade if not degrade their historical subjects do so because they cannot transcend their own Leftist paradigms, or because they simply cannot help but project themselves onto their subjects. Either way, the effects are the same: history has increasingly and unabashedly been made to confirm and conform to Leftist paradigms and priorities, with little protest.

Having considered some modern distortions concerning Godfrey and the First Crusaders, Louis, the Cid, and Richard, it is interesting to note that little academic mischief has been foisted against the rest—namely, Ferdinand, Hunyadi, Skanderbeg, and Vlad. Two reasons account for this. First, unlike the Crusaders, every one of these men was ultimately defending against or liberating home territories from Islam. As such, it is much more difficult to portray them as "initiating" any conflict—unlike the Crusaders who left their homes to march onto and war in Muslim-controlled territory. (Of course and as shown, even the Crusaders were acting in accordance with the principles of Just War, not least because the Holy Land, indeed, the entire region, was originally Christian before being conquered by Islam; that said, and due to their logistical movements, it is simply *easier* to make the Crusaders appear the aggressor.)

The second reason is that, being less a part of "Western history" proper—which tends to trace its lineage to nations such as England, France, and later Germany—Eastern or Southern Europeans such as Ferdinand, Hunyadi, and Skanderbeg are already little known in the Western tradition.* In other words, whereas those heroes from nations such as England and France (Richard and Louis for example) were once naturally popular and therefore had to be taken down, it has been far better for those who seek to discredit history's Western heroes simply to say nothing about the other four, to let sleeping dogs lie—that is, to let already prevailing oblivion continue to do its work for them.

While this conclusion has focused on how the past has been distorted or suppressed by and in the present, there is, in fact, one way in which the past sheds light on the present that should not be passed over in silence. Aside from those who were unchallenged kings, virtually every Defender in this book—especially the Cid, Hunyadi, Skanderbeg, and Vlad—were as loved and supported by the common man or peasants, as they were hated, demonized, and conspired against by the nobles and upper classes—history's "elites"—who tended to place their own interests and agendas first, including by siding with the common Islamic enemy against their own. In this, history has little changed.

Before closing and to reiterate, this book has been exclusively interested in examining how its eight subjects "stood against Islam"—that and little more. As such, it has not tried to argue that any one of them were exemplars par excellence in all walks of life, to be extolled or emulated uncritically. Whether one wishes to see them as saints or sinners, heroes or villains, in the end they were just men—and that means fallible.

Even so, without them and so many more Defenders like them over the centuries, there would not have been a West to speak of today.† Accordingly, if there is anything about them worth emulating, it is precisely their firm and unapologetic stance against unprovoked Islamic aggression—a thing which is sorely lacking these days.‡

---

* As discussed, the Cid and Vlad are the exceptions. Due to their "accidental" popularity, they too have been targeted and reduced, respectively to a cynical mercenary and a bloodsucking vampire.

† For substantiation of this otherwise "far-fetched" sounding claim, see *Sword and Scimitar: Fourteen Centuries of War between Islam and the West.*

‡ These final words were written during and in response to the U.S.'s disastrous capitulation—which included the abandonment of billions of dollars' worth of weapons—to radical Islam in the guise of the Taliban in Afghanistan, September 2021.

Works Cited

Adam, Graeme Mercer, ed. *Spain and Portugal*. Philadelphia: John D. Morris and Company, 1906.

Akbar, M. J. *The Shade of Swords: Jihad and the Conflict between Islam and Christianity*. London: Routledge, 2003.

Albert of Aachen. *Albert of Aachen's History of the Journey to Jerusalem. Volume 1: Books 1-6*. Trans. Susan B. Edington. Burlington: Ashgate, 2013.

Allen, S. J., ed. *The Crusades: A Reader*. Toronto: University of Toronto Press, 2010.

"American Commissioners to John Jay, 28 March 1786," Founders Online, National Archives: http://founders.archives.gov/documents/Jefferson/01-09-02-0315. Original source: Julian P. Boyd, ed. 1954. *The Papers of Thomas Jefferson*, vol. 9, 1 November 1785–22 June 1786. Princeton: Princeton University Press, pp. 357–359.

Andressohn, John C. *The Ancestry and Life of Godfrey of Bouillon*. Bloomington: Indiana University, 1947.

Anna Comnena. *The Alexiad*. Trans. E. R. A. Sewter. London: Penguin Books, 1969.

Archer, Thomas Andrew. *The Crusade of Richard I, 1189-92*. London: David Nutt, 1889.

Babinger, Franz. *Mehmet the Conqueror and His Time*. Trans. Ralph Manheim. Princeton: Princeton University Press, 1978.

Baha' al-Din ibn Shaddad. *The Rare and Excellent History of Saladin (Al-Nawadir al-Sultaniyya wa'l Mahasin al-Yusifiyya)*. Trans. D. S. Richards. Burlington: Ashgate, 2001.

Bain, Nisbet. "The Siege of Belgrade by Muhammad II, July 1-23, 1456." *The English Historical Review*, vol. 7, No. 26 (April 1982), pp. 235-252.

Bartolomeo de Giano. "A Letter of the Cruelty of the Turks." Trans. W. L. North. *Patrologia Graeca*, vol. 158. Paris: Imprimerie Catholique, n.d. Accessed online, https://apps.carleton.edu/curricular/mars/assets/Bartholomeus_de_Giano.pdf.

Barton, Simon and Richard Fletcher, trans. *The World of the Cid: Chronicles of the Spanish Reconquest*. New York: Manchester University Press, 2000.

Belloc, Hilaire. *The Great Heresies*. London: Sheed and Ward, 1938 (retypeset and republished by Cavalier Books, Milwaukee, 2015).

Bertrand, Louis. *The History of Spain*. 2d ed., rev. and continued to the year 1945. London: Eyre & Spottiswoode, 1952.

Bostom, Andrew, ed. *The Legacy of Jihad: Islamic Holy War and the Fate of Non-Muslims*. New York: Prometheus Books, 2005.

Brackob, A.K. *Scanderbeg: A History of George Castriota and the Albanian Resistance to Islamic Expansion in Fifteenth Century Europe*. Las Vegas: Vita Histria, 2018.

Brewer, Clifford. *The Death of Kings: A Medical History of the Kings and Queens of England*. London: Abson, 2000.

Brundage, James A, ed. *The Crusades: A Documentary Survey*. Milwaukee: Marquette University Press, 1962.

Butler, Alban. *The Lives of the Fathers, Martyrs, and Other Principal Saints*. Volume 5. London: John Murphy, 1815.

Cardini, Franco. *Europe and Islam*. Trans. Caroline Beamish. Oxford: Blackwell Publishers, 2001.

Chalkokondyles, Laonikos. *The Histories*. Volume 1. Trans. Anthony Kaldellis. Cambridge: Harvard University Press, 2014.

Churchill, Winston Spencer. *The River War: A Historical Account of the Reconquest of the Soudan*. London: Longmans, Green, and Co., 1899.

———. *The Second World War: The Gathering Storm*. London: Cassell, 1948.

Cohen, Richard. *By the Sword: A History of Gladiators, Musketeers, Samurai, Swashbucklers, and Olympic Champions*. New York: Random House, 2002.

Constable, Olivia Remie, ed. *Medieval Iberia: Reading from Christian, Muslim, and Jewish Sources*. Philadelphia: University of Pennsylvania Press, 1997.

Crowley, Roger. *1453: The Holy War for Constantinople and the Clash of Islam and the West*. New York: Hachette Books, 2014.

Daniel, Norman. *Islam and the West: The Making of an Image*. Edinburgh: Edinburgh University Press, 1962.

Dillon, George, F. *The Virgin Mother of Good Counsel: A History of the Ancient Sanctuary*. New York: Catholic Publication Society, 1884.

Długosz, Jan. *The Annals of Jan Długosz*. Trans. Maurice Michael. West Sussex: IM Publications, 1997.

Doukas. *Decline and Fall of Byzantium to the Ottoman Turks*. Trans. Harry J. Magoulias. Detroit: Wayne State University Press, 1975.

Drizari, Nelo. *Scanderbeg: His Life, Correspondence, Orations, Victories, and Philosophy*. Palo Alto: The National Press, 1968.

Edbury, Peter W, trans. *The Conquest of Jerusalem and the Third Crusade: Sources in Translation*. Burlington: Ashgate, 1998.

Efrosin. *The Tale of Prince Dracula*. n.p., 1486. Accessed online: http://hypocritereader.com/52/tale-of-dracula

Fernandez-Morera, Dario. *The Myth of the Andalusian Paradise*. Wilmington: ISI Books, 2016.

———. "Christian Slavery under Islam." *The Postil Magazine*, April 1, 2021. Accessed online: https://www.thepostil.com/author/dario-fernandez-morera/

Fields, Larry F. *The Sanctity of Louis IX: Early Lives of Saint Louis by Geoffrey of Beaulieu and William of Chartres*. Ithaca: Cornell University Press, 2014.

Fitzhenry, James. *El Cid: God's Own Champion*. St. Mary's (KS): Catholic Vitality Publications, 2008.

———. *Defenders of Christendom*. St. Mary's (KS): Catholic Vitality Publications, 2015.

Fletcher, Richard. *The Quest for El Cid*. New York: Knopf, 1990.

Florescu, Radu R. and Raymond T. McNally. *Dracula: Prince of Many Faces*. New York: Back Bay Books, 1989.

Fortescue, Adrian. *The Lesser Eastern Churches*. New York: AMS Press, 1972.

Frankopan, Peter. *The First Crusade: The Call from the East*. London: Vintage Books, 2013.

Frashëri, Kristo. *George Kastrioti-Scanderbeg: The National Hero of the Albanians (1405-1468)*. Tirana: State Publishing Enterprise, 1962.

Fuller, J. F. C. *Military History of the Western World. Vol. 1, From the Earliest Times to the Battle of Lepanto*. New York: Da Capo Press, 1987.

Gabrieli, Francesco, trans. *Arab Historians of the Crusades*. New York: Barnes and Noble, 1993.

Gaposchkin, M. Cecilia, ed. *Blessed Louis, the Most Glorious of Kings: Texts Relating to the Cult of Saint Louis of France*. Trans. Phyllis B. Katz. Indiana: University of Notre Dame, 2012.

Gibbon, Edward. *The Decline and Fall of the Roman Empire*. Vol. 2. Chicago: University of Chicago, 1952.

Gillingham, John. *Richard the Lionheart*. New York: Times Books, 1978.

Gilo of Paris. *The Historia Vie Hierosolimitane of Gilo of Paris and a Second, Anonymous Author*. Ed and trans. C. W. Grocock and J.E. Siberry. Oxford: Clarendon Press, 1997.

Guéranger, Dom Prosper. *The Liturgical Year*. Volume II. Trans. Dom Laurence Shepherd. Dublin: James Duffy, 1871.

Guibert of Nogent. *The Deeds of God through the Franks*. Middlesex: Echo Library, 2008.

Guindy, Adel. *A Sword over the Nile: A Brief History of the Copts under Islamic Rule*. London: Austin Macauley Publishers, 2020.

Gullen, M. Fethullah. *Essentials of the Islamic Faith*. Trans. Ali Unal. New Jersey: Light, 2006. al-Hakam, Ibn 'Abd. *The History of the Conquest of Spain*. Trans. John Harris Jones. New York: B. Franklin, 1969.

———. *Futūḥ Miṣr wa'l Maghrab wa'l Andalus* [The Conquests of Egypt, North Africa, and Spain]. New York: Cosimo Classics, 2010. Excerpts translated by author.

Hamilton, Rita and Janet Perry, ed. and trans. *The Poem of the Cid*. New York: Penguin Books, 1984.

Held, Joseph. *Hunyadi: Legend and Reality*. New York: Columbia University Press, 1985.

Hillenbrand, Carole. *Turkish Myth and Muslim Symbol: the Battle of Manzikert*. Edinburgh: Edinburgh University Press, 2007.

Humphreys, R. Stephen, "Ayyubids, Mamluks, and the Latin East in the Thirteenth Century." *Mamluk Studies Review*, 1998. Accessed online: https://mamluk.uchicago.edu/MSR_II_1998-Humphreys.pdf

Ibn al-Athir. *The Chronicle of Ibn al-Athir for the Crusading Period from al-Kamil fi'l Ta'rikh*. Part 1. Trans. D.S. Richards. Burlington: Ashgate, 2006.

———. *The Chronicle of Ibn al-Athir for the Crusading Period from al-Kamil fi'l Ta'rikh*. Part 2. Trans. D.S. Richard. Burlington.: Ashgate, 2007.

Ibrahim, Raymond. *Sword and Scimitar: Fourteen Centuries of War between Islam and the West*. New York: Da Capo Press, 2018.

———. *Crucified Again: Exposing Islam's New War on Christians*. Washington, DC: Regnery Publishing, 2013.

———. *The Al Qaeda Reader*. New York: Doubleday, 2007.

Jackson, Peter. *The Seventh Crusade, 1244-1254: Sources and Documents*. London: Routledge, 2016.

Jamieson, Alan G. *Faith and Sword*. London: Reaktion Books, 2006.

Jefferson, John. *The Holy Wars of King Wladislas and Sultan Murad: The Ottoman-Christian Conflict from 1438–1444*. Leiden: Brill, 2012.

John, Simon. *Godfrey of Bouillon: Duke of Lower Lotharingia, Ruler of Latin Jerusalem, c. 1060-1100*. London: Routledge, 2019.

Joinville and Villehardouin. *Chronicles of the Crusades*. Trans. Sir Frank Marzials. Mineola: Dover Publications, 2007.

Jordan, William Chester. *The Apple of His Eye: Converts from Islam in the Reign of Louis IX*. Princeton: Princeton University Press, 2019.

Kennedy, Hugh. *Muslim Spain and Portugal: A Political History of al-Andalus*. London: Longman, 1996.

Kinross, Lord (Patrick Balfour). *The Ottoman Centuries*. New York: Morrow Quill, 1979.

Krey, August, ed. *The First Crusade: The Accounts of Eyewitnesses and Participants*. London: Oxford University Press, 1921.

Lewis, Bernard, ed. and trans. *Islam (from the Prophet Muhammad to the Capture of Constantinople, Vol 1: Politics and War)*. New York: Oxford University Press, 1987.

———. *Islam and the West*. New York: Oxford University Press, 1994.

———. *The Middle East: A Brief History of the Last 2,000 Years*. New York: Scribner, 2003.

Madden, Thomas F. *The New Concise History of the Crusades*. New York: Barnes & Noble, 2007.

al-Maqqari, Ahmad ibn Muhammad. *The History of the Mohammedan Dynasties in Spain*. Vol. 1. Trans. Sir Gore Ouseley. New York: Johnson Reprint Corp, 1964.

———. *The History of the Mohammedan Dynasties in Spain*. Vol. 2. Trans. Sir Gore Ouseley. New York: Johnson Reprint Corp, 1964.

al-Maqrizi, Taqi al-Din. *A Short History of the Copts and Their Church*. Trans. S. C. Malan. London: D. Nutt, 1873.

———. *Essulouk li Mariset il Muluk*. n.p. Fordham University's Medieval Sourcebook: "Al-Makrisi: Account of the Crusade of St. Louis," 1969. Accessed online: https://sourcebooks.fordham.edu/source/makrisi.asp.

Maria del Carmen. *The Life of the Very Noble King of Castile and León, Saint Ferdinand III*. Trans. Fernandez de Castro Cabeza. New York: The Foundation for a Christian Civilization, 1987.

Mariana, Juan. *The general history of Spain from the first peopling of it by Tubal, till the death of King Ferdinand, who united the crowns of Castile and Aragon*. Trans. John Stevens. London: Richard Sare and Thomas Bennet, 1699. Accessed online: https://quod.lib.umich.edu/e/eebo/a51926.0001.001/1:5.9.4?vid=54233;view=toc

Matthew of Edessa. *Armenia and the Crusades, Tenth to Twelfth Centuries: The Chronicle of Matthew of Edessa*. Trans. Ara Edmond Dostourian. Lanham:

National Association for Armenian Studies and Research; University Press of America, 1993.

Melville-Jones, John R. *The Siege of Constantinople 1453: Seven Contemporary Accounts*. Amsterdam: Hakkert, 1973.

Mihailović, Konstantin. *Memoirs of a Janissary*. Trans. Benjamin Stolz. Princeton: Markus Wiener Publishers, 2011.

Moczar, Diane. *Islam at the Gates: How Christendom Defeated the Ottoman Turks*. Manchester: Sophia Institute Press, 2008.

Moore, Clement, C. *George Castriot, Surnamed Scanderbeg, King of Albania*. New York: D. Appleton & Company, 1850.

Mourad, Suleiman A. and James E. Lindsay. *Muslim Sources of the Crusader Period*: An Anthology. Indianapolis: Hackett, 2021.

Mureşanu, Camil. *Hunyadi: Defender of Christendom*. Oxford: Center for Romanian Studies, 2019.

Nicholson, Helen J., trans. *Chronicle of the Third Crusade: A Translation of the Itinerarium Peregrinorum et Gesta Regis Ricardi*. Burlington: Ashgate, 1997.

Noli, Fan Stylian. *George Castrioti Scanderbeg (1405–1468)*. Tirana: International University Press, 1947.

O'Callaghan, Joseph F. *A History of Medieval Spain*. Ithaca: Cornell University, 1975.

———, trans. *The Latin Chronicle of the Kings of Castile*. Tempe: Arizona Center for Medieval and Renaissance Studies, 2002.

———. *Reconquest and Crusade in Medieval Spain*. Philadelphia: University of Pennsylvania Press, 2004.

Perry, Frederick. *Saint Louis (Louis IX of France): The Most Christian King*. London: G. P. Putnam's Son, 1901.

Peters, Edward, ed. *First Crusade: Chronicle of Fulcher of Chartres and Other Source Materials*. Philadelphia: University of Pennsylvania Press, 1971.

Piccolomini, Aeneas Silvius (Pope Pius II). *Europe (c.1400-1458)*. Trans. Robert Brown. Washington D.C.: The Catholic University Press, 2013.

Pidal, Ramon Menendez. *The Cid and His Spain*. Trans. Harold Sunderland. London: John Murray, Albemarle Street, W., 1934.

Purser, Toby. *Medieval England, 1042-1228*. Oxford: Heinemann Educational Publishers, 2004.

Ralph of Caen. *The Gesta Tancredi of Ralph of Caen: A History of the Normans on the First Crusade*. Trans. Bernard S. Bachrach and David S. Bachrach. Burlington: Ashgate, 2005.

Richard of Devizes. *The Chronicle of Richard of Devizes*. Trans. J. A. Giles. London: James Bohn, 1853.

Riley-Smith, Jonathan. *The Crusades, Christianity, and Islam*. New York: Columbia University Press, 2008.

———, ed. *The Oxford Illustrated History of the Crusades*. Oxford: Oxford University Press, 1995.

Robert the Monk. *History of the First Crusade (Historia Iherosolimitana)*. Trans. Carol Sweetenham. Burlington: Ashgate, 2005.

Roosevelt, Theodore. *The Works of Theodore Roosevelt: Memorial Edition*, Vol. XX. New York: Charles Scribner's Sons, 1925.

Rubenstein, Jay, ed. *The First Crusade: A Brief History with Documents*. Boston: Bedford/St. Martin's, 2015.

Sphrantzes, Georgios. *The Fall of the Byzantine Empire: A Chronicle*. Trans. Marios Philippides. Amherst: University of Massachusetts Press, 1980.

Stark, Rodney. *God's Battalions: The Case for the Crusades*. New York: Harper One, 2009.

Stern, Fritz, ed. *The Varieties of History: From Voltaire to the Present*. New York: Vintage Books, 1973.

Thomas the Eparch and Joshua Diplovatatzes. "Account of the Taking of Constantinople." Trans. William L. North, from the Italian version in A. Pertusi, ed., *La Caduta di Costantinopoli: Le Testimonianze dei Contemporanei*. Milan: Mondadori, 1976, pp. 234–239. Accessed online: https://apps.carleton.edu/curricular/mars/assets/Thomas_the_Eparch_and_Joshua_Diplovatatzes_for_MARS_website.pdf.

Thorp, Nigel R. *The Old French Crusade Cycle (La Chanson de Jerusalem)*. Volume VI. Tuscaloosa: University of Alabama Press, 1992.

Tolan, John V. *Saracens: Islam in the Medieval European Imagination*. New York: Columbia University Press, 2002.

Treptow, Kurt W, ed.. *Dracula: Essays on the Life and Times of Vlad the Impaler*. Oxford: Center for Romanian Studies, 2019.

———. *Vlad III Dracula: The Life and Times of the Historical Dracula*. Oxford: The Center for Romanian Studies, 2020.

Tursun Beg. *The History of Mehmed the Conqueror*. Trans. Halil Inalcik and Rhoads Murphey. Minneapolis: Bibliotheca Islamica, 1978.

Twain, Mark (Samuel Clement). *The Innocents Abroad*. Pleasantville: The Reader's Digest, 1990.

Tyerman, Christopher. *God's War: A New History of the Crusades*. Cambridge: Belknap Press of Harvard University Press, 2006.

Watts, Henry Edward. *The Christian Recovery of Spain: Being the Story of Spain from the Moorish Conquest to the Fall of Granada (711–1492 A.D.)*. New York: G.P. Putnam's Sons, 1894.

Wheatcroft, Andrew. *Infidels: A History of the Conflict between Christendom and Islam*. New York: Random House Trade Paperbacks, 2005.

William of Tyre. *A History of Deeds Done Beyond the Sea*. Vol. 1. Trans. Emily Atwater Babcock and A.C. Krey. New York: Columbia University Press, 1943.

——. *Godefroy of Boloyne, or The Siege and Conqueste of Jerusalem*. Ed. Mary Noyes Colvin. Trans. William Caxton. Millwood: Kraus Reprint Co, 1893.

William, Leonard. *The Arts and Crafts of Older Spain*. London: T.N. Foulis, 1907.

Wolf, Kenneth Baxter, trans. *Conquerors and Chroniclers of Early Medieval Spain*. Liverpool: Liverpool University Press, 1990.

Ye'or, Bat. *The Decline of Eastern Christianity under Islam: From Jihad to Dhimmitude*. Cranbury, NJ: Associated University Presses, 2010.

Endnotes

Introduction

1 Peters, 24.
2 Madden 2007, 213.
3 Lewis 1994, 13.
4 Ibrahim 2018, 122–129.
5 Cardini 2001, 3.
6 "American Commissioners" n.d.
7 Belloc 1938, 51, 71.
8 Churchill 1948, 272.
9 Jamieson 2006, 215.
10 Stern, 101, 103.
11 Ibid., 103.
12 Ibid., 102–103.
13 Mihailović, 2.
14 Tyerman, 30–31.
15 Ibid.
16 Riley-Smith 2008, 12.
17 Ibid., 13–16.
18 Madden, 8.
19 Riley-Smith 2008, 16.
20 https://www.nationalreview.com/2007/05/islamic-apologetics-raymond-ibrahim/
21 Riley-Smith 2008, 4–5.
22 Madden, 223.

Chapter 1

1 Ralph of Caen, 65.
2 Peters, 90.
3 Stark 2009, 85.
4 al-Maqrizi 1873, 86.
5 Ibrahim 2013, 39–42; Stark 2009, 91.
6 William of Tyre 1943, 70.
7 Lewis 2003, 88, 95.
8 Bostom 2005, 609.
9 Fuller 1987, 404.

10 https://greekcitytimes.com/2021/06/01/turkish-dna-project-greeks-turkified/
11 Robert the Monk, 219.
12 Guibert of Nogent, 32–33.
13 William of Tyre 1943, 71.
14 Ibid., 81.
15 Ye'or, 292.
16 Brundage, 18–19.
17 Matthew of Edessa, 164.
18 Ibid.
19 Andressohn, 28.
20 John, 56.
21 Ibid., 57.
22 William of Tyre 1943, 387.
23 Robert the Monk, 83–84.
24 William of Tyre 1943, 387.
25 Ralph of Caen, 36–37; 53.
26 William of Tyre 1943, 389.
27 Robert the Monk, 83–84.
28 William of Tyre 1943, 390–391.
29 John, 80.
30 William of Tyre 1893, xxxi; Andressohn, 48.
31 William of Tyre 1943, 391; William of Tyre 1893, xxxiii.
32 John, 106.
33 William of Tyre 1943, 392.
34 Ibid., 140.
35 Albert of Aachen, 59.
36 Peters 1971, 129.
37 William of Tyre 1943, 130.
38 Peters 1971, 144.
39 Guibert of Nogent, 58; Robert the Monk, 104.

40 Albert of Aachen, 68.
41 Ibid., 68.
42 William of Tyre 1943, 162.
43 Albert of Aachen, 64.
44 Robert the Monk, 105.
45 Guibert of Nogent, 60.
46 Robert the Monk, 105.
47 Anna Comnena 1969, 312; cf., Fulcher of Chartres in Peters 1971, 42.
48 Guibert of Nogent 2008, 45.
49 William of Tyre 1943, 169.
50 Robert the Monk, 107.
51 William of Tyre 1943, 170.
52 Robert the Monk, 108.
53 Guibert of Nogent, 58–61.
54 William of Tyre 1943, 172.
55 Ralph of Caen, 53, 46.
56 William of Tyre 1943, 172.
57 John, 131.
58 William of Tyre 1943, 171–172.
59 Gabrieli 1993, 38–39.
60 Guibert of Nogent, 61; cf. Robert the Monk, 115.
61 Ibid., 66.
62 Peters, 43.
63 Albert of Aachen, 81.
64 William of Tyre 1943, 176.
65 Albert of Aachen, 81–82; Albert in John, 132.
66 John, 132; William of Tyre 1943, 176.
67 Albert of Aachen, 82.
68 Peter, 51.
69 William of Tyre 1943, 188.
70 Albert of Aachen, 101.
71 William of Tyre 1943, 241.
72 Frankopan, 91.
73 Peters, 55.
74 William of Tyre 1943, 228.
75 Robert the Monk, 131.
76 William of Tyre 1943, 221.
77 Albert of Aachen, in John, 139-140.
78 John, 139.
79 William of Tyre 1943, 233.
80 Albert of Aachen, 129.
81 Robert the Monk, 133.
82 Ibid., 133.
83 Ibid., 137.
84 Rubenstein, 56.
85 Robert the Monk, 137–138.
86 Andressohn, 83.
87 Robert the Monk, 126.
88 Ibid., 147.
89 William of Tyre 1943, 258.
90 Albert of Aachen, 151.
91 Matthew of Edessa, 167.
92 Robert the Monk, 153.
93 John, 144.
94 William of Tyre 1943, 282.
95 Robert the Monk, 165.
96 Albert of Aachen, 166.
97 Robert the Monk, 165.
98 Ibid., 165.
99 Guibert of Nogent, 98.
100 Ibid., 98; William of Tyre 1943, 284.
101 John, 145.
102 Rubenstein, 121–123.
103 William of Tyre 1943, 295.
104 Wheatcroft, 170.
105 Ibn al-Athir 2006, 17.
106 Robert the Monk, 172.
107 Ibn al-Athir 2006, 14.
108 John, 157.
109 Albert of Aachen, 203.
110 Rubenstein, 75.
111 Peters, 72.
112 John, 158.
113 William of Tyre 1943, 330.
114 Krey 1921, 242–243.
115 Madden 2007, 33.
116 William of Tyre 1943, 334.
117 William of Tyre 1893, xxxviii.
118 Albert of Aachen, 208.
119 Gilo of Paris, 243.
120 Robert the Monk, 198.
121 Ralph of Caen, 139.
122 Gilo of Paris, 243.
123 William of Tyre 1943, 352–353.
124 Peters, 85.
125 Ibid., 210.
126 Ibid., 211.
127 Gilo of Paris, 243.
128 Rubenstein 2015, 142.
129 William of Tyre 1943, 359.

DEFENDERS OF THE WEST

130 Albert of Aachen, 215.
131 William of Tyre 1943, 359.
132 Rubinstein, 143–144.
133 William of Tyre 1943, 366; cf. Robert the Monk, 217.
134 William of Tyre 1943, 362.
135 Ibid., 362.
136 Peters, 212.
137 William of Tyre 1943, 365.
138 Robert the Monk, 199.
139 Ibid., 199.
140 Albert of Aachen, 220; cf. Andressohn, 100.
141 Andressohn, 101.
142 Raymond of Aguilers in Peters, 213.
143 Ralph of Caen, 147.
144 John, 163.
145 William of Tyre 1943, 370.
146 Ibid., 370.
147 Albert of Aachen, 223.
148 Ibid., 200.
149 Ibid., 200.
150 Matthew of Edessa, 173.
151 William of Tyre 1943, 371–372.
152 Gibbon, 401.
153 William of Tyre 1893, xxxix.
154 Robert the Monk, 201.
155 William of Tyre 1943, 373.
156 Ralph of Caen, 65. Although these words were spoken by a Crusader named Ursinus concerning the conquest of another Muslim held city during the First Crusade, they were no doubt even more applicable for Jerusalem.
157 Robert the Monk, 202.
158 William of Tyre 1943, 382.
159 Ibid., 382.
160 Robert the Monk, 202.
161 John, 157.
162 William of Tyre 1893, xxxii.
163 Ibid., xxxix.
164 Gibbon, 388–392.
165 William of Tyre 1943, 394.
166 Robert the Monk, 204.
167 Andressohn, 109.
168 Robert the Monk, 205.

169 Ibid., 207.
170 Albert of Aachen, 241.
171 Robert the Monk, 209.
172 Ibid., 209.
173 Ralph of Caen, 79.
174 William of Tyre 1943, 413.
175 Albert of Aachen, 244.
176 William of Tyre 1943, 408.
177 John, 198, 201.
178 Thorp, 197.
179 Matthew of Edessa, 175–176.
180 Ralph of Caen, 157.
181 John, 205.
182 William of Tyre 1943, 392.
183 John, 1.
184 Twain, 363–364.
185 Ibid., 295–296.
186 William of Tyre 1943, 391.

Chapter 2

1 Hamilton, 61–63.
2 Ibid., 115.
3 Wolf, 167.
4 al-Hakam 2010, 208; cf. al-Hakam 1969, 22.
5 al-Maqqari, vol 1, 275.
6 Ibid., 275, 288.
7 Ibid., 275, 279–280.
8 Wolf, 132.
9 Fernandez-Morera 2016, 39–40
10 Ibid., 39–40.
11 Wolf, 132. Contrary to widespread belief, the northwest quadrant of Spain appears never to have been conquered by the Moors. See the University of Salamanca's Felipe Maíllo Salgado's seminal *Acerca de la conquista* árabe *de Hispania: Imprecisiones, equívocos y patrañas*, 2016.
12 Ibid., 165.
13 Ibid., 166.
14 O'Callaghan 2004, 5; Wolf, 167.
15 al-Maqqari, vol 2, 34–35; 260–261.
16 Bertrand, 87.
17 Watts, 27.
18 Bostom, 597.
19 Fernandez-Morera 2016, 162, 159.

326

20 Adam, 132.

21 O'Callaghan 2004, 12.

22 Watts, 9.

23 Bertrand, 93.

24 Pidal, 27.

25 Ibid., 76.

26 Barton, 81.

27 Mariana, 141–142.

28 Bertrand, 115.

29 Ibid., 113.

30 Pidal, 427.

31 Bertrand, 113.

32 Hamilton, 63, 203, 131, 191–193.

33 Although this episode was widely reported in several chronicles and poems stretching back to the thirteenth century, because it does not appear in the *Historia Roderici* or the *Poem of the Cid*, some modern historians question its historicity.

34 https://www.dailymail.co.uk/news/article-8187193/Crucifix-confirmed-El-Cids-famous-medieval-warlord.html

35 Hamilton, 23.

36 See Fernandez-Morera 2016, chapter 1.

37 Pidal, 32.

38 al-Maqqari, vol 2, Appendix C, xxvii- xxviii.

39 Barton, 143.

40 al-Maqqari, vol 2, 262.

41 Barton, 84.

42 O'Callaghan 2004, 30.

43 al-Maqqari, vol 2, C, xxxii-iii.

44 Ibid., 264.

45 Ibid., 290.

46 Pidal, 215.

47 al-Maqqari, vol 2, 274.

48 Ibid., 264.

49 Ibid., C, xxxiii.

50 Pidal, 216.

51 al-Maqqari, vol 2, 275; 279.

52 Ibid., 280; C, xxxiii.

53 Ibid., 280; C, xxxv.

54 Ibid., 283.

55 Ibid., 285.

56 Pidal, 218.

57 al-Maqqari, vol 2, C, xxxvi.

58 Pidal, 219.

59 al-Maqqari, vol 2, C, xxxvi.

60 Ibid., 279.

61 Pidal, 219.

62 Ibid., 219.

63 al-Maqqari, vol 2, 286.

64 Ibid., 287.

65 al-Maqqari, vol 2, C, xxxvi.

66 Pidal, 221.

67 al-Maqqari, vol 2, 288.

68 Ibid., 288.

69 Pidal, 434.

70 al-Maqqari, vol 2, 289.

71 Mariana, 157.

72 Pidal, 249.

73 Ibid., 288.

74 Ibid., 244.

75 Barton, 255.

76 Bertrand, 127.

77 Pidal, 265.

78 al-Maqqari, vol 2, 295.

79 Fletcher, 159.

80 Pidal, 267.

81 Ibid., 268; 269; 275.

82 Ibid.279.

83 Ibid., 280.

84 Ibid., 279–280.

85 Barton, 134.

86 Mariana, 157.

87 al-Maqqari, vol 2, C, xxxix.

88 Pidal, 304; 309.

89 Ibid., 279–280.

90 Barton, 136.

91 Ibid., 136.

92 Barton, 137.

93 Pidal, 319.

94 Barton, 137.

95 Pidal, 319.

96 Ibid., 330–331.

97 al-Maqqari, vol 2, 333.

98 Pidal, 435.

99 https://en.caminodelcid.org/cid-history-legend/cid-history/

100 Hamilton, 107; Barton, 137; Pidal, 352.

101 Pidal, 352.
102 Ibid., 312.
103 Barton, 137.
104 Hamilton, 109.
105 Pidal, 354.
106 Fletcher, 172.
107 Barton, 138.
108 Ibid., 138.
109 Ibid., 138; Hamilton, 88–89.
110 Fletcher, 173.
111 Fitzhenry 2008, 155.
112 Pidal, 354.
113 Ibid., 356.
114 Fletcher, 173.
115 Pidal, 366.
116 Ibid., 341.
117 Bertrand, 116.
118 Pidal, 322.
119 Ibid., 351.
120 Pidal, 365.
121 Barton, 139.
122 Ibid., 140.
123 Ibid., 140–141.
124 Pidal, 375.
125 Hamilton, 149.
126 Pidal, 375.
127 Fitzhenry 2008, 168.
128 Pidal, 375.
129 Barton, 141.
130 Hamilton, 149–151.
131 Ibid., 153.
132 Pidal, 322.
133 See "Loyalty and Enmity" by al-Qaeda's Ayman al-Zawahiri in Ibrahim 2007, p. 63–115.
134 Ibrahim 2007, 84.
135 Pidal, 4.
136 Ibid., 426.
137 Ibid., 376.
138 Ibid., 377.
139 Ibid., 406.
140 Ibid., 406–407.
141 Barton, 146.
142 Pidal, 379.
143 O'Callaghan 1975, 214.
144 Pidal, 428, 433.
145 Barton, 99.

146 Pidal, 437.
147 Ibid., 426.
148 Hamilton, 87.
149 Ibid., 109–111.
150 Ibid., 113; 115.
151 O'Callaghan 2004, 30.
152 Pidal, 428.

Chapter 3

1 Nicholson, 261.
2 Ibid., 231, 367
3 Gabrieli, 144.
4 Guindy, 127–142.
5 Gabrieli, 164.
6 Ibid., 163.
7 Nicholson, 47.
8 Ibid., 48.
9 Ibid., 69.
10 Ibid., 47.
11 Edbury, 179.
12 Richard of Devizes, 77.
13 Baha' al-Din, 34.
14 Brewer, 41.
15 Nicholson, 190.
16 Ibid., 146.
17 Madden, 80.
18 Nicholson, 83.
19 Edbury, 93.
20 Nicholson, 167.
21 Ibid., 186.
22 Richard of Devizes, 48.
23 Edbury 176.
24 Nicholson, 196.
25 Ibid., 202.
26 Baha' al-Din, 150.
27 Richard of Devizes, 48; Nicholson, 196–197.
28 Nicholson, 197.
29 Gillingham, 172; cf. Edbury, 104.
30 Nicholson, 198.
31 Ibid., 198.
32 Ibid., 198–199.
33 Baha' al-Din, 151; Ibn al-Athir 2007, 387.
34 Nicholson, 199.
35 Baha' al-Din, 151.
36 Nicholson, 204.
37 Baha' al-Din, 146.

38 Nicholson, 209.
39 Ibn al-Athir 2007, 387.
40 Baha' al-Din, 153.
41 Called Arnoldia (or Leonardia) in the sources, see Nicholson, 204; Gillingham, 175.
42 Nicholson, 209.
43 Ibid., 209.
44 Ibid., 205.
45 Ibid., 210.
46 Ibid., 211–212.
47 Baha' al-Din, 184.
48 Nicholson, 213.
49 Ibid., 218.
50 Ibid., 75.
51 Ibid., 218.
52 Ibn al-Athir 2007, 388.
53 Gillingham, 178.
54 Richard of Devizes, 54.
55 Archer, 172.
56 Richard of Devizes, 72.
57 Nicholson, 229.
58 Ibid., 231.
59 Ibid., 380.
60 Ibid., 232.
61 Edbury, 180.
62 Baha' al-Din, 164–165.
63 Richard of Devizes, 53.
64 Ibn al-Athir 2007, 390.
65 Nicholson, 241.
66 Ibid., 244–245.
67 Baha' al-Din, 177.
68 Ibid., 170.
69 Nicholson, 250.
70 Ibid., 248.
71 Ibid., 247.
72 Ibid., 248–249.
73 Ibid., 253–260.
74 Ibid., 253–255.
75 Ibn al-Athir 2007, 391.
76 Edbury, 180.
77 Ibid., 180.
78 Nicholson, 259.
79 Ibid., 260.
80 Ibid., 260–261.
81 Ibn al-Athir 2007, 391.
82 Edbury, 181.
83 Baha' al-Din, 186.
84 Ibid., 186.
85 Ibid., 186.
86 Nicholson, 273.
87 Baha' al-Din, 188.
88 Nicholson, 279.
89 Ibid., 285.
90 Gillingham, 199.
91 Nicholson, 309.
92 Ibid., 341.
93 Baha' al-Din, 207.
94 Nicholson, 311.
95 Ibid., 290.
96 Ibid., 311.
97 Ibid., 316–319.
98 Gillingham, 209.
99 Richard of Devizes, 67.
100 Nicholson, 327.
101 Ibid., 328.
102 Archer, 250.
103 Nicholson, 336.
104 Ibid., 345.
105 Ibid., 335; cf. Ibn al-Athir 2007, 394.
106 Gillingham, 198; Nicholson, 271–272.
107 Nicholson, 266–267.
108 Baha' al-Din, 182.
109 Richard of Devizes, 76.
110 Nicholson, 349.
111 Ibid., 352.
112 Baha' al-Din, 219.
113 Nicholson, 350-358.
114 Ibid., 353.
115 Baha' al-Din, 222.
116 Nicholson, 354.
117 Edbury, 117; Nicholson, 355.
118 Nicholson, 355–356.
119 Baha' al-Din, 222.
120 Nicholson, 357.
121 Baha' al-Din, 222–223.
122 Nicholson, 358.
123 Gillingham, 214.
124 Baha' al-Din, 223;
125 Nicholson, 359.
126 Ibid., 361–364.
127 Gillingham, 215.
128 Nicholson, 364.

129 Baha' al-Din, 225–226.
130 Nicholson, 367.
131 Ibid., 368–369.
132 Nicholson, 369.
133 Richard of Devizes, 68–69.
134 Baha' al-Din, 224.
135 Nicholson, 383.
136 Baha' al-Din, 213.
137 Nicholson, 371.
138 Ibn al-Athir 2007, 402.
139 Nicholson, 373–9; Baha' al-Din, 239.
140 Nicholson, 375.
141 Richard of Devizes, 78.
142 Gabrielli, 101.
143 Purser, 161.
144 Nicholson, 389.
145 Ibid., 372.
146 Ibid., 368.
147 Joinville, 135.

Chapter 4
1 O'Callaghan 1975, 331.
2 al-Maqqari, vol 2, 34.
3 Barton, 225.
4 Ibid., 204.
5 Ibid., 207-208.
6 O'Callaghan 1975, 216.
7 O'Callaghan 2002, 7.
8 Ibid., 8.
9 Ibid., 9.
10 al-Maqqari, vol 2, 303.
11 Ibid., C, xlv.
12 Ibid., 304.
13 Ibid., C, xlvi.
14 O'Callaghan 2004, 48.
15 al-Maqqari vol 2, 309.
16 O'Callaghan 2004, 40.
17 Barton, 186.
18 O'Callaghan 1975, 285.
19 al-Maqqari, vol 2, 307.
20 Bertrand, 126–127.
21 O'Callaghan 2002, 9.
22 Barton, 188.
23 al-Maqqari, vol 2, C, xlvi.
24 O'Callaghan 2004, 201.
25 Barton, 178.
26 Ibid., 180.
27 Ibid., 220.

28 Ibid., 247.
29 Ibid., 153.
30 al-Maqqari, vol 2, 318.
31 O'Callaghan 2004, 46.
32 O'Callaghan 1975, 231.
33 Ibid., 231.
34 Allen, 306.
35 Ibid., 306.
36 Barton, 243.
37 Kennedy, 198.
38 Constable, 187.
39 Watts, 109.
40 Barton, 249.
41 Bertrand, 126.
42 Ibid., 127–128.
43 O'Callaghan 1975, 234.
44 al-Maqqari, vol 2, 321; D, lxv.
45 O'Callaghan 2002, 27.
46 al-Maqqari, vol 2, 322.
47 O'Callaghan 2002, 37.
48 Ibid., 41.
49 O'Callaghan 2004, 67–69.
50 al-Maqqari, vol 2, 323 D, lxviii.
51 O'Callaghan 2002, 134; Guéranger, 689.
52 Maria del Carmen, 9.
53 Ibid., 9.
54 Ibid., 18.
55 Ibid., 20.
56 O'Callaghan 2002, 76.
57 Maria del Carmen, 58.
58 O'Callaghan 1975, 355.
59 O'Callaghan 2002, 84.
60 Ibid., 85.
61 Maria del Carmen, 67.
62 Ibid., 137.
63 Ibid., 62.
64 Tolan, 184–185.
65 Maria del Carmen, 62.
66 O'Callaghan 2004, 84.
67 O'Callaghan 2002, 92.
68 Ibid., 89.
69 O'Callaghan 2004, 84; cf. O'Callaghan 2002, 88.
70 O'Callaghan 2002, 89.
71 O'Callaghan 2004, 81.
72 Maria del Carmen, 82.

73 Ibid., 89.
74 Butler, 413.
75 O'Callaghan 2002, 97.
76 Butler, 412–413.
77 Maria del Carmen, 97.
78 Ibid., 97.
79 O'Callaghan 2004, 84.
80 Maria del Carmen, 92–93.
81 O'Callaghan 1975, 344.
82 Butler, 411.
83 Ibrahim 2018, 199–203.
84 O'Callaghan 2002, 101–102.
85 O'Callaghan 2004, 204.
86 Tolan, 188.
87 O'Callaghan 2002, 106–107.
88 Maria del Carmen, 103.
89 Pidal, 437.
90 al-Maqqari, vol 2, 335.
91 Maria del Carmen, 125.
92 O'Callaghan 2002, 132.
93 Butler, 414.
94 O'Callaghan 2002, 133–134.
95 Ibid., 136.
96 Ibid., 134.
97 al-Maqqari, vol 2, 335.
98 O'Callaghan 2002, 140.
99 O'Callaghan 1975, 344.
100 O'Callaghan 2002, 142.
101 Ibid., 141, cf. O'Callaghan 2004, 204.
102 Fernandez-Morera 2016, 67.
103 O'Callaghan 2002, 141; cf. Tolan, 185.
104 Fernandez-Morera 2016, 135.
105 Maria del Carmen, 170.
106 Ibid., 176.
107 al-Maqqari, vol 2, 337.
108 Maria del Carmen, 208.
109 Ibid., 206–207.
110 Ibid., 209.
111 O'Callaghan 2004, 112.
112 al-Maqqari, vol 2, 344.
113 Maria del Carmen, 252.
114 O'Callaghan 2004, 112.
115 Maria del Carmen, 241.
116 Ibid., 216.
117 Ibid., 224.
118 Guéranger, 694.
119 Maria del Carmen, 255.
120 Ibid., 254.
121 O'Callaghan 2004, 117; cf. Constable 221–222.
122 Maria del Carmen, 263.
123 Guéranger, 695.
124 O'Callaghan 2004, 8.
125 William, 250.
126 O'Callaghan 2004, 120–122.
127 Guéranger, 696.
128 O'Callaghan 2004, 112.
129 Maria del Carmen, 279.
130 al-Maqqari, vol 2, 34–35; 260–261.

Chapter 5

1 Gaposchkin, 205.
2 Jackson, 129.
3 Sibt ibn al-Jawzi in Lindsay & Mourad, 107–116.
4 Perry, 133.
5 al-Maqrizi 1969, 3.
6 Ibid., 3.
7 Perry, 134.
8 al-Maqrizi 1969, 3.
9 Jackson, 25.
10 Ibid., 25–26.
11 Perry, 26.
12 Jackson, 160.
13 Fields, 74.
14 Gaposchkin, 111.
15 Ibid., 235.
16 Jackson, 19.
17 Perry, 156.
18 Jackson, 83.
19 Ibid., 77.
20 Ibid., 77, 81.
21 Ibid., 79.
22 al-Maqrizi 1969, 5.
23 Perry, 166.
24 Jackson, 88.
25 Ibid., 87.
26 Ibid., 88, 92.
27 Perry, 166–167; cf Joinville, 152.
28 Joinville, 151.
29 Jackson, 86.
30 al-Maqrizi 1969, 5; Jackson, 155.
31 Perry, 168; Jackson, 89.
32 Jackson, 88.

33 Ibid., 90.
34 Ibid., 89.
35 Ibid., 95.
36 Ibid., 93.
37 Ibid., 96, 91.
38 Ibid., 129, 155.
39 Ibid., 136.
40 Joinville, 155–156.
41 Jackson, 132.
42 Perry, 173.
43 Jackson, 109.
44 Joinville, 162.
45 Perry, 178.
46 Guindy, 180.
47 Joinville, 166–167.
48 Ibid., 168.
49 Ibid., 170.
50 Jackson, 100.
51 Joinville, 175.
52 Jackson, 100.
53 Jordan, 29.
54 Guindy, 120.
55 Jackson, 110.
56 Joinville, 179–182.
57 Jackson, 115.
58 Joinville, 179–182.
59 Perry, 184.
60 Jackson, 115.
61 Joinville, 183.
62 Jackson, 101.
63 Joinville, 118.
64 Jackson, 116.
65 Perry, 184.
66 Joinville, 183.
67 Jackson, 160.
68 al-Maqrizi 1969, 10.
69 Ibid., 10.
70 Jackson, 110.
71 Ibid., 160.
72 Jackson, 102.
73 al-Maqrizi 1969, 10.
74 Jackson, 101.
75 Perry, 186; cf. Gaposchkin, 135.
76 Jackson, 160.
77 Ibid., 114.
78 Joinville, 188.
79 Jackson, 127.
80 al-Maqrizi 1969, 10.
81 Fields, 136–137.
82 Jackson, 117.
83 Joinville, 193.
84 Gaposchkin, 189.
85 Joinville, 195.
86 Ibid., 198; cf. Gaposchkin, 67, 129, 189.
87 Fields, 135–136.
88 Gabrieli, 299.
89 Jackson, 111.
90 Ibid., 154.
91 Joinville, 197.
92 Jackson, 112–113.
93 Ibid., 113.
94 Ibid., 170.
95 Ibid., 186–187.
96 Ibid., 191.
97 Ibid., 183.
98 Ibid., 188.
99 Ibid., 188.
100 Ibid., 189.
101 Ibid., 193.
102 Perry, 200.
103 Ibid., 208.
104 Jackson, 119.
105 Joinville, 224.
106 Jackson, 91.
107 Fields, 137–138; cf. Joinville, 244.
108 Perry, 228.
109 Joinville, 238.
110 Stark, 229.
111 Gaposchkin, 119.
112 Fields, 102.
113 Gaposchkin, 59.
114 Perry, 272; cf. Gaposchkin, 61, 127.
115 Gaposchkin, 59.
116 Perry, 273.
117 Joinville, 123.
118 Gaposchkin, 121.
119 Perry, 270.
120 Fields, 132.
121 Perry, 271.
122 Gaposchkin, 267.
123 Perry, 272.
124 Ibid., 273.
125 Ibid., 280.

126 Ibid., 283.
127 Guindy, 179–190.
128 See Guindy's highly detailed *A Sword over the Nile*, pp.179–200.
129 Ibid., 190.
130 Fortescue, 247.
131 Allen, 358–359.
132 Gabrieli, 310.
133 Madden, 181.
134 Gabrieli, 311.
135 Fields, 144.
136 Ibid., 117.
137 Fields, 116–18; cf. Gaposchkin, 76–78.
138 See William C. Jordan's *The Apple of His Eye: Converts from Islam in the Reign of Louis IX.*
139 Gaposchkin, 77.
140 Ibid., 43–45.
141 Gabrieli, 303.
142 Tolan, 203.
143 Gaposchkin, 79.
144 Joinville, 127.
145 Fields, 147, 120–22; Jordan, 145.
146 Gaposchkin, 81.
147 Stark, 234.
148 Gabrieli, 337.
149 Ibid., 342.
150 Daniel, 111.
151 Gabrieli, 345–349.
152 Akbar, 62.
153 Gabrieli, 346.
154 Jackson, 31.
155 Guéranger, 691.

Chapter 6
1 Held, 129.
2 Bain, 239.
3 Bostom, 463–469.
4 Ibid., 63.
5 Doukas, 144–145.
6 Bostom, 480.
7 Ibid., 463.
8 Ibid., 489; Doukas, 88.
9 Riley-Smith 1995, 250–251.
10 For *Houris* in Islamic scriptures, see Koran 44:54, 52:20, 55:72, 56:22; for serving boys see Koran 52:24, 56:17, and 76:19; for other aspects of a corporeal and/or hedonistic paradise, see Koran 35:33, 43:71, 47:15, 52:22.
11 Doukas, 171–172; Bostom, 614–615.
12 Bartolomeo, 3, 6.
13 Ibid., 6.
14 Ibid., 3.
15 Ibid., 5.
16 Ibid., 8.
17 Mureşanu, 48.
18 Ibid., 53.
19 Chalkokondyles, 425–427.
20 Mureşanu, 54–55.
21 Ibid., 82.
22 Długosz, 485.
23 Bartolomeo, 6.
24 Mureşanu, 81.
25 Ibid., 64.
26 Ibid., 145.
27 Ibid., 86.
28 Babinger, 20.
29 Ibid., 21.
30 Mureşanu, 83.
31 Lord Kinross, 85–86.
32 Mureşanu, 81–82.
33 Babinger, 21.
34 Mureşanu, 93–94.
35 Jefferson, 152.
36 Mureşanu, 96.
37 Babinger, 25.
38 Moczar, 56.
39 Mureşanu, 99–100.
40 Bostom, 569.
41 Bartolomeo, 3.
42 Mureşanu, 102.
43 Długosz, 489.
44 Ibid., 490.
45 Lord Kinross, 86.
46 Mureşanu, 105.
47 Ibid., 105
48 Piccolomini, 82.
49 Ibid., 82–83.
50 Kinross, 91.
51 Mureşanu, 112–113.
52 Długosz, 490.
53 Ibid., 492–493.

54 Jefferson, 447.
55 Mureșanu, 119.
56 Lewis 1987, 143.
57 Ibid., 143.
58 Ibid., 143–144.
59 Doukas, 184–185.
60 Długosz, 496.
61 Treptow 2019, 68.
62 Mihailović, 40–41.
63 Jefferson, 482.
64 Ibid., 72.
65 Mureșanu, 128–129.
66 Ibid., 130.
67 Piccolomini, 90.
68 Mureșanu, 67.
69 Ibid., 175.
70 Ibid., 168.
71 Mureșanu, 175.
72 Held, 129.
73 Długosz, 503.
74 Mureșanu, 183.
75 Hillenbrand, 171–172.
76 Piccolomini, 91–92.
77 Długosz, 504; Mihailović, 43.
78 Długosz, 504.
79 Doukas, 192.
80 Mihailovic, 44.
81 Sphrantzes, 131.
82 Melville-Jones, 123.
83 Sphrantzes, 131.
84 Thomas the Eparch and Diplovatatzes 1976, 235 (3 in pdf).
85 Melville-Jones, 124.
86 Doukas, 234.
87 Tursun Beg, 37.
88 Bostom, 492.
89 Bain, 236.
90 Mureșanu, 205.
91 Ibid., 209.
92 Bain, 240.
93 Ibid., 236.
94 Ibid., 236.
95 Ibid., 237.
96 Ibid., 237.
97 Piccolomini, 101.
98 Bain, 239.
99 Ibid., 239–240.
100 Tursun Beg, 38.
101 Bain, 240.
102 Held, 157.
103 Bain, 240.
104 Piccolomini, 102.
105 Bain, 241.
106 Ibid., 242.
107 Chalkokondyles, 233.
108 Bain, 242.
109 Ibid., 238.
110 Mureșanu, 219.
111 Piccolomini, 101–102.
112 Bain, 242-243.
113 Mureșanu, 220.
114 Held, 159.
115 Bain, 244.
116 Chalkokondyles, 245.
117 Bain, 246.
118 Mureșanu, 222.
119 Bain, 246.
120 Held, 161.
121 Chalkokondyles, 233.
122 Bain, 246.
123 Held, 161.
124 Mureșanu, 224.
125 Bain, 247.
126 Ibid., 247.
127 Ibid., 247–248.
128 Piccolomini, 102.
129 Bain, 248.
130 Mureșanu, 225.
131 Ibid., 225.
132 Bain, 249.
133 Ibid., 249.
134 Ibid., 249–250.
135 Ibid., 250.
136 Ibid., 250–251; Mureșanu, 226.
137 Bain, 251.
138 Chalkokondyles, 237–239.
139 Bain, 251.
140 Ibid., 251.
141 Ibid., 251.
142 Mureșanu, 226–227.
143 Piccolomini, 102–103.
144 Bain, 252.
145 Ibid., 252.
146 Piccolomini, 60.

147 Mureşanu, 227.
148 Ibid., 227.
149 Ibid., 229.
150 Ibid., 233.
151 Ibid., 229.

Chapter 7

1 Drizari, 57–58.
2 Ibid., 16–17; 53–54.
3 Jefferson, 82.
4 Fernandez Morera, 2021, p.2.
5 Doukas, 133–134.
6 Bostom, 472.
7 Doukas, 135–136.
8 Bostom, 557.
9 Ibid., 558.
10 Florescu, 15.
11 Moczar, 39.
12 Bostom, 558.
13 Mihailović, 50–51.
14 Ibid., 51.
15 Bostom, 487–488.
16 Mihailović, 68.
17 Drizari, 91–92.
18 Fitzhenry 2015, 103.
19 Cohen, 151.
20 Drizari, 91–92.
21 https://fencingclassics.
wordpress.com/2011/10/04/
saber-combat-turkey-143/
22 Drizari, 91.
23 Brackob, 46.
24 Jefferson, 36.
25 Brackob, 48.
26 Ibid., 49; Moczar, 58.
27 Ibid., 53.
28 Ibid., 56–57.
29 Ibid., 56–57.
30 Drizari, xii.
31 Gibbon, 536.
32 Mihailović, 36.
33 Drizari, 2–5.
34 Ibid., xviii.
35 Mihailović, 68.
36 Drizari, 9–13.
37 Moore, 44.
38 Drizari, xix.
39 Ibid., xix.

40 Ibid., 14.
41 Ibid., 16–17.
42 Ibid., 20–22.
43 Ibid., 23.
44 Brackob, 76.
45 Jefferson 72.
46 Drizari, 26–27.
47 Mihailović, 15.
48 Drizari, 28–29.
49 Chalkokondyles, 117.
50 Akbar, 90.
51 Drizari, 29.
52 Ibid., 39–40.
53 Ibid., 34.
54 Ibid., 35–36.
55 Ibid., 39.
56 Ibid., 40–41.
57 Ibid., 41.
58 Brackob, 86.
59 Chalkokondyles, 125.
60 Drizari, 80.
61 Brackob, 87–88.
62 Ibid., 86.
63 Dillon, 126–127.
64 Moore, 200.
65 Chalkokondyles, 127.
66 Moore, 202.
67 Brackob, 88.
68 Drizari, 42.
69 Ibid., 42.
70 Brackob, 96.
71 Moore, 212.
72 Drizari, 43–44.
73 Ibid., 48.
74 Ibid., 2–3.
75 Ibid., 55.
76 Ibid., 56.
77 Ibid., 57–58.
78 Frashëri 30–32.
79 Ibid., 32.
80 Ibid., 32.
81 Drizari, 53–54.
82 Florescu, 24.
83 Moczar, 90.
84 Ibid., 90.
85 Drizari, 68.
86 Ibrahim 2018, 246.

87 Drizari, 70.
88 Ibid., 71.
89 Gibbon, 540.
90 Frashëri, 33.
91 Noli, 35–36.
92 Drizari, 77.
93 Brackob, 118.
94 Tursun Beg, 55.
95 Brackob, 118.
96 Frashëri, 36–37.
97 Tursun Beg, 55.
98 Brackob, 120.
99 Ibid., 119–120.
100 Bostom, 493.
101 Brackob, 124.
102 Drizari, 83–84.
103 Ibid., 84–85.
104 Ibid., 83.
105 Brackob, 125.
106 Ibid., 126.
107 Drizari, 86.
108 Brackob, 126–127.
109 Drizari, 86.
110 Ibid., 86–87.
111 Ibid., 87–88.
112 Brackob, 153.
113 Babinger, 495.
114 Brackob, 145.
115 Ibid., 160.
116 https://www.historytoday.com/
history-matters/skanderbeg-man-
our-times#:~:text=Rejecting%20
the%20Islam%20of%20his,a%20
Christian%20bulwark%20
against%20Islam.&text=Pope%20
Calixtus%20III%20provided%20
funds,of%20Naples%20became%20
another%20supporter
117 Brackob, 9.
118 Ibid., 10.
119 https://biography.yourdictionary.
com/gjergj-kastrioti-skanderbeg
120 Ibid.
121 Gibbon, 536.
122 Mihailović, 68.
123 https://www.congress.
gov/bill/109th-congress/
house-resolution/522/text
124 Gibbon, 536.

Chapter 8

1 Treptow 2019, 417–419.
2 Treptow 2020, 191.
3 Ibid., 40–41.
4 Ibid., 37.
5 Mureşanu, 38.
6 Florescu, 49–50.
7 Mureşanu, 40.
8 Doukas, 177.
9 Ibid., 177.
10 Florescu, 46.
11 Ibid., 85.
12 Treptow 2019, 394, 398, 402, 407.
13 Florescu, 56.
14 Treptow 2019, 63.
15 Ibid., 59.
16 Florescu, 57–60.
17 Treptow 2020, 69.
18 Mureşanu 218.
19 Chalkokondyles, 369.
20 Treptow 2019,429; cf. Chalkokondyles, 369.
21 Treptow 2019, 429; cf. Chalkokondyles, 369
22 Treptow 2020, 113.
23 Treptow 2019, 413.
24 Treptow 2020, 126–130.
25 Ibid., 133.
26 Florescu, 56, 60.
27 Doukas, 201.
28 Treptow 2019, 68.
29 https://www.cnn.com/videos/
international/2014/08/21/
isis-the-power-of-terror-tom-fore-
man-orig-jtb.cnn
30 Treptow 2019, 247.
31 Treptow 2020, 122.
32 Florescu, 99; cf. Treptow 2019, 430;
cf. Chalkokondyles, 369.
33 Chalkokondyles, 371.
34 http://hypocritereader.com/52/
tale-of-dracula

35 Chalkokondyles, 371; cf. Treptow 2019, 430.
36 Treptow 2019, 417.
37 Ibid., 417–418.
38 Ibid., 401–402.
39 Chalkokondyles, 373.
40 Treptow 2019, 417–419.
41 Chalkokondyles, 373.
42 http://hypocritereader.com/52/tale-of-dracula
43 Mihailović, 65.
44 http://hypocritereader.com/52/tale-of-dracula
45 Treptow 2019, 24.
46 Florescu, 137.
47 Treptow 2019, 394.
48 Ibid., 401–402.
49 Ibid., 417–419.
50 Ibid., 431, 395–398; Doukas, 260.
51 Treptow 2019, 346.
52 Florescu, 141.
53 Treptow 2020, 17.
54 Mihailović, 67.
55 Treptow 2019, 408.
56 Chalkokondyles, 381; cf. Treptow 2019, 151.
57 Treptow 2019, 402.
58 Doukas, 260.
59 Treptow 2019, 395.
60 Ibid., 433.
61 Ibid., 433; cf. Chalkokondyles, 383.
62 Chalkokondyles, 379.
63 Treptow 2020, 161.
64 Treptow 2019, 396–398.
65 Ibid., 434.
66 Ibid., 347.
67 Florescu, 146.
68 Chalkokondyles, 385–387; cf. Treptow 2019, 434–435.
69 Florescu, 147; cf. Mihailović 67.
70 Treptow 2019, 409–410.
71 Ibid., 404.
72 Ibid., 398.
73 Treptow 2020, 155.
74 http://hypocritereader.com/52/tale-of-dracula
75 Treptow 2019,148–149.
76 Ibid., 399; cf. Tursun Beg, 49; Mihailović, 67.
77 Treptow 2019, 402.
78 Chalkokondyles, 389.
79 Ibid., 391.
80 Treptow 2019, 347, 436, 149; cf. Tursun Beg, 47.
81 Florescu, 147–148; cf. Doukas, 260.
82 Treptow 2019, 436; cf. Chalkokondyles, 391.
83 Doukas 260–261.
84 Florescu, 148.
85 Treptow 2019, 437; cf. Chalkokondyles, 397.
86 Treptow 2020, 170; cf. Treptow 2019, 348.
87 Treptow 2019, 274.
88 Ibid., 348.
89 Treptow 2020, 148.
90 Treptow 2019, 151.
91 Ibid., 437; cf. Chalkokondyles, 397.
92 Treptow 2019, 410.
93 Chalkokondyles, 367–369.
94 Florescu, 151.
95 Chalkokondyles, 433.
96 Ibid., 397.
97 Florescu, 151; Treptow 2019, 438.
98 Florescu, 57.
99 Treptow 2019, 438.
100 Ibid., 321.
101 Treptow 2019, 438; Chalkokondyles, 399.
102 Florescu, 150.
103 Treptow 2019, 348–349.
104 Treptow 2020, 179.
105 Ibid., 177.
106 Florescu, 202.
107 Treptow 2019, 226; Florescu, 105.
108 Florescu, 105.
109 Treptow 2019, 242.
110 Ibid., 243.
111 Ibid., 226, 264.
112 http://hypocritereader.com/52/tale-of-dracula
113 Treptow 2019, 231
114 Florescu, 100–104.
115 Ibid., 101.

116 Treptow 2019, 318.
117 Florescu, 106.
118 Treptow 2019, 350.
119 Florescu, 167.
120 Ibid., 163.
121 Treptow 2019, 186, 193.
122 Ibid., 187.
123 Ibid., 180–181.
124 Ibid., 351.
125 Treptow 2020, 189.
126 Ibid., 189.
127 Ibid., 190.
128 Treptow 2019, 425.
129 Florescu, 174.
130 Treptow 2019, 29.
131 Treptow 2020, 11.
132 Florescu, 239.
133 Treptow 2020, 191.
134 Florescu, 241.
135 Treptow 2020, 137–138.
136 Florescu, 97.
137 Treptow 2019, 30, 145.
138 Ibid., 266.
139 https://kutztownenglish.files.
    wordpress.com/2015/09/jds_
    v4_2002_rezachevici.pdf

Conclusion

1 Roosevelt, 367.
2 https://www.youtube.com/watch?
  v=k-KaFRbdXMI
3 https://old.post-gazette.com/
  magazine/19981004walkside6.asp
4 Based on contemporary sources; see
  chapters 4 and 5 of *Sword and Scimitar* which cites and documents some
  of these accounts and their figures.
5 https://web.archive.org/web/
  20040207120343/http://www.opinion-
  journal.com/extra/?id=95001224
6 http://www.stlamerican.com/news/
  local_news/catholics-and-alt-right-
  clashed-with-protestors-in-forest-
  park-as-activists-called-for-removal/
  article_9702459c-b8ee-11ea-b462-
  ff1dc6577f64.html
7 https://www1.cbn.com/cbnnews/
  us/2020/june/attack-catholics-pray-
  ing-elderly-man-who-were-protect-
  ing-king-louis-ix-statue
8 Ibid.
9 According to historian of Medieval
  Spain, Dario Fernández-Morera, in an
  email exchange.
10 Gillingham, 6.
11 Ibid., 6–7.
12 Ibid., 162.
13 Ibid., 107, 162.